10th

CANADIAN
EDITION

Study Guide for use with
Macroeconomics

McCONNELL
BRUE
BARBIERO

Prepared by
Torben Andersen
Red Deer College

William B. Walstad
University of Nebraska, Lincoln

Robert C. Bingham

McGraw-Hill
Ryerson

Toronto   Montréal   Boston   Burr Ridge, IL   Dubuque, IA   Madison, WI   New York
San Francisco   St. Louis   Bangkok   Bogotá   Caracas   Kuala Lumpur   Lisbon
London   Madrid   Mexico City   Milan   New Delhi   Santiago   Seoul   Singapore
Sydney   Taipei

McGraw-Hill Ryerson

**Study Guide for use with
Macroeconomics,
Tenth Canadian Edition**

ISBN: 0-07-092240-3

3 4 5 6 7 8 9 10 MP 0 9 8 7 6 5

Printed and bound in Canada.

Vice President, Editorial and Media Technology: Patrick Ferrier
Executive Sponsoring Editor: Lynn Fisher
Economics Editor: Ron Doleman
Developmental Editor: Daphne Scriabin
Marketing Manager: Kelly Smyth
Supervising Editor: Joanne Murray
Production Coordinator: Madeleine Harrington
Formatter: Jay Tee Graphics Ltd.
Printer: Maracle Press Ltd.

Contents

Preface

Welcome to the study of economics. This **Study Guide** complements the course textbook, **Macroeconomics**, 10th Canadian edition, by McConnell, Brue and Barbiero. The design of the **Study Guide** is based on the conviction that active study beats passive study. To benefit from an aerobics class, it is not enough to watch the instructor demonstrate—you must also do the exercises yourself. To learn carpentry you cannot merely read a book—you must practice using the tools. And so it is with economics; you must actively do exercises and work with the tools.

The **Study Guide** provides you opportunities for this practice and gives you feedback along the way. Here you will find a range of questions that require verbal, numerical, and graphical answers. These are the three main modes of analysis in economics, and skill in all three areas will likely be expected of you in your exams.

I hope that you will use this **Study Guide** often, and that it will help you to have more success and more fun in your economics course.

Study Guide Organization

For each chapter in the text there is a chapter in the **Study Guide** with a set of common features as follows.

The **Overview** puts the chapter in context and briefly highlights and summarizes the key ideas.

The **Chapter Outline** is divided into the same main sections as the text chapter and for each one provides: specific learning objectives (indicated by ◈), a summary of the main points, a *Quick Quiz* (two or three multiple choice questions dealing specifically with each section), and sometimes special hints or tips (indicated by ➲).

A list of **Terms and Concepts** shows which new terms and concepts are introduced in the chapter.

The remainder of the chapter consists of practice questions and answers. **Fill-In** and **True-False** questions mainly test your recall of

the reading. There are more questions of the **Multiple-Choice** variety because such questions are most common on exams in most colleges and universities. Many of these questions involve analysis and application of concepts (including graphs, calculations, and other technical aspects). **Problems and Projects** require analysis and application, frequently with graphs, charts and calculations. The **Discussion Questions** may serve as review questions for study groups, and give some suggestion of possible short essay questions for exams. The **Answers** section provides solutions, often with a bit of explanation, for all questions except the **Discussion Questions**.

The last section of the Study Guide provides detailed answers to the **Key Questions** found at the end of chapters in the text.

A Bit of Advice

Try to work several times each week with your text and the **Study Guide**. Economics is absorbed most effectively in small, frequent doses.

It may be useful to preview the **Overview** and **Chapter Outline** sections before tackling a new chapter in the textbook. However, most of your time with the **Study Guide** should come after reading the chapter in the textbook, and probably after your instructor has addressed the material in class.

Make a serious attempt to answer a question before looking at its solution. Evaluate your results to identify your strengths and weaknesses. Especially if you don't have time to do all of the questions, stress those that seem more important given your instructor's emphasis of topics and style of exam questions. If you are thinking like an economist, you will strive to know the most important things extremely well and the less important things not so well!

When reviewing for exams, you may not have time to re-read all of the textbook chapters. Use the **Overview** and **Chapter Outline** sections for quick review and to zero in on key areas that will require more detailed review of the textbook.

Acknowledgments

Thanks to Tom Barbiero for the encouragement and advice, and for writing such a fine textbook for Canadian students. I owe a great deal also to the authors of previous editions of the **Study Guide**: Cyril Grant, William Walstad, and Robert Bingham. I am grateful for helpful comments from my colleague, Chandan Shirvaikar, and from numerous students, especially Ruth Krentz. Daphne Scriabin and Ron Doleman at McGraw-Hill Ryerson were most generous with their guidance and support.

If you have any comments on the **Study Guide** I would be delighted to hear from you. Please email me at torben.andersen@rdc.ab.ca.

--- Torben Andersen
    Red Deer, Alberta

Chapter 1

The Nature and Method of Economics

Overview

Economics is the social science concerned with the efficient use of scarce resources to achieve maximum satisfaction of wants. Chapter 1 introduces you to the kinds of topics economists study, how economists analyze these topics, and why economics is useful and important. You also learn about eight widely accepted economic goals that are important to our society.

The central idea in economics is scarcity of resources. Our resources are limited, but our wants are unlimited, so we must choose how to allocate our resources. In these choices we face tradeoffs. When we choose to spend resources to produce one thing we sacrifice the production of something else. This sacrifice is known as an opportunity cost. Economics consists of analyzing how humans behave in response to the problem of scarcity. The analysis is based on the assumptions of "rational self-interest" and on "marginal analysis."

The field of economics uses the scientific method. Based on observations of human behaviour (facts or data), we formulate hypotheses that are possible explanations of the causes and effects of these behaviours. Therefore, we test the predictions of our hypotheses to see whether they are supported by the data. Explanations that produce predictions that are highly consistent with the data become accepted theories. Policy economics applies theories and data to formulate policies to solve economic problems or achieve our economic goals. Policy controversies often centre on the interpretation and relative importance of goals that may be in conflict with each other. Such issues move us from positive economics (which investigates *what is*) to normative economics (which incorporates subjective views of *what ought to be*).

Economics is divided into two main categories. Microeconomics studies individual or specific economic units. Macroeconomics studies economy-wide aggregates.

Clear thinking requires that we avoid many common pitfalls or errors in thinking. These include: bias, loaded terminology, imprecise definitions, fallacies of composition, and causation fallacies.

Chapter Outline

◇ What is the definition of economics?

• Economics is the social science concerned with the efficient use of scarce resources to obtain the maximum satisfaction of society's unlimited wants.

1.1 Ten Key Concepts to Retain for a Lifetime

◇ What are the ten key concepts?

• There are ten key concepts that we hope you will recall long after this course is over. These concepts are merely listed in this chapter, but they recur throughout the text. Wherever one appears it is identified with the "key" icon.

• The ten key concepts fall into three categories: (a) those that pertain to the individual; (b) those that explain the interaction among individuals; and (c) those that deal with the economy as a whole and the standard of living.

Quick Quiz

1. Which of the following is not among the key concepts related to the individual?
   (a)   the effectiveness of markets
   (b)   facing tradeoffs
   (c)   choosing a little more or a little less
   (d)   the influence of incentives

2. To say that "choices are made at the margin" means that:
   (a)   we choose the best option
   (b)   we choose a little more or a little less
   (c)   government makes the choices for us
   (d)   we sometimes make incorrect choices

3. In the economy as a whole, the standard of living improves when there is more:
  (a)   inflation
  (b)   unemployment
  (c)   government involvement
  (d)   production of goods and services

1.2 The Economic Perspective

◈ What is the economic way of thinking?
  o   What is scarcity?
  o   What is an opportunity cost?
  o   What is rational behaviour?
  o   How does marginal analysis work?

•   The economic perspective on human behaviour is described in three interrelated ideas: scarcity, rational behaviour, and marginal analysis.

•   Scarcity of resources forces people to make choices and incur opportunity costs. The opportunity cost of a choice is the value of the next best alternative forgone.

•   People make rational decisions based on their own self-interest. Whatever gives a person maximum satisfaction (or utility) is deemed to be in that person's self-interest.

•   People make choices by comparing marginal costs and marginal benefits.

Quick Quiz

4. A major feature of the economic perspective is:
  (a)   equating rational self-interest with selfishness
  (b)   comparing marginal benefits with marginal costs
  (c)   the validity of normative economics for decision making
  (d)   the recognition of the abundance of economic resources

5. Because our resources are limited:
  (a)   we face the problem of scarcity
  (b)   we must make choices
  (c)   we must incur opportunity costs
  (d)   all of the above

6. People are behaving rationally only if:
  (a)   they behave selfishly
  (b)   they consistently pursue their own self-interest
  (c)   government makes the choices for us
  (d)   they never make any choices they later regret

1.3 Economic Methodology

◈ How do economists construct theories?
  o   What are the five elements of the scientific method?
  o   What constitutes a good economic theory?
  o   Why do economists use the other-things-are-equal assumption?

•   The scientific method consists of: (1) observing facts (data); (2) formulating possible cause-effect explanations (hypotheses); (3) testing hypotheses by comparing their predictions with data from specific real world events: (4) accepting, rejecting or modifying hypotheses based on test results; (5) continued testing.

•   Economists develop economic principles (also called theories, laws or models) to explain the economy and formulate policies to solve economic problems.

•   Economic principles are expressed as generalizations or tendencies. Good theories are those that explain and predict well. Predictions of a theory need not hold true in every single case in order for the theory to be useful.

•   The *ceteris paribus* or other-things-equal assumption is used in order to focus on only the variables of main interest in a theory.

•   Economic theories are abstractions from reality because they are intentionally simplified to omit irrelevant facts.

•   An explanation that has not yet been tested is often called a hypothesis; one that has been tested and supported by the data is often called a theory; one that has been tested many times, and is regularly supported by the data, is often called an economic law or principle.

➲ You may have difficulty accepting that economics is a science, especially because economic theories are inexact. Economics is a science by virtue of the methodology it uses to arrive at generalizations. Think of generalizations from cancer research or meteorology. Scientists have proven a link between smoking and lung cancer, even though their knowledge is not exact enough to identify which specific smokers will get cancer. Meteorologists' weather forecasts are not always correct, yet we rely on these forecasts because they are generally better than the forecasts we could generate ourselves without the benefit of the inexact science of meteorology.

◇ What is policy economics?

   o Distinguish between policy economics and theoretical economics.

   o What are the basic steps in policy-making?

   o List the eight widely accepted goals of economic policy in Canada.

• Policy economics involves the application of economic theories and data to formulate policies designed to achieve specific goals.

• The three steps in policy-making are: (1) stating the goals; (2) determining the policy options for achieving the chosen goals; and (3) implementing the chosen policy and evaluating its effects.

• Eight major economic goals are widely accepted in Canada: economic growth, full employment, economic efficiency, price-level stability, economic freedom, equitable distribution of income, economic security, and balance of trade.

• Economic goals may be complementary or conflicting. When goals conflict, the tradeoffs must be assessed and value judgments made about how to balance them.

Quick Quiz

7. When economists state that "consumer spending rises when personal income increases," this is an example of:

  (a) a generalization

  (b) loaded terminology

  (c) a normative statement

  (d) a fallacy of composition

8. Economists usually test their theories by:

  (a) mathematical calculations and proofs

  (b) making assumptions

  (c) comparing their predictions with data from the real world

  (d) doing experiments in a laboratory

9. The three basic steps in economic policy making are:

  (a) gather facts, make abstractions, show findings

  (b) state the goal, determine the options, evaluate results

  (c) create the theory, analyze assumptions, derive conclusions

  (d) form hypothesis, simplify the model, assume other things are equal

1.4 Macroeconomics and Microeconomics

◇ What is the difference between macroeconomics and microeconomics?

• Macroeconomics deals with the nation's economy as a whole by examining aggregate measures (such as the overall price level in Canada). Microeconomics looks at specific economic units (such as the price of houses in one city).

◇ What is the difference between positive and normative economics?

• Positive economics concerns the study of facts to determine *what is*, whereas normative economics involves value judgments to determine *what ought to be*. Theoretical economics is positive in nature, whereas policy economics must involve both positive and normative.

Quick Quiz

10. When we look at the whole economy or its major aggregates, our analysis would be at the level of:

  (a) microeconomics

  (b) macroeconomics

  (c) positive economics

  (d) normative economics

11. Which would be studied in microeconomics:

  (a) the output of the entire community

  (b) the total number of workers employed in Canada

  (c) the general level of the prices in the Canadian economy

  (d) the output and price of wheat in Canada

12. Which is a normative statement?

  (a) the consumer price index rose 5.6% last month

  (b) an unemployment rate of 6.8% is too high

  (c) the average rate of interest on loans is 8.6%

  (d) the economy will grow by 2.6% next year

1.5 Pitfalls to Objective Thinking

◇ What are six common pitfalls to objective thinking?

   o Give examples of: the fallacy of composition, the post hoc fallacy, and confusion between correlation and causation.

- Common pitfalls to avoid in order to think clearly and logically using the economic perspective include:
  - bias or preconceptions not warranted by facts
  - loaded terminology that appeals to emotions
  - careless use of terms whose precise technical definitions differ from common usage
  - the fallacy of composition, or the assumption that what is true for one is necessarily true for the group
  - the *post hoc* fallacy, or the mistaken belief that if event A precedes event B, A is the cause of B
  - confusion of correlation with causation, or the mistaken belief that if A and B are correlated that must be a cause and effect relationship between A and B

⮑ To remember them more easily, associate each pitfall with a specific example: perhaps one that is funny or has personal meaning for you. For example: "Last summer when it was really hot I ate lots of ice cream, so if I eat more ice cream now the weather will warm up." Which fallacy does this example illustrate?

Quick Quiz
13. If one fan can get a better view of a hockey game by standing up, then every fan can get a better view of the game by standing up. This is a case of:
- (a)   the after this, therefore because of this fallacy
- (b)   the fallacy of composition
- (c)   economic bias
- (d)   using loaded terminology

14. What pitfall to objective thinking is reflected in a person's view that corporate profits are always excessive?
- (a)   bias
- (b)   definition
- (c)   the fallacy of composition
- (d)   confusing correlation and causation

15. During World War II, price controls were used to prevent inflation; some people called this "a fascist and arbitrary restriction of economic freedom," while others said it was a "necessary

and democratic means of preventing ruinous inflation." Both labels are examples of:
- (a)   economic bias
- (b)   the fallacy of composition
- (c)   misuse of commonsense definitions
- (d)   loaded terminology

Terms and Concepts

economics	policy economics
economic perspective	tradeoffs
utility	macroeconomics
marginal analysis	aggregate
scientific method	microeconomics
theoretical economics	positive economics
principles	normative economics
generalizations	fallacy of composition
"other-things-equal" assumption	post hoc, ergo propter hoc fallacy

Fill-In Questions

1. Economics is concerned with the _____ use of _____ resources to attain the _____ satisfaction of human wants.

2. Deriving principles or theories is called _____ economics, whereas applying economic principles to solve problems is called _____ economics.

3. The three steps involved in the formulation of economic policy are:
- (a) _____
- (b) _____
- (c) _____

4. Eight economic goals that are widely accepted in Canada include:
- (a) _____
- (b) _____
- (c) _____
- (d) _____
- (e) _____
- (f) _____
- (g) _____
- (h) _____

5. The economic perspective has three interrelated features: It recognizes that (a) scarcity requires _____; (b) that people make decisions in a _____ manner based on their _____; and (c) that weighing the costs and benefits of a decision is based on _____ analysis.

True-False

Circle T if the statement is true, F if it is false.

1. We use the "other things equal" or ceteris paribus assumption in order to simplify the reasoning process. **T F**

2. Abstraction in economic theory is useful because it eliminates unnecessary complexity and irrelevant facts. **T F**

3. A common reason that individuals disagree on what economic policy should be chosen is that they disagree on the goal or desired result. **T F**

4. Making value judgments as to preferred goals of an economy is known as positive economic analysis. **T F**

5. The statement: "Increased patent protection for the Canadian pharmaceutical industry will result in increased research and development activity in Canada" is a positive statement. **T F**

6. If two variables are correlated with one another, changes in one must be causing changes in the other. **T F**

7. Scarcity is caused by the fact that people make choices. **T F**

8. In economics the word "marginal" means additional, or extra. **T F**

Multiple-Choice

Circle the letter that corresponds to the best answer.

1. Which statement is the best one to complete a short definition of economics? "Economics is the study of:
- (a) profit maximization by businesses."
- (b) the triumph of the capitalistic system over communism."
- (c) monetary transactions."
- (d) the efficient use of scarce resources."

2. The statement that "there is no free lunch" refers to what economic concept?
- (a) correlation does not imply causality
- (b) everything has an opportunity cost
- (c) nothing is free because government taxes everything
- (d) individuals have different tastes and preferences

3. If Ben is rational, when he buys soup he will:
- (a) never donate any cans of soup to the food bank
- (b) always choose the same brand of soup
- (c) always choose the cheapest brand of soup
- (d) choose the brand of soup that offers the most utility in relation to the price

4. One economic principle states that, *ceteris paribus*, the lower the price of a commodity the greater will be the quantity of the commodity consumers will wish to purchase. On the basis of this principle alone, it can be concluded that:
- (a) if the price of mink coats falls, consumers will purchase more mink coats
- (b) if the price of mink coats falls, there must have been a decrease in the demand for clothes made of fur
- (c) if the price of mink coats falls and there are no important changes in the other factors affecting their demand, consumers will purchase more mink coats
- (d) if more mink coats are purchased this month than last month, it is because the price of mink coats has fallen

5. An economic model is *not*:
- (a) an ideal type of economy or economic policy that we should strive to achieve
- (b) a tool economists employ to enable them to predict
- (c) an abstract representation of the economy or some part of the economy

(d) an explanation of how the economy or a part of the economy functions in its essential details

6. Which of the following is *not* among the dangers encountered when constructing or applying an economic model?
(a) it may contain irrelevant facts and be more complex than necessary
(b) it may come to be accepted as "what ought to be" rather than as "what is"
(c) it may be overly simplified and so be a very poor approximation of the reality it explains
(d) it may result in a conclusion that is unacceptable to people

7. A theory in economics:
(a) is useless if it uses simplifying assumptions
(b) is of little use if it is abstract
(c) is useful if the predictions of the theory usually correspond to actual economic occurrences
(d) is useless if its predictions are not always correct

8. Which of the following would not be contained in an economic theory?
(a) predictions that follow from that theory
(b) definitions that clearly set out the variables included in the model
(c) statements of the relationships among the variables in the model
(d) normative statements about the most preferred outcomes

9. If one individual decides to consume less beef, there will be little or no effect on beef prices. To argue, therefore, that if all individuals consume less beef there will be little or no effect on beef prices is an example of:
(a) the post hoc, ergo propter hoc fallacy
(b) the fallacy of composition
(c) an oversimplified generalization
(d) using loaded terminology

10. The Great Depression that began in 1929 was preceded by a stock market crash. To conclude that the Depression was therefore caused by the stock market crash is an example of:
(a) the post hoc, ergo propter hoc fallacy
(b) the fallacy of composition

(c) the ceteris paribus assumption
(d) using loaded terminology

11. Which of the following is not a widely accepted economic goal?
(a) price-level stability
(b) zero taxation
(c) economic efficiency
(d) economic freedom

12. Which economic goal is associated with the idea that we want to get the maximum benefit at the minimum cost from the limited productive resources available?
(a) economic security
(b) economic growth
(c) economic efficiency
(d) economic freedom

13. Which of the following might be studied in microeconomics?
(a) the output of the entire economy
(b) the national unemployment rate
(c) the effect of money supply changes on the Consumer Price Index
(d) the price and output of apples from the Annapolis Valley

14. If economic growth tends to produce a more equitable distribution of income among people in a nation, then the goals of growth and equitable income distribution seem to be:
(a) a tradeoff
(b) conflicting
(c) complementary
(d) mutually exclusive

15. To say that two economic goals are conflicting means that:
(a) there is a tradeoff in the achievement of the goals
(b) some people do not agree with these goals
(c) the achievement of one goal results in achievement of the other goal
(d) it is impossible to quantify both goals

16. Which of the following is a macroeconomic topic?
(a) the effect of cigarette tax reductions on cigarette smoking
(b) the effect of government set stumpage fees on the amount of lumber exported to the United States

(c)   the effect of the cod fishery closure on the unemployment rate in Halifax

(d)   the effect of the falling Canadian dollar on Canada's exports and imports

Problems and Projects

1. Opportunity Cost
Use the idea of opportunity cost to provide some possible explanations for these observations:

(a) Ashley turned down an "all-expenses-paid" trip to California because the trip was the week before her midterms.

(b) Dennis decided to use a realtor to sell his house, even though he could have avoided the realtor's fee by selling it himself.

(c) The St. Amand family buys a dishwasher from Sears because they didn't know that the same model was available at a lower price at a discount warehouse store.

2. Marginal Analysis
Kim Mitchell is at Canadian Tire shopping for patio lanterns. He must choose between a pack of 10 lights for $50 and a pack of 20 lights for $75. Explain the thought process he might use if he applies marginal analysis.

3. Positive and Normative Statements
Indicate in the space beside each statement whether it is positive (P) or normative (N).

(a) Tuition fee increases are causing university enrolments to decrease. _____

(b) Agricultural subsidies in Europe are killing small towns in Saskatchewan. _____

(c) Higher automobile insurance premiums increase the number of people willing to drive without insurance. _____

(d) The Employment Insurance program is too generous because it gives people the incentive to quit their jobs. _____

(e) It is unfair for the government to tax scholarship income. _____

(f) The federal government should do more to eliminate regional disparities in Canada. _____

4. Economic Methodology
Match the terms on the left-hand list with the descriptions on the right-hand list.

(a) hypothesis   (i)   explanation supported by data

(b) law   (ii) proposed explanation

(c) theory   (iii) explanation supported by data many times

5. Pitfalls to Objective Thinking
Below are five statements, each containing an example of a common pitfall in thinking about economics. Indicate, in the space following each statement, the type of pitfall involved.

(a) The Second World War resulted in forty-five years of economic expansion in Canada. _____

(b) "An unemployed worker can find a job if he or she looks diligently and conscientiously for employment; therefore, all unemployed workers can find employment if they search diligently and conscientiously." _____

(c) "Just tell me when rain will be needed and I will schedule my vacation for that week." _____

(d) "The players, not the team owners, deserve to benefit from the recent jump in revenues earned by the National Basketball Association; after all, it is the players that fans pay to see." _____

(e) "The North American Free Trade Agreement is making Canadian workers pawns of the powerful corporations who can move their sweat shops to Mexico." _____

Discussion Questions

1. What are some issues that you face in your personal or work life for which some knowledge of economics could provide useful skills?

2. What is a "laboratory experiment under controlled conditions?" Why are such experiments not normally possible in economics? What does economics have instead of a laboratory?

3. What is the relationship between facts and theory?

4. Why are economic principles and models necessarily generalizations and abstractions?

5. Sketch a map showing me how to get from your home to the nearest grocery store. In what ways is your map realistic, and in what ways is it unrealistic (abstract)? Would your map necessarily be more helpful to me in finding the store if it was more realistic? Would it be worth making it more realistic? How do these issues concerning your map relate to issues concerning economic theories?

6. Explain each of the following: (a) fallacy of composition; (b) loaded terminology; (c) the *post hoc, ergo propter hoc* fallacy.

7. Explain briefly the difference between: (a) macroeconomics and microeconomics; (b) correlation and causation

Answers

Quick Quiz
1. p. 3
2. p. 5
3. p. 9
4. pp. 4-6
5. p. 4
6. pp. 4-5
7. p. 8
8. p. 7
9. p. 9
10. (b) pp. 10-11
11. p. 11
12. (b) p. 11
13. (b) pp. 12-13
14. p. 12
15. p. 12

Fill-In Questions
1. efficient, scarce, maximum
2. theoretical, policy
3. stating goals; analyzing policy options; evaluating policy effectiveness
4. full employment; economic growth; price-level stability; balance of trade; equitable distribution of income; economic efficiency; economic security; economic freedom
5. choices; rational; self-interest; marginal

True-False
1. T
2. T
3. T
4. F   Value judgments imply normative economics
5. T   The statement is positive, whether true or false
6. F   Don't confuse correlation with causation
7. F   The other way around
8. T

Multiple-Choice
1. (d)   This one is the most comprehensive
2. (b)   Everything has a cost in some form
3. (d)   He may have charitable motives, he may buy different brands due to price changes, and he may buy more expensive soup because it gives him more utility
4. (c)   *Ceteris paribus* means "other things remaining constant"
5. (a)   An economic model explains how the world is, not how we want it to be
6. (d)   Perhaps the conclusion will be unacceptable to some people, but this does not affect the validity of the theory
7. (c)   Good theories always involve assumptions and abstractions, and may not predict correctly in *every* case.
8. (d)   Theories are limited to positive aspects
9. (b)   What is true for one need not be true for all
10. (a)   Because B happened *after* A does not prove that B *caused* A
11. (b)   Zero taxation is not on the list of eight goals
12. (c)
13. (d)   This topic deals with a single market rather than with the economy in aggregate
14. (c)   Complementary because they can be achieved together, without tradeoff
15. (a)   To move towards one goal entails moving away from the other
16. (d)   All the others deal with specific markets

Problems and Projects
1. Each of these decisions was presumably made because the opportunity cost was too high: (a) by going to Disneyland, Ashley would lose study time and her exam results would suffer; (b) selling his own house would have cost Dennis some time, and perhaps some money if a realtor could get a higher price; (c) shopping at every store to find the absolute lowest price is not usually worth the cost of time and travel.
2. Mitchell would compare the extra enjoyment or use he would get from the 10 extra lights in the larger pack with what other enjoyment he could get by spending on something else the $25 extra cost for the larger pack. That is, he would compare marginal benefit and marginal cost.
3. (a) P; (b) P; (c) P; (d) N; (e) N; (f) N. In principle it is possible to test whether positive statements are true or false, while normative statements depend on values.
4. (a)-(ii); (b)-(iii); (c)-(i)
5. (a) *post hoc ergo propter hoc* fallacy; (b) the fallacy of composition; (c) confusing correlation and causation; (d) bias; (e) loaded terminology

Appendix to Chapter 1

Graphs and Their Meaning

Overview

The old saying that "a picture is worth a thousand words" is true in economics because economists use graphs to "picture" relationships between variables. A graph can display a lot of information in a manner that is precise yet quick to comprehend. Because we rely so much on these "pictures," you need to be skilled in constructing and interpreting graphs. If you are already skilled with the basics of graphing, you may only need to review this appendix quickly. On the other hand, if this material seems unfamiliar, relax and work carefully through the appendix; all of the basics you need are here.

The appendix shows how to construct a graph from a table of data on two variables (using the example of income and consumption). Each variable is represented on one of the two axes, so each axis should be labelled with the variable name, its units of measurement, and marked off with a consistent measurement scale. We often plot data to determine whether two variable are related, and if so, whether directly or inversely.

Economists usually, but not always, measure the independent variable on the horizontal axis and the dependent variable on the vertical axis of a graph. The curve plotted to illustrate the relationship between the two variables is drawn based on the ceteris paribus condition. If any other variable affecting the dependent variable happens to change, then we must plot a whole new curve passing through a different set of points. This is called a shift in the curve.

A relationship that is linear (a straight line) can be defined by two simple elements: the slope and the vertical intercept of the line. A linear relationship is easily expressed in equation form once the slope and the vertical intercept are found from a graph or table of data. Slope often has economic meaning, because slopes measure how a marginal change in the independent variable causes a marginal change in the dependent. For a nonlinear curve the slope is not constant; it varies as one moves along the curve.

Appendix Outline

◇ What is a graph?

◇ How is a graph constructed?

• A graph is a visual representation of the relationship between variables and is helpful in describing economic theories and models.

• To construct a simple graph, plot numerical data about two variables from a table. Sometimes the tabular data must be found first by using an equation relating the two variables.

    o Each graph has a horizontal and a vertical axis that is labelled for each variable and then scaled for the range of the data points that will be measured on the axis. Along a given axis a certain increment of distance represents a consistent increment in the variable.

    o Data points are plotted on the graph by drawing perpendiculars from the scaled points on the two axes to the place on the graph where the perpendiculars intersect.

    o A line or curve can then be drawn to connect the points plotted on the graph. If the line is straight the relationship is "linear."

➲ Some students are comfortable with economic graphs right away, but others initially have an aversion to graphs. If you are in the first group, you are fortunate because economics will come more easily to you. If you are in the second group, do not run because you cannot hide! It is incredibly important that you quickly develop basic skills with graphing. If you find this appendix very difficult you should seek extra help with these tools.

➲ All graphs in this appendix have actual numerical values marked on the axes. Later in the text you will see graphs without any numbers on the axes. In such cases the specific numbers are not necessary for the explanation, but you should recognize that there are numbers implicit on the axes. If at first you have difficulty comprehending such abstract graphs, you could pencil in arbitrary values on the axes until you get used to such graphs.

◇ What are direct and inverse relationships?

◇ What are dependent and independent variables?

• The slope of the line on a graph indicates the relationship between the two variables.
  o A line that is upsloping to the right indicates a positive or direct relationship between the two variables: an increase (a decrease) in one is associated with an increase (a decrease) in the other.
  o A line that is downsloping to the right indicates a negative or inverse relationship between the two variables because the variables are changing in opposite directions: an increase (a decrease) in one is associated with a decrease (an increase) in the other.
• Economists are concerned with determining cause and effect in economic events.
  o An independent variable is the variable that changes first, and causes another variable to change.
  o A dependent variable is one that changes as a result of a change in another variable.
  o Economists do not always follow the convention used in mathematics whereby an independent variable is placed on the horizontal axis and a dependent variable on the vertical axis.
• A two-variable graph is a simplified representation of an economic relationship. In such a graph there is an implicit assumption that all other factors are being held constant.
• This "other things equal" or ceteris paribus assumption is a simplification that helps us focus on the two variables of interest. If another variable that influences the dependent variable does change, then the curve on the graph will shift to a new position.

◇ How is a relationship defined by a line defined in algebraic terms?
  o What is the slope of a line?
  o What is the vertical intercept of a line?
• A slope and vertical intercept can be calculated for a linear relationship (straight line graph). These values also define the equation of the line.
  o The slope of a straight line is the ratio of the vertical change to the horizontal change between two points.
  o The slope measures the marginal effect on one variable of a small change in the other.
  o A positive (negative) slope indicates a direct (inverse) relationship between the two variables.
• The vertical intercept is the value where the line intersects the vertical axis of the graph.
• A linear equation is written as $y = a + bx$. If the values for the intercept a and the slope b are known, then given any value of variable x, the value of variable y can be determined.
• A straight line has a constant slope, but a nonlinear curve has a continually changing slope. To estimate the slope of a nonlinear curve at a point, calculate the slope of a line tangent to the curve at that point.

➲ Some graphs in the text use real world data showing relationships between two variables. Such graphs often take the form of a "scatter diagram" with a "best-fitting line." That is, the data points may be somewhat scattered, rather than lying exactly on a curve. Therefore, no *precise* relationship is evident in the data, but there is a discernible tendency or pattern in the data, indicating that the variables are related. A "best-fitting line" through the data points indicates this pattern. If you take a statistics course you will learn the proper techniques for determining best-fitting lines, and for judging when you can be confident that the points in a scatter diagram do indicate some relationship. To understand this textbook you need only have a rough idea of a "best-fitting line."

Quick Quiz

1. If an increase in variable A is associated with a decrease in variable B, then we can conclude that A and B are:
  (a)   nonlinear
  (b)   directly related
  (c)   inversely related
  (d)   positively related

2. In the relationship between average birthweight of babies and the rate of cigarette smoking of their mothers, we would expect:

(a)   birthweight to be dependent
(b)   rate of smoking to be dependent
(c)   both variables to be dependent
(d)   both variables to be independent

3. Given the equation of a line as $y = 100 - 5x$. Then the point with the horizontal coordinate of 12 will have a vertical coordinate of:
(a)   160
(b)   112
(c)   88
(d)   40

Terms and Concepts

horizontal axis
vertical axis
direct relationship
inverse relationship

independent variable
dependent variable
slope of a straight line
vertical intercept

Fill-In Questions

1. The relationship between two variables can be visualized with a two-dimensional graph.
(a)   The (dependent, independent) _____ variable is said to change because of a change in the _____ variable.
(b)   The vertical and horizontal (scales, ranges) _____ on the graph are calibrated to reflect the _____ of values in a table of data points on which the graph is based.

2. The graph of a straight line that slopes downward to the right indicates that there is (a direct, an inverse) _____ relationship between the two variables. A graph of a straight line that slopes upward to the right tells us that the relationship is (direct, inverse) _____. When the value of one variable increases and the value of the other variable increases, then the relationship is _____; when the value of one increases, and the other decreases, the relationship is _____.

3. The slope of a straight line between two points is defined as the ratio of the (horizontal, vertical) _____ change over the _____ change. The point at which the line meets the vertical axis is called the _____.

4. We can express the graph of a straight line with a linear equation written as $y = a + bx$

(a)   a is the (slope, intercept) _____ and b is the _____.
(b)   If a = 2, b = 4, and x = 5, then y would be _____.

5. The slope of a (straight line, nonlinear curve) _____ is constant throughout; the slope of a _____ varies from point to point. The slope of a nonlinear curve at a point can be estimated by calculating the slope of a straight line that is _____ to the point on the curve.

True-False

Circle T if the statement is true, F if it is false.

1. If the straight line on a two-variable graph is upward sloping to the right, then there is a positive relationship between the two variables.   **T F**

2. A variable that changes as a consequence of a change in another variable is considered to be a dependent variable.   **T F**

3. *Ceteris paribus* means that the value of all other variables is set equal to zero.   **T F**

4. In the ratio for the calculation of the slope of a straight line, the horizontal change is divided by the vertical change.   **T F**

5. If the slope of the linear relationship between consumption (on the vertical axis) and income (on the horizontal axis) is 0.90, then it tells us that for every $1 increase in income there will be a $0.90 increase in consumption.   **T F**

6. If the slope of a straight line on a two-variable (x, y) graph is 2 and the vertical intercept is 6, then if the value for x is 10, the value for y is 22.   **T F**

7. If there is an inverse relation between price and quantity demanded, the graph of this function will be downward-sloping.   **T F**

8. In the relationship between snowfall and demand for snowblowers, snowfall is the dependent variable.   **T F**

9. If the line tangent to a nonlinear curve is up-sloping, this indicates that the slope of the curve is positive at that point.   **T F**

10. If two points described by the (x, y) combinations of (13, 10) and (8, 20) lie on a straight line, then the slope is 2.   **T F**

11. On a graph relating the number of visitors to Canada's national parks to the price of admission to the parks, an increase in levels of rainfall would likely shift the curve to the left.   **T F**

Multiple-Choice

Circle the letter that corresponds to the best answer.

1. If an increase in variable A is associated with a decrease in variable B, then we can conclude that A and B are:
(a)   nonlinear
(b)   directly related
(c)   inversely related
(d)   positively related

2. Economists:
(a)   always put the independent variable on the vertical axis
(b)   always put the independent variable on the horizontal axis
(c)   sometimes put the dependent variable on the horizontal axis
(d)   use only linear functions

3. If y is plotted on the vertical axis and x is on the horizontal axis, which of the following is a false statement regarding the equation $y = 100 + 0.4x$?
(a)   the vertical intercept is 100
(b)   the slope is 0.4
(c)   when x is 20, y is 108
(d)   the graph is nonlinear

4. The equation of a line is: $y = 10 + 5x$. If the value of $x = 6$, then what is the value of y?
(a)   30
(b)   40
(c)   50
(d)   none of the above

5. Which of the following has a slope of zero at all points?

(a)   a vertical line
(b)   a horizontal line
(c)   a curved line
(d)   a straight line

6. If a straight line drawn tangent to a nonlinear curve has a slope of zero, then at the point of tangency the curve is:
(a)   vertical
(b)   horizontal
(c)   upsloping
(d)   downsloping

Answer questions 7 through 10 on the basis of the following diagram.

7. The graph indicates that price and quantity supplied are:
(a)   positively related
(b)   negatively related
(c)   indirectly related
(d)   nonlinear

8. The slope of the line is:
(a)   0.15
(b)   0.20
(c)   1.50
(d)   6.67

9. The vertical intercept is:
(a)   0
(b)   10
(c)   20

(d)   80

10. The linear equation for the function is:
  (a) $p = 20 + 0.15q$
  (b) $q = 20 + 6.67p$
  (c) $p = 20 + 6.67q$
  (d) $q = 20 + 0.15p$

11. Consider a graph relating gasoline consumption (on the vertical axis) to population (on the horizontal axis). All of the following will affect gasoline consumption, but which one will **not** shift the curve?
  (a)   increased consumer incomes
  (b)   increased availability of public transit
  (c)   increased population
  (d)   more efficient gasoline engines

12. Which of the following statements is true?
  (a)   a vertical line has a slope of zero
  (b)   a horizontal line has a slope of infinity
  (c)   a nonlinear curve has different slopes at different points
  (d)   an upsloping line has a negative slope

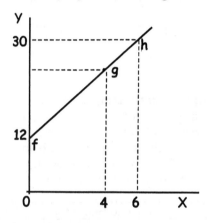

13. The slope of the line is:
  (a)   9
  (b)   3
  (c)   5
  (d)   2

14. The equation of the line is:
  (a) $y = 12 + 3x$
  (b) $y = 30 + 6x$
  (c) $y = 12 + 2x$
  (d) $y = 30 - 3x$

15. The y-axis coordinate of the line at point g is:
  (a)   16
  (b)   18

(c)   22
(d)   24

Problems and Projects

1. Graphing: Dependent and Independent Variables
The data below represent the relationship between the mortgage interest rate and the number of new houses built.

Mortgage Rate (% per year)	Housing Starts (thousands per year)
12	70,000
10	90,000
8	110,000
6	130,000
4	150,000

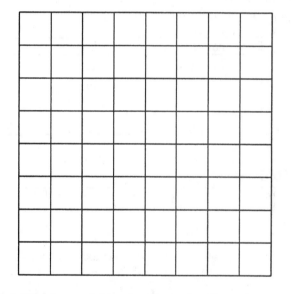

(a) Which variable is dependent? _____
Which is independent? _____
(b) On the axes of the graph below, set up the scales to best suit these data. Label each axis of the graph (including the units of measurement).
(c) Plot the five data points given in the table.
(d) The curve is (up-, down-) _____ sloping, meaning that the relationship between the mortgage interest rate and housing starts is (direct, inverse) _____.

2. Shifts and Movements Along a Curve
(a) Based on the relationship found in question 1, if the mortgage rate increases by 1%, ceteris

paribus, then housing starts will (decrease, increase) _____ by ____ thousands per year.

(b) If household incomes rise, new homes would become more affordable, so there would be more new housing starts at the same interest rate as before. On the graph, this would cause a (leftward, rightward) _____ shift of the curve in question 1.

(c) If lumber prices increase, new homes would become less affordable, so there would be fewer new housing starts at the same interest rate as before. On the graph, this would cause a (leftward, rightward) _____ shift of the initial curve.

3. The Graph and Equation of a Line

The Hammerheads, a very mediocre club band, have just released a CD. They will immediately sell 10 copies to their parents and friends. Thereafter, they can sell 4 copies for each performance they give in a club.

(a) Use this information to complete the table.

Performances	CD Sales
0	_____
5	_____
10	_____
15	_____
20	_____

CD Sales

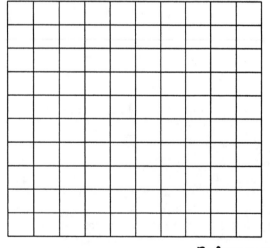

Performances

(b) Which variable is dependent? _____ Which is independent? _____

(c) Plot the data on the graph below.

(d) The vertical intercept value is _____.

(e) The slope value is _____.

(f) Write the equation for this relationship:

_____.

4. The Slope of a Line

(a) The function in the graph below has a negative slope between the X values of _____ and _____. Over this range the relationship between X and Y is (direct, inverse) _____.

(b) Find the slope of the curve at these points:
A: _____, B: _____, C: _____

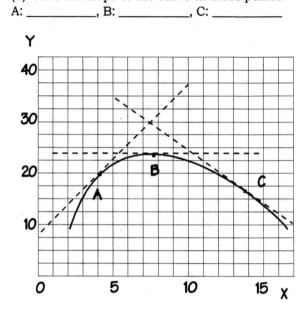

5. Finding a Best-Fitting Line and Equation

An economist is hired to determine the relationship between real estate value and proximity to the waterfront in a Manitoba lakeshore resort community. The table below gives recent selling prices for undeveloped building lots.

Lot	Distance to Shore (m)	Price ($)
A	200	9,000
B	0	18,000
C	50	16,000
D	100	15,000
E	50	17,000
F	150	10,000
G	200	7,000
H	125	12,000

(a) On the graph provided, create a "scatter diagram" with lot prices on the vertical axis and distance to shore on the horizontal axis.

(b) The scatter diagram suggests that lot prices are (directly, inversely, not) _____ related to their proximity to the waterfront.

(c) With a ruler, draw in what appears to be the "best-fitting" line through these data points.

(d) The value of the vertical intercept is _____. This value indicates price for a lot that is _____.

(e) The value of the slope is _____. This value indicates that price (falls, rises) _____ by $_____ for each metre from the waterfront.

(f) The expression for the equation of this line is: _____.

Price (thousand $)

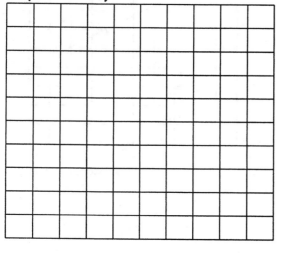

Distance to shore (m)

Discussion Questions

1. Why do economists use graphs?

2. If the vertical intercept increases in value but the slope of a straight line stays the same, what happens to the graph of the line? If the vertical intercept decreases, what happens to the line?

3. If you know that variables X and Y are inversely related, what does this tell you about the slope of a line showing the relationship between these two variables? What do you know about the slope when X and Y are positively related?

4. Identify the dependent and independent variables in the following statement: "A decrease in business taxes gave a big boost to investment spending." How does one tell the difference between a dependent and independent variable when examining economic relationships?

5. Why is it assumed that all other variables are held constant when we construct a two-variable graph of the price and quantity of a product?

6. If you were to plot a two-variable graph of the price of gasoline versus per capita use of gasoline, using the data for various nations, what sort of graph would you expect, and what sort of relationship would this represent? The data points would probably be somewhat scattered, rather than consistently located along a precise line or curve. Give some reasons why the data points might be somewhat scattered.

Answers

Quick Quiz
1. (c) p. 18
2. (a) p. 18
3. (d) pp. 20-21

Fill-in Questions
1. (a) dependent, independent; (b) scales, ranges
2. an inverse; direct; direct, inverse
3. vertical, horizontal; vertical intercept
4. (a) intercept, slope; (b) 22
5. straight line; nonlinear curve; tangent

True-False
1. T   This is also termed a direct relationship
2. T
3. F   It means "other things equal"
4. F   Vertical change divided by horizontal change
5. T
6. F   The equation is $y = 6 + 2x$; at $x = 10$, $y = 26$
7. T
8. F   The amount of snowfall does not depend on how many snowblowers are purchased
9. T   An upsloping curve
10. F $(20-10)/(8-13) = -2$
11. T   Rainfall would likely be one of the variables held constant on the original graph, so if rainfall changes the curve will shift

Multiple-Choice
1. (c) Variables changing in opposite directions are inversely or negatively related
2. (c) There is no consistent convention
3. (d) Because the slope is a fixed number, the graph is a straight line
4. (b)

5. (b) There is no vertical change
6. (b)
7. (a) The curve is upsloping
8. (a) (80-20)/(400-0) = 0.15
9. (c)
10. (a) See the answers to questions 8 and 9
11. (c) Population is held constant along the initial curve
12. (c) The slope of the tangent line keeps changing
13. (b) (30-12)/(6-0) = 3
14. (a)
15. (d) 12+(3)(4) = 24

Problems and Projects
1. (a) housing starts; mortgage interest rates; (d) down; inverse; (b) and (c):

2. (a) decrease, 10; (b) rightward; (c) leftward
3. (a) 10, 30, 50, 70, 90; (b) CD sales; performances; (c) see graph; (d) 10; (e) 4; (f) CD Sales = 10 + 4 Performances

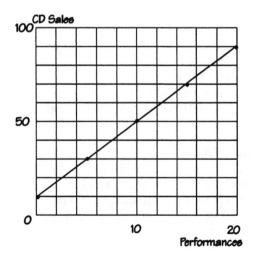

4. (a) 8; 17; inverse; (b) 3.0; 0; -2.1.
5. (a) see graph; (b) inversely; (c) see graph; (d) about $19,000; on the waterfront; (e) vertical change/horizontal difference is approximately = (8,000-19,000)/(200-0) = -11,000/200 = about -55; falls; about $55. (f) Price = 19,000 - 55 Distance.

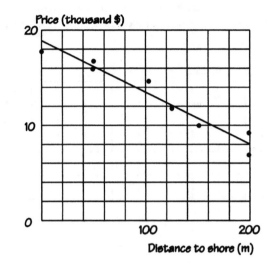

Chapter 2

The Economic Problem: Scarcity, Wants, and Choices

Overview

The field of economics is based on two key facts: our wants are unlimited or insatiable, and the resources available for satisfying these wants are limited, or scarce. Consequently, we face the economic problem: the need to make choices about how to allocate our scarce resources. These resources are land, capital, labour, and entrepreneurial ability. Given scarcity, all resources must be fully employed and used efficiently if we are to satisfy wants to the fullest possible extent. Efficiency has two elements: productive efficiency is achieved if resources are used in the least cost manner, and allocative efficiency is achieved if resources are used to produce those goods society wants most.

The production possibilities table and the production possibilities curve are very basic and important tools that illustrate many concepts in this chapter: scarcity, choice, the law of increasing opportunity cost, allocative and productive efficiency, unemployment, and economic growth.

Every society uses some sort of economic system to address the problem of scarcity. Most use some combination of the two basic types: the market system and the command system. In a market system most resources are owned privately and economic activity is coordinated spontaneously, with little government interference. In a command system government owns most of the property resources and economic activity is centrally planned. Canada uses a market system with some elements of a command system.

Chapter Outline

2.1 The Foundation of Economics

◈ What is the economic problem, and what two key facts create this problem?

• The study of economics rests on two facts:
  o Society's wants are essentially unlimited and insatiable.
  o The resources for producing goods and services to satisfy society's wants are limited or scarce.

• These two facts create the problem of scarcity, whereby we are forced to make choices.

• The four categories of resources are land, capital, labour, and entrepreneurial ability. The payments received by suppliers of these resources are, respectively: rental income, interest income, wages, and profits.

Quick Quiz

1. Which of the following statements is false:
   (a) human wants outstrip the ability of our resources to satisfy our wants
   (b) economists believe that improvements in technology will eventually eliminate the scarcity problem
   (c) scarcity exists in all human societies
   (d) if there was no scarcity problem we would not face opportunity costs

2. Which is the correct match of an economic resource and payment for that resource?
   (a) land and wages
   (b) labour and interest income
   (c) capital and rental income
   (d) entrepreneurial ability and profit

2.2 Efficiency: Getting the Most from Available Resources

◈ What is the nature of economic efficiency?

◈ Distinguish between:
  o full employment and full production
  o productive efficiency and allocative efficiency

• Economics is the social science concerned with the problem of using scarce resources to attain the maximum fulfillment of society's unlimited wants.

• To achieve this goal society must use its resources efficiently, achieving both:
  o full employment (available resources are being used)

o   full production (the resources are being used as efficiently as possible)
- Two kinds of efficiency must be achieved:
  o   productive efficiency (goods and services are produced in the least costly way)
  o   allocative efficiency (the resources are used to produce that particular mix of goods and services most wanted by society)

◈ What is a production possibilities table or curve, and how does it illustrate scarcity, efficiency, choice, and opportunity cost?

◈ What assumptions are made when a production possibilities table or curve is presented?

- The production possibilities table, or production possibilities curve, indicates the alternative combinations of goods and services an economy can produce.
- Four assumptions are made in constructing a production possibilities table or curve:
  o   full employment and productive efficiency
  o   fixed resources
  o   fixed technology
  o   two goods are being produced

➲ The production possibilities curve is the first of many instances in the textbook where graphing skills are needed. If you have serious difficulty with this graph you probably have a general weakness in graphing that you should remedy immediately. Spend extra time on the graphical questions in this study guide, the relevant sections of the chapter, and on Appendix 1A of the textbook and this study guide. Your instructor may have additional resources or advice for you.

- Any point on the production possibilities curve is attainable, but society must choose one point (one particular combination of goods). If the chosen combination provides the greatest satisfaction, the economy is said to be allocatively efficient.

➲ Many students initially confuse the coordinates of a point on the production possibilities curve with the intercepts of the curve. The intercepts indicate the *maximum*, or *potential*, production for each good (if all resources are dedicated to producing that good), whereas the coordinates

of the production point show *actual* production for each good.

- Points outside the curve are unattainable, so the production possibilities curve illustrates the condition of scarcity.
- Given full employment and full production, society can produce more of one good only by producing less of the other good. This foregone output is termed the opportunity cost and arises because resources must be shifted from one production activity to another.
- The marginal opportunity cost of producing additional units of a product usually increases as more of that product is produced. This generalization is the law of increasing opportunity costs.
  o   Opportunity costs are increasing because resources are not perfectly adaptable from one production use to another.
  o   Increasing opportunity costs cause the production possibilities curve to be concave (bowed out from the origin).

◈ How is allocative efficiency related to marginal benefit and marginal cost?

- The amount of resources allocated to the production of a good is optimal where the marginal benefit (MB) received from the last unit produced equals its marginal cost (MC). MC is the opportunity cost in terms of other goods that could have been produced with the same resources.
  o   The optimal production level on the production possibilities curve corresponds to the point of allocative efficiency.
  o   MB falls as more is produced.
  o   MC rises as more is produced.

Quick Quiz

3. When a production possibilities table is written (or a production possibilities curve is drawn), four assumptions are made. Which of the following is one of those assumptions?
- (a)   more than two products are produced
- (b)   the state of technology changes
- (c)   the economy has both full employment and productive efficiency
- (d)   the quantities of all resources available to the economy are variable, not fixed

4. A point outside today's production possibilities curve:
- (a)   represents allocative inefficiency

(b)   represents productive inefficiency
(c)   represents unemployment
(d)   represents a production level unattainable with current resources and technology

5. The changing slope of the production possibilities curve when moving along the curve reflects:
(a)   increasing resource supplies
(b)   increasing production of both goods
(c)   increasing opportunity cost as production of one good increases
(d)   increased productive and allocative efficiency

6. Society is said to be underallocating resoures to the production of a good if for the last unit produced:
(a)   marginal benefit is greater than the marginal cost
(b)   marginal benefit is less than the marginal cost
(c)   opportunity cost of production is rising
(d)   consumption of the product is falling

2.3 Unemployment, Growth, and the Future

◈ How is economic growth achieved?

•   This section examines the effects of dropping some of the assumptions underlying the production possibilities model.

•   An economy experiencing unemployment or productive inefficiency is operating at a point inside its production possibilities curve, and is therefore failing to meet its productive potential.

•   Economic growth occurs through improvements in technology or expansions in resource supplies, causing the production possibilities curve to expand, or shift outward.

➲ A movement from one point on the production possibilities curve to another point on the same curve shows a change in what combination of products society *chooses*. In contrast, a shift of the whole production possibilities curve indicates a change in the *set of choices* available to society.

•   Today's resource allocation decisions shape our future production possibilities; the more capital or future goods that we produce today, the more the production possibilities curve will expand in the future.

•   If a nation specializes and trades with other nations, then the nation is not limited to consuming combinations of products represented by points on the production possibilities curve.

Quick Quiz

7. A nation's production possibilities curve will shift outwards if:
(a)   the nation reduces its unemployment rate
(b)   the nation discovers new mineral resources
(c)   the nation increases its foreign trade
(d)   any of the above occurs

8. Canada could expect to grow faster in the coming years if, *ceteris paribus,* Canada today increases her production of:
(a)   food
(b)   video games
(c)   clothing
(d)   highways

9. When an economy slides into a recession:
(a)   the production possibility curve will shift inwards
(b)   the production possibility curve will become steeper
(c)   the production possibility curve will become flatter
(d)   the production point will fall below the production possibility curve

2.4 Economic Systems

◈ What are the characteristics of the two main types of economic systems?

•   Different societies use different economic systems for addressing the fundamental economic problem of scarcity. Systems differ mainly in the ownership of resources, and in the method used to coordinate and direct economic activity.

•   At one extreme is the market system, or capitalism, which relies upon private ownership of resources, the profit motive, and coordination through the use of prices and markets. The type of capitalism used in Canada also gives government a significant role in the economy.

•   At the other extreme, the command economy uses public ownership of resources and decisions are made by central planning. In recent years a number of command economies have incorporated elements of the market system.

Quick Quiz

10. The private ownership of property resources and use of the market system to direct and coordinate economic activity is characteristic of:
 (a)   pure capitalism
 (b)   the command economy
 (c)   market socialism
 (d)   the traditional economy

11. In a centrally planned economy resource allocation decisions are made by the:
 (a)   the command system
 (b)   the market system
 (c)   the capitalist system
 (d)   the laissez-faire system

2.5 The Circular Flow Model

◇ What is the circular flow model?

•   The circular flow model illustrates the interaction between businesses and households in resource markets and product markets. In exchange for resources that households supply to firms, firms pay incomes that households in turn use to demand goods and services produced by firms.

Quick Quiz

12. The two kinds of markets found in the circular flow model are:
 (a)   real and money markets
 (b)   real and traditional markets
 (c)   money and authoritarian markets
 (d)   product and factor markets

13. In the circular flow model, businesses:
 (a)   demand both products and resources
 (b)   supply both products and resources
 (c)   demand products and supply resources
 (d)   supply products and demand resources

Terms and Concepts

economic problem
economic resources
land
capital
investment
labour
entrepreneurial ability
factors of production

capital goods
production possibilities table
production possibilities curve
opportunity cost
law of increasing opportunity cost
economic growth

full employment
full production
productive efficiency
allocative efficiency
consumer goods

economic system
market system
command system
factor market
product market
circular flow model

Fill-In Questions

1. The two fundamental facts that provide the foundation of economics are:
 (a)   Society's wants are _____.
 (b)   Society's resources are _____.

2. Economic efficiency requires that there be both full _____ of resources and full _____. Full production implies that both _____ efficiency and _____ efficiency are achieved.

3. Below is a production possibilities curve for ropes and ladders.

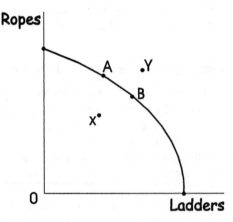

(a) If the economy moves from point *A* to point *B*, it will produce (more, fewer) _____ ropes and (more, fewer) _____ ladders.
(b) If the economy is producing at point *X*, some of the resources of the economy are either _____ or _____.
(c) In order for the economy to produce at point *Y*, it must either expand its supply of _____ or improve its _____.

4. If Canada attempts to expand her apple industry, the opportunity cost per apple will tend to increase because resources are not completely _____ to different uses. This is an example of the generalization known as the law of _____.

True-False

Circle T if the statement is true, F if it is false.

1. If you must stand in line for six hours to get into a free concert by the Rolling Stones, there is no opportunity cost to you for seeing the concert.
T   F

2. Money is a resource and is classified as "capital."
T   F

3. Profit is the reward paid to those who provide the economy with capital.
T   F

4. The opportunity cost of producing wheat tends to increase as more wheat is produced because land less suited to its production must be reallocated from other uses.
T   F

5. A production possibilities curve that is concave to the origin reflects the law of increasing opportunity costs.
T   F

6. The problem of scarcity is likely to be solved someday by technological progress.
T   F

7. An economy that is employing the least cost productive methods has achieved allocative efficiency.
T   F

8. Given full employment and full production, it is impossible for an economy that can produce only two goods to increase production of both.
T   F

9. The more capital goods an economy produces today, the greater will be its ability to produce all goods in the future, ceteris paribus.
T   F

10. Most nations use economic systems somewhere between the extremes of pure capitalism and command economy.
T   F

11. In a command economy most resources are privately owned and are allocated by the market system.
T   F

12. In the circular flow model, households act on the demand side of resource and product markets.
T   F

Multiple-Choice

Circle the letter that corresponds to the best answer.

1. In her role as an "innovator" an entrepreneur:
(a) makes policy decisions in a business firm
(b) combines factors of production to produce a good or service
(c) invents a new production process
(d) takes risks in the market place

2. An economy is efficient when it has achieved:
(a) full employment
(b) full production
(c) full employment or full production
(d) full employment and full production

3. When a production possibilities curve is drawn, four assumptions are made. Which is not one of those assumptions?
(a) only two goods are produced
(b) wants are unlimited
(c) the economy has both full employment and full production
(d) the quantities of all resources available to the economy are fixed

The next three questions are based on the following production possibilities table for Nashia Twang, a singer who can use her time and other resources to perform concerts or write new songs.

Alternative	A	B	C	D	E
Concerts	0	20	40	60	80
Songs	10	9	7	4	0

4. The opportunity cost of writing one more song as Twang moves from alternative C to B is:
(a) 40 concerts per song
(b) 20 concerts per song
(c) 10 concerts per song
(d) 8 concerts per song

5. The opportunity cost of playing one more concert as Twang moves from alternative C to D is:
(a) 3/20 song per concert
(b) 3 songs per concert
(c) 20 songs per concert
(d) 6 2/3 songs per concert

6. Twang's highest opportunity cost for producing one more song occurs in the neighbourhood of alternative:
  (a)   A
  (b)   B
  (c)   C
  (d)   D

7. If opportunity costs are constant, instead of increasing, the production possibilities curve will be:
  (a)   concave to the origin
  (b)   convex to the origin
  (c)   a downward sloping straight line
  (d)   parallel to the horizontal axis

Answer the next three questions on the basis of the following diagram.

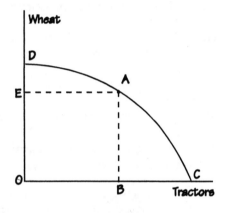

8. At point *A* on the production possibilities curve:
  (a)   less wheat than tractors is being produced
  (b)   fewer tractors than wheat are being produced
  (c)   the economy is employing all its resources
  (d)   the economy is not employing all its resources

9. The opportunity cost of producing 0*B* of tractors is:
  (a)   0*D* of wheat
  (b)   0*E* of wheat
  (c)   *ED* of wheat
  (d)   0*C* of tractors

10. If there occurred a technological improvement in the production of tractors but not wheat:
  (a)   point *D* would remain fixed and point *C* shift to the left
  (b)   point *C* would remain fixed and point *D* shift upward
  (c)   point *D* would remain fixed and point *C* shift to the right
  (d)   point *C* would remain fixed and point *D* shift inward

11. From one point to another along the same production possibilities curve:
  (a)   resources remain fixed but are reallocated between the production of the two goods
  (b)   resources are increased and are reallocated between the two goods
  (c)   resources are increased and production of both goods increased
  (d)   idle resources are put to work to increase the production of one good

12. Which of the following would cause a nation's production possibilities curve to shift inward toward the origin?
  (a)   more people in the labour force
  (b)   increased international trade
  (c)   rising unemployment of workers
  (d)   not replacing capital equipment as it wears out

13. Which of the following will slow down the rate at which Canada's production possibilities curve shifts rightward?
  (a)   increasing rate of technological change
  (b)   increased immigration
  (c)   depletion of Canada's oil and gas deposits
  (d)   freer trade between Canada's provinces

14. If there is an increase in the resources available within the economy:
  (a)   more goods and services will be produced in the economy
  (b)   the economy will be capable of producing more goods and services
  (c)   the standard of living in the economy will rise
  (d)   the technological efficiency of the economy will improve

15. The opportunity cost of providing a governmentally financed stadium for a city's baseball team is:

(a) the interest on the money borrowed to finance the stadium

(b) the future tax increase the public will be forced to bear to pay for the stadium

(c) the other goods and services that must be sacrificed so that resources can be used for stadium construction

(d) there is no opportunity cost since Ottawa will finance the stadium under a regional development program

16. Private ownership of property resources, use of the market system to direct and coordinate economic activity, and the presence of the profit motive are characteristic of:

(a) pure capitalism

(b) the command economy

(c) market socialism

(d) communism

17. Central planning is associated with which economic system?

(a) pure capitalism

(b) laissez-faire capitalism

(c) market economy

(d) command economy

18. Productive efficiency is attained when:

(a) resources are all employed

(b) output is produced at least possible cost

(c) there is no government involvement in the economy

(d) the production possibilities curve is concave

19. The term "laissez-faire" refers to:

(a) the absence of government intervention in markets

(b) the absence of monopoly

(c) the absence of competition in markets

(d) efficient use of employed resources

Problems and Projects

1. Resource Incomes

Match the resources on the left with the corresponding resource payments on the right.

(a) labour   (i) rent
(b) capital   (ii) wages
(c) land   (iii) profits
(d) entrepreneurial (iv) interest
    ability   income

2. Types of Resources

Below is a list of resources. Indicate in the space to the right of each whether the resource is land (Ld), capital (K), labour (L), or entrepreneurial ability (EA).

(a) fishing grounds in the North Atlantic _____

(b) a farmer's inventory of wheat _____

(c) Maple Leaf Gardens in Toronto _____

(d) the work performed by Bill Gates _____

(e) Cavendish beach in Prince Edward Island _____

(f) Stelco's steel plant in Hamilton ___

(g) the tasks accomplished in making the Apple Computer a commercial success _____

(h) the work of a cashier at Zeller's _____

3. Production Possibilities

An economy produces coolers (C) and heaters (H), according to the production possibilities table below. The usual assumptions apply.

(a) Plot the data on the graph provided, and label the curve PPC.

Coolers	Heaters	Heaters (f)
0	6	_____
7	5	_____
13	4	_____
18	3	_____
22	2	_____
25	1	_____
27	0	_____

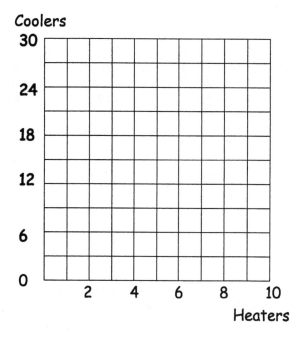

(b) Can the economy produce 4 of H and 22 of C? _____ If not, why? _____ What is the maximum amount of C that can be produced in combination with 4H?_____

(c) If the economy is producing 2H and 15C, what problem is being experienced? _____

(d) Assuming that the economy is productively efficient, what is the opportunity cost of producing 1H instead of none? _____ What is the opportunity cost of the second unit of H? _____ And the third H? _____

(e) As more units of H are produced, what is the trend in the number of units of C that must be given up to get the extra H? _____. Due to this trend, the shape of the production possibilities curve is _____ to the origin.

(f) A technological breakthrough makes it possible to produce 50% more heaters with the same resources as before. Fill in the new values for the column labelled Heaters (f), use this data to plot the new production possibilities curve PPCf.

4. Consumer Goods and Capital Goods

Below is a list of economic goods. Indicate in the space beside each whether the good is a consumer good (C), a capital good (K), or that it depends (D) upon who is using it and for what purpose.

(a) a dairy cow   ____
(b) a tractor   ____
(c) a telephone pole   ____
(d) a telephone   ____
(e) your refrigerator   ____
(f) a refrigerator in a restaurant ____

5. Production Possibilities Curve Shifts

For each case below you are given an initial production possibilities curve between timber and fish. For each event, sketch a new curve to show the result.

(a) Supplies of labour and capital expand.

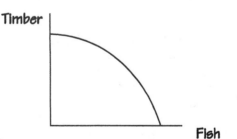

(b) New tree-planting techniques improve the success of reforestation operations.

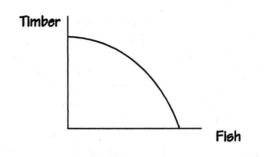

(c) An ecological disaster wipes out a large part of the fish stocks.

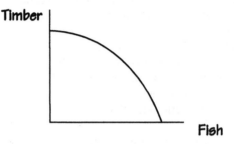

6. The Impact of Technological Change

An economy is achieving full production, producing automobiles and food at point X.

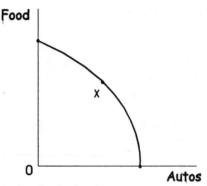

Now a technological advance occurs which enables this economy to produce automobiles with fewer resources than previously. How is it possible for the society to consume more automobiles *and* more food as a result? Illustrate using the production possibilities diagram.

7. Allocative Efficiency

A department store is installing video cameras to reduce shoplifting. The marginal costs and marginal benefits of additional cameras are:

Camera	MB ($/month)	MC ($/month)
1	300	100
2	250	125
3	160	150
4	50	175

(a) If the store must choose one of the options listed in the table, then allocative efficiency is reached by installing __ cameras.
(b) How much better off is the store with the optimal number than with one fewer camera? $___
(c) How much better off is the store with the optimal number than with one more camera? $___

Discussion Questions

1. Explain what is meant by the "economic problem." Why are resources scarce?

2. When is a society economically efficient? What is meant by "full production," and how does it differ from "full employment"?

3. What four assumptions are made in drawing a production possibilities curve? How do technological progress and an increased supply of resources in the economy affect the curve?

4. Why cannot an economist determine which combination in the production possibilities table is "best"? What determines the optimum product-mix?

5. What is opportunity cost? What is the law of increasing opportunity costs? Why do opportunity costs increase?

6. Would the economic problem disappear if the affluent countries, including Canada, offered to pay more for the products of the Third World countries? Explain.

7. During the Cold War, Russia seemed to be quite competitive with the United States in terms of military strength even though Russia's overall production capabilities were much lower than America's. Use the production possibility curve model to resolve this paradox.

8. If resources in an economy are fully employed, what would be the effect on living standards if the government decided to increase the output of goods for the future? Explain using the production possibilities curve.

9. Explain why you agree or disagree with the statement: "The opportunity cost of allocating large numbers of people to clean up Ontario's lakes during a recession is different from the opportunity cost during a period of full employment."

10. Explain the difference between productive and allocative efficiency.

11. What are the roles of households and of businesses in the resource market and the product market?

Answers

Quick Quiz
1. (b) p. 26
2. (d) pp. 27-28
3. (c) pp. 28-29
4. (d) p. 30
5. (c) pp. 30, 32
6. (a) p. 33
7. (b) p. 35
8. (d) pp. 36-37
9. (d) p. 34
10. (a) p. 40
11. (a) p. 40
12. (d) pp. 40-42
13. (d) pp. 41-42

Fill-In Questions
1. (a) unlimited; (b) scarce (or limited)
2. employment, production; productive, allocative
3. (a) fewer, more; (b) unemployed, underemployed; (c) resources, technology
4. adaptable; increasing opportunity costs

True-False
1. F   Your time has value
2. F   Money is not an economic resource
3. F   Profit goes to entrepreneurs; capitalists earn interest income
4. T
5. T
6. F   Even as we become able to produce more our wants will continue to expand
7. F   Allocative efficiency is not achieved unless the most wanted combination of goods is being produced
8. T
9. T   As we produce more capital goods, or goods for the future, our PPC expands more in the future
10. T

11. F The statement describes capitalism or market system

12. F Households are suppliers, not demanders, in resource markets

Multiple-Choice

1. (c) The others are roles of entrepreneurs, but not the innovator role

2. (d) Both are necessary conditions

3. (b) Demands for goods do not determine the position of the PPC

4. (c) (20-40)/(9-7)= -10; 10 concerts are sacrificed per song written

5. (a) (4-7)/(6-40) = -3/20; 3/20 song sacrificed per concert

6. (a) A

7. (c) Such a line would have a constant slope, or trade-off ratio between the two goods

8. (c) Any point on the curve involves full employment

9. (c) Wheat production falls from D to E

10. (c) Maximum tractor output increases; maximum wheat does not change

11. (a) Increased resources would imply a shift; if resources were previously idle the economy was not on the curve

12. (d) The capital stock would shrink, meaning a reduction in the supply of resources

13. (c) Reduction in our supply of resources

14. (b) The PPC will shift out, meaning that the economy is *capable* of producing more, and reaching a higher standard of living; but this potential may not be realized

15. (c) Ultimately the opportunity cost must be measured in other goods given up

16. (a) All are critical to a capitalist or market economy

17. (d) Including socialism and communism

18. (b) Using resources in the most productive way, and minimizing cost of production go hand in hand

19. (a) "Let it be" is government's attitude toward the economy in a "laissez faire" system

Problems and Projects

1. labour/wages; capital/interest income; land/rental income; entrepreneurial ability/profits

2. (a) Ld; (b) K; (c) K; (d) EA; (e) Ld; (f) K; (g) EA; (h) L

3. (a) see graph below; (b) No; this combination lies outside the PPC (see point b); 13C; (c) productive inefficiency (unemployment or underem-

ployment) (see point C); (d) 2C = 27C – 25C, 3C, 4C; (e) increasing, concave; (f) in the table, add 50% to the values in the Heaters column: 9, 7.5, 6, 4.5, 3, 1.5, 0; the result is PPCf on the graph.

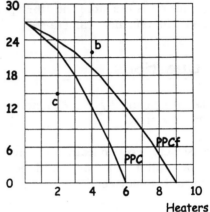

4. (a) K, (b) K, (c) K, (d) D, (e) C, (f) K

5. For each case below, PPC1 is before the event, and PPC2 is after.

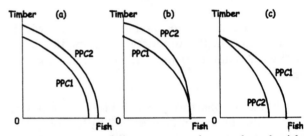

6. More automobiles can now be produced with a given amount of resources, so the automobiles intercept shifts out. If there is no reallocation of resources, production would move from *X* to *X'*, but by moving some resources from autos to food, the society can produce more food and more automobiles. This is shown by the movement along the new PPC from *X'* to *Y*.

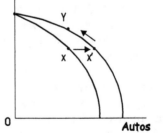

7. (a) 3 cameras, because for each of the first three, the MB > MC; (b) $10/month is the net benefit for the 3rd camera ($160-150); (c) $125/month is the net loss for the 4th camera ($50-175)

Chapter 3 | Individual Markets: Demand and Supply

Overview

This chapter presents the most important tool of economic analysis: the demand and supply model. We use this model to analyze how various events affect the price and quantities of goods and services traded in highly competitive markets with many buyers and sellers trading a standardized product. The model can be expressed in several ways: as algebraic equations, schedules in tables, or graphs.

The law of demand asserts an inverse relationship between price and quantity demanded, *ceteris paribus*. The law of supply states a positive relationship between price and quantity supplied, *ceteris paribus*. Given the demand and supply in a market, equilibrium is found at the one price at which the quantity demanded by consumers exactly equals the quantity supplied by sellers.

Starting from an equilibrium, a change in any demand or supply determinant will shift the demand or supply curve, and throw the market out of equilibrium — creating either a shortage or a surplus. To eliminate the shortage (or surplus) the price must rise (or fall) to restore the balance between how much consumers are willing and able to buy and producers are willing and able to sell.

Mastery of the supply and demand model depends on clear understanding of the definitions of demand and supply, and the key distinctions between "demand" and "quantity demanded" and between "supply" and "quantity supplied." Practice with the graphical model of demand and supply will greatly help clarify these concepts.

Sometimes governments implement price controls to keep the price higher or lower than the equilibrium price that would result from market forces. Price ceilings create shortages, and price floors create surpluses, and in both cases there is a rationing problem. Price controls also create a host of unintended side effects, including black market transactions, as disappointed or frustrated market participants try to get around the intended effects of the price controls.

Chapter Outline

3.1 Markets

✧ What is a market?

• A market is any institution or mechanism that brings together the buyers and sellers of a particular good or service.

• In this chapter we assume that markets are highly competitive, meaning that there are many buyers and sellers of a standardized product.

➲ This chapter is the most important one in the book. Be sure to spend extra time on it, and to return to it to review the fundamentals if you run into difficulties in later chapters.

Quick Quiz

1. The markets examined in this chapter:
   (a) sell nonstandard or differentiated products
   (b) have buyers cooperating to determine prices
   (c) are controlled by a single producer
   (d) are highly competitive

3.2 Demand

✧ What is demand?
   o What is the law of demand?
   o What does a demand curve show?
   o How is the market demand found?

• Demand is the relationship between the price of a product and the amount of the product that the consumer is willing and able to purchase in a specific time period. The relationship can be expressed in a table, graph, or equation.

• The law of demand states that, other things being equal, as price falls, the quantity demanded rises. That is, there is an inverse relationship between price and quantity demanded.

• Along with plenty of strong evidence for the law of demand are three analytical reasons:
   o If consumers experience diminishing marginal utility then they will be willing

to buy additional units of a good only if price is reduced.

   o   When price falls there is an income effect: the consumer's overall buying power increases so the consumer buys more of the good.
   o   When price falls there is a substitution effect: the consumer is motivated to buy more of the good that is now relatively less expensive instead of other goods for which it is a substitute.

•   The demand curve is a graphic representation of the law of demand.

   o   The graph has price on the vertical axis, and quantity demanded on the horizontal axis.
   o   A change in price leads to a movement along the demand curve. This is called a change in quantity demanded.

•   The market demand is derived by "adding up" the individual consumer demands at each possible price. The law of demand applies to both individual and market demand curves.

➲   Perhaps more than any other chapter, this chapter requires active practice. Pick up your pencil and draw graphs. Begin by plotting demand and supply schedules onto graphs. Study carefully the examples in the text and study guide to learn the appropriate labels for such graphs. Once you are confident of working with graphs with concrete numbers, go to the next step of drawing abstract graphs where numbers are implied on the axes, but not explicitly given.

◇   What are the determinants of demand, and how do they influence demand?

◇   What is the difference between a change in demand and a change in quantity demanded?

•   The price determines the quantity demanded of a good, but factors other than price determine the location of the whole demand curve. These factors are known as the demand determinants:

   o   tastes (or preferences) of buyers;
   o   number of buyers in the market;
   o   incomes of consumers;
   o   prices of related goods (substitutes and complements);
   o   expectations.

•   A change in a demand determinant will shift demand to the left (a decrease) or the right (an increase), creating an entirely new demand curve. This is called a change in demand.

   o   If tastes shift in favour of a good, its demand will increase.
   o   If the number of buyers of a good increases, its demand will increase.
   o   If consumer incomes increase, demand will increase if the good is normal, and demand will decrease if the good is inferior.
   o   If an increase in the price of one good causes the demand for another good to decrease, the two goods are complements; if the price increase causes demand for the other good to increase, the two goods are substitutes.
   o   If consumers expect prices or incomes to rise in the future they may increase their demand now.

•   A change in demand and a change in the quantity demanded are not the same thing. This is obvious on the graph where a change in the price of the good causes a change in the quantity demanded, or movement along the curve, whereas a change in demand shifts the entire curve to a new location.

Quick Quiz

2. A schedule which shows the various amounts of a product consumers are willing and able to purchase at each price in a series of possible prices during a specified period of time is called:
   (a)   supply
   (b)   demand
   (c)   quantity supplied
   (d)   quantity demanded

3. The reason for the law of demand is best explained in terms of:
   (a)   complementary goods
   (b)   substitutable goods
   (c)   law of increasing costs
   (d)   diminishing marginal utility

4. Which factor will decrease the demand for a product?
   (a)   a favourable change in consumer tastes
   (b)   an increase in the price of a substitute good
   (c)   a decrease in the price of a complementary good
   (d)   a decrease in the number of buyers

3.3 Supply

◈ What is supply?
  ○ What is the law of supply?
  ○ What does a supply curve show?
  ○ How is the market supply found?

• Supply is the relationship between the price of a product and the amount of the product that suppliers will offer to sell in a specific time period.

• The law of supply states that, other things being equal, as price rises, the quantity supplied rises. That is, there is a positive relationship between price and quantity supplied. The quantity supplied rises with price because the supplier can profitably produce more output at a higher price.

• The supply curve is a graphic representation of supply and the law of supply.
  ○ The graph has price on the vertical axis, and quantity supplied on the horizontal.
  ○ A change in price leads to a movement along the supply curve. This is called a change in quantity supplied.

◈ What are the determinants of supply, and how do they influence demand?

◈ What is the difference between a change in supply and a change in quantity supplied?

• The determinants of supply are:
  ○ factor prices;
  ○ technology;
  ○ taxes and subsidies;
  ○ prices of other goods;
  ○ price expectations;
  ○ number of sellers in the market.

• A change in any of the determinants will shift supply to the left (a decrease) or the right (an increase), creating an entirely new supply curve. This is called a change in supply.
  ○ If prices of factors (production resources) fall, supply will increase.
  ○ A technological change will improve the efficiency of production and increase the supply.
  ○ A new tax will raise the producer's costs and reduce the supply; a new subsidy will increase the supply.
  ○ Producers may reallocate their resources if the price of a related good changes. Depending on the case, supply could increase or decrease.
  ○ It is also difficult to generalize about how

a change in expectations about the future price will change today's supply.
  ○ An increase in the number of sellers will increase the supply.
• A change in supply and a change in the quantity supplied are different things. The difference is most obvious on a graph. A change in the price of the good causes a change in the quantity supplied, which on the graph is a movement to a different point on the same supply curve, whereas a change in supply involves a shift to a whole new supply curve.

➲ You have not mastered the chapter until you can clearly distinguish between a change in demand and a change in quantity demanded; the same for supply vs. quantity supplied. You should be able to articulate the difference verbally, and graphically.

Quick Quiz

5. A decrease in the supply of a product would most likely be caused by:
  (a) an increase in business taxes
  (b) an increase in consumer incomes
  (c) a decrease in factor prices
  (d) a decrease in the price of a complementary good

6. Which of the following could not cause an increase in the supply of cotton?
  (a) an increase in the price of cotton
  (b) better technology for producing cotton
  (c) a decrease in the price of the machinery and tools employed in cotton production
  (d) a decrease in the price of corn

7. An "increase in supply" means:
  (a) a rightward shift of the supply curve
  (b) a leftward shift of the supply curve
  (c) a movement up along a given supply curve
  (d) a movement down along a given supply curve

3.4 Supply and Demand: Market Equilibrium

◈ What is a market equilibrium?
  ○ What happens when there is a shortage or a surplus?
  ○ What does a supply curve show?
  ○ How is equilibrium affected by a shift in demand or supply?

- The market-clearing or equilibrium price of a good is that price at which quantity demanded and quantity supplied are equal; the equilibrium quantity is equal to the quantity demanded and supplied at the equilibrium price.
  - o If price is above the equilibrium, quantity demanded is less than quantity supplied, so there is a surplus. This will cause price to fall.
  - o If price is below the equilibrium, quantity demanded is greater than quantity supplied, so there is a shortage. This will cause price to rise.
  - o The only sustainable price is the equilibrium price.
  - o The rationing function of price is to create consistency between the decisions of sellers and of buyers, so as to eliminate any shortages or surpluses.
- Any change in a determinant of demand or supply will cause the curve to shift, and result in a new equilibrium price and quantity.
  - o Most changes shift only one of the two curves.
  - o When demand changes, and supply is unchanged, equilibrium price and quantity change in the same direction as demand.
  - o When supply changes, and demand is unchanged, quantity moves in the same direction as supply, but equilibrium price moves in the opposite direction.
  - o In complex cases where both supply and demand change, both curves will shift; either the direction of price change or quantity change will be predictable, the other will be indeterminate.

➲ The first step in analyzing how an event affects the market equilibrium is to determine which curve is directly affected by the event: supply or demand. The second step is to decide whether that curve increases or decreases. From there it is a simple matter to decide the direction of change for the equilibrium price and quantity.

➲ If algebraic work with demand and supply is relevant in the economics course you are studying, please look at the Appendix to Chapter 3.

Quick Quiz

8. If the quantity supplied of a product is greater than the quantity demanded for a product, then:
(a)   there is a shortage of the product
(b)   there is a surplus of the product
(c)   the product is a normal good
(d)   the product is an inferior good

9. What would be the effect on the market for houses in a city that experiences a rise in population?
(a)   demand would increase, raising the equilibrium price and quantity of houses
(b)   supply would decrease, raising the equilibrium price and quantity of houses
(c)   demand would decrease, lowering the equilibrium price and quantity of houses
(d)   supply would increase, lowering the equilibrium price and quantity of houses

10. If the demand for tuna increases at the same time that the supply of tuna decreases:
(a)   the equilibrium price of tuna will rise, but the change in the equilibrium quantity of tuna cannot be predicted
(b)   the equilibrium quantity of tuna will fall, but the change in the equilibrium price of tuna cannot be predicted
(c)   the equilibrium price and quantity of tuna will both rise
(d)   the equilibrium price and quantity of tuna will both fall

3.5 Application: Government-set Prices

◈ What are government-set prices and how do they affect market equilibrium?
- o What are price ceilings?
- o What are price floors?
- Sometimes governments impose price ceilings when prices seem unfairly high to buyers, or impose price floors when prices seem unfairly low to sellers. Such controls prevent market forces from performing the rationing function.
- A price ceiling is a maximum legal price. It results in a shortage of the commodity; may bring about formal rationing by the government and a black market; and causes a misallocation of resources.
- A price floor is a minimum legal price. It results in a surplus of the commodity which may induce government to take measures to restrict the supply, increase demand, or purchase the surplus; and causes a misallocation of resources.
- Examples of price ceilings are: rent controls

on apartments, proposed controls on gasoline prices, and proposed credit card interest rate ceilings. Examples of price floors are agricultural price supports and minimum wage laws.

• Price controls always involve controversial tradeoffs because any benefits provided by the controls entail costs for some people, and create various unintended and undesirable side effects.

Quick Quiz

11. A price ceiling is intended to:
   (a)   create a surplus
   (b)   create a shortage
   (c)   lower price for consumers
   (d)   raises price for producers

12. Which is an example of a price floor?
   (a)   rent controls on apartments
   (b)   a minimum wage law
   (c)   a maximum on university tuition rates
   (d)   limits on interest rates charged by credit card companies

Terms and Concepts

market	supply
demand	law of supply
law of demand	supply curve
marginal utility	determinants of supply
income effect	
substitution effect	change in supply
demand curve	change in quantity supplied
determinants of demand	
	surplus
normal good	shortage
inferior good	equilibrium price
substitute goods	equilibrium quantity
complementary goods	rationing function of prices
change in demand	
change in quantity demanded	price ceiling
	price floors

Fill-In Questions

1. A market is the institution or mechanism that brings together the _____ and the _____ of a particular good or service.

2. The Latin phrase meaning "all other things being equal" is _____.

3. The graph of the demand schedule is called the demand _____ and according to the law of demand is _____ sloping.

4. A change in price causes a change in (demand, quantity demanded) _____, and results in a (movement along, shift in) _____ the demand curve. A change in consumer incomes causes a change in (demand, quantity demanded) _____, and results in a (movement along, shift in) _____ the demand curve.

5. Marianne tends to buy more books when the price of books falls because:
(a) her purchasing power is increased, so she can afford to buy more books and other goods; this is called the _____ effect.
(b) books become less expensive relative to magazines, so Marianne tends to buy more books and fewer magazines; and this is called the _____ effect.

6. Jean enjoys fashion magazines. She is willing to pay less for each additional subscription because she is successively less likely to actually read each extra one she buys. This is an example of the principle known as diminishing _____.

7. A change in price causes a change in (supply, quantity supplied) _____, and results in a (movement along, shift in) _____ the supply curve. A change in resource costs causes a change in (supply, quantity supplied) _____, and results in a (movement along, shift in) _____ the supply curve.

True-False

Circle T if the statement is true, F if it is false.

1. The classified ads section of a student newspaper could be considered a market.   **T F**

2. The law of demand states that as price increases, the demand for the product decreases, *ceteris paribus.*   **T F**

The next three questions are based on the accompanying graph.

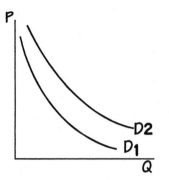

3. If the demand curve changes from D_1 to D_2 demand has increased.   **T F**

4. The shift of the demand curve from D_1 to D_2 could be caused by a decrease in the price of complements.   **T F**

5. The shift of the demand curve from D_1 to D_2 could be caused by a decrease in supply.   **T F**

6. If two goods are complements, an increase in the price of one will cause the demand for the other to decrease.   **T F**

7. A fall in the price of cable internet access will cause the demand for telephone internet access to decrease.   **T F**

8. Since the amount purchased must equal the amount sold, demand and supply must always equal each other.   **T F**

9. A decrease in quantity supplied can be caused by an increase in production costs.   **T F**

10. If the supply curve for lipstick shifts to the right, the supply of lipstick has decreased.   **T F**

11. When quantity supplied exceeds quantity demanded, the market price will tend to fall.   **T F**

12. The equilibrium price is also referred to as the market-clearing price.   **T F**

13. The rationing function of prices is the elimination of shortages and surpluses.   **T F**

14. If government sets a price floor that is above the equilibrium price, this will raise the price and quantity in the market.   **T F**

15. A government-set ceiling on credit card inter-est rates would lead to actions by the issuers to reduce their costs or increase service charges.

T F

Multiple-Choice

Circle the letter that corresponds to the best answer.

1. An increase in the quantity demanded of oranges can be caused by:
  (a)   a shift to the left of the supply curve of oranges
  (b)   a shift to the right of the supply curve of oranges
  (c)   a decline in the demand for orange juice
  (d)   a rise in the demand for orange juice

2. A decrease in the quantity demanded:
  (a)   shifts the demand curve to the left
  (b)   shifts the demand curve to the right
  (c)   is a movement down along the demand curve
  (d)   is a movement up along the demand curve

3. If skiing at Banff and skiing at Whistler are substitutes, an increase in the price of skiing at Banff will:
  (a)   decrease demand for skiing at Whistler
  (b)   increase demand for skiing at Whistler
  (c)   decrease quantity demanded of skiing at Whistler
  (d)   increase quantity demanded of skiing at Whistler

4. Which pair of goods would most consumers regard as complementary goods?
  (a)   coffee and tea
  (b)   hockey sticks and skates
  (c)   hamburger meat and bus rides
  (d)   books and televisions

5. Which of the following is **not** among the determinants of demand?
  (a)   consumer incomes
  (b)   consumer expectations of future prices
  (c)   prices of substitute goods
  (d)   cost of resources

6. If an increase in income causes the demand for gumboots to decrease, then gumboots are:

(a) normal
(b) inferior
(c) substitute goods
(d) complementary goods

7. According to the law of supply:
(a) equilibrium quantity will increase when equilibrium price increases
(b) equilibrium quantity will decrease when equilibrium price increases
(c) the supply curve has a negative slope
(d) if other things remain the same, the quantity supplied increases whenever price increases

8. A supply curve indicates:
(a) the profit-maximizing quantities sellers place on the market at alternative prices
(b) the minimum quantities sellers place on the market at alternative prices
(c) the maximum quantities sellers will place on the market at different prices for inputs
(d) the quantities sellers place on the market in order to meet consumer demand at that price

9. The supply curve of the firm slopes upward in the short run because:
(a) the increased production requires the use of inferior inputs
(b) hiring more inputs for the extra production requires the payment of higher input prices
(c) the increased technology to produce more output is expensive
(d) productive efficiency declines because certain productive resources cannot be expanded quickly

10. A movement along a supply curve for a good would be caused by:
(a) improvements in production technology
(b) an increase in the price of the good
(c) an increase in the number of suppliers of the good
(d) a change in expectations

11. Which of the following would increase the supply of books?
(a) an increase in the demand for books
(b) an increase in the price of books
(c) an increase in the cost of paper

(d) a decrease in the wages paid to printers

12. Which of the following events would likely cause a furniture manufacturer to increase his supply of oak tables:
(a) an increase in the price of oak tables
(b) an increase in the cost of oak lumber
(c) a decrease in the demand for pine tables
(d) an increase in wages paid to staff

The next four questions are based on the following diagram.

13. Given the original demand and supply curves are D and S:
(a) the equilibrium price and quantity were P and Q1
(b) the equilibrium price and quantity were P and P1
(c) the equilibrium price and quantity were P1 and Q1
(d) the equilibrium price and quantity were P and Q3

14. The shift of the supply curve from S to S_1 is termed:
(a) an increase in supply
(b) an increase in quantity supplied
(c) a decrease in supply
(d) a decrease in quantity supplied

15. The shift in the supply curve from S to S_1 could be caused by:
(a) an increase in the price of the good
(b) a technological improvement in the production of the good
(c) a decrease in demand
(d) an increase in the cost of the resources used in the production of the good

16. If the price were prevented from adjusting when the supply shifted from S to S_1 the result

would be:
- (a) a surplus of Q3 - Q1
- (b) a shortage of Q2 - Q1
- (c) a shortage of Q3 - Q1
- (d) a surplus of Q3 - Q2

17. A market is in equilibrium when:
- (a) inventories of the good are not rising
- (b) suppliers can sell all of the good they decide to produce at the prevailing price
- (c) quantity demanded equals quantity supplied
- (d) demanders can purchase all of the good they want at the prevailing price

18. An increase in supply and an increase in demand will:
- (a) increase price and increase the quantity exchanged
- (b) decrease price and increase the quantity exchanged
- (c) affect price in an indeterminate way and decrease the quantity exchanged
- (d) affect price in an indeterminate way and increase the quantity exchanged

19. If scalping NHL playoff game tickets is profitable, this is a sign that the initial price at which the tickets were issued was:
- (a) below the equilibrium price
- (b) equal to the equilibrium price
- (c) above the equilibrium price
- (d) unreasonably high

20. A shortage of paper would cause the price of paper to rise. This would alleviate the shortage by:
- (a) giving buyers incentives to use less paper
- (b) giving producers incentives to find ways to supply more paper
- (c) . increasing the amount of paper being recycled
- (d) all of the above

21. In 2001 fewer tents were sold, and the price of tents was higher, as compared to 2000. Which event alone might have caused the change?
- (a) demand for tents was greater in 2001
- (b) demand for tents was less in 2001
- (c) supply of tents was greater in 2001
- (d) supply of tents was less in 2001

22. Which of the following could raise the price of movie rentals in Saskatoon?

- (a) a drop in the number of movie stores
- (b) an increase in the price of VCRs
- (c) a decrease in the population of Saskatoon
- (d) a decrease in the price of admission to movie theatres

23. If new reserves of natural gas were discovered and brought into production, and population were to fall at the same time:
- (a) the price of natural gas would rise
- (b) the price of natural gas would fall
- (c) the price of natural gas would not change
- (d) the price of natural gas might rise or fall

This graph is used for the next two questions.

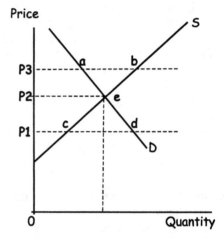

24. The distance *cd* measures:
- (a) the shortage at a price ceiling of P1
- (b) the surplus at a price ceiling of P1
- (c) the shortage at a price floor of P1
- (d) the surplus at a price floor of P1

25. A price floor set at which price would create a surplus?
- (a) P1
- (b) P2
- (c) P3
- (d) none of the above prices

26. An effective minimum wage law can be expected to:
- (a) raise incomes for all workers who previously earned below the minimum wage
- (b) have no effect on teenage unemployment
- (c) create more jobs for teenagers
- [d] reduce employment among teenagers

27. If the government fixes apartment rents below their equilibrium level, the effects in the long run

will include:
- (a) an increased supply of apartments
- (b) a decrease in the demand for apartments
- (c) conversion of condos into rental units
- (d) a reduction in the construction of new apartment units

Problems and Projects

1. Market Demand for Hockey Sticks
(a) Three individuals' demand schedules for hockey sticks are shown below. Assuming these are the only buyers, fill in the market demand schedule for sticks.
(b) If the market supply of sticks is fixed at 48 per year, what will be the equilibrium price and number of sticks bought by each consumer?
Price = $_____ per stick
Quantity = Elmer: _____ sticks; Toe: _____ sticks; Maurice: _____ sticks

Price (per stick)	Quantity Demanded (sticks per year)			
	Elmer	Toe	Maurice	Total
$5	10	6	8	_____
4	12	8	10	_____
3	15	11	12	_____
2	19	15	14	_____
1	24	18	16	_____

2. Demand and Supply Graphing
(a) Plot the demand and supply schedules below on the graph provided. Indicate the equilibrium price and quantity by drawing lines from the intersection of the demand and supply curves to the axes, labelling the values P* and Q*.
(b) At equilibrium, P* = _____, and Q* = _____.
(c) Fill in the last column of the table showing the amount of shortage or surplus that would exist at each price shown.

Price per Unit	Quantity Demanded	Quantity Supplied	Shortage (-) or Surplus (+)
$13	18	54	_____
12	21	48	_____
11	24	42	_____
10	27	36	_____
9	30	30	_____
8	33	24	_____
7	36	18	_____
6	39	12	_____

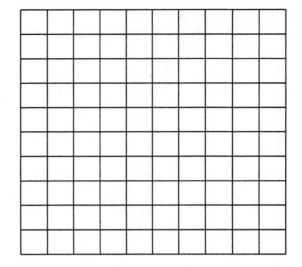

3. Determinants of Demand and Supply of Wine
Below are some events that affect the market for wine. In each space, indicate whether the event shifts demand (D) or supply (S), and whether it is an increase (+) or decrease (-) in the curve.
- (a) Increase in the price of grapes   _____
- (b) Increase in population of consumers   _____
- (c) Increase in the price of cheese   _____
- (d) Improvement in production technology   _____
- (e) New subsidies for wine production   _____
- (f) Increase in the price of beer   _____
- (g) Consumers expect a new tax on wine   _____

4. Supply and Demand for Beef
Consider the demand and supply model for the market for beef produced in Canada. For each of the following events, sketch a demand and supply graph showing the effect on the equilibrium price and quantity of Canadian beef.

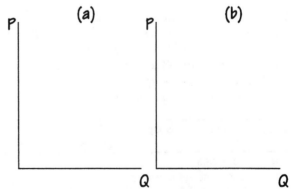

(a) A popular singer remarks that red meat in the diet may be a contributing factor in heart and

circulatory diseases.
(b) The East Coast cod fishery is closed due to depleted fish stocks.

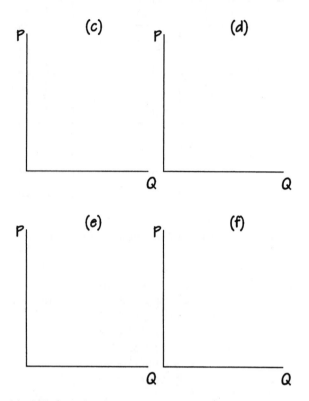

(c) Hoof and mouth disease in Europe leads to destruction of much of the supply of beef produced in that country.
(d) The price of livestock feed grains rises sharply due to a record harvest.
(e) Agriculture Canada discovers a new growth hormone that will increase the weight of beef cattle by 20% with the same feed intake.
(f) Many burger shops close down because of sharp increases in the minimum wage rate.

5. Shifts in Demand and Supply
The following table shows a number of different cases of a change in demand and/or supply. In the blank columns fill in the direction of which in equilibrium price and quantity: increase (+), decrease (-), or indeterminate (?).

Case	Demand	Supply	Price change	Quantity change
a	increases	constant	_____	_____
b	constant	increases	_____	_____
c	decreases	constant	_____	_____
d	constant	decreases	_____	_____
e	increases	increases	_____	_____

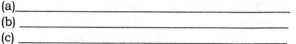

f	increases	decreases	_____	_____
g	decreases	decreases	_____	_____
h	decreases	increases	_____	_____

6. Golf and the Law of Demand
In the 1990s, most golf courses raised their prices but also had more golfers coming to play at their courses. This case (is, is not) _____ a violation of the law of demand. Three possible reasons for the observed behaviour are:
(a)_____
(b) _____
(c) _____

7. Market Demand and Supply for Firewood
The table below shows the demand and supply schedules for firewood in two small towns, Eastwick and Westwood. At first each town is a separate market because there is no passage across the river separating the towns.

	Eastwick		Westwood		Total	
Price	Qd	Qs	Qd	Qs	Qd	Qs
$225	80	100	45	105	____	____
200	90	90	55	95	____	____
175	100	80	65	85	____	____
150	110	70	75	75	____	____
125	120	60	85	65	____	____

(a) In Eastwick the equilibrium price is _____ per cord, and the equilibrium quantity is _____ cords per year.
(b) In Westwood the equilibrium price is _____ per cord, and the equilibrium quantity is _____ cords per year.
Now a bridge is built across the river, turning Eastwick and Westwood into one combined market.
(c) Fill in the market demand and supply schedules in the blank columns.
(d) The new equilibrium price is _____ per cord. This represents an increase in (Westwood, Eastwick) _____ and a decrease in _____.
(e) In Westwood quantity demanded is now _____ cords per year, and quantity supplied is now _____ cords per year. In Eastwick quantity demanded is now _____ cords per year, and quantity supplied is now _____ cords per year. Therefore, the town of _____ must import _____ cords per year from the town of _____.

8. Substitutes and Complements
How would a lengthy strike by transit drivers in

Winnipeg affect the market for gasoline in Winnipeg? Work this out by considering the relationships between buses and cars, and between cars and gasoline.

9. Price Controls and Taxes on Parking Spots
The graph below shows the demand and supply for daily parking spots in the downtown core of a Canadian city.

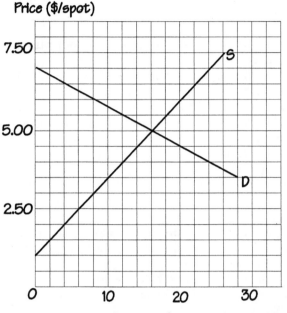

Price ($/spot)

(a) The current equilibrium price is _____ per spot, and _____ spots are rented each day.
(b) Citizen complaints about the cost of parking prompt the city council to impose a price ceiling of $4.00 per spot. The result will be a (shortage, surplus) _____ of ___ spots/day.
(c) Suppose that city council levies a new tax on parking lot operators in order to raise revenue to pay for a rapid transit system. The tax is set at $1.50 per spot. If the consumer pays $6.00, the supplier keeps $6.00-$1.50=$4.50. If the consumer pays $5.00, the supplier keeps _____.
(d) Show the new supply curve reflecting the tax. (The supply curve will shift upward by the amount of the tax because suppliers require this much extra in order to be willing to maintain the same supply as before.)
(e) The new equilibrium price is _____ per spot, and _____ spots are rented each day. Accordingly, the price consumers pay for one spot has (fallen, risen) _____ by $_____, and the price that suppliers keep has _____ by $_____. There-

fore, the consumers' burden of the tax is _____ percent, and the suppliers' burden is _____ percent.

Discussion Questions

1. What is a market? For what kinds of goods does a laundromat bulletin board, or classified pages in a student newspaper, often serve as a market?

2. Carefully state the law of demand and explain the three reasons presented in this chapter to justify downward sloping demand curves.

3. The last time OPEC succeeded in sharply increasing the price of oil, drivers reacted by significantly reducing their gasoline consumption. Explain this in terms of the income effect and substitution effect.

4. Explain the difference between an increase in demand and an increase in quantity demanded. What factors cause a change in demand?

5. Define supply and explain why supply curves are upward sloping.

6. Explain the difference between a change in supply and a change in quantity supplied. What factors cause a change in supply?

7. Neither demand nor supply remains constant for long. Economic circumstances are always changing so the actual prices we see are often not equilibrium prices. Why then do economists spend so much time trying to determine the equilibrium price and quantity if these magnitudes change so frequently?

8. How are normal, inferior, substitute, complementary, and independent goods defined? During a recession (when consumer incomes are falling), who would fare better, firms that sell normal goods, or firms that sell inferior goods?

9. Analyze the following quotation and explain the fallacies contained in it. "An increase in demand will cause price to rise; with a rise in price, supply will increase and the increase in supply will push price down. Therefore, an increase in demand may or may not result in a price increase."

10. To reduce emissions of greenhouse gases, Canada wants to reduce the burning of fossil fuels. Explain why a new tax on automobiles or a subsidy for bicycles would help?

11. From the supply and demand perspective, what would you say has happened in the market for cell phones in the last decade? Are the falling prices and increased numbers of cell phones in use consistent with our economic theory?

12. Ticket agencies have usually set prices at a level where the best seats for concerts sell instantly and are then scalped (or resold for higher prices). In 2003 Ticketmaster announced plans to hold on-line auctions to sell the premium seats to some events. Why did the traditional pricing practice amount to a price control? Who stands to benefit and who stands to lose from the new auction scheme?

Answers

Quick Quiz
1. (d) p. 48
2. (b) p. 48
3. (d) p. 48
4. (d) p. 52
5. (a) p. 58
6. (a) p. 58
7. (a) p. 56
8. (b) p. 61
9. (a) p. 63
10. (a) p. 64
11. (c) p. 65
12. (b) p. 67

Fill-in Questions
1. buyers, sellers (either order)
2. ceteris paribus
3. curve, downward (negative)
4. quantity demanded, movement along; demand, shift in
5. (a) income; (b) substitution
6. marginal utility
7. quantity supplied, movement along; supply, shift in

True-False
1. T   It brings together buyers and sellers

2. F   The change is in quantity demanded, not demand
3. T
4. T
5. F   A supply shift has no bearing on the position of the demand curve
6. T
7. T   The two forms of internet service are substitutes
8. F   The two curves are not equal, though at equilibrium the two curves intersect, sharing a point where Qd equals Qs.
9. F   The decrease is in supply, not quantity supplied
10. F   The supply has increased
11. T   This is a surplus situation
12. T
13. T   Thus determining who gets the available output
14. T   Though quantity produced will exceed quantity demanded
15. T

Multiple-Choice
1. (b) There is a movement along the demand curve when the supply shifts, changing the equilibrium price
2. (d) This is caused by a rise in price
3. (b) Some skiers choose Whistler instead of Banff
4. (b) Complementary goods are used together
5. (d) Cost of resources affects supply, not demand
6. (b) Likely because consumers can substitute higher quality but more expensive footwear
7. (d) This law states a positive relationship between quantity supplied and price
8. (a) Sellers try to maximize profits
9. (d) For example, a restaurant cannot quickly expand its kitchen facilities
10. (b) All of the others shift the supply curve
11. (d) Lower wages means lower production costs and an increase in supply
12. (c) The supply of oak tables could shift right if producers move their resources away from making pine tables to make more oak tables
13. (d) Where S and D intersect
14. (c) Less is supplied at every possible price
15. (d) Increased costs for resources decreases supply
16. (c) If price cannot change, Qd is still at Q3, but Qs is now at Q1
17. (c) All of the other options are only partially correct

18. (d) Depending on which shifts more, demand or supply, price could rise or fall
19. (a) Scalpers profit from the shortage existing at the price at which tickets are first issued
20. (d) These are all aspects of the rationing function of prices
21. (d) Of the possibilities given, only the supply decrease affects both price and quantity as specified
22. (a) Fewer stores would mean a decrease in supply
23. (b) The supply shifts right, while demand shifts left, so both events contribute to a drop in the price
24. (c) Qd – Qs = *cd*. If P1 was a price floor the price would simply rise to equilibrium at P2
25. (c) A surplus of *ab*. None of the other prices would be an effective floor price.
26. (d) The higher wage increases the Qs (number willing to work) but reduces the Qd (number of workers demanded), causing some layoffs
27. (d) Developers will be deterred from supplying more apartment buildings

Problems and Projects
1. (a) 24, 30, 38, 48, 58; (b) $2 (where Qd = Qs). Elmer: 19; Toe: 15; Maurice: 14.
2. (a)

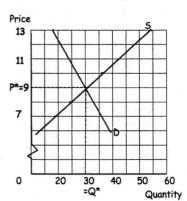

(b) $9, 30; (c) from top to bottom: +36, +27, +18, +9, 0, -9, -18, -27
3. (a) S-; (b) D+; (c) D- (complements for consumers); (d) S+; (e) S+; (f) D+ (substitutes for consumers); (g) D+ (buy more now before price rises).
4. (a) D shifts left: P -, Q -; (b) Fish and beef are substitutes for consumers, so as fish prices rise, then in the beef market D shifts right: P +, Q +; (c) Some buyers switch to Canadian beef, so D shifts right: P +, Q +; (d) Resource prices rise, so S shifts left: P +, Q -; (e) Improved production technology causes S to shift right; P -, Q +; (f) Less buyers of beef, so D shifts left: P -, Q -.

5. (a) +, +; (b) -,+; (c) -,-; (d) +,-; (e) ?,+; (f) +,?; (g) ?,-; (h) -,?
6. is not; (a) population growth, (b) increased incomes, (c) increased preferences for golf, or increased prices for substitute recreation activities, etc.
7. (a) $200, 90; (b) $150, 75; (c) Qd = 125, 145, 165, 185, 205; Qs = 205, 185, 165, 145, 125; (d) $175, Westwood, Eastwick; (e) 65, 85; 100, 80; Eastwick, 20, Westwood.
8. Cars and buses are substitutes, so when buses are out of service more people will drive cars. Cars and gasoline are complements, so more gasoline will be used. The demand for gasoline shifts to right. Equilibrium price and quantity both increase.
9. (a) $5.00, 16,000; (b) Shortage of Qd – Qs = 24,000 – 12,000 = 12,000; (c) $3.50; (d) the new S curve is parallel to the original and $1.50 above it; (e) about 5.50, 12,000, risen, 0.50, fallen, 1.00; 33, 67.

Overview

This appendix shows how the demand and supply model can be represented mathematically. The demand curve and the supply curve can be expressed in equation form as functions of price. Only at the equilibrium price do both functions generate the same value for quantity. Therefore, given the equations for demand and supply, we can set the two equal to solve for equilibrium price and quantity.

This appendix deals with only straight-line demand and supply curves, so their equations can be represented as simple linear equations. Demand is given by $P = a - bQd$, and supply is given by $P = c + dQs$. Each parameter in the equations has an economic meaning. If the price reaches a or higher, the amount demanded will be zero. If the price reaches c or lower, the amount supplied will be zero. The value b indicates the amount by which price would have to rise to reduce quantity demanded by one unit. The value d indicates the amount by which price would have to increase to increase quantity supplied by one unit.

Normally the values for a, b, c, and d are known. With these parameters known, P and Qd are unknown in the demand equation, and P and Qs are unknown in the supply equation. There appear to be three unknowns (P, Qd, and Qs), but at the equilibrium price, Qd and Qs are equal. Therefore the only unknowns are equilibrium price and quantity, which can be represented as Q^* and P^*.

Appendix Outline

◇ How is equilibrium found in a mathematical model of demand and supply?

• A market equilibrium can be expressed as the price-quantity pair (Q^*, P^*) where quantity demanded equals quantity supplied ($Qd = Qs$).

• The market equilibrium results from the negotiating process that brings together the sellers' behaviour and the buyers' behaviour.
• The buyers' behaviour is represented in the equation: $P = a - bQd$. Buyers will buy only at prices below a, and b reflects how quantity demanded and price are related.
• The sellers' behaviour is represented in the equation: $P = c + dQs$. Sellers will sell only at prices above c, and d reflects how quantity supplied and price are related.
• The equilibrium values are solved from the parameter values as follows:
$$P^* = (ad + bc)/(a + d)$$
$$Q^* = (a - c)/(b + d)$$

⮑ Solving for the equilibrium price at which the demand and supply equations are equal is the mathematical equivalent of locating the intersection on a demand and supply graph to find the equilibrium price. There is only one value for price at which the two equations, or the two curves, have the same value for quantity.

⮑ If price is not at the equilibrium value there will be a shortage or a surplus, which can also be determined from the equations by substituting the given price into both equations and then comparing the resulting values for quantity demanded and quantity supplied.

Quick Quiz
1. For the demand equation $P = 20 - 5Qd$:
   (a)   the price axis intercept is 20
   (b)   the price axis intercept is 5
   (c)   the price axis intercept is 4
   (d)   the price axis intercept cannot be solved

2. Consider a demand equation of the general form $P = a - bQd$. If $b = 6$ and $a = 40$, then at what price will quantity demanded be 5?
   (a)   the price axis intercept is 20
   (b)   the price axis intercept is 5
   (c)   the price axis intercept is 4

(d)   the price axis intercept cannot be solved

3. If the demand equation is $P = 20 - 5Qd$, and the supply equation is $P = 4 + 3Qs$, the equilibrium quantity is:
  (a)   2
  (b)   3
  (c)   4
  (d)   5

4. If the demand equation is $P = 20 - 5Qd$, and the supply equation is $P = 4 + 3Qs$, the equilibrium price is:
  (a)   4
  (b)   5
  (c)   10
  (d)   20

Fill-In Questions

1. The maximum price that buyers are willing to pay for a product is given by the (slope, intercept) _____ term in the (demand, supply) _____ equation.

2. The extent to which the producers are willing to supply more when price increases is reflected in the (slope, intercept) _____ term in the (demand, supply) _____ equation.

3. If demand is given by $P = a - bQd$, an increase in the value of parameter a indicates that the demand curve shifts to the (left, right) _____, and equilibrium price will (decrease, increase) _____.

4. If supply is given by $P = c + dQs$, a decrease in the value of parameter c indicates that the supply curve shifts to the (left, right) _____, and equilibrium price will (decrease, increase) _____.

True-False

Circle T if the statement is true, F if it is false.

1. If the demand curve is given by $P = 12 - 2Qd$, then quantity demanded is 3 if price is 6.   **T F**

2. If the supply curve is given by $P = 5 + 4Qs$, then price will be 7 if quantity supplied is 2.   **T F**

3. A change in either of the parameters in the demand equation will change the market equilibrium price.   **T F**

4. A change in either of the parameters in the supply equation will change the market equilibrium price.   **T F**

5. A change in either of the parameters in the demand equation will change the parameters in the supply equation.   **T F**

Multiple-Choice

Circle the letter that corresponds to the best answer.

Answer questions 1 through 6 on the basis of the following demand and supply equations:
$P = 100 - 2Qd$
$P = 40 + 4Qs$

1. The equilibrium price, P^*, will be:
  (a)   50
  (b)   60
  (c)   70
  (d)   80

2. The equilibrium quantity, Q^*, will be:
  (a)   10
  (b)   20
  (c)   30
  (d)   40

3. The lowest price at which producers are willing to begin selling output is:
  (a)   10
  (b)   20
  (c)   30
  (d)   40

4. Quantity demanded would become zero if the price rises above what level?
  (a)   70
  (b)   80
  (c)   90
  (d)   100

5. If price were 60, what would the situation be in this market?
- (a)   a surplus of 15
- (b)   a shortage of 15
- (c)   a surplus of 20
- (d)   a shortage of 20

6. The demand equation given could also be re-written as:
- (a) $Qd = 100 - 2P$
- (b) $P = 50 - Qd$
- (c) $Qd = 100 - 0.5 Qd$
- (d) $Qd = 50 - 0.5P$

Problems and Projects

1.   Demand and Supply in the Shoe Market

The demand and supply in the market for shoes are given by the following equations:

$P = 100 - 0.1 Qd$ $P = 50 + 0.4 Qs$

(a)   Rewrite the demand equation as a function of Qd: _____
(b)   Rewrite the supply equation as a function of Qs: _____
(c)   Using these new equations, fill in the table.
(d)   Solve for the equilibrium price: _____

Price ($/pair)	Qd (pairs/yr)	Qs (pairs/yr)
100	_____	_____
90	_____	_____
80	_____	_____
70	_____	_____
60	_____	_____
50	_____	_____

2.   The Market for Lemons

Suppose that the market for lemons can be characterized by the following equations:

$P = 4 - 0.01 Qd$
$P = 1 + 0.02 Qs$

(a)   Solve for the equilibrium quantity: _____
(b)   Solve for the equilibrium price: _____
(c)   If price was fixed by government policy at P = 2, would there be a shortage or a surplus, and what would the amount be?
(d)   If price was fixed by government policy at P = 3.5, would there be a shortage or a surplus, and in what amount?

3.   The Market for Computer Printers

The data below represents the market for computer printers.

Price ($/printer)	Qd (printers/yr)	Qs (printers/yr)
100	4000	0
200	3000	0
300	2000	1000
400	1000	2000
500	0	3000

(a) Based on the demand schedule, what is the demand equation? _____
(b) Based on the supply schedule, what is the supply equation? _____
(c) Use the supply and demand equations to solve for equilibrium: P^* = _____ , Q^* = _____

Discussion Questions

1. What aspect of a demand equation shows that the equation is consistent with the law of demand? What aspect of the supply equation ensures that there is a positive relation between price and quantity supplied?

2. Sketch a hypothetical straight-line demand curve. How would the position of this curve change if there were an increase in the parameter *a*? What if there were an increase in *b*?

3. Sketch a hypothetical straight-line supply curve. How would the position of this curve change if there were an increase in the parameter *c*? What if there were an increase in *d*?

Answers

Quick Quiz
1. (a) p. 73
2. (d) p. 73
3. (a) p. 74
4. (c) pp. 74-75

Fill-in Questions
1. intercept, demand
2. slope, supply
3. right, increase
4. right, decrease

True-False
1. T   Substitute in 6 for P and solve for Q_d
2. F   Substitute in 2 for Q_s and $P = 13$
3. T   If a or b changes the demand curve will shift
4. T   If c or d changes the supply curve will shift
5. F   The two equations are independent of each other

Multiple-Choice
1. (d) Set $Q_d = Q_s$ and solve for P^*
2. (a) Substitute $P^* = 80$ into either the Q_d or the Q_s equation
3. (d) Set $Q_s = 0$
4. (d) Set $Q_d = 0$
5. (b) Find that $Q_d = 20$ and $Q_s = 5$ at this P
6. (d) Rearrange the equation to solve for Q_d

Problems and Projects
1. (a) $Q_d = 1000 - 10\,P$; (b) $Q_s = -125 + 2.5\,P$: (c) from top to bottom: Q_d: 0, 100, 200, 300, 400, 500; Q_s: 375, 350, 325, 300, 275, 250: (d) by setting the two equations equal, or by reading the table, we see that $P^* = 90$, where $Q_d = Q_s = 100$.
2. (a) 100; (b) 3; (c) $Q_d = 200$, $Q_s = 50$, so a shortage of 150; (d) surplus of 75
3. (a) $P = 500 - 0.1\,Q_d$; (b) $P = 200 + 0.1\,Q_s$; (c) $P^* = 350$, $Q^* = 1500$

Chapter 4   The Market System and International Trade

Overview

Chapter 3 explained how prices and quantities are determined in individual markets. This chapter widens the focus to consider the nature of the market system as a whole, with emphasis on describing the Canadian economy.

The market system or capitalism has six defining characteristics: private property rights; freedom of choice for consumers and freedom of enterprise for suppliers; the pursuit of self-interest; competition among economic units; coordination through markets and prices; and an active, but limited, role for government. The many demand and supply decisions made by households and firms determine market prices which in turn provide incentives and signals to these decision-makers, thereby coordinating the allocation of society's resources.

In a competitive market setting, with consumers and producers following their self-interest, their choices will coincide with the interests of society — as though individuals are guided by an "invisible hand" to serve the public interest. Accordingly, the role of government is quite limited.

Modern industrial economies have three other characteristics that increase dramatically the amount of goods and services that can be produced: (1) extensive use of advanced technology and capital goods; (2) specialization in production; and (3) use of money.

The challenge for any market economy can be summarized in four fundamental questions: (1) what goods and services will be produced; (2) how will the goods and services be produced; (3) who will get the goods and services; and (4) how will the system accommodate change?

The market system features three key virtues: efficiency, incentives, and freedom. However, where there are spillover costs or benefits, or public goods, the market fails to produce an efficient allocation of resources. Therefore there is a role for government to correct the inefficiencies.

The final section describes how globalization links the Canadian economy with the rest of the world. The theory of comparative advantage explains how all nations can gain if they specialize in production of goods in which they have lower opportunity costs, and then trade some of their output for goods produced by other nations.

Chapter Outline

4.1 Characteristics of the Market System

◈ What are the six defining characteristics of the market system?

• The market system, or capitalism, is an economic system is defined by: private property, freedom of enterprise and choice, self-interest, competition, self-regulating markets, and an active, but limited role for government.

   o   Resources are the private property of households and firms who are free to obtain, control, employ, and dispose of their property as they see fit.

   o   Freedom of enterprise means that firms are free to make business decisions about what to produce, where to sell, etc. Freedom of choice means that consumers can spend their incomes on whatever goods they want, and resource owners can supply their land, labour, etc. as they see fit.

   o   Self-interest is the motivating force behind decisions: consumers try to maximize their satisfaction, and entrepreneurs try to maximize their profits.

   o   A market is competitive if it has many independent buyers and sellers, each free to enter or exit the market, so that no individual buyer or seller has much power.

   o   Signals and incentives are conveyed through prices. Because buyers and sellers respond spontaneously to price changes, resource allocation is coordinated in a decentralized and spontaneous fashion, as if by an "invisible hand."

- o Markets create a sufficiently self-regulating, self-adjusting, and efficient allocation of resources that the government's role is limited. Due to certain shortcomings of the market (discussed later in the chapter) government's role is nevertheless important.
- All modern industrial economies have three other main characteristics:
  - o There is extensive use of advanced technologies and roundabout production. By producing complex capital goods (e.g., machinery or computers) we raise the efficiency in producing final goods for consumers (e.g. food).
  - o Specialization prevails at all levels. Division of labour among workers means that each person produces only a very narrow range of goods and relies on the existence of markets and prices to trade for goods that others have produced. The same is true of regions and nations. Specialization creates efficiencies by making use of ability differences, by allowing learning by doing, and by saving time.
  - o To overcome the inconvenience and transactions costs of bartering, some system of money is inevitable. It is impossible to sustain a highly specialized economy without some form of money to facilitate exchanges. Anything that is generally accepted by sellers in exchange for goods and services is considered money.

Quick Quiz

1. Which is one of the main features of pure capitalism?
- (a) central economic planning
- (b) limits on freedom of choice
- (c) the right to own private property
- (d) an expanded role for government in the economy

2. In pure capitalism, freedom of enterprise means that:
- (a) businesses are free to produce products that consumers want
- (b) consumers are free to buy goods and services that they want

- (c) resources are distributed freely to businesses that want them
- (d) government is free to direct the actions of businesses

3. In pure capitalism, the role of government is best described as:
- (a) nonexistent
- (b) active but limited
- (c) significant
- (d) extensive

4.2 The Market System at Work

◈ What are the four fundamental questions that every economy must answer?

- The competitive market system functions with two groups of decision makers: households (consumers) and firms (businesses). Households are the ultimate suppliers of resources, and firms are the suppliers of goods purchased by consumers with the incomes from their resources. The market system communicates the decisions of millions of individual households and firms, and coordinates these decisions in a coherent allocation of resources.
- Faced with scarcity, every economy must find answers for the Four Fundamental Questions:
  - o What goods and services will be produced?
  - o How will the goods and services be produced?
  - o Who will get the goods and services?
  - o How will the system accommodate change?
- The market system, or price mechanism, is a communication and coordination system that provides answers to the Four Fundamental Questions.
  - o Consumers' "dollar votes" for the products they want, and firms' desires for profits determine the types and amounts of goods to be produced, and at what price.
  - o The profit motive drives businesses to use production methods that economize on resources, especially those resources that are relatively expensive.
  - o Goods are distributed to those consumers willing and able to pay the current market price. Consumers' incomes are determined by the quantities and prices of the labour, property, and other resources

they supply in resource markets. The market system does not guarantee an equitable distribution of income and consumer goods.

- o   Changes in consumer tastes, technology, and resource supplies are signalled by price changes that give households and firms incentives to adjust their choices. Thus price changes guide the reallocation of resources to accommodate change.

- Competition in the economy compels firms and households acting in their own self-interest to promote (as though led by an "invisible hand") the interests of society as a whole, though this is not their intention. Adam Smith first noted this concept in his 1776 book, The Wealth of Nations.

➲ The crux of the market system is the dual role played by prices: to provide both signals and incentives. An increase in the price of a product signals that for some reason scarcity of this product has increased. The price increase gives consumers the incentive to reduce their consumption (as they ration their limited incomes) and gives producers the incentive to produce more (in order to maximize profits).

- The market system has several merits. The two economic arguments for the system are the efficient allocation of resources and the incentives for using resources productively. The personal freedom allowed in a market economy is its major non-economic virtue.

➲ Consider how amazing it is that a market system works at all! How can millions of independent decisions by consumers and producers possibly add up to a coherent allocation of resources that virtually guarantees that your neighbourhood store will have milk and bread every time you come to buy them? Nobody is in control of the whole economy; nobody has the responsibility to coordinate the allocation of resources. Yet, as if guided by an "invisible hand," the economy is coordinated in a manner that is spontaneous and decentralized.

Quick Quiz

4.   The maximization of profit tends to be the driving force in the economic decision making of:
- (a)   entrepreneurs
- (b)   workers
- (c)   consumers
- (d)   legislators

5.   To decide how to use its scarce resources to satisfy human wants pure capitalism relies on
- (a)   central planning
- (b)   roundabout production
- (c)   markets and prices
- (d)   barter

6.   Which of the following would necessarily result, sooner or later, from a decrease in consumer demand for a product?
- (a)   a decrease in the profits of firms in the industry
- (b)   an increase in the output of the industry
- (c)   an increase in the supply of the product
- (d)   an increase in the prices of resources employed by the firms in the industry

4.3 Market Failure

◈   Why does market failure occur?
- o   What are spillover costs?
- o   What are spillover benefits?
- o   What are public goods?

◈   How can government correct market failure?

- Market failure occurs when the competitive market system results in the "wrong" production level for some goods, or fails to produce any of certain goods.
- o   Spillover costs exist when production or consumption of a good inflicts costs on a third party without compensation. Environmental pollution is an example. Such goods tend to be overproduced. Government can correct the overproduction by legislation or by specific taxes.
- o   Spillover benefits exist when production or consumption of a good creates benefits for third parties. Not enough is produced of such goods. Government can correct the allocation problem by subsidizing producers or consumers or by directly providing the good.
- o   Public goods are neither rivalrous nor excludable. Because everybody can use them simultaneously free of cost, they are subject to the free-rider problem and will tend to be underproduced. Government will tend to directly provide public goods.
- Government can be added to the circular flow model. Government buys goods and services from the product market, employs labour, capital, etc.

from resource markets, and finances its expenditures from net tax revenues collected from businesses and households.

Quick Quiz

7. Which economic situation would result in overallocation of resources to the production of a good?
(a)   spillover benefits
(b)   spillover costs
(c)   a free-rider program
(d)   inflation

8. How does government correct for spillover benefits?
(a)   by taxing consumers
(b)   by taxing producers
(c)   by subsidizing producers
(d)   by separating ownership from control

9. Which of the following is included in the circular flow diagram?
(a)   businesses
(b)   households
(c)   government
(d)   all of the above

4.4 Canada and International Trade

◈ How is Canada's economy connected to the rest of the world?

◈ According to the principle of comparative advantage how do nations gain from specializing and trading with each other?

• Canada is linked to other nations through flows of: goods and services, capital and labour, information and technology, and financial instruments. Through the process of globalization such links are becoming stronger and more numerous, and the economy is becoming more competitive.

• Specialization and trade among economic units (individuals, firms, provinces, regions, or nations) are based on the principle of comparative advantage. Specialization and trade increase productivity and output. Adam Smith wrote about this in 1776, and the idea was fully explained by David Ricardo in the early 1800s.

• The principle of comparative advantage is shown with an example of two individuals able to do two jobs, or with an example of two nations producing two goods.

o A chartered accountant (CA) needing her house painted can paint it herself or hire a house painter. The CA will try to minimize her opportunity cost. By comparative advantage, even if the CA can do the job in less time than the painter can, if the CA incurs a lower opportunity cost by hiring the painter, the CA will specialize in accounting. Likewise, the painter will specialize in painting, and hire a CA to prepare his tax return, if this minimizes his opportunity costs.

o Mexico and Canada both can produce corn and soybeans. Assuming each nation has a constant opportunity cost ratio, each nation has the lower opportunity cost — and therefore comparative advantage — in producing one of the two goods. By specializing in producing one good, each nation can trade for the other nation's good. The terms of trade, or ratio at which one good is traded for another, lies between the cost ratios for the two nations.

➲ If the data on production possibilities reflect constant costs, opportunity costs can be found easily by dividing a producer's maximum outputs of each of the two goods. For example, suppose Norway's maximum outputs are 100 fish or 20 tables. What is the cost of 1 table? Divide the number of tables into the number of fish: 100 fish/20 tables = 5 fish per table. What is the cost of 1 fish? Divide the number of fish into the number of tables: 20 tables/100 fish = 1/5 table per fish.

• When two nations specialize and trade according to their comparative advantage, both nations can consume more of both goods than their domestic production possibilities curves would permit. This reduces the scarcity problem.
• The circular flow model can be adapted to include a government sector and "rest of the world" sector.

Quick Quiz

10. Why do nations specialize and engage in trade?
(a)   to protect multinational corporations
(b)   to increase output and income
(c)   to improve communications
(d)   to control other nations

11. Bolivia sacrifices production of 2 blankets to produce 10 potatoes. Chile sacrifices 1 blanket to produce 8 potatoes. Which country has a comparative advantage?
  (a)   Bolivia in blankets
  (b)   Bolivia in potatoes
  (c)   Chile in blankets
  (d)   Bolivia in both blankets and potatoes

Terms and Concepts

private property	dollar votes
freedom of enterprise	derived demand
freedom of choice	guiding function of
self-interest	prices
competition	creative destruction
roundabout	"invisible hand"
production	market failure
specialization	spillover costs
division of labour	spillover benefits
medium of exchange	exclusion principle
barter	public good
money	free-rider problem
household	quasi-public goods
firm	absolute advantage
Four Fundamental	comparative advantage
Questions	terms of trade
consumer sovereignty	

Fill-In Questions

1. The ownership of resources by private individuals and organizations is the institution of _____.

2. In a market system private businesses have freedom of _____ and consumers have freedom of _____.

3. List the six characteristics of the market system.
  (a)   _____
  (b)   _____
  (c)   _____
  (d)   _____
  (e)   _____
  (f)   _____

4. If Robinson Crusoe spends time building a canoe to help him to catch more fish, he is engaging in _____ production.

5. Adam Smith believed that economic units seeking to further their own self-interest and operating within the capitalistic system will simultaneously, as though directed by an _____, promote the _____ interest.

6. List the Four Fundamental Questions to which every society must respond.
  (a)   _____
  (b)   _____
  (c)   _____
  (d)   _____

7. Three ways in which division of labour enhances a society's output are:
  (a)   _____
  (b)   _____
  (c)   _____

8. Exchange by barter requires a _____ of wants.

9. Government frequently reallocates resources when it finds instances of _____ failure. The two major cases of such failure of the competitive market involve _____ effects and _____ goods.

10. Spillovers occur when benefits or costs associated with the production or consumption of a good are incurred by a _____ party. Spillovers are also called _____.

11. Governments can resolve the problem of spillover benefits through _____ paid to the _____ or the _____ of the good.

12. Public goods are not subject to the _____ principle. Once a public good is produced, the benefits from the good cannot be confined to the purchaser. This results in a _____ effect.

13. In the circular flow model, imports and exports are added as flows to the _____ market. Canadian expenditures pay for (exports, imports) _____, and foreign expenditures pay for _____.

14. If Nigeria can produce 10 kg of coffee at a cost of 1 barrel of oil, and Kenya can produce 25 kg of coffee at a cost of 1 barrel of oil, then _____ has the lower cost for producing oil, and _____ has the lower cost of producing coffee. The comparative advantage for oil lies with _____ and for coffee lies with _____.

15. The amount of one product that a nation must export in order to import one unit of another product is the _____.

True-False

Circle T if the statement is true, F if it is false.

1. Self-interest means the same as selfishness.
T F

2. In a competitive market every seller has significant influence over the market price.   **T F**

3. In the market system most prices are set by a government agency.   **T F**

4. If property rights did not exist for intellectual property, individuals would have less incentive to create music, books, and computer software.
T F

5. In the market system prices serve as signals for the allocation of resources.   **T F**

6. Because the market system is efficient in resource use, every person is better off under this form of economic organization than any alternative.   **T F**

7. In capitalism the distribution of output depends upon the distribution of resources.   **T F**

8. The market system ensures that all households will receive an equitable share of the economy's output of goods and services.   **T F**

9. The "invisible hand" refers to government intervention in the market.   **T F**

10. Pollution is a cause of market failure because the price of the polluting product does not reflect all the resource costs used in its production. **T F**

11. A spillover or externality is a cost or benefit that is imposed upon an individual or group external to the market transaction.   **T F**

12. A public good is any good or service that is provided free by the government.   **T F**

13. A free-rider problem occurs when people can receive benefits of a good without contributing to the cost of providing it.   **T F**

14. The first economists to explain the principle of comparative advantage were Adam Smith and David Ricardo.   **T F**

15. The principle of comparative advantage applies just as well to individuals or regions as it does to nations.   **T F**

16. If two nations produce only coal and lumber, one of the nations could have the comparative advantage over the other in both coal and lumber.   **T F**

Multiple-Choice

Circle the letter that corresponds to the best answer.

1. Which of the following is not one of the six characteristics of the market system?
- (a)   competition
- (b)   freedom of enterprise and choice
- (c)   self-interest
- (d)   central economic planning

2. The "invisible hand" is used to explain how in the market system:
- (a)   property rights are defined
- (b)   taxes and subsidies are determined
- (c)   the self-interest of individuals is harnessed for the benefit of society
- (d)   spillover effects occur

3. In the market system a decrease in the demand for a good should result in all but:
- (a)   an increase in the price of the resources producing the good
- (b)   a decrease in the profitability of producing the good
- (c)   a movement of resources out of the production of the good
- (d)   a decrease in the price of the good

4. Roundabout production refers to:
- (a)   the use of resources by government

(b)   the use of resources to produce consumer goods directly

(c)   the use of resources to produce services

(d)   the use of resources to produce capital goods that in turn are used to produce other goods

5. Which of the following is **not** an example of a capital good?

(a)   money

(b)   a warehouse

(c)   a forklift

(d)   a computer

6. Which of the following is **not** a condition for a market to be highly competitive:

(a)   the presence of a large number of buyers

(b)   the freedom to enter or leave a particular market

(c)   the presence of a large number of sellers

(d)   a fair price determined by a public agency

7. Which of the following is a reason that specialization in production increases efficiency?

(a)   trade is rendered unnecessary

(b)   barter transactions are rendered unnecessary

(c)   individuals usually possess very similar resources and talents

(d)   experience or "learning-by-doing" results in increased output

8. Barter:

(a)   is the main method of trading in a market economy

(b)   is the action of haggling over the price of a good

(c)   is the exchange of a good for money

(d)   is the exchange of a good for a good

9. Which of the following is **not** a necessary consequence of specialization?

(a)   people will barter

(b)   people will engage in trade

(c)   people will be dependent upon each other

(d)   people will produce more of one thing than they would produce in the absence of specialization

10. Which of the following is **not** a virtue of the market system?

(a)   allocative efficiency

(b)   productive efficiency

(c)   equitable distribution of income

[d]   ability to adapt to changes in tastes, technologies, and resource supplies

11. The term "division of labour" means the same as:

(a)   specialization

(b)   barter

(c)   economies of scale

(d)   coincidence of wants

12. All modern economies have the following characteristics except for:

(a)   specialization

(b)   limited government interference

(c)   use of money

(d)   roundabout means of production

13. The economist who first wrote about the "invisible hand" was:

(a)   John Maynard Keynes

(b)   Karl Marx

(c)   David Ricardo

(d)   Adam Smith

14. If external benefits accompany the production of a good:

(a)   too much of the good will be produced by a competitive market

(b)   too little of the good will be produced in a competitive market

(c)   a tax on the production of the good will result in the optimum production of the good

(d)   the good is exported to foreign countries

15. In the case where producing a good creates spillover costs, government could promote the optimal output by:

(a)   banning production of the good

(b)   taxing the producers of the good

(c)   subsidizing consumers of the good

(d)   subsidizing producers of the good

16. Which of the following is a good example of a good or service providing spillover benefits?

(a)   a cup of hot tea

(b)   a new muffler on a car

(c)   a sofa

(d)   a pair of skis

17. Suppose that in order to relieve traffic congestion, user charges are imposed on drivers using

urban expressways. This would be a response to what economic problem?
(a)   spillover benefits
(b)   spillover costs
(c)   the free-rider problem
(d)   inequitable income distribution

18. Public goods differ from private goods in that public goods are:
(a)   divisible
(b)   subject to the exclusion principle
(c)   not subject to the free-rider problem
(d)   nonrivalrous and not subject to the exclusion principle

19. Quasi-public goods are goods and services:
(a)   to which the exclusion principle could be applied
(b)   that have large spillover benefits
(c)   that private producers would overproduce
(d)   that have large spillover benefits, and to which the exclusion principle could be applied

20. If the market system tends to overallocate resources to the production of good X:
(a)   good X could be a public good
(b)   good X could involve spillover benefits
(c)   good X could involve spillover costs
(d)   good X could be prone to the free-rider problem

21. Government expenditures, taxes, and transfer payments in the circular flow affect:
(a)   the distribution of income
(b)   the allocation of resources
(c)   the level of economic activity
(d)   all of the above

22. If Canada can produce 1 bottle of syrup at a cost of 2 cigars, and Cuba can produce 1 bottle of syrup at a cost of 6 cigars, what would be a mutually beneficial term of trade:
(a)   2 cigars per 1 syrup
(b)   3 cigars per 1 syrup
(c)   6 cigars per 1 syrup
(d)   8 cigars per 1 syrup

The next four questions are based on the data in the table that shows maximum production levels for the regions of Heath and Cliff, both of which have constant costs of production, and are able to trade with one another.

Heath		Cliff	
Wool	Peat	Wool	Peat
100	20	120	40

23. In Heath, the domestic opportunity cost of:
(a)   1 wool is 5 peat
(b)   1 wool is 1/5 peat
(c)   1 peat is 1.2 wool
(d)   1 peat is 1/5 wool

24. In Cliff, the domestic opportunity cost of:
(a)   1 peat is 3 wool
(b)   1 peat is 2 peat
(c)   1 wool is 3 peat
(d)   1 peat is 1/3 wool

25. Which of the following statements is **false**?
(a)   Heath has the comparative advantage in wool
(b)   Cliff should specialize in peat
(c)   Heath and Cliff could both gain from trading with one another
(d)   Heath has the comparative advantage in both wool and peat

26. The terms of trade will be:
(a)   more than 3 wool for 1 peat
(b)   fewer than 5 wool for 1 peat
(c)   between 3 and 5 wool for 1 peat
(d)   not between 3 and 5 wool for 1 peat

27. Countries A and B will be unable to mutually gain from trade and specialization if:
(a)   A has more resources than B
(b)   A's resources are more productive in both goods than B's
(c)   A and B have identical opportunity cost ratios between the two goods
(d)   none of the above

Problems and Projects

1. Rationing of Parking Spots

Consider a college with fewer parking spots than students who want to drive to school. At present the college offers free parking on a first-come-first-served basis. They are considering charging for parking, setting the fee high enough that there would always be a few spots open.

(a) Why would the system of charging for parking change the allocation of parking spots?

(b) Why would some students be in favour of the change while others would not?

(c) What socially beneficial incentives would be created by the proposed parking fee?

2. Cost Minimization

A firm can produce 100 units of product X by combining labour, land, capital, and entrepreneurial ability in three different ways as shown in the table below. It can hire labour at $2 per unit, land at $3 per unit, capital at $5 per unit, and entrepreneurial ability at $10 per unit.

| | Method | | |
Resource	A	B	C
Labour	8	13	10
Land	4	3	3
Capital	4	2	4
Entrepreneurial ability	1	1	1

(a) Which is the least cost method of producing 100 units of X? _____

(b) If the wage for labour rises from $2 to $3 per unit, which is the least cost method to produce 100 units of X? _____

(c) If the firm produces 100 X, the increase in the wage rate gives the firm the incentive to (increase, decrease) its use of labour from _____ units to _____ units.

3. Electricity and the Price Mechanism

In 2001 electric power prices increased sharply in Alberta.

(a) What did the price increase signal?

(b) What incentives for power consumers and producers were created by the price increase?

(c) If households and firms responded to these incentives, how would this be socially beneficial?

(d) What is the primary motivation for consumers and producers to make choices that are socially beneficial?

4. Circular Flow Diagram

The circular flow diagram below includes business firms, households, and government (the public sector). Product and resource markets are also shown.

(a) Identify the sector that corresponds to each box:

a. _____

b. _____

c. _____

d. _____

e. _____

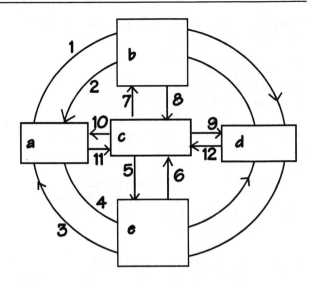

(b) Supply a label or an explanation for each of the twelve flows in the model:

1: _____

2: _____

3: _____

4: _____

5. _____

6: _____

7: _____

8: _____

9: _____

10: _____

11: _____

12: _____

(c) If government wished to increase the production of public goods and decrease the production of private goods in the economy, which flows could it increase? _____, _____, _____.

5. Property Rights in Grades

The grade that you earn in your economics course this term will be the product of your work, and you probably consider this grade your private property.

(a) How would your incentives to study change if you did not have the right to communicate your grade to potential employers or other colleges or universities?

(b) How would your incentives change if you had to share your "output" on exams with your classmates (i.e., everybody is awarded the class average grade)?

(c) Are there any reasons for restricting your property rights in your grade? For example, should you be able to sell or give your grade to another student?

6. Types of Market Failure

Match each example on the right with the type of situation on the left:

(a) spillover cost   (1) a radio broadcast
(b) spillover benefit   (2) a noisy house party
(c) public good   (3) vaccinations

7. Comparative Advantage in Tailoring

Julius and Murray are tailors. Their production possibilities tables for trousers and jackets are given below. Initially they work independently, with Julius choosing production alternative D, and Murray choosing E from his alternatives.

JULIUS: Production Possibilities Table

Product	Production Alternative					
	A	B	C	D	E	F
Trousers	75	60	45	30	15	0
Jackets	0	10	20	30	40	50

MURRAY: Production Possibilities Table

Product	Production Alternative						
	A	B	C	D	E	F	G
Trousers	60	50	40	30	20	10	0
Jackets	0	5	10	15	20	25	30

(a) For Julius 1 pair of trousers costs _____ jackets, and 1 jacket costs _____ pairs of trousers.

(b) For Murray 1 pair of trousers costs _____ jackets, and 1 jacket costs _____ pairs of trousers.

(c) The comparative advantage in making trousers lies with _____ because his opportunity cost is (lower, higher) _____. The comparative advantage in making jackets lies with _____ because his opportunity cost is (lower, higher) _____.

(d) If Julius and Murray form a partnership, Julius should specialize in making _____, and Murray should specialize in _____.

(e) Working independently Julius and Murray would produce a total of 50 pairs of trousers and 50 jackets. If each specializes fully, their combined output will be _____ pairs of trousers, and _____ jackets. Thus, the gain from specialization is _____ pairs of trousers and _____ jackets.

8. Comparative Advantage in Fruit

Venezuela and Costa Rica have the production possibilities tables shown below.

(a) Find the opportunity costs:

Venezuela: 1 apple costs _____
            1 banana costs _____
Costa Rica: 1 apple costs _____
            1 banana costs _____

(b) Determine which country has the comparative advantage in each good:

Apples: _____   Bananas: _____

VENEZUELA: Production Possibilities Table

Product	Production Alternative					
	A	B	C	D	E	F
Apples	40	32	24	16	8	0
Bananas	0	4	8	12	16	20

COSTA RICA: Production Possibilities Table

Product	Production Alternative					
	A	B	C	D	E	F
Apples	75	60	45	30	15	0
Bananas	0	5	10	15	20	25

(c) From the information given we cannot determine specifically what the terms of trade will be. However, the terms of trade must be greater than _____ apples per banana, and less than _____ apples per banana.

(d) Suppose that each nation would choose production alternative C if specialization and trade were impossible. The combined production in the two countries would be _____ apples and _____ bananas.

(e) If each nation specializes completely according to comparative advantage, their combined production will be _____ apples and _____ bananas.

(f) Their combined gains from specialization will be _____ apples and _____ bananas.

(g) Suppose that the nations specialize and then agree to trade 25 apples for 10 bananas. This trade will leave Venezuela consuming _____ apples and _____ bananas. Costa Rica will consume _____ apples and _____ bananas.

(h) Compared to production alternative C, this leaves Venezuela with a gain of _____ apples and _____ bananas. Compared to production alternative C, this leaves Costa Rica with a gain of _____ apples and _____ bananas.

Discussion Questions

1. List the Four Fundamental Questions that all economies must answer. Which of these questions does the market system answer, and how so?

2. What property rights does the owner of a motor vehicle have? What restrictions or limits are there on those rights, and why do these restrictions exist? Do these restrictions increase or decrease the value of owning a vehicle?

3. How does the pursuit of self-interest by all economic units in the market system model ultimately benefit society? Give an example of a choice you make that is in your self-interest, but not selfish.

4. At one time the world price of oil was expected to hit $100 a barrel by the 1990s. If so, the Canadian economy would presumably have allocated more resources to oil production. How would market forces have produced such a result? How would market forces have changed the gasoline consumption habits of Canadian households?

5. What are the advantages of "indirect" or "roundabout" production? If you were stranded on a tiny island in the Pacific, what roundabout production might you undertake?

6. In order for a market to be competitive, why must there be many buyers and many sellers? What might be some consequences if there are few buyers or few sellers?

7. How does an economy benefit from specialization and division of labour?

8. What are the disadvantages of barter, and how does money overcome these disadvantages?

9. What is "market failure" and what are the two major kinds of such failures?

10. If the person living down the hall from you plays her music very loudly, is there a spillover cost or spillover benefit? If a homeowner builds an extra high fence between his house and his neighbours', is there a spillover cost or spillover benefit?

11. Based on ideas from this chapter, what is the case for government supporting needle exchange programs for intravenous drug users?

12. Discuss how the concepts of spillover effects and public goods might apply to the Internet?

13. How are private goods different from public goods? Why does there tend to be underallocation of resources to public goods in the absence of government intervention?

14. What basic method does government employ in Canada to reallocate resources away from the production of private goods and toward the production of public goods?

15. Sketch how the international trade component can be built into the circular flow model.

16. Explain how comparative costs determine which producer has the comparative advantage. What determines the terms of trade? What is the gain that results from specialization and trade according to comparative advantage?

17. Suppose that Dr. Ocula is an outstanding eye surgeon with good enough hand-eye coordination that he keyboards faster than anyone else in town. Use the principle of comparative advantage to explain why he hires someone else to do the word-processing in his office, even though he could do it faster himself.

Answers

Quick Quiz
1. (c) p. 77
2. (a) pp. 77-78
3. (b) pp. 79
4. (a) p. 82
5. (c) pp. 83-84
6. (a) p. 84
7. (b) pp. 86-87
8. (c) pp. 87-88
9. (d) p. 91
10. (b) p. 96
11. (a) p. 95

Fill-in Questions
1. private property
2. enterprise, choice
3. private property; freedom of enterprise and choice; self-interest; markets and prices; competition; limited, but active government
4. roundabout

5. "invisible hand," social (or public)
6. what goods and services will be produced?; how will the goods and services be produced?; who will get the goods and service?; how will the system accommodate change?
7. making use of differences in ability, fostering learning by doing, saving time
8. coincidence
9. market; spillover, public
10. third; externalities
11. subsidies, consumers, producers
12. exclusion; free-rider
13. product; imports, exports
14. Nigeria, Kenya; Nigeria, Kenya
15. terms of trade

True-False
1. F You might consider it in your self-interest to help other people, or donate to charities
2. F No seller has significant influence
3. F Most prices are set mainly by market forces
4. T The prospect of earning royalties is an incentive to produce
5. T
6. F Some individuals fare poorly under a market system, particularly those who have few resources
7. T Those with more resources can earn higher incomes and have more spending power
8. F The market offers no guarantees of equitability
9. F The "invisible hand" refers to market forces
10. T
11. T
12. F Many goods provided by government free of charge are not public goods
13. T Because the exclusion principle does not apply
14. T
15. T
16. F If one nation has the comparative advantage in coal the other nation has the comparative advantage in lumber

Multiple-Choice
1. (d) Central planning is characteristic of the command system
2. (c) Socially beneficial results stem from self-interested behaviour, without any central control
3. (a) Less demand for the good means less demand and lower price for resources used in producing the good

4. (d) Making a better axe allows us to cut more firewood later
5. (a) All of the others are human-made resources designed to help produce other things
6. (d) There is no assumption that government or any public agency would be involved
7. (d) As we gain experience we become more efficient at those tasks in which we specialize
8. (d) Price haggling is "bargaining"
9. (a) When we specialize we must trade, but it need not be by the inefficient barter system
10. (c) The market system often produces extreme discrepancies in incomes that do not seem equitable
11. (a)
12. (b) Many modern economies have a great deal of government interference
13. (d) In his book *The Wealth of Nations*
14. (b) Too little is produced because the producer will not take into account all of the benefits of the good
15. (b) Banning the product would reduce output to zero, which is not typically the optimal amount
16. (b) Cutting sound pollution for neighbours
17. (b) Each driver adds to the highway congestion, thereby imposing added time costs on other drivers
18. (d) They can be consumed simultaneously by many people, and those who do not pay cannot be excluded from using them
19. (d) Both aspects of this description are necessary
20. (c) All of the others are prone to underproduction
21. (d) Check the circular flow diagram
22. (b) Anything more than 2 and less than 6 cigars per syrup
23. (b) 20 peat / 100 wool = 1/5 peat / wool
24. (a) 120 wool / 40 peat = 3 wool/peat
25. (d) The comparative advantage in peat lies with Cliff
26. (c) The terms of trade must be between the two producers' opportunity cost ratios
27. (c) There is no reason to trade in this case

Problems and Projects
1. (a) Some students who are willing and able to arrive early or to spend time hunting for a spot may be unwilling to pay for a spot, whereas others may be willing and able to pay; (b) differences in availability of money and time; (c) students who place a low value on parking would have

incentive to walk, bus, carpool, thus leaving spots for those who value them more; firms seeking profit would have more incentive to provide near campus parking for a fee.

2. (a) B at $55; (b) A at $66; (c) decrease, 13, 8.

3. (a) increased scarcity of electricity; (b) to consume less by economizing on energy or switching to alternate sources; and to produce more; (c) there would be electric power available, and the available amount would be allocated to highest valued uses, thus minimizing the effects of increased scarcity.

4. (a) a: business firms, b: resource markets, c: government, d: households, e: product markets; (b) 1: businesses pay costs for resources that become money income for households, 2: households provide resources to businesses, 3: household expenditures become receipts for businesses, 4: businesses provide goods and services to households, 5: government spends money in product market, 6: government receives goods and services from product market, 7: government spends money in resource market, 8: government receives resources from resource market, 9: government provides goods and services to households, 10: government provides goods and services to businesses, 11: businesses pay net taxes to government, 12: households pay net taxes to government; (c) 9, 10, 11.

5. (a) If you could not use a good grade to help you get jobs, scholarships, etc. you may have less incentive to study; (b) If you get a better mark on an exam, your share of that improved mark would be very small, so you would have less incentive to study; (c) Restricted property rights in grades are probably justified because if students could sell their grades to other people then good grades would no longer indicate what they are supposed to, and would therefore no longer be meaningful or valuable.

6. (a) 2: neighbours suffer cost; (b) 3: one person being vaccinated reduces the risk of disease for other people, too; (c) 1: everybody can listen to a radio broadcast.

7. (a) 2/3, 1 1/2; (b) 1/2, 2; (c) Murray, lower, Julius, lower; (d) jackets, trousers; (e) 60, 50; 10, 0

8. (a) 1/2 banana, 2 apples, 1/3 banana, 3 apples; (b) Costa Rica, Venezuela; (c) 2, 3; (d) 69, 18; (e) 75, 20; (f) 6, 2; (g) 25, 10, 50, 10; (h) 1, 2, 5, 0

Chapter 5

Measuring the Economy's Output

Overview

Among the main topics in macroeconomics are the causes of short run fluctuations and long run trends in the economy's total output and income. This chapter defines measures of these variables and discusses what the measures can and cannot tell us about the macroeconomy.

The key measure is gross domestic output (GDP): the total market value of all final goods and services produced in the country in a year. To avoid the problem of multiple counting, we count only final goods. We also exclude various non-production transactions. GDP can be determined through either the "income approach" or the "expenditure approach." In total, incomes and expenditures must be equal because the value of the nation's output equals the total expenditures on this output, and these expenditures become the incomes of those in the nation who have produced this output.

By the expenditures approach, GDP has four components: personal consumption (C), gross investment (I_g), government purchases (G), and net exports (X_n). This same GDP (after a few adjustments) is also distributed to households as incomes in the form of: wages, rent, interest, and profit. The chapter also explains briefly several other national income concepts. The circular flow model (first presented in Chapter 2) illustrates the relationship between income flows and expenditure flows.

GDP tallied up in terms of the current money value of the nation's output is known as "nominal GDP." Fluctuations from year to year are caused by changes in both the amount of goods produced and in their prices. To separate price changes and real production changes, economists have developed a constant dollar measure, known as "real GDP," which is found by deflating nominal GDP by the GDP price index.

The final section of the chapter points out some shortcomings of the real GDP measure. It proves to be seriously flawed as an indicator of the society's well-being, and even as a measure of our total output.

Chapter Outline

5.1 Measuring the Economy's Performance: GDP

◈ What is gross domestic product (GDP), and how is it measured?

• National income accounting enables economists and policy-makers to:
   o assess the health of the economy by measuring and comparing output at regular intervals
   o track the long-run course of the economy's growth or decline in output
   o formulate policies to maintain and improve the economy's health

• The gross domestic product (GDP) is the total market value of all final goods and services produced in a country during a given year.
   o GDP is measured in monetary terms.
   o To avoid multiple counting, GDP includes only final goods and services (goods and services that are not for resale or further processing). The same result can be found by summing up the value added by producers at all stages of production.
   o GDP excludes non-production transactions such as purely financial transactions and second-hand sales.

• GDP can be calculated by either the expenditure or the income approach, and the same result is obtained.

• In the expenditure approach, GDP is computed by adding the four components of spending for final goods and services:
   o Personal consumption expenditures (C) are the expenditures of households on durable and nondurable goods and services.
   o Gross investment (I_g) includes all final spending by business firms for machin-

ery, equipment, and tools; building construction spending (including residential construction); and changes in inventories.

- A change in inventories is included in investment because it is part of the year's output (even though it was not sold during the year).
- Investment does not include expenditures for stocks or bonds or for second-hand capital goods.
- Net investment equals gross investment less the capital consumption allowance (or depreciation) for capital used up during the year.

o Government purchases (*G*) include all expenditures on final goods and services and investment goods made by all levels of government. Transfer payments are excluded.

o Net exports (*X*$_n$) equal the expenditures made by foreigners on goods and services produced in the economy (exports) less the expenditures made by consumers, government, and businesses for goods and services produced in foreign nations (imports). In symbols: $X_n = X - M$.

o The sum of the four major expenditure components gives gross domestic product. $GDP = C + I_g + G + X_n$.

➲ Memorize the GDP equation right away. It is also important to remember what types of expenditures fall in each of the four components of GDP. These concepts appear regularly in the chapters that follow.

- To compute GDP by the income method, add the four categories of income derived from the production and sale of final goods and services, and make three adjustments, as follows:

o wages, salaries, and supplementary labour income

o profits of corporations and government enterprises before taxes

o interest and investment income

o net income from farms and unincorporated businesses

o taxes less subsidies on factors of production (direct and indirect)

o capital consumption allowances (depreciation).

Quick Quiz

1. Which good should not be included in GDP because it is not a final good?
- (a) surgical equipment bought by a hospital
- (b) furniture purchased by a hotel
- (c) a snow blower purchased by a household
- (d) bread bought by a restaurant

2. An example of an investment expenditure is:
- (a) Kate's purchase of an Emily Carr painting
- (b) John's purchase of a new Mustang car
- (c) the Manning family's construction of a new home in Calgary
- (d) Don's purchase of shares in Air Canada

3. Which is not included in Canada's GDP?
- (a) trucks produced by Ford Canada but not yet sold
- (b) police services provided by the City of Toronto
- (c) Michael Ondaatje novels printed in Canada and sold to a store in Switzerland
- (d) the GST tax credit paid by the federal government to low-income Canadians

5.2 Other National Accounts

◈ What are some other measures of a nation's production of goods and services?

- Several other national income measures are also useful.

o Gross national product (GNP) measures the total income the country's residents earn during the year, regardless of whether the goods and services they produced were produced in the country or abroad.

o Net domestic product (NDP) nets out the portion of the year's output needed to replace the capital goods used up during the year.

o Net national income (NNI) adjusts NDP for indirect taxes and subsidies to arrive at the income earned by the nation's resources, whether located at home or abroad.

o Personal income (PI) is the total income actually received by households, earned or unearned.

o Disposable income (DI) is PI less personal taxes and other transfers to government.

o   Figure 5-2 is a more realistic and com-
    plex circular flow diagram showing the
    flows of expenditures and incomes among
    households, businesses, governments,
    and the rest of the world.

➡ Find out from your instructor how familiar
you need to be with these "other" income measures. Subsequent chapters in the text deal almost exclusively with the GDP measure.

Quick Quiz

4. Kerri is a Canadian owning an environmental
consulting company. If she moves her business
from Vancouver to Seattle, but still lives in Canada, what is the effect on Canada's national income statistics?
   (a)   GNP and GDP both fall
   (b)   GDP falls
   (c)   GNP falls
   (d)   GDP falls and GNP rises

5. If the government increases the personal income tax, which measure of income would be
directly reduced?
   (a)   GNP
   (b)   NNP
   (c)   PI
   (d)   DI

5.3 Nominal GDP Versus Real GDP

◈ What is the difference between nominal GDP
and real GDP?

• Because GDP is a monetary measure, it is
meaningful to compare a nation's GDP level in
different years only if the value of money itself
does not change.
   o   Inflation decreases the value of money,
       and deflation increases the value of
       money.
   o   GDP calculated at current prices, and
       unadjusted for price level changes, is
       called nominal GDP. GDP calculated to
       adjust for price level changes, or meas-
       ured in constant dollars, is called real
       GDP.

➡ It is almost impossible to analyze and discuss
macroeconomic topics without clearly understanding the difference between real and nominal
GDP. Later chapters assume that you understand this difference.

• One way to adjust nominal GDP to correct for
price changes is to use a price index.
   o   The price index is a number that meas-
       ures the ratio of the price of a market
       basket of goods in a given year to the
       price of the same market basket of goods
       in a base year, with this ratio multiplied
       by 100.
   o   To adjust nominal GDP figures for infla-
       tion, divide the year's nominal GDP by
       the year's price index and multiply the
       result by 100. The result is the real GDP.
• An alternative method of finding real GDP is
to calculate the value of each year's output using
base year prices.
• The GDP price index can then be found by
dividing nominal GDP by real GDP multiplied by
100.
• In the real world of many, many goods, our
national income accountants measure price data
on some 380 categories of goods and services,
assigning a "weight" to each category based on its
proportion in the nation's output.
• Since 2001, Statistics Canada has used a
chain weighted index in which the weight given
to each category of goods is updated annually
according to changes in the mixture of output of
the economy.

Quick Quiz

6. A rising level of nominal GDP can occur in
which situation?
   (a)   more output is produced
   (b)   prices of goods rise
   (c)   prices rise and more output is produced
   (d)   any of the above situations

7. If nominal GDP is rising and real GDP is falling, this indicates that:
   (a)   prices are rising but output is falling
   (b)   prices and output are both falling
   (c)   prices and output are both rising, but
         prices are rising faster
   (d)   prices and output are both falling, but
         output is falling faster

8. If 2004 nominal GDP is $150 billion, and the
2004 price index is 125, then what is real GDP in
2004?
   (a) $1.20 billion
   (b) $83.33 billion
   (c) $120.0 billion
   (d) $187.5 billion

5.4 Shortcomings of GDP

◈ What are the shortcomings of GDP as a measure of domestic output and well-being?

- GDP is a reasonably accurate and very useful measure of a nation's economic performance, but it is a flawed measure of the nation's output.
  - o GDP does not capture the value of non-market transactions (e.g. home production).
  - o GDP does not capture activity in the underground economy (whether illegal activities or legal).
  - o GDP does not capture changes in how much leisure time we enjoy.
  - o GDP does not capture improvements in product quality.
- GDP is also a flawed measure of society's well-being.
  - o GDP does not record the environmental costs that invariably accompany the production of final goods and services.
  - o GDP does not measure changes in the composition and the distribution of society's output.
  - o GDP does not reflect many non-material aspects of well-being such as levels of crime, civility, peace, and human rights.

Quick Quiz

9. What happens if some home renovation companies begin doing their work on a "cash only" basis to avoid paying GST and income tax?

- (a)   measured GDP will rise, but the true GDP is unchanged
- (b)   measured GDP will fall, but the true GDP is unchanged
- (c)   measured GDP does not change, but true GDP falls
- (d)   there is no effect on either measured to true GDP

10. The difference between the well-being of Canadians today versus Canadians a century ago may be overstated by the growth in GDP per person in the last century if:

- (a)   today's Canadians enjoy less leisure time
- (b)   today's Canadians grow less of their food and make less of their clothing at home
- (c)   a greater fraction of today's GDP must be spent on police protection
- (d)   all of the above

Terms and Concepts

national income accounting
gross domestic product (GDP)
intermediate goods
final goods
multiple counting
value added
expenditures approach
income approach
personal consumption expenditures
gross investment
net investment

capital consumption allowance
government purchases
net exports
indirect taxes
net domestic product (NDP)
net national income (NNI)
personal income
disposable income
nominal GDP
real GDP
price index
GDP deflator

Fill-In Questions

1. GDP is the abbreviation for _____, and measures the total market _____ of all final goods and services (produced, sold) _____ in an economy in a year. The goods and services are valued at their _____ prices.

2. Value added is the difference between the market value of a firm's _____ and its _____ from other firms. The total value added to a product at all stages of production equals the _____ of the final product; and the total value added to all final products produced in the economy during a year is the _____.

3. GDP can be computed by adding up all spending on final goods and services produced this year. This method is the _____ approach. GDP can also be computed by adding all incomes derived from the production of this year's output. This method is the _____ approach.

4. In the expenditures approach, expenditures on final goods and services are divided into four categories or expenditure streams:

- (a)   _____
- (b)   _____
- (c)   _____
- (d)   _____

5. Gross investment includes all final purchases of _____ goods (e.g. machinery, equipment, and tools) by businesses, all _____ of new buildings and houses, and changes in _____.

6. If gross investment is less than depreciation, net investment is (positive, zero, negative) _____ and the economy's stock of capital is (constant, declining, increasing) _____.

7. Government transfer payments are not counted as part of government purchase of goods and services because transfer payments do not represent a payment for goods _____.

8. An economy's net exports equal its _____ less its _____.

9. The net incomes of _____ businesses represent a mixture of labour income and investment income that is impossible to segregate.

10. Disposable income equals _____ income minus personal _____ and other personal _____ to government.

11. The price index used to adjust the nominal GDP for changes in the price level is called the _____ or the _____.

12. Reasons that real GDP is not a good measure of social well-being in an economy include that:
(a) It excludes _____ transactions that result in the production of goods and services, and the amount of _____ time enjoyed by the citizens of the economy.
(b) It fails to record improvements in the _____ of the products, changes in the composition and distribution of the economy's total _____, the _____ costs that are an undesirable side-effect of producing the GDP, and the goods and services produced in the _____ economy.

True-False

Circle T if the statement is true, F if it is false.

1. Both the nominal GDP and the real GDP of the Canadian economy are measured in constant dollars. **T F** (F circled)

2. Value added is the market value of a firm's output less the value of the inputs it has purchased from others. **T F** (T circled)

3. The gross domestic product would be understated if intermediate goods were included in its calculation. **T F** (T circled)

4. Your bank account balance is a stock variable whereas your calorie intake is a flow variable. **T F** (T circled)

5. If a DVD player was produced in 1991 and sold in 1992, it would be included in 1992's gross domestic product. **T F** (F circled)

6. The expenditure approach to finding GDP is also known as the factor payment approach. **T F** (F circled)

7. The expenditure made by a household to have a new home built counts as a personal consumption expenditure. **T F**

8. A price index measures the price of a specific set of goods and services in a given period relative to the price of an identical (or very similar) set of goods and services in a base period. **T F**

9. A GDP value that reflects current prices is called current dollar or nominal GDP. **T F**

10. In a year when nominal GDP rises, real GDP must also rise, though not necessarily by the same percentage. **T F**

11. The existence of an underground economy causes an overstatement of the GDP value. **T F**

Multiple-Choice

Circle the letter that corresponds to the best answer.

1. Which of these is not an important purpose for national income accounting?
(a) to provide a basis for the formulation and application of policies designed to improve the economy's performance
(b) to permit the measurement of the amount of unemployment in the economy
(c) to permit the estimation of the output of final goods and services in the economy

(d) to enable the economist to chart the growth of the economy over a period of time

2. In the computation of GDP, to include both the value of a loaf of bread and the value of the flour that goes into the bread would be an example of:
(a) including a non-market transaction
(b) including a non-production transaction
(c) including a non-investment transaction
(d) multiple counting

3. In the definition of GDP the term "final goods and services" refers to:
(a) goods and services that are in the final stage of production
(b) goods and services that have been produced and purchased this year
(c) goods and services produced for final use and not for resale or further processing
(d) goods and services produced in prior years and finally sold this year

4. Excluded from the measurement of GDP are all of the following with the exception of:
(a) government transfer payments
(b) purchases of stocks and bonds
(c) second-hand sales
(d) investment expenditures by business firms

5. Net investment equals gross investment less:
(a) gross national product
(b) net inventory change
(c) capital consumption allowances
(d) government investment expenditure

6. Which is the correct equation for calculating GDP?
(a) GDP = C + I_g + G + X_n
(b) GDP = C + I_g + G - X_n
(c) GDP = C + I + G + X_n
(d) GDP = C + I_g + G + X

7. If Canada has a positive value for net investment, then Canada's stock of capital is:
(a) increasing
(b) declining
(c) staying constant
(d) not enough information provided to reach a conclusion

8. Which of the following does not represent investment?
(a) an increase in the quantity of shoes on the shelves of a shoe store
(b) the construction of a condominium
(c) the purchase of shares of stock in Canadian Pacific Limited
(d) the construction of a factory building using money borrowed from a bank

9. A refrigerator is manufactured in 1998, sold during 1998 to a retailer, and sold by the retailer to a final consumer in 1999. The refrigerator is:
(a) counted as consumption in 1998
(b) counted as investment in 1999
(c) counted as investment in 1998
(d) not included in the gross domestic product of 1998

10. The income approach to GDP sums the total income earned by resource suppliers and adds two adjustments:
(a) saving and investment
(b) depreciation and indirect taxes less subsidies
(c) indirect business taxes and dividends
(d) depreciation and net investment

Questions 11 to 13 are based on the following national income accounting data.

	Billions
Personal consumption expenditure	$60
Savings	11
Gross investment	15
Capital consumption allowance	5
Gov't purchases of goods and services	23
Exports	17
Imports	21

11. Gross domestic product is equal to:
(a) $83 billion
(b) $94 billion
(c) $102 billion
(d) $105 billion

12. Disposable income is equal to:
(a) $60 billion
(b) $71 billion
(c) $83 billion
(d) $94 billion

13. Net investment is equal to:
(a) $10 billion

(b) $11 billion
(c) $15 billion
(d) $26 billion

14. In national income accounting personal income is:
(a) income earned by the factors of production for their current contribution to production
(b) income received by households before personal taxes
(c) income received by households less savings
(d) income received by households less personal consumption expenditure

15. Which is not a category of profits of private corporations?
(a) dividends
(b) undistributed earnings
(c) corporate income taxes
(d) investment

16. If both nominal GDP and the level of prices are rising, it is evident that:
(a) real GDP is constant
(b) real GDP is rising but not as rapidly as prices
(c) real GDP is declining
(d) no conclusion can be drawn concerning the real GDP of the economy on the basis of this information.

17. The real GDP in 1989 was $566 billion and in 1991 it was $553 billion. It can be concluded that:
(a) the price level declined between 1989 and 1991
(b) the price level rose between 1989 and 1991
(c) the quantity of goods and services produced fell between 1989 and 1991
(d) the quantity of goods and services produced increased between 1989 and 1991

18. In an economy, the total expenditure for a market basket of goods in year 1 (the base year) was $400 million. In year 2, the total expenditure for the same basket of goods was $450 million. What was the GDP price index for year 2?
(a) 88
(b) 112.5
(c) 188
(d) 103

19. Goods are produced in a factory in New Brunswick that is owned by a firm based in Italy. The profits earned by the factory would be included in which measure of the Canadian economy?
(a) both GNP and GDP
(b) neither GNP nor GDP
(c) GNP but not GDP
(d) GDP but not GNP

20. Statistics Canada now uses a chain weighted price index to deal with the problem of:
(a) rapid changes in the relative prices of information technology goods
(b) improved product quality
(c) unobserved activity in the underground economy
(d) inflation in the prices of all goods

21. Changes in the real GDP from one year to the next do not reflect:
(a) changes in the quality of goods produced
(b) changes in the nation's population
(c) changes in the average length of the work week
(d) any of the above changes

22. GDP is deficient as a measure of social well-being because GDP does not reflect:
(a) increased leisure enjoyed by members of society
(b) the composition and distribution of output
(c) transactions in the underground economy
(d) all of the above

23. Which of the following is **not** another term for nominal GDP?
(a) current dollar GDP
(b) unadjusted GDP
(c) real GDP
(d) money GDP

Problems and Projects

1. Value Added in a Three-stage Production Process
Suppose the toy industry consists of three firms: a wood producer, a manufacturer, and a retailer. The tables below show their financial data.

Wood Producer			
Purchases of material inputs	$0	Sales to toy manufacturer	$84
Wages	65		
Profits	19		

Toy Manufacturer			
Purchases from wood producer	$84	Sales to toy retailer	$110
Wages	16		
Profits	10		

Toy Retailer			
Purchases from toy manufacturer	$110	Sales to consumers	$150
Wages	30		
Profits	10		

(a) Based on the firms' data, complete this table:

Firm	Sales Value of Product	Purchases from other Firms	Value Added
Wood producer	$_____	$_____	$_____
Toy manufacturer	_____	_____	_____
Toy retailer	_____	_____	_____
TOTALS	_____	_____	_____

(b) Compute the total incomes, or factor payments:
Wages $_____; Profit $_____; Total Incomes $_____
(c) Explain why the totals in (a) and (b) should be the same.

2. Gross Investment, Net Investment and Changes in Inventories

In 1998 a steel company purchased $100 million worth of new machinery, $25 million worth of used machinery, and spent $113 million building new corporate headquarters. The company had $520 million worth of inventory of steel products at the beginning of the year and $482 million worth of inventory at year end. Depreciation was $30 million in 1998.
(a) Determine this company's contribution to the nation's gross investment for 1998.
(b) Determine the company's contribution to net investment for 1998.

3. National Income Accounting

Use the data in the following table to compute the following:

(a) GDP by expenditure approach $_____
(b) GDP by income approach $_____
(c) GNP $_____
(d) NDP $_____
(e) NNI $_____
(f) PI $_____
(g) DI $_____

Exports	94
Profits of corporations and government enterprises before taxes	46
Capital consumption allowances	76
Government current purchases of goods and services	113
Net income of farm and unincorporated businesses	24
Taxes less subsidies on factors of production	75
Wages, salaries, supplementary labour income	371
Gross investment	167
Indirect taxes less subsidies	11
Personal saving	154
Government transfer payments	89
Interest and investment income	59
Net investment income from non-residents	-15
Personal consumption expenditure	463
Imports	175
Undistributed corporate profits	7
Personal taxes	25

4. Nominal GDP and Real GDP

The next table contains data on Canada's nominal GDP, constant dollar GDP, and the GDP price index for a number of years.
(a) Complete the missing entries.
(b) Which is the base year for the price index?

Year	Nominal GDP (Billion $)	Real GDP (Billion $)	GDP Price Index
1984	$444.7	$_____	95.2
1985	477.9	489.6	_____
1986	_____	505.7	100.0
1987	551.6	526.8	_____
1988	605.9	_____	109.5
1989	_____	565.6	114.9

5. Two Approaches to Calculating Real GDP

An economy produces four different goods. Below are shown the output quantities and prices for each in 2000 and 2001, and also the prices in 1992, which is used as the base year by statisticians in this economy.

(a) Find nominal GDP in each year by finding the total market value of each year's output using the prices current in that year.
Nominal GDP 2000 = $_____
Nominal GDP 2001 = $_____

(b) Construct a price index for each year using the 2000 quantities as weights, and 1992 as the base year.
Price index 2000 = _____
Price index 2001 = _____

(c) Find real GDP for each year using your answers in (a) and (b). [This approach is called Method 1 in Table 5-7.]
Real GDP 2000 in 1992 $ = $_____
Real GDP 2001 in 1992 $ = $_____

(d) Find real GDP for each year by determining the value that each year's output would have sold for using 1986 prices. [This approach is called Method 2 in Table 5-7.]
Real GDP 2000 in 1992 $ = $_____
Real GDP 2001 in 1992 $ = $_____

(e) Your results in (b) would have been somewhat different had you used the 2001 quantities as weights. What solution does Statistics Canada currently use to deal with this sort of discrepancy?

Good	Output in 2000	Output in 2001	Price in 1992	Price in 2000	Price in 2001
Books	20	22	$8	$10	$12
Cards	1000	900	$1	$1	$1
Dolls	8	10	$15	$20	$21
Grain	100	80	$2	$2	$4

6. What's Included in GDP?

The objective of measuring gross domestic product is to reflect the value of all final goods and services produced in Canada during a year. Given this, and what you have learned in this chapter about how GDP accounting works, classify each of the following as: (A) Included in calculated GDP; (B) Excluded from GDP, and correctly so; (C) Excluded from GDP, but ideally should be included.

(a) the sale from Burke to Solomon of shares in the Nortel company
(b) repairs that Slade performs on his own car
(c) the increase in inventories at Zellers stores
(d) health care provided in a provincially-funded hospital in Prince Edward Island
(e) construction services provided in Indonesia by a Canadian-based firm

(f) Wilson's purchase of a second-hand radio from Pickett

7. Real GDP or Nominal GDP?

In each case below, explain whether the speaker is discussing real GDP or nominal GDP.
(a) "Last year the nation's GDP rose by 3.5%, most of which was growth because prices rose by only 1.2%."
(b) "Rising GDP improves our standard of living by expanding the size of the economic pie."
(c) "GDP will continue to rise this year: if for no other reason than inflation."

Discussion Questions

1. Of what use are national income accounts to the economist and to the government's economic policy makers?

2. Why must GDP be measured in monetary terms, and what problem does this cause?

3. Why does GDP exclude non-production transactions? What are the two principal types of such transactions? List examples of each.

4. Why are there two ways, both yielding the same answer, for computing GDP?

5. Why are transfer payments excluded from GDP but included in Personal Income?

6. Is residential construction counted as investment or consumption? Why? Why is a change in inventories counted as an investment?

7. Why do economists find it necessary to inflate and deflate GDP when comparing GDP in different years? How do they do this?

8. Why is GDP not a good measure of the well-being of a society? Are there any omissions from GDP that are likely to be particularly problematic if you are trying to use GDP data to compare well-being in the Bahamas with well-being in Canada? What if you want to compare social well-being in modern day Canada with Canada a century ago?

Answers

Quick Quiz
1. (d) p. 106
2. (c) p. 108
3. (d) p. 109
4. (b) p. 113
5. (d) p. 114
6. (d) p. 116
7. (a) p. 116
8. (c) p. 118
9. (b) p. 120
10. (d) pp. 120-122

Fill-in Questions
1. gross domestic product, value, produced, market
2. output, purchases, market price, GDP
3. expenditures, income
4. (a) personal consumption expenditure; (b) gross investment; (c) government current purchase of goods and services; (d) net exports
5. capital, construction, inventories
6. negative, declining
7. produced
8. exports, imports
9. unincorporated
10. personal, taxes, transfers
11. GDP deflator, implicit price index
12. (a) nonmarket, leisure; (b) quality, output, environment, underground

True-False
1. F   only real GDP is in constant dollars
2. T
3. F   it would be overstated by multiple counting
4. T   a flow variable has a time dimension (e.g., calories per day); a stock variable does not
5. F   it would be included in 1991 GDP as inventory investment
6. F   the factor payment approach is also known as the income approach
7. F   construction of housing counts as investment
8. T
9. T
10. F   if real GDP falls, but prices rise by a larger percentage, nominal GDP can rise
11. F   understatement (because some production is excluded from the GDP accounts)

Multiple-Choice
1. (b)

2. (d)   include only the final product
3. (c)   the goods need not have been purchased this year, but they must have been produced this year
4. (d)   the others are non-productive transactions
5. (c)   this is the same thing as depreciation
6. (a)
7. (a)   net investment represents the addition to the capital stock
8. (c)   this is purely a financial transaction
9. (c)   it is added to the retailer's inventories in 1991
10. (b)
11. (b)   60 + 15 + 23 + (17-21)
12. (b)   60 + 11
13. (a)   15 - 5
14. (b)
15. (d)   investment is an expenditure
16. (d)   it depends whether or not prices are rising faster than nominal GDP
17. (c)   since both figures are for real GDP we can infer nothing about how prices changed
18. (b)   (450/400) x 100
19. (d)
20. (a)   such price changes cause distortion in a fixed weight system
21. (d)
22. (d)
23. (c)

Problems and Projects
1. (a) Wood producer: $84; 0; $84; Toy manufacturer: $110; $84; $26; Toy retailer: $150; $110; $40; Totals: $344; $194; $150; (b)   111; 39; 150; (c) Total incomes = total expenditures
2. (a) 100 + 113 + (482 - 520) = $175 million; (b) 175 - 30 = $145 million
3. (a)   463 + 167 + 13 + (94-175) = 662: (b) 371 + 46 + 59 + 24 + 75 + 11 + 3 = 662; (c) GDP – 15 = 647; (d) GNP – 76 = 571; (e) NDP – 11 = 560; (f) NNI – 7 + 89 = 642; (g) NI – 25 = 617
4. 1984: (447.7/95.2) x 100= $467.1; 1985: (477.9/489.6) x 100 = 97.6; 1986: (505.7/100) x 100 = $505.7; 1987: (551.6/526.8) x 100 = 104.7; 1988: (605.9/109.5) x 100 = $553.3; 1989: (565.6/100) x 114.9 = $649.9
5. (a) 2000: (20 x 10) + (1000 x 1) + (8 x 20) + (100 x 2) = $1560; 2001: (22 x 12) + (900 x 1) + (10 x 21) + (80 x 4) = $1694; (b) the 2000 quantities cost would have cost $1480 at 1992 prices, $1560 at 2000 prices, and $1808 at 2001 prices. Thus, 2000 index = (1560/1480) x 100 = 105.4;

2001 index = (1808/1480) x 100 = 122.1; (c)
2000 real GDP = ($1560/105.4) x 100 = $1480;
2001 real GDP = ($1694/122.1) x 100 = $1387;
(d) 2000: (20 x 8) + (1000 x 1) + (8 x 15) + (100 x
2) = $1480; 2001: (22 x 8) + (900 x 1) + (10 x 15)
+ (80 x 2) = $1386; (e) chain-weighted price index
6. (a) B – non-productive financial transaction;
(b) C – a nonmarket, but productive, activity; (c)
A – included in investment; (d) A – included in
government expenditures; (e) B – production is
outside Canada; (f) B – non-productive transaction
7. (a) Most of the 3.5% increase in nominal GDP
is caused by price increases; (b) real GDP must
grow for the "pie" to get bigger; (c) nominal GDP
can be increased by either price or output increases.

Chapter 6

Introduction to Economic Growth, Unemployment, and Inflation

Overview

This chapter introduces the topic of long run growth of real GDP, and short run fluctuations in real GDP, unemployment, and inflation. The chapters that follow will explain how these variables are determined, why they fluctuate, and what policies may be used to control them for the well-being of society.

Economic growth can be defined as either an increase in real GDP or in real GDP per capita. Either way, growth is an important goal because it lessens the burden of scarcity. Growth stems from increases in the supply of resource inputs and increases in the productivity of these inputs. Over the long haul, Canada's real GDP has shown a clear trend of growth (giving us a rising standard of living), but we see continual short-run deviations from the long-run trend. Sometimes we enjoy the prosperity that comes with rapidly growing output and employment, while at other times we suffer shrinking output and employment. Such periodic fluctuations in output, employment, and price levels are called "business cycles."

There are three types of unemployment: frictional, structural, and cyclical. Cyclical unemployment exists only when the economy is in recession, whereas frictional and structural unemployment exist even when the economy is at "full employment" – or operating at the natural rate of unemployment. Economists estimate that Canada's current natural rate of unemployment is about 6 to 7%.

Official unemployment statistics may lead to overstatement or understatement of the unemployment problem. As well as the hardship experienced by unemployed workers themselves, society loses the output that the unemployed could have produced. The relationship between unemployment and lost production is captured in Okun's Law. The burden of unemployment varies between men and women, between provinces, between younger and older workers, and between occupations.

Inflation is a second problem resulting from economic instability. The inflation rate is the annual percentage increase in the general price level. If inflation is not extreme, its most significant effects are arbitrary redistributions of income and wealth, particularly when the inflation is unanticipated. Some individuals suffer while others benefit. But inflation may not only affect how the pie is divided, it may also affect the size of the pie. The fear of inflation is rooted in the lesson of history that hyperinflation can lead to a severe breakdown in the economy that can devastate people's lives.

Chapter Outline

6.1 Economic Growth

◇ How is economic growth defined?

◇ What are the causes of economic growth?

• Canada has experienced a long-run trend of growth in real output. Economic growth is defined in two different ways:
  o Increase in real GDP over some period.
  o Increase in real GDP per capita over some period.
• By either definition, growth is calculated as an annual percentage change.
• Growth is a widely held economic goal because it lessens the burden of scarcity.
• As shown by the rule of 70, even a small improvement in the annual growth rate of the economy can over a number of years imply a dramatic change in the standard of living.
• The main sources of growth are increases in the supply of resource inputs, and increases in the productivity of these inputs.
• Since 1950 Canada has averaged about 4% per year growth. This figure must be qualified because this measure does not reflect the im-

pacts of improved products, increased leisure time, and other impacts such as increased environmental damage that have accompanied this growth.

Quick Quiz

1. A nation's real GDP is $120 billion in 2002 and $126 billion in 2003. What is the growth rate in real GDP?

(a) 0.05%
(b) 0.5%
(c) 5%
(d) 6%

2. At an average annual growth rate of 5%, how many years would it take for the Canadian economy to double its real GDP?

$\frac{70}{5}$

(a) 10
(b) 12
(c) 14
(d) 20

3. If growth is defined in terms of real GDP per capita, growth will occur only if:

(a) population does not grow
(b) population diminishes
(c) population grows faster than production of goods and services
(d) population grows more slowly than production of goods and services

6.2 The Business Cycle

◈ What is the nature of the business cycle?

◈ What causes business cycles?

• The long-run trend of economic growth is punctuated by business cycles (periods of short-term economic instability).

• A business cycle entails alternating periods of prosperity and recession (or depression). Cycles are of irregular duration and intensity but typically follow a four-phase pattern:

o peak
o recession
o trough
o recovery

➲ The term business cycle is misleading if it implies to you a sense of regularity or predictability. The next recession isn't likely to last exactly as long, or be exactly as deep, as the last one. Therefore, some economists use the term

"business fluctuations" rather than "business cycles."

• The business cycle affects the entire economy, but it does not affect every industry or province in the same way or to the same degree.

• The most important cause of fluctuations in the levels of output and employment is fluctuation in the level of total spending or demand.

• During a cycle, the output of capital goods and consumer durables fluctuates more than the output of services and consumer non-durables because the purchase of capital and durable goods can be postponed.

Quick Quiz

4. Employment and output will be at their lowest levels during which phase of the business cycle?

(a) peak
(b) recession
(c) trough
(d) recovery

5. Most economists believe that the immediate cause of business cycles is fluctuations in:

(a) the amount of money in circulation
(b) productivity of labour
(c) government policies
(d) total spending

6. Which business would be likely to experience the biggest fluctuations in demand due to the business cycle?

(a) grocery store
(b) telephone company
(c) brake repair shop
(d) furniture manufacturer

6.3 Unemployment

◈ How is unemployment measured?

◈ What is the nature of unemployment?

• Measurement of unemployment starts with the definition of three groups in the population: (1) those not eligible to work (under 15 or institutionalized), (2) those eligible but choosing not to participate in the labour force (homemakers, full-time students, retired people), and (3) the labour force (those eligible and available to work – whether employed or unemployed).

- The labour force participation rate is the percentage of the population 15 years and over that is in the labour force.

⮑ Don't confuse "in the labour force" with "employed." The labour force includes both employed and unemployed workers.

- The unemployment rate is defined as the percentage of the labour force unemployed; that is, people who are not working but are actively seeking work.
- This definition is criticized for understating unemployment because:
  - o part-time workers are counted as the same as full-time workers
  - o "discouraged workers" who have given up seeking jobs are not counted as unemployed.

⮑ Another common error is to assume that the categories "employed" and "unemployed" account for everyone. In fact, some people are in neither category and therefore are not counted as members of the labour force. Movements in and out of the labour force can explain many otherwise puzzling changes in labour market statistics.

- There are three kinds of unemployment:
  - o Frictional unemployment refers to workers "between jobs": searching for jobs, or waiting to take jobs very soon. Some frictional unemployment is inevitable and, to an extent, desirable.
  - o Structural unemployment results when changes in technology or consumer demands create a mismatch between the skills or location of workers compared to the skills or location required for the available jobs. Structural unemployment is a serious and longer term problem.
  - o Cyclical unemployment refers to the shortage of jobs caused by a drop in total spending. It is therefore associated with recessions.
- Even when the economy is "fully employed" some frictional and structural unemployment exist. The natural rate of unemployment (NRU), or full-employment unemployment rate, occurs when the economy is achieving its potential GDP and there is no cyclical unemployment. The NRU is the sum of frictional and structural unemployment.

- The economy does not usually operate at full employment, so the unemployment rate is usually above the natural rate, but can be below.
- Canada's current NRU is estimated to be around 6 to 7 percent. Demographic and institutional changes can shift the NRU.
- The economic cost of unemployment is measured by the GDP gap (or foregone output) that results during a recession. The GDP gap is the amount by which actual GDP falls short of potential GDP.
- Okun's law indicates that for every 1% which the actual unemployment rate exceeds the natural rate of unemployment, there is a GDP gap of about 2%.

⮑ Even when the economy is at full employment there is some unemployment; this is the natural rate of unemployment. Therefore, it is also possible — such as during World War II — for the economy to exceed its potential GDP for a period of time.

- The burden of unemployment is unequally distributed among different groups. Younger workers, blue-collar workers, less-educated workers, and workers in the Maritimes have typically suffered higher than average unemployment rates in recent years.
- Unemployment also has non-economic costs such as increased incidence of serious social problems.
- In the last decade, Canada's unemployment rate has fallen, but remains higher than that of many of other industrialized countries.

Quick Quiz

7. A town has 1000 people 15 years and over. There are 800 people employed, and 100 unemployed. What is the town's unemployment rate?
- (a)   10.0%
- (b)   11.1%
- (c)   20.0%
- (d)   25.0%

8. Wayne is an unemployed welder. There are jobs for welders in the town where he lives, but he hasn't found one yet. What type of unemployment describes Wayne's case?
- (a)   frictional
- (b)   structural
- (c)   cyclical
- (d)   natural

9. At the natural rate of unemployment:
  (a)   there is no GDP gap
  (b)   there is no cyclical unemployment
  (c)   all unemployment is structural or frictional
  (d)   all of the above

6.4 Inflation

◇ How is inflation defined?

◇ What is the nature of inflation?

• Inflation is a rise in the general level of prices, and is measured by the annual percentage rise in the Consumer Price Index (CPI).

• The CPI measures the price of a fixed "market basket" of goods and services purchased by the typical Canadian consumer. The CPI is scaled to equal 100 in the base year.

• Since 1960, the general level of prices in Canada has risen every year. Inflation was very low in the 1960s, highest in the 1970s and 1980s, and low again since the early 1990s. Canada's inflation rate is now low relative to other industrialized countries.

• The rule of 70 can be used to calculate how many years it would take for the price level to double at any given rate of inflation.

• As a provisional theory, we distinguish between demand-pull inflation, caused by an excess of total spending on goods compared to the economy's capacity to produce, and cost-push inflation, caused by increasing per unit production costs. Demand-pull inflation can continue indefinitely whereas cost-push inflation is self-limiting.

Quick Quiz

10. When there is inflation:
  (a)   all goods are rising in price
  (b)   all consumer goods are rising in price
  (c)   all prices are rising, though some rise faster than others
  (d)   the general level of prices is rising

11. The CPI is based on:
  (a)   actual patterns of expenditures by Canadian consumers in each year
  (b)   actual patterns of expenditures by Canadian consumers in a base year
  (c)   actual patterns of production of goods in the Canadian economy in each year
  (d)   the actual pattern of production of goods in the Canadian economy in a base year

12. Which statement is false?
  (a)   Canada's inflation rate in the last few years is significantly lower than during the 1970s and 1980s.
  (b)   Canada has a lower inflation rate than many nations around the world
  (c)   Canada's inflation rate has been falling quite consistently for the last twenty years.
  (d)   Canada's inflation rate peaked in the early 1980s.

6.5 Redistribution Effects of Inflation

◇ How does inflation redistribute real income?

• Nominal income refers to the money amount of income, whereas real income refers to the purchasing power of nominal income.

• The percentage change in real income can be approximated by subtracting the percentage change in the price level from the percentage change in nominal income.

• Unanticipated inflation redistributes income away from fixed-income receivers. Flexible-income receivers (especially those whose incomes are subject to automatic cost-of-living adjustment – or COLA clauses) are not harmed by inflation.

• Unanticipated inflation hurts savers by decreasing the real value of savings, the nominal value of which is fixed.

• Unanticipated inflation benefits debtors and hurts creditors because it lowers the purchasing power or the real value of the money when it is repaid.

• When the inflation is anticipated, and people can adjust their affairs to reflect the expected rise in the price level, the redistribution of income is lessened. This occurs with COLA clauses in labour agreements and with adjustments to nominal interest rates in financial agreements.

• The nominal interest rate equals the real interest rate plus the premium for the expected inflation rate.

• Three final points about the redistribution effects of inflation:
  o The results of unanticipated deflation are exactly the opposite of unanticipated inflation.
  o Most people experience mixed effects from inflation because they have several

roles in the economy (e.g. wage earner, borrower, and saver).

o   Inflation wreaks its effects in a purely arbitrary (and unfair) manner.

⮕ How inflation affects the distribution of wealth and income depends crucially on whether or not the inflation is correctly anticipated. Learn to ask, whenever you are assessing the redistribution effects in an inflation scenario: "what level of inflation had been anticipated?"

Quick Quiz

13. If Cheryl gets a 10% raise at her part-time job, but the CPI goes up by 4% at the same time, then Cheryl's real income has: *10 - 4 = 6%*
   (a)   decreased by 6%
   (b)   increased by 4%
   (c)   increased by 6%
   (d)   increased by 10%

14. Unexpected inflation will benefit:
   (a)   debtors
   (b)   fixed-income receivers
   (c)   creditors
   (d)   savers

15. If the expected rate of inflation jumps by 3%:
   (a)   the real interest rate should rise by 3%
   (b)   the real interest rate should fall by 3%
   (c)   the nominal interest rate should rise by 3%
   (d)   the nominal interest rate should fall by 3%

6.6 Effects of Inflation on Output

◈ How does inflation affect real output?

•   Sharp increases in the cost of resources (such as energy) can cause cost-push inflation, reduce the demand for goods, causing GDP to fall and unemployment to rise.

•   Some economists stress that even mild inflation inflicts a cost on the economy as households and businesses spend time and other resources trying to minimize the impact of inflation. Other economists believe that mild demand-pull inflation may a necessary side effect of maintaining sufficient demand in the economy to maintain full employment.

•   Very rapid inflation (hyperinflation) will lead people to expect yet further price increases, so they will accelerate their spending in order to

stay ahead of the anticipated price increases. Speculative behaviour of all sorts will ensue, and money eventually will become worthless. Complete economic and social collapse is a possibility (such as in Weimar Germany). Hyperinflations have occurred recently in several countries.

Quick Quiz

16. In a country suffering rising inflation:
   (a)   firms will spend additional resources changing their prices more frequently
   (b)   households will try to hold more money than usual in their wallets
   (c)   there will be less demand for real assets than for monetary assets
   (d)   all of these statements are correct

17. Hyperinflation tends to cause:
   (a)   drastic redistribution effects
   (b)   increased use of barter
   (c)   expectations of continuing inflation
   (d)   all of the above effects

Terms and Concepts

real GDP per capita	potential GDP
economic growth	GDP gap
rule of 70	Okun's law
productivity	inflation
business cycle	consumer price index (CPI)
peak	
recession	demand-pull inflation
trough	cost-push inflation
recovery	nominal income
labour force	real income
unemployment rate	anticipated inflation
discouraged workers	unanticipated inflation
frictional unemployment	cost-of-living adjustment (COLA)
structural unemployment	real interest rate
cyclical unemployment	nominal interest rate
natural rate of unem-ployment (NRU)	deflation
	hyperinflation
	inflation

Fill-In Questions

1. The main sources of economic growth are increases in the _____ or _____ of resource inputs.

2. The term "business cycle" refers to the recurrent _fluctuations_ in the level of business activity around the long-run growth trend in the economy. The four phases of a typical business cycle are _peak_, _recession_, _trough_, and _recovery_.

3. Frictional unemployment refers to that group of workers who are _seeking_ for jobs or _waiting_ to take jobs in the near future. Structural unemployment means the lack of job opportunities due to changes in product _demand_ or _technology_. Cyclical unemployment arises in the _recession_ phase of the business cycle.

4. The full-employment unemployment rate is: (a) also called the _NRU_ rate of unemployment; (b) equals the total of the _frictional_ and the _structural_ unemployment in the economy; (c) realized when the _cyclical_ unemployment in the economy is equal to zero and when the _actual_ output of the economy is equal to its _potential_ output; and (d) currently estimated to be about _6_ to _7_ % in Canada.

5. The cost to society of unemployment is the lost _output_ that the unemployed resources could have produced. The GDP gap is equal to _potential_ GDP minus _actual_ GDP; and for every percentage point the unemployment rate rises above the natural rate of unemployment, the GDP gap will, according to Okun's law, (increase, decrease) _increase_ by _2_ %.

6. The burdens of unemployment are borne more heavily by (adult, teenage) _teenage_ and (blue-collar, white-collar) _blue collar_ workers.

7. If one's (real, nominal) _nominal_ income rises by 10% over the same period that the price level rises by 7%, the percentage increase in _real_ income would be 3%.

8. Inflation:
(a) hurts those whose money incomes are relatively (fixed, flexible) _fixed_;
(b) penalizes savers when the inflation is (anticipated, unanticipated) _unanticipated_, and benefits (borrowers, lenders) _borrowers_.

9. The redistributive effects of inflation are less severe when it is (anticipated, unanticipated) _anticipated_.

10. Clauses in labour contracts that call for automatic adjustments of workers' income from the effects of inflation are called _____.

11. The percentage increase in purchasing power that the lender receives from the borrower is the (real, nominal) _____ rate of interest; the percentage increase in money that the lender receives is the _____ rate of interest.

12. Real income measures the _____ power of nominal income. To obtain real income for a year divide the _____ income by a _____ index for that year, and multiply the result by ____. If nominal income increases at a faster rate than the price index, real income will _____; if the price index is increasing at a faster rate, real income will _____.

True-False

Circle T if the statement is true, F if it is false.

1. When the nominal GDP is increasing the nation is experiencing economic growth.   T **F**

2. Individual business cycles tend to be of roughly equal duration and intensity.   T **F**

3. One reason for structural unemployment is a mismatch between worker skills and the skills required to fill vacant jobs.   **T** F

4. Workers can be frictionally unemployed because they find it difficult to relocate or retrain to qualify for available jobs.   T **F**

5. Cyclical unemployment is sometimes termed deficient-demand unemployment.   **T** F

6. If unemployment is at its natural rate, the actual GDP and potential GDP are equal.   **T** F

7. At the natural rate of unemployment, the number of job vacancies is equal to the number of job seekers.   **T** F

8. It is possible for the unemployment rate and the number of people employed to rise at the same time.   **T** F

9. By not counting discouraged workers as unemployed, the official unemployment data tends to overstate the unemployment rate.　T F

10. If some people who report themselves as "unemployed" are employed in the underground economy, the reported unemployment rate may be overstated.　T F

11. The economy's GDP gap is measured by deducting actual GDP from potential GDP.　T F

12. An economy cannot reach an actual real GDP level higher than its potential real GDP.　T F

13. If the inflation rate exceeds the percent rise in nominal income, real income will drop.　T F

14. Unanticipated deflation would benefit creditors (lenders) and hurt debtors (borrowers).　T F

15. The real interest rate is the nominal interest rate plus the expected rate of inflation.　T F

16. Whether the inflation is anticipated or unanticipated, the effects of inflation on the distribution of income are much the same.　T F

17. The world has not experienced hyperinflation since the 1920s in Germany.　T F

Multiple-Choice

Circle the letter that corresponds to the best answer.

1. Which one of the following is not one of the four phases of an idealized business cycle?
- (a) inflation
- (b) recession
- (c) recovery
- (d) trough

2. At an average annual growth rate of 4%, the Canadian economy would double its real GDP in about:
- (a) 10 years
- (b) 12 years
- (c) 18 years
- (d) 25 years

3. An economy with real output growing 6% per year and population growing 2% per year will experience growth of:
- (a) 2% per year
- (b) 4% per year
- (c) 6% per year
- (d) 4% or 6% per year, depending on the definition of growth

4. Which of the following factors must be considered when interpreting real GDP growth rates?
- (a) improved products and services
- (b) increased leisure time
- (c) increased environmental degradation
- (d) all of the above

5. Since 1945, the deepest recession experienced in Canada occurred in:
- (a) 1954
- (b) 1973
- (c) 1982
- (d) 1991

6. Production and employment in which of the following industries would be least affected by a recession?
- (a) dairy products
- (b) furniture
- (c) factory equipment
- (d) construction

7. A worker who loses her job because her job is computerized is an example of:
- (a) frictional unemployment
- (b) structural unemployment
- (c) cyclical unemployment
- (d) disguised unemployment

8. A worker who has quit one job and is taking two weeks off before reporting to a new job is an example of:
- (a) frictional unemployment
- (b) structural unemployment
- (c) cyclical unemployment
- (d) disguised unemployment

9. Insufficient total spending in the economy results in:
- (a) frictional unemployment
- (b) structural unemployment
- (c) cyclical unemployment
- (d) disguised unemployment

10. The unemployment rate is computed as a ratio of the number unemployed over:
- (a) the labour force population
- (b) the labour force
- (c) the number employed
- (d) total population

11. If there are 150 people in the labour force, and the unemployment rate is 10%, the number of employed workers in the economy is:
- (a) 120
- (b) 135
- (c) 125
- (d) 130

12. The labour force data collected by Statistics Canada have been criticized because:
- (a) part-time workers are counted as if they are fully-employed
- (b) discouraged workers are treated as a part of the civilian labour force
- (c) part-time workers are not included in the labour force
- (d) none of the above

13. The full-employment unemployment rate in the economy has been achieved when:
- (a) frictional unemployment is zero
- (b) structural unemployment is zero
- (c) cyclical unemployment is zero
- (d) the natural rate of unemployment is zero

14. Which of the following could increase Canada's natural rate of unemployment?
- (a) increased participation of women and teenagers in the Canadian labour force
- (b) increases in employment insurance benefits in Canada
- (c) increases in the legal minimum wage
- (d) all of the above

15. An increase in the GDP gap indicates that:
- (a) potential output has decreased
- (b) real output has fallen compared to nominal output
- (c) the natural rate of employment has decreased
- (d) actual output has decreased compared to potential output

16. Okun's law predicts that when the actual unemployment rate is two percentage points above

the natural rate of unemployment, the GDP gap will equal:
- (a) 1% of the potential GDP
- (b) 3% of the potential GDP
- (c) 4% of the potential GDP
- (d) 5% of the potential GDP

17. If the GDP gap were equal to 6% of the potential GDP, the actual unemployment rate would exceed the natural rate of unemployment by:
- (a) two percentage points
- (b) three percentage points
- (c) four percentage points
- (d) five percentage points

18. The rate of unemployment is lowest among the following groups:
- (a) the uneducated
- (b) teenagers
- (c) workers 15-24 years of age
- (d) workers 25 years of age and older

19. During periods of inflation the purchasing power of money:
- (a) rises
- (b) falls
- (c) stays constant
- (d) could rise or fall

20. If a person's nominal income increases by 8% while the price level increases by 10%, the person's real income will have:
- (a) increased by 2%
- (b) increased by 18%
- (c) decreased by 18%
- (d) decreased by 2%

21. John earns $6,000 at his summer job. He owes $20,000 in student loans, and he owns a $4,000 GIC. Suddenly, at the end of the summer, the CPI rises by 10%. The effect John of this unanticipated inflation is approximately the same as:
- (a) losing $600 in cash
- (b) losing $1,000 in cash
- (c) gaining $1,000 in cash
- (d) gaining $2,000 in cash

22. If no inflation were anticipated, a bank would be willing to lend a business firm $10 million at an annual interest of 8%. If the rate of inflation were expected to be 6%, the bank would charge the firm an annual interest rate of:
- (a) 2%

(b)   6%
(c)   8%
(d)   14%

23. Of the following, who would not be hurt by inflation?
(a)   those living on company pensions that are fixed in money terms
(b)   those who find prices rising more rapidly than their money incomes
(c)   those who have loaned money at fixed interest rates
(d)   those who took out mortgage loans prior to the inflation

24. A cost-of-living adjustment clause (COLA) in a union contract:
(a)   states that the last worker hired will be the first one fired in a cyclical downturn
(b)   guarantees a worker a stated percentage of regular income during layoffs
(c)   adjusts worker incomes automatically to inflation
(d)   provides early retirement benefits for long-term employees in case of permanent layoffs

25. Which of the following is not often associated with hyperinflation?
(a)   war or its aftermath
(b)   rising output in the economy
(c)   the hoarding of goods and speculation
(d)   a halt to the use of money as a medium of exchange and unit of account

26. Which of the following is not among the inefficiencies caused by even a mild inflation?
(a)   households spend more time acquiring information about prices
(b)   businesses incur more costs in updating their prices
(c)   households begin holding larger quantities of cash
(d)   all of the above are among the inefficiencies created by inflation

Problems and Projects

1. Interpreting Business Cycles
The solid line in the graph shows twenty years of history of real output for some nation. The points

labelled as years refer to the beginning of the years. The broken line shows potential GDP.

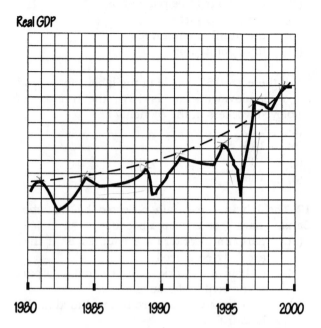

Real GDP

1980   1985   1990   1995   2000

(a) During this period the nation experienced six full business cycles. Identify the six peaks that marked the beginnings of these cycles.
(b) Which cycle lasted the longest from peak to peak?
(c) In which recession did real output fall the farthest?
(d) Which recovery was the quickest?
(e) What does the slope of the broken line indicate?
(f) In what year was the output gap the largest? What does this indicate?
(g) Were there any years when the output gap was negative? What does this indicate?
(h) In what year was the level of cyclical unemployment probably highest? Why?

2. Employment, Unemployment and Labour Force
In the following table are a nation's labour force statistics for 2003 and 2004. (Numbers of persons are in millions.)

	2003	2004
Non-institutionalized population (15+)	15.2	15.3
Labour force	11.5	12.3
Not in labour force	____	____
Employed		11.0
Unemployed	1.2	____

Unemployment rate (%)   _____   _____

(a) Fill in the missing entries in the table.

(b) How is it possible that both employment and unemployment increased in 2004?

(c) Which year, 2003 or 2004, seems more likely to have been a year of recession?

(d) Why is the task of maintaining full employment over the years more than just a problem of finding jobs for those who happen to be unemployed at any given time?

3. Purchasing Power Effects of Inflation

Janice consumes only one good, "Pepsi," and measures her purchasing power in terms of litres of "Pepsi."

(a) At the beginning of the year when "Pepsi" was $1 a litre Janice loaned $100 interest free for one year to a friend. During the course of the year the price of "Pepsi" increased to $1.25.

(1) How many litres of "Pepsi" did Janice lend to her friend?

(2) How many litres of "Pepsi" were returned to Janice when the loan was paid back?

(3) By how much did the unanticipated inflation reduce Janice's wealth?

(b) Suppose that Janice knew that the price of "Pepsi" would increase to $1.25. What nominal interest rate would she charge in order to keep the purchasing power of the loan constant?

(c) Suppose that Janice wants to receive a 3% increase in purchasing power from the loan. Given that she knows that the price of "Pepsi" will increase to $1.25, how much money must she receive when the loan is repaid? What nominal interest rate will she charge?

4. GDP Gaps and Okun's Law

The nation whose GDP data appears in the following table had a natural rate of unemployment of 5% throughout the three years shown.

(a) In 1994 the nation's real GDP gap was ___, and the unemployment rate was _____%.

(b) In 1995 actual real GDP was _____, and the unemployment rate must have been (above, below) _____ the natural rate of 5%.

(c) Suppose that in 1996 the nation had 7% unemployment. By Okun's law, actual real GDP must have been approximately _____% below potential real GDP. Therefore, the real GDP gap was about _____, and actual real GDP was about _____.

Year	Potential Real GDP	Actual Real GDP	Real GDP Gap
1994	600	600	_____
1995	618	_____	28
1996	630	_____	_____

5. Inflation, Real Income and Real Interest Rates

The following table shows the price index in the economy at the end of four different years.

Year	Price Index	Rate of Inflation
1	100.00	
2	112.00	_____%
3	123.20	_____%
4	129.36	_____%

(a) Compute and enter in the table the rates of inflation in years 2, 3 and 4.

(b) Using the "rule of 70," how many years would it take for the price level of double at each of these three inflation rates?

(c) If nominal income increased by 15% from year 1 to 2, what was the approximate percentage increase in real income?

(d) If nominal income was $25,000 in year 2, what was the real income (measured in year 1 $)?

(e) If the nominal interest rate was 14% to borrow money from year 1 to year 2, what was the approximate real rate of interest over that period?

6. The Real Increase in Tuition Fees

In 1974 a full-time student in the Bachelor of Arts program at the University of British Columbia paid $462.00 in tuition.

(a) Use the CPI data provided at the very back of your textbook to compute the value of this amount expressed in 2002 terms.

(b) How much higher is the full-time tuition in your program at your current school?

7. Interest Rates and Unanticipated Inflation

The Atlantic Bank lends M. Laberge $100,000 at a nominal interest rate of 11%. Both he and the bank expect that this will yield a real interest rate of 8%.

(a) What inflation rate do the bank and Laberge expect?

(b) Suppose that inflation turns out to be 5%. What is the error in the inflation prediction, what does the error do to the real interest rate, and to whose benefit is this surprise?

Discussion Questions

1. Since the 1960s, what is the historical record of the Canadian economy with respect to economic growth, full employment, and price-level stability?

2. Define the business cycle. Why do some economists prefer the term "business fluctuation" to "business cycle"? Describe the four phases of an idealized cycle.

3. What, in the opinion of most economists, is the main cause of most business cycles?

4. Why are some industries particularly susceptible to downturn when the economy goes into recession? Can you give an example of an industry in your area that would be hit particularly hard, and one that would be affected only slightly?

5. Distinguish between frictional, structural, and cyclical unemployment.

6. When is there full employment in the Canadian economy? (Answer in terms of the unemployment rate, the actual and potential output of the economy, and the markets for labour.)

7. How is the unemployment rate measured in Canada? What criticisms have been made of Statistics Canada's method of determining the unemployment rate?

8. What is the economic cost of unemployment, and how is the cost measured? What does Okun's law say is the relationship between the unemployment rate and the cost of unemployment?

9. What groups in the economy tend to bear the burdens of unemployment, and what do you think are the reasons for their high unemployment rates?

10. What is inflation and how is the rate of inflation measured? If the price of gasoline rises, is

this inflation? If the price of computers falls, is this deflation?

11. What is real income and how can real income be obtained from nominal income figures?

12. What groups benefit from and what groups are hurt by inflation? How do the effects of inflation depend on whether it is anticipated or unanticipated?

13. What are the different ways in which inflation can affect the level of real output?

14. How have Canada's unemployment rate and inflation rate compared with those for other industrialized nations in recent years?

15. When there is a sharp rise or fall in the average price of stocks, what does this imply for the economy as a whole?

Answers

Quick Quiz
1. (c) p. 128
2. (c) p. 129
3. (d) p. 128
4. (c) p. 131
5. (d) p. 132
6. (d) pp. 132-133
7. (b) p. 133
8. (a) p. 135
9. (c) p. 135
10. (d) p. 140
11. (b) p. 140
12. (c) pp. 141-142
13. (c) p. 144
14. (a) pp. 145-146
15. (c) pp. 146-147
16. (a) pp. 148-149
17. (d) pp. 149-150

Fill-in Questions
1. supplies, productivity
2. fluctuations; recession, trough, recovery, peak
3. searching, waiting, demand, technology, recession
4. (a) natural; (b) frictional, structural; (c) cyclical, actual, potential; (d) 6 to 7
5. output, potential, actual, increase, 2
6. teenage, blue-collar

7. nominal, real

8. (a) fixed; (b) unanticipated, borrowers

9. anticipated

10. cost-of-living adjustments (COLA)

11. real, nominal

12. purchasing, nominal, price, 100, increase, decrease

True-False

1. F   growth refers to real GDP, not nominal the increases and decreases are in real GDP, not the inflation rate

2. F   they vary significantly

3. T

4. F   workers in this situation are suffering structural unemployment

5. T   there is not enough demand during a recession

6. T

7. T   in other words, there is not a shortage of jobs

8. T   with an expansion in the labour force

9. F   for this reason, it tends to understate the problem

10. T   there would be less unemployed than reported

11. T

12. F   it can for brief periods (WWII for example)

13. T

14. T   the creditors would be repaid money that has a higher purchasing power than expected

15. F   the nominal interest rate minus the expected inflation rate

16. F   when inflation is anticipated people take steps to hedge (protect themselves)

17. F   Serbia, Nicaragua, and Democratic Republic of Congo

Multiple-Choice

1. (a)

2. (c)   70/4 = approx 18

3. (d)   4% is in terms of real output per capita

4. (d)

5. (c)

6. (a)   purchases of consumer non-durables are not easily postponed

7. (b)   there is no longer a match between her skill and the skill demanded in the labour market

8. (a)

9. (c)

10. (b)

11. (b)   150 - 15

12. (a)   when, in fact, many part-time workers desire full-time work

13. (c)

14. (d)   all would tend to make jobs harder to find, or enable people to remain unemployed longer

15. (d)

16. (c)   2% of GDP per 1% of unemployment

17. (b)

18. (d)

19. (b)

20. (d)   8% - 10%

21. (c)   he gains $2,000 in drop in real value of debt, and loses $600 and $400 in drop in real value of assets: net effect is $1,000 better off

22. (d)   the real interest rate plus the expected inflation premium

23. (d)   they benefit because their mortgage payments have lower real value than expected because their nominal interest rate did not include the correct inflation premium

24. (c)

25. (b)   hyperinflation makes the economy less efficient, not more

26. (c)   if anything, people hold less cash in order to avoid the loss of purchasing power caused by inflation

Problems and Projects

1. (a) 1981, 1984, 1988, 1991, 1994, 1996, 1999; (b) 1984 to 1988; (c) 1994 to 1996; (d) 1994 to 1996; (e) trend of growth in potential GDP; (f) 1995; economy was very far below potential; (g) parts of each year from 1996 to 1999; economy was temporarily operating above its normal full employment potential; (h) end of 1995 when the gap was the largest.

2. (a) The following figures complete the table: 2003: 15.2–11.5 = 3.7, 11.5–1.2= 10.3, (1.2/11.5) x 100% = 10.4%; 2004: 15.3 – 12.3 = 3.0, 12.3 – 11.0 = 1.3, (1.3/12.3) x 100% = 10.6%; (b) The labour force increased more than employment increased; (c) Probably 2004. Because the unemployment rate was higher than in 2003, the output gap was likely also larger, unless the NRU had increased substantially from 2003 to 2004; (d) The number of people looking for work is continually expanding, and the structure of the demand for labour is continually changing.

3. (a) (1) 100 litres; (2) $100/$1.25 per litre = 80 litres: (3) 20 litres; (b) 25%; (c) $128.75; 28.75%

4. (a) 0, 5% (the natural rate); (b) 618–28 = 590, above; (c) (7%-5%) x 2% gap per 1% U = 4%; 630 x 0.04 = 25.2, 630 – 25.2 = 604.8

5. (a) ((112-110)/100) x 100% = 12%, ((123.2-112.0)/112.0) x 100% = 10%, ((129.36-123.2)/123.2) x 100% = 5%; (b) 70/12 = approx. 6, 70/10 = 7, 70/5 = 14; (c) 15%-12% = 3%; (d) $25,000 x (100/112) = $22,321 (in year 1 $); (e) 14%-12%=2%

6. (a) $462 x (CPI 2002/CPI 1974) = 462 x (119.0/31.1) = $1768 in 2002; (b) While the $1768 in 2002 $ would be a bit higher by now (because of CPI increase since 2002), your school almost certainly charges a substantially higher tuition rate!

7. (a) nominal – real = expected inflation: %11-8%= 3%; (b) the prediction is low by 2%; the effective real interest rate falls by 2%, to 6%; Laberge, as the borrower, benefits.

Chapter **7**

The Aggregate Expenditures Model

Overview

Chapter 6 discussed business cycles but said very little about how the level of GDP is determined and why the GDP fluctuates. This chapter tackles these remaining questions using the aggregate expenditures model, beginning with the very simplified "private closed economy" model. Later an international sector and a government sector are added to complete the model.

The basic premise of the aggregate expenditures model is that the output level depends only on the demand for output because the economy is assumed to have enough excess production capacity and unemployed workers to increase real output without driving prices up. In the "private closed economy" model demand has only two components: consumption and investment. Consumption spending depends mainly on the level of disposable income. Investment depends mainly on the rate of return that businesses expect from investment projects compared to the real rate of interest they must pay on the funds.

The equilibrium level of output is that output the production of which will create planned aggregate spending just sufficient to purchase that much output. Here the total of consumption and planned investment equals the level of real GDP.

If demand does not match the output level, the economy is in disequilibrium. Businesses will experience undesired changes in inventory levels, so they will adjust their production levels, in turn leading to a change in aggregate output.

A shift in the consumption or the investment schedule will change the equilibrium GDP, and by a larger amount than the initial expenditure change itself! This is the multiplier effect.

The closed economy model is extended to an open economy model by adding exports and imports. Exports are treated as a constant addition to the demand for Canada's output, whereas imports reduce the demand for our output because they represent expenditures on goods produced in other countries. Equilibrium GDP in the open economy model -- as in the closed economy

model -- is where real GDP equals aggregate expenditures. However, because aggregate expenditures now include net exports, equilibrium real GDP will equal $C + I_g + X_n$. The multiplier effect is also different in this version of the model. Because import spending is a leakage from the flow of domestic income, the open-economy multiplier is smaller than the simple multiplier in the closed economy model.

The final extension of the model adds a public sector. Government spending (G) is added as an extra source of aggregate expenditures and taxes (T) are added as a new leakage from spending. The revised expression for equilibrium, where output equals aggregate expenditures is: GDP = $C + I_g + X_n + G$. Because taxes are assumed to be a fixed amount, the open economy multiplier applies to this model also.

The economy's equilibrium need not be at the full-employment level of GDP. Typically the economy will have either a recessionary gap (GDP is below full employment and there is cyclical unemployment) or an inflationary gap (GDP is above full employment and unemployment is below the natural rate). This insight was at the heart of John Maynard Keynes' *General Theory*, an important book written in response to the Great Depression and the shortcomings of classical economic theory for explaining the behaviour of the macroeconomy. The Last Word box gives details of the differences between Keynes and his classical predecessors.

Chapter Outline

7.1 The Aggregate Expenditures Model: Consumption and Saving

◇ What factors determine consumption spending and saving?

• The basic premise of the aggregate expenditures model is that the amount of goods produced depends on the aggregate expenditures (total spending). The economy has excess production capacity and unemployed labour.

- Our initial aggregate expenditures model for "a private closed economy" assumes that: (1) the economy is closed (no imports or exports); (2) there is no government sector involved in spending or taxation; (3) all saving is personal saving; (4) depreciation is zero.
- Under these assumptions: (1) consumption and investment are the only expenditure components in the model, and (2) all income or output measures (GDP, NDP, PI, DI) are equivalent.
- Disposable income is divided between consumption (C) and saving (S) and is the main determinant of both C and S.
- Consumption and saving both increase as income increases.
  o The consumption schedule shows the amounts households plan to spend for consumer goods at various levels of disposable income.
  o The saving schedule indicates the amounts households plan to save at different disposable income levels.
- The average propensities to consume and to save and the marginal propensities to consume and to save can be computed from the consumption and saving schedules.
  o The APC and the APS are the percentages of income spent for consumption and saved; and their sum is equal to 1.
  o The MPC and the MPS are the percentages of additional income spent for consumption and saved; and their sum is equal to 1. On the graphs, these are the slopes of the C and S schedules.
- Changes in several other determinants of consumption and saving can shift the C and S schedules
  o wealth
  o expectations
  o household debt
  o real interest rates
  o taxation
- A change in the amount consumed (or saved) refers to a move from one point to another on a given schedule, due to a change in disposable income. A change in consumption (or saving) refers to a shift in the schedule, due to a change in one of the non-income determinants. When these two schedules change, they normally change in opposite directions. These two schedules are normally very stable.

⮕ Get lots of exercise with the concepts in this chapter. Be sure to work with tabular examples, graphs, and verbal explanations – instead of perhaps sidestepping an approach that doesn't come easily to you.

Quick Quiz

1. Consumption spending rises from $620 to $660 when disposable income rises from $750 to $800. What are the marginal propensity to consume and the marginal propensity to save?
(a) MPC = 0.825 but MPS cannot be determined
(b) MPC = 0.80 but MPS cannot be determined
(c) MPC = 0.825 and MPS = 0.175
(d) MPC = 0.80 and MPS = 0.20

2. If the graph of the *C* schedule becomes steeper, then:
(a) MPC has decreased
(b) MPS has decreased
(c) the S schedule also becomes steeper
(d) there is not necessarily any effect on the slope of the S schedule

3. The entire *C* schedule will shift upwards if:
(a) the level of disposable income increases
(b) households receive news that their future pension incomes will be higher than expected
(c) households decide that their levels of debt are too high and must be reduced
(d) government enacts new taxes on individuals

7.2 Investment

◇ What factors determine investment spending?
- The two key determinants of the level of investment spending are the expected rate of return from the purchase of additional capital goods and the real rate of interest.
  o The expected rate of return is higher the more revenues are expected to increase due to an investment, and lower the greater the cost of making an investment in capital goods.
  o The rate of interest is the price paid for the use of the money capital needed to buy real capital. If the expected rate of return is greater than the real rate of in-

terest, a business will invest because the investment will be profitable.

- o Therefore, the lower the real rate of interest, the greater will be the level of investment spending – resulting in a down-sloping investment demand curve (graphed as real interest rate vs. amount of investment).
- Any change in these non-interest-rate determinants of investment demand will shift the curve:
  - o acquisition, maintenance, and operating costs
  - o business taxes
  - o technological change
  - o the stock of capital goods on hand
  - o expectations
- The model in this chapter assumes investment to be independent of income, so the investment schedule is horizontal when plotted against real GDP.
- Because investment goods are durable and the five non-interest-rate determinants of investment are subject to sudden changes, investment spending is volatile.

Quick Quiz

4. If the real interest rate increases:
- (a) some previously unprofitable investment opportunities will now be profitable
- (b) the investment demand curve will shift to the left
- (c) there will be a movement upwards to the left along the existing investment demand curve
- (d) investment spending will increase

5. Suppose there is an increased demand worldwide for oil from Alberta's tar sands. Which of the following would not be included among the expected results?
- (a) an increase in the expected return from investing in capital equipment to extract oil from the tar sands
- (b) an increase in the real interest rate
- (c) a rightward shift in the investment demand curve in Alberta
- (d) an increased amount of investment in the Alberta economy

6. Which of the following would tend to increase the level of investment spending:
- (a) technological breakthroughs make solar

heating systems more economical
- (b) the level of unused capacity in factories increases
- (c) the federal government implements additional taxes on corporate profits
- (d) the probability increases that there will be a recession in the near future

7.3 Equilibrium GDP

◈ How is equilibrium GDP determined?
- The determination of the equilibrium level of real GDP can be shown in several different ways:
  - o Equilibrium real GDP is the real GDP at which aggregate expenditures $(C + I_g)$ equal the real GDP.
  - o On a graph, equilibrium is where the aggregate expenditures curve cuts the 45 degree line.
  - o Equilibrium is at the real GDP level where saving (leakage) equals planned investment (injection).
  - o Equilibrium is at the real GDP level where there are no unplanned changes in inventories.

➲ A key feature of the graphs for the aggregate expenditures model is the "45 degree line." The line is actually 45 degrees only if the measurement scale is identical on both the vertical and horizontal axes. If the scales differ, the line showing points where expenditures equal GDP will have a different angle.

- If GDP is not at the equilibrium level, market forces will push it back to equilibrium. If the level of GDP is below equilibrium:
  - o $C + I_g$ will exceed GDP, so planned spending exceeds production, causing a depletion of inventories.
  - o Planned investment will exceed saving, causing unplanned inventory decreases (so that actual investment equals saving).
  - o The unintended disinvestment through shrinking inventories will cause firms to increase production (up to equilibrium GDP).
- If the level of GDP is above equilibrium:
  - o GDP will exceed $C + I_g$, so production exceeds planned spending, causing an accumulation of inventories.

o   Saving will exceed planned investment, causing unplanned inventory increases (forcing actual investment to equal saving).

o   The unintended investment in rising inventories will cause firms to reduce output (until equilibrium GDP is reached).

➲ The distinction between actual and planned investment is key to understanding equilibrium. Actual investment includes both planned and unplanned investment. Unplanned investment refers to unplanned changes in inventories when businesses have based their production plans on faulty forecasts of how much their customers will buy.

Quick Quiz

7. GDP is currently above equilibrium if:
(a) $(C + I_g) >$ GDP
(b) $S = I_g$
(c) $C > I_g$
(d)   contrary to plans, inventories are shrinking

8. If planned investment exceeds saving:
(a)   inventories are being used up
(b)   GDP is above its equilibrium level
(c)   firms will want to reduce output
(d)   there is excess supply of output

9. At equilibrium GDP:
(a)   there are no unintended changes in inventories
(b)   planned investment equals actual investment
(c)   saving equals planned investment
(d)   all of the above

7.4 Changes in Equilibrium GDP and the Multiplier

◈ What is the multiplier and how does it affect changes in equilibrium GDP?

•   A shift in the investment schedule (or consumption schedule) will cause the equilibrium real GDP to change in the same direction, and by a larger amount than the initial change in spending. This is called the multiplier effect.

•   The multiplier effect occurs because if a business or household spends $100 extra then another person's income will rise by $100. That will cause that person to spend some fraction of the $100, causing yet another person's income to rise, and their consumption to rise, and so on.

•   There are several versions of the formula for calculating the multiplier:
o   Multiplier = change in real GDP / initial change in spending
o   Multiplier = 1/(1-MPC)
o   Multiplier = 1/MPS

➲ In using the first version of the formula, take care not to confuse a movement along the aggregate expenditures curve ($C + I_g$) with a shift in the curve. "Change in initial spending" refers to a shift in the vertical intercept of the curve.

•   A higher propensity to save implies a smaller multiplier.

•   In reality the multiplier is not as large as the formula 1/MPS would suggest. A more complete story of the multiplier must account for leakages into imports and taxes, as well as effects of inflation. All of these factors weaken the multiplier.

➲ The multiplier is a vital concept. It is simply the ratio of the change in equilibrium real GDP to the initial change in expenditures that caused the equilibrium to change. Play with numerical examples until you have a good grasp. Be sure you understand why a higher rate of leakages creates a smaller multiplier.

Quick Quiz

10. An economy has a marginal propensity to consume equal to 0.75. What is the multiplier?
(a)   0.25
(b)   0.75
(c)   1.33
(d)   4.0

11. When new government tax incentives for investment cause businesses to boost capital spending by $3 billion, the real GDP rises by $5 billion. What is the multiplier and how much *more* would GDP rise if the investment increases a further $2 billion?
(a)   the multiplier is 2.0; GDP would rise another $1.0 billion
(b)   the multiplier is 1.67: GDP would rise another $3.33 billion
(c)   the multiplier is 0.60; GDP would rise another $1.2 billion

(d)   the multiplier is 1.50; GDP would rise another $3.0 billion

12. The size of the multiplier will increase if:
(a)   investment spending rises
(b)   investment spending falls
(c)   the MPS falls
(d)   the MPC falls

7.5 International Trade and Equilibrium Output

◈ How does adding exports and imports to the model affect equilibrium output?

• In an open economy, exports (X) add to the nation's aggregate expenditures, and imports (M) subtract from its aggregate expenditures.

• Aggregate expenditures now equal the sum of consumption spending, planned investment spending, and net exports (X_n) with $X_n = X - M$.

• Canada's imports are positively related to Canada's GDP, whereas our exports are positively related to GDP in other countries.

• An appreciation of the Canadian dollar will lead to increased imports and decreased exports. A depreciation of our dollar relative to foreign currencies will have the opposite effect.

• The net export schedule is a decreasing function of domestic GDP, with the marginal propensity to import (MPM) controlling the rate at which X_n falls as GDP rises.

• Because our imports are leakage from spending on domestically produced goods, the open economy multiplier will be smaller than the closed economy multiplier. The open economy multiplier = 1/(MPS + MPM).

• Equilibrium real GDP in an open economy occurs where the real GDP is equal to consumption plus planned investment plus net export spending (GDP = C + I_g + X_n).

• By the leakages-injections approach, equilibrium occurs where $I_g + X = S + M$.

• If net exports are negative (positive), the effect of net exports is to reduce (increase) Canada's equilibrium GDP.

• Any increase (decrease) in Canada's X_n will increase (decrease) our equilibrium real GDP with a multiplier effect.

• In the open economy model, Canada's GDP can change due to changes in prosperity levels abroad, changes in tariffs or quotas, or changes in exchange rates.

Quick Quiz
13. As GDP increases, net exports decrease because:
(a)   imports are directly related to GDP
(b)   imports are inversely related to GDP
(c)   exports are directly related to GDP
(d)   exports are inversely related to GDP

14. Suppose the MPS is 0.10 and the MPM is 0.15. Then the open economy multiplier is:
(a)   0.25
(b)   4.0
(c)   5.0
(d)   10.15

15. If the Canadian dollar depreciates from 0.75 US$ to 0.73 US$, what will be the result for Canada's economy?
(a)   the net exports schedule will shift down, and equilibrium GDP will increase
(b)   the net exports schedule will shift up, and equilibrium GDP will increase
(c)   the net exports schedule will shift down, and equilibrium GDP will decrease
(d)   the net exports schedule will shift up, and equilibrium GDP will decrease

7.6 Adding the Public Sector

◈ How do exports and imports affect equilibrium output?

• A public sector is added to the aggregate expenditures model under the following assumptions:
  o   Government spending levels have no effect on consumption or investment spending plans
  o   Government's net tax revenues (taxes minus transfer payments) are derived entirely from personal taxes.
  o   The amount of taxes collected is fixed, regardless of GDP.

• Government purchases of goods and services (G) are an injection of spending that add to the aggregate expenditures schedule and increase equilibrium real GDP (with a multiplier effect).

• Taxes (T) are a leakage of spending that reduce the aggregate expenditures schedule and decrease equilibrium real GDP. A change in the level of lump-sum taxes has a multiplier effect on GDP.

• Taxes cause disposable income (DI) to fall short of GDP, forcing households to reduce consumption, saving, and imports below what they

would be in the absence of taxes. The after-tax versions of these variables in symbols are as follows:
o consumption is C_a
o saving is S_a
o imports are M_a, and net exports are X_{na}
• Equilibrium real GDP in an open economy with a public sector can be expressed in two ways:
o where output equals aggregate expenditures: GDP = $C_a + I_g + X_{na} + G$.
o where leakages equal injections: $S_a + T + M_a = I_g + X + G$.

➲ Although the model becomes more complex with the addition of the trade sector and the public sector, the basic mechanics of the model do not change. Equilibrium GDP is always found where aggregate expenditures equal output, and there is always a multiplier effect when any of the expenditures schedules shift.

➲ When faced with questions about the aggregate expenditures model — whether in this study guide or on an exam! — take time to assess which version of the model is indicated by the question. Is the economy open or closed? Is there a government sector? Are taxes fixed relative to income?

Quick Quiz
16. When government levies taxes, households finance the payment of these taxes by reducing which of the following?
(a) consumption
(b) saving
(c) imports
(d) all of the above

17. If G exceeds T, then the net impact of the public sector on equilibrium GDP is:
(a) an increase
(b) a decrease
(c) zero change
(d) not predictable without more information

18. Which is a false statement regarding equilibrium in an open economy with a public sector?
(a) injections equal leakages
(b) there are no unplanned changes in inventories
(c) the aggregate expenditures schedule intersects the 45 degree line

(d) saving equals gross investment

7.7 Equilibrium Versus Full-Employment GDP
✦ What is the distinction between equilibrium GDP and full-employment GDP?
• The equilibrium level of real GDP can be below, above, or equal to, full-employment GDP.
o If equilibrium GDP is less than full-employment GDP, there is a recessionary gap equal to the amount by which actual GDP is below full-employment GDP.
o If equilibrium GDP is greater than full-employment GDP, there is an inflationary gap equal to the amount by which actual GDP exceeds full-employment GDP.
• In the late 1990s Canada experienced strong economic growth and falling unemployment without developing much inflation at the same time. There must have been a recessionary gap at the beginning of this period of expansion, but it is also apparent that the full-employment GDP level was growing remarkably quickly.
• The aggregate expenditures model has three key limitations (that will be addressed in subsequent chapters):
o It does not show price-level changes.
o It does not address cost-push inflation.
o It does not allow for "self-correction."

Quick Quiz
19. The economy has a multiplier of 3 and a recessionary gap of 15. What shift in the aggregate expenditures schedule would close this gap?
(a) a decrease of 45
(b) a decrease of 5
(c) an increase of 5
(d) an increase of 45

20. In an inflationary gap situation:
(a) demand-pull inflation is likely to result
(b) equilibrium GDP is below potential GDP
(c) the economy is at full employment
(d) cyclical unemployment is high

• As explained in "The Last Word," the Great Depression revolutionized macroeconomic theory.
o Classical economists believed that an economy in depression would automatically return to full employment without any need for government policy intervention. This conclusion was based on Say's Law which states that supply creates its own demand. An oversupply of goods

(and an oversupply of labour) would force prices (and wages) would drop until the equilibrium was restored at full employment and potential output.

o During the Great Depression unemployment was so high for so long that the classical conclusions were thrown into question. In his book, *The General Theory of Employment, Interest and Money*, John Maynard Keynes developed the aggregate expenditures model which rejected Say's Law and the classical theories. Keynes argued that while output creates enough income to purchase all of the output, there is no guarantee that all of the income will be spent on the current output because savings and investment decisions are not necessarily coordinated. Secondly, wages and prices are downwardly inflexible, so recessions may be deep and prolonged. Overall, Keynes did not believe the market economy to be capable of stabilizing itself, so government involvement is necessary.

Terms and Concepts

45-degree line
consumption schedule
saving schedule
break-even income
average propensity to
    consume
average propensity to
    save
marginal propensity
  to consume
marginal propensity to
  save
wealth effect
expected rate of return
investment demand
  curve

planned investment
investment schedule
aggregate expenditures
  schedule
equilibrium GDP
leakage
injection
unplanned changes in
  inventory
actual investment
multiplier
marginal propensity to
  import
lump-sum tax
recessionary gap
inflationary gap

Fill-In Questions

1. The first model in this chapter is based on four assumptions: a(n) (open, closed) _____ economy; no _____ or _____ by government; all saving is (personal, business) _____; and depreciation is _____. These

assumptions imply that: the only relevant expenditure components are _____ and _____.

2. Because there is assumed to be _____ production capacity and _____ labour, the level of output in the economy depends directly on the level of _____ expenditures, and changes in the level of output (do, do not) _____ change the price level.

3. A shift of the entire consumption schedule is referred to as a change in _____; but a movement from one point on a given consumption schedule to another point on the schedule is referred to as a change in _____.

4. Investment is defined as spending for additional _____ goods. The amount of investment spending depends on the expected rate of _____ and on the real rate of _____.

5. Five non-interest-rate determinants of investment demand are: (a) _____, _____, and _____ costs; (b) _____ taxes; (c) _____ change; (d) stock of _____; and (e) _____.

6. In a private closed economy, the equilibrium can be expressed in at least three ways. It is that level of real GDP at which:
(a) aggregate _____ equal real _____; (b) real GDP equals _____ plus _____; (c) the aggregate expenditures schedule or curve intersects the _____ line.

7. If:
(a) aggregate expenditures exceed real output, saving is (greater, less) _____ than planned investment, there is unplanned (investment, disinvestment) _____ in inventories, and real GDP will (rise, fall) _____.
(b) aggregate expenditures are less than real output, savings is _____ than planned investment, there is unplanned _____ in inventories, and real GDP will _____.
(c) aggregate expenditures are equal to real output, saving is _____ planned investment, unplanned investment in inventories is _____, and real GDP will _____.

8. The demand abroad for Canadian exports depends upon the GDP in (Canada, other countries) _____, whereas the demand for Cana-

dian imports depends upon the GDP in
_____.

9. An appreciation of the Canadian dollar generally causes Canada's imports to (increase, decrease) _____, and causes Canada's exports to _____.

10. If exports are constant and imports increase with an increasing domestic GDP, the open economy multiplier will be (greater than, less than) _____ the closed economy multiplier and is given by 1/(_____ + _____).

11. According to classical economic theory, if the economy were in recession, wages and prices of goods and services would tend to (rise, fall) _____ and thereby automatically restore the economy to the _____ level of output.

12. Another element of classical economics was _____ Law, which stated that _____ creates its own _____.

True-False

Circle T if the statement is true, F if it is false.

1. In the model in this chapter the price level remains constant so any change in GDP is a change in real output.   **T F**

Questions 2 through 5 are based on the data in the following table. Assume that there is no government and no business saving, so GDP and disposable income (DI) are equal.

GDP	Consumption
160	168
200	196
240	224
280	252
320	280

2. When the GDP is 240, the average propensity to consume is 0.95.   **T F**

3. At a GDP level of 320 there is dissaving.   **T F**

4. The break-even level of GDP is somewhere below 240.   **T F**

5. The marginal propensity to consume in the table is 0.95 at all income levels.   **T F**

6. MPS + APS = 1.   **T F**

7. Other things equal, a rise in wealth will shift the consumption schedule up and result in an increase in saving at any given level of *DI*.   **T F**

8. The consumption schedule and the saving schedule tend to be more stable over time than the investment schedule.   **T F**

9. A business firm will purchase additional capital goods if the real rate of interest exceeds the expected rate of return from the investment.   **T F**

10. A decrease in the corporate profits tax will shift the investment demand curve to the left.   **T F**

11. At the equilibrium level of income, potential and actual GDP are equal.   **T F**

12. The equilibrium level of GDP is that GDP that where the aggregate expenditure schedule intersects the 45-degree line.   **T F**

13. If the multiplier is 2.5, and planned investment spending drops by 10, equilibrium real GDP will increase by 25.   **T F**

14. If the GDP in the United States is growing, we can expect an increase in Canadian GDP, *ceteris paribus*.   **T F**

15. If the price of a U.S. dollar has risen from $1.40 Canadian to $1.50 Canadian, an increase in Canadian exports to the United States can be expected.   **T F**

16. A higher marginal propensity to import in Canada means that Canadian households are spending a larger percentage of their disposable income on foreign produced goods.   **T F**

17. If MPC is 0.3 and MPM is 0.2, the open-economy multiplier is 2.   **T F**

18. A recessionary gap is the amount by which full-employment GDP falls short of actual GDP. **T F**

19. When the economy is in a recessionary gap, unemployment is above its natural rate. **T F**

20. The classical economists thought that the economy had enough wage and price flexibility to restore full employment equilibrium. **T F**

Multiple-Choice

Circle the letter that corresponds to the best answer.

1. Which of the following is **not** one of the assumptions made in developing the aggregate expenditure model in this chapter?
(a) the price level is constant
(b) business saving is zero
(c) any taxes are lump-sum taxes
(d) investment spending is related to the level of income

2. In the aggregate expenditure model, output and employment depend:
(a) directly on the level of total expenditures
(b) inversely on the quantity of resources available
(c) directly on the level of saving
(d) directly on the rate of interest

3. As disposable income decreases, *ceteris paribus*:
(a) both consumption and saving increase
(b) consumption increases and saving decreases
(c) consumption decreases and saving increases
(d) both consumption and saving decrease

4. If consumption spending increases from $358 to $367 when disposable income increases from $412 to $427, then the MPC must be:
(a) 0.4
(b) 0.6
(c) 0.8
(d) 0.9

5. If when disposable income is $375 billion the average propensity to consume is 0.8, then:

(a) the MPC is also 0.8
(b) consumption is $325 billion
(c) saving is $75 billion
(d) the marginal propensity to save is 0.2

Use the following graph to answer questions 6 through 9.

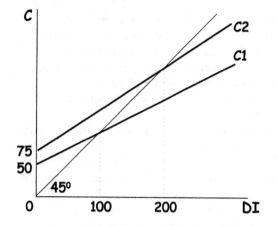

6. Which of the following could **not** cause the consumption curve to shift from C1 to C2?
(a) a decrease in the level of income taxes on households
(b) an increase in consumers' ownership of financial assets
(c) a decrease in the amount of consumers' indebtedness
(d) an increase in the income received by consumers

7. Which of the following is a true statement concerning the shift from C1 to C2?
(a) the marginal propensity to consume has increased
(b) the marginal propensity to save has increased
(c) the break even level of income has decreased
(d) the average propensity to save has decreased

8. What is the equation of consumption curve C2?
(a) C = 75 + 0.50 DI
(b) C = 50 + 0.50 DI
(c) C = 75 + 0.625 DI
(d) C = 50 + 0.625 DI

9. What are the marginal propensities to consume for the C1 and C2 consumption curves?
 (a)   0.50 for C1 and 0.625 for C2
 (b)   0.50 for C1 and 0.375 for C2
 (c)   0.25 for C1 and 0.75 for C2
 (d)   0.25 for both C1 and C2

10. Which of the following relationships is an inverse one in the aggregate expenditure model?
 (a)   the relationship between consumption spending and disposable income
 (b)   the relationship between investment spending and the rate of interest
 (c)   the relationship between saving and the level of income
 (d)   the relationship between investment spending and GDP

11. A leftward shift of the investment demand curve could be caused by:
 (a)   a decline in the rate of interest
 (b)   a decline in the level of wages paid
 (c)   a decline in business taxes
 (d)   growing pessimistic about the economy

Questions 12 and 13 are based on the consumption schedule below and assume a closed economy with no government sector.

Real GDP	Consumption
$350	$320
400	360
450	400
500	440
550	480
600	520

12. If planned investment is $60, what is equilibrium real GDP?
 (a) $400
 (b) $450
 (c) $500
 (d) $550

13. If planned investment is $60, and GDP is $450, unplanned investment is:
 (a)   -$20
 (b)   -$10
 (c) $0
 (d) $10

The next graph is the basis for questions 14 through 16. The equation for the consumption is C = 50 +.50 GDP.

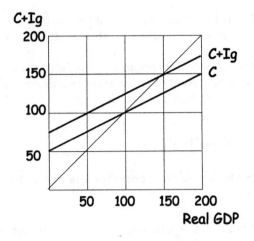

14. The level of planned investment is
 (a) $15
 (b) $25
 (c) $40
 (d) $50

15. The equilibrium level of real GDP is:
 (a) $120
 (b) $150
 (c) $175
 (d) $200

16. At a GDP level of $200, unintended investment is:
 (a) $25
 (b) $50
 (c) $75
 (d)   cannot be calculated with the information supplied

17. If GDP is below equilibrium:
 (a)   inventories will be zero
 (b)   inventories will be diminishing
 (c)   inventories will be increasing
 (d)   inventories will be stable

18. The volume of Canada's exports depends on:
 (a)   the price in foreign currency of a Canadian dollar
 (b)   the level of Canadian prices relative to the price level abroad
 (c)   the level of GDP in foreign countries
 (d)   all of the above

19. Generally, a depreciation of the Canadian dollar will lead to:
(a) an increase in exports and an increase in imports
(b) an increase in exports and no change in imports
(c) a decrease in exports and an increase in imports
(d) an increase in exports and a decrease in imports

20. An increase in GDP in Canada will increase our imports and:
(a) increase our exports
(b) increase our net exports
(c) decrease our exports
(d) decrease our net exports

21. Which of the following would increase Canadian imports of fruits from California?
(a) an increase in the price of Canadian fruit
(b) an appreciation of the U.S. dollar relative to the Canadian dollar
(c) an increase in fruit prices in California
(d) all of the above

22. A movement along Canada's net export schedule would be caused by:
(a) an increase in export demand
(b) an increase in our marginal propensity to import
(c) an increase in the foreign exchange rate for our dollar
(d) an increase in Canada's income

23. What is the correct formula for the open economy multiplier?
(a) 1/MPS
(b) 1/MPM
(c) 1/MPS + MPM
(d) 1/(MPS + MPM)

The following table of data represents the situation of an open economy with no government sector. Use the data to answer questions 24 through 27.

GDP	S	Ig	M	X
1000	200	150	150	340
1100	220	150	165	340
1200	240	150	180	340
1300	260	150	195	340
1400	280	150	210	340

24. For the economy in this table:
(a) MPC = 0.80 and MPM = 0.15
(b) MPS = 0.80 and MPM = 0.15
(c) MPC = 0.80 and MPM = 0.10
(d) MPS = 0.20 and MPM = 0.10

25. Equilibrium GDP is:
(a) 1100
(b) 1200
(c) 1300
(d) 1400

26. The open economy multiplier is:
(a) 0.95
(b) 2.86
(c) 3.50
(d) 4.32

27. If export expenditures fall by 35, equilibrium GDP will:
(a) decrease by 35
(b) increase by 35
(c) decrease by 100
(d) increase by 100

28. Other things remaining constant, which of the following would decrease an economy's real GDP and employment?
(a) the imposition of tariffs on goods imported from abroad
(b) an increase in the level of national income among the trading partners for this economy
(c) a decrease in the marginal propensity to consume
(d) a decrease in the marginal propensity to import

29. The effect of an increase in exports on GDP is similar to the effect of an increase in:
(a) interest rates
(b) saving
(c) investment
(d) business taxes

The data in the following table relate to an open economy with no public sector. Use the data to answer questions 30 through 33.

30. The equilibrium real GDP is:
(a) $960
(b) $980
(c) $1000

(d) $1020

GDP	C + Ig	Xn
$900	$913	$3
920	929	3
940	945	3
960	961	3
980	977	3
1000	993	3
1020	1009	3

31. If net exports are increased by $4 at each level of GDP, the equilibrium real GDP would become:
   (a) $960
   (b) $980
   (c) $1000
   (d) $1020

32. The multiplier in this economy is:
   (a)   2
   (b)   3
   (c)   4
   (d)   5

33. In the complete model with both government and foreign trade sectors, what is the proper expression of where equilibrium output is found?
   (a) $GDP = C_a + I_g + G + X$
   (b) $GDP = C_a + I_g + G + X_n$
   (c) $GDP = C_a + I_g + G + X + M$
   (d) $GDP = C_a + I_g + G + X_n - M$

Questions 34 through 37 are based on the next graph.

34. The multiplier in this economy is:
   (a)   2
   (b)   2.5
   (c)   3
   (d)   3.5

35. This diagram assumes that government purchases, net exports, and planned investment total:
   (a)   130 and are constant at all levels of GDP
   (b)   80 and are constant at all levels of GDP
   (c)   130 and increase as GDP increases
   (d)   80 and increase as GDP increases

36. What is the equilibrium level labelled GDP*?
   (a)   300
   (b)   390
   (c)   420
   (d)   450

37. If full-employment GDP happens to be 400, then what is the gap at GDP*?
   (a)   recessionary gap of 10
   (b)   inflationary gap of 10
   (c)   recessionary gap of 30
   (d)   none of the above

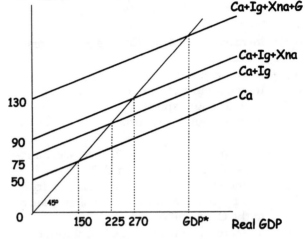

38. A change in which variable would change the slope of the C_a+I_g+Xn+G curve?
   (a)   the level of planned investment
   (b)   the level of lump-sum taxes
   (c)   the level of government purchases
   (d)   the marginal propensity to import

39. An inflationary gap is:
   (a)   the amount by which actual GDP falls short of full-employment GDP
   (b)   the amount by which actual GDP exceeds full-employment GDP
   (c)   the number of workers that would be employed at full employment minus the number actually employed
   (d)   the increase in investment spending needed to reach full-employment GDP from present GDP

40. If equilibrium real GDP is below full-employment GDP:
   (a)   there is a recessionary gap and aggregate expenditures must increase to close the gap
   (b)   there is a recessionary gap and aggregate expenditures must decrease to close the gap

(c) there is an inflationary gap and aggregate expenditures must increase to close the gap

(d) there is an inflationary gap and aggregate expenditures must decrease to close the gap

41. A nation that enters a free trade agreement can expect that:

(a) their multiplier will decrease because their MPM will rise

(b) their multiplier will increase because their MPM will decrease

(c) their multiplier will increase because their exports will increase

(d) their multiplier will be unaffected

42. Classical economics suggests that in a market economy:

(a) unemployment is a persistent problem

(b) market forces ensure full employment

(c) a recession will cause automatic increases in prices and wages

(d) demand creates its own supply

Problems and Projects

1. Consumption and Saving

Following is a consumption schedule. Assume taxes and transfers are zero and that all saving is personal saving.

GDP	C	S	APC	APS
$1500	$1540	$ ____	1.027	
1600	1620	____	____	-0.013
1700	1700			
1800	____	20	____	____
1900	____	____	____	____

(a) Compute saving at each of the first three levels of GDP listed.

(b) Compute consumption at GDP = $1800.

(c) The break-even level of income (GDP) is: $ ____ .

(d) The marginal propensity to consume (MPC) between GDP = $1500 and $1600 equals $ ____ divided by $ ____ = ____ . Between GDP = $1600 and $1700 MPC equals $ ____ divided by $ ____ = ____ .

(e) The marginal propensity to save (MPS) between GDP = $1500 and $1600 equals $ ____ divided by $ ____ = ____ . Between GDP = $1600 and $1700 MPS equals $ ____ divided by $ ____ = ____ .

(f) Since the MPC is constant, the consumption level at GDP = $1900 is $ ____ , and saving level is $ ____ .

(g) Given the value of APC at GDP = $1500, APS at this level of income is ____ .

(h) At GDP = $1600, APC ____ .

(i) Fill in the remaining APC and APS values.

(j) As income rises, the APC (rises, falls) ____ , and the APS ____ .

2. Graph of Consumption and Saving

This question is based on the graph that follows.

(a) At GDP = 0, consumption is $ ____ .

(b) The MPC = ____ .

(c) The break-even income level is GDP = $ ____ .

(d) When GDP = 0, saving is $ ____ .

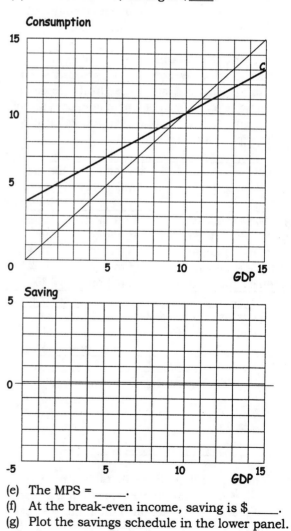

(e) The MPS = ____ .

(f) At the break-even income, saving is $ ____ .

(g) Plot the savings schedule in the lower panel.

(h) Based on answers (a) through (g), fill in the parameters in the equations:

$C = \_\_\_ + \_\_\_$ GDP

$S = \_\_\_ + \_\_\_$ GDP

3. Shifts in Consumption and Saving Schedules

Indicate in the space next to each of the following events whether the event will increase (+), decrease (-), or not change (0) the consumption schedule and the saving schedule.

(a) Consumers begin to expect that prices will be higher in the future. C: ☐ S: ☐

(b) Falling real estate prices reduce households' wealth. C: ☐ S: ☐

(c) A rise in the actual level of disposable income. C: ☐ S: ☐

(d) The government suddenly increases income tax rates. C: ☐ S: ☐

(e) A rise in the level of household credit card debt. C: ☐ S: ☐

4. Investment Demand

A corporation's investment opportunities are shown in the following schedule. (In the economy as a whole, each firm has a similar schedule of its own.) For each project is given the dollar cost, and the expected rate of return.

Project	Investment Amount ($)	Expected Rate of Return
A: new warehouse	12 million	8%
B: new delivery vehicles	10 million	9%
C: computer upgrades	3 million	11%
D: office expansion	5 million	10%
E: retail store renovation	8 million	7%

Real Interest Rate (%)	Profitable Projects	Investment Amount (million $)
12	_____	_____
11	_____	_____
10	_____	_____
9	_____	_____
8	_____	_____
7	_____	_____

(a) From the data indicate in table (by letters) which projects are profitable investments at each possible real interest rate, and then find the total amount of investment spending that would be undertaken at each real interest rate.

(b) Graph the data in the table completed in (a) as an investment demand curve.

Real Interest Rate

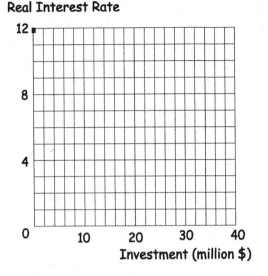

Investment (million $)

(c) The graph and the table show that the relation between the real rate of interest and the amount of investment spending is _____. When the real rate of interest increases, investment will (increase, decrease) _____.

5. Shifts in Investment Demand

Indicate in the box to the right of each event whether the event would tend to increase (+) or decrease (-) the investment demand curve. If the event does not shift the curve, indicate (0).

(a) An increase in the price of energy used for operating factory machinery.   ☐

(b) A new expectation of higher taxes on business profits.   ☐

(c) A mild recession.   ☐

(d) A belief that the economy is due for a period of "slow" consumer demand.   ☐

(e) Decreasing costs in the construction industry.   ☐

(f) A period of a high level of investment spending that has resulted in productive capacity in excess of the current demand for goods and services.   ☐

6. Aggregate Expenditures Model: Closed Economy

The table below shows consumption and saving at some levels of real GDP. The equation for the consumption schedule is: $C = 10 + .80$ GDP. Planned investment expenditures are fixed at $I_g = 20$.

(a) Complete the table. UI stands for unplanned inventory investment which is negative in the case of unplanned disinvestment and positive in the case of unplanned accumulation. In the GDP Change column, indicate "+" if GDP must rise to from the current level to reach equilibrium, and "–" if it must fall.

Real GDP	C	S	I_g	$C+I_g$	UI	GDP Change (+/-)
0	—	—	—	—	—	—
50	—	—	—	—	—	—
100	—	—	—	—	—	—
150	—	—	—	—	—	—
200	—	—	—	—	—	—
250	—	—	—	—	—	—

(b) The equilibrium real GDP will be $____, because at this income level, real GDP and _____ are equal, or savings and _____ are equal.

(c) For the given data, the value of the MPC = _____ and the value of MPS = ____.

7. The Multiplier Effect

A closed economy with no public sector has a marginal propensity to consume of 0.6. This economy experiences an increase of $10 in planned investment because businesses become more optimistic about future profits. Work through the rounds of the multiplier effect to fill in the table below.

	Change in income	Change in C	Change in S
Increase in I_g	$10	—	—
2nd round	—	—	—
3rd round	—	—	—
4th round	—	—	—
5th round	—	—	—
all other rounds	—	—	—
Total	—	—	—

8. Aggregate Expenditures Model and the Multiplier

The table below shows consumption levels for various GDP levels in an economy that has no foreign trade or government sector. The table shows two columns of values for planned investment: (I_g and I_g^*).

(a) Assuming planned investment is equal to I_g, complete the aggregate expenditures column labeled $C + I_g$.

(b) Equilibrium GDP at this level of I_g is ____.

(c) Now assuming planned investment at I_g^*, complete the aggregate expenditures column labeled $C + I_g^*$.

(d) Equilibrium GDP when investment is + I_g^* is ____.

(e) When planned investment rises by ___, equilibrium GDP rises by ___. Therefore the multiplier is ___/___ = ___.

GDP	C	I_g	$C+I_g$	I_g^*	$C+I_a^*$
100	120	30	____	55	____
200	195	30	____	55	____
300	270	30	____	55	____
400	345	30	____	55	____
500	420	30	____	55	____
600	495	30	____	55	____

9. Injections and Leakages in an Open Economy with Marginal Taxes

Suppose that households spend 80% of each dollar of disposable income on consumption goods, imports are 10% of disposable income, and personal taxes take 25% of each dollar of personal income.

(a) For each $100 of new personal income, $____ goes to taxes, and the other $____ goes to new disposable income.

(b) Of the $____ in new disposable income, $____ goes to consumption, and the other $____ goes to saving.

(c) Of the $____ in new consumption, $____ is spent on imported goods.

(d) In summary, of the $100 of new income, the total new leakages is $____ + $____ + $____ = $____.

(e) The fraction of the new $100 that leaks is ___, so the multiplier is 1/___ = ___

(f) Given this multiplier value, a new injection of $1 would raise equilibrium GDP by $____.

10. Aggregate Expenditures Model: Open Economy with Public Sector

The tables below pertain to an open economy with a public sector. The full-employment level of GDP is $450. The consumption and import data are shown in the tables. At all GDP levels, taxes are $50, exports are $50, and government purchases are $55. Planned investment is given by the equation Ig = 60 - i, where i is the interest rate in percent. At present i = 20.

(a) Fill in the first table.

(b) Find the equilibrium GDP by finding where GDP equals aggregate expenditures (AE).

(c) Confirm your result in (b) by proving that leakages equal injections at this GDP level.

(d) At equilibrium, is there a recessionary gap or an inflationary gap, and what size is the gap?

(e) Calculate the value of the multiplier.

(f) If the interest rate falls from 20% to 14%, what is the change in I_g, and according to the multiplier effect, what is the change in GDP?

(g) If foreigners decreased by $12 their purchases from this economy, what will be the impact on equilibrium income, according to the multiplier value found in (e)?

(h) What will the new gap be after the change in interest rate, and after the drop in purchases by foreigners?

(i) How much, and in what direction, would government purchases need to change in order to close the gap calculated in (h)?

(j) Confirm your conclusion in (i) by completing the second table including the appropriate new value for G. To start, remember to change I_g and X from their values in the original table.

GDP	T	DI	Ca	Sa	Ig	X	Ma	Xna	G	AE
$400	___	___	$340	___	___	$40	___	___	___	___
450	___	___	380	___	___	45	___	___	___	___
500	___	___	420	___	___	50	___	___	___	___
550	___	___	460	___	___	55	___	___	___	___
600	___	___	500	___	___	60	___	___	___	___

GDP	T	DI	Ca	Sa	Ig	X	Ma	Xna	G	AE
$400	___	___	$340	___	___	$40	___	___	___	___
450	___	___	380	___	___	45	___	___	___	___
500	___	___	420	___	___	50	___	___	___	___
550	___	___	460	___	___	55	___	___	___	___
600	___	___	500	___	___	60	___	___	___	___

11. Aggregate Expenditures Shifts and Equilibrium Changes in an Open Economy

Indicate whether each of the following will increase (+) or decrease (-) equilibrium real GDP in an open economy.

(a) An increase in its imports ☐

(b) An increase in its exports ☐

(c) An increasing level of national income among trading partners ☐

(d) An increase in trade barriers imposed by trading partners ☐

(e) Depreciation of the nation's currency ☐

12. Equilibrium Versus Full-Employment

The graph shows the economy with aggregate expenditures at level AE0.

(a) What is the equilibrium GDP, and what sort of gap exists at this point?

(b) If the aggregate expenditures shifts up to AE1 then full employment would be reached. This could be achieved by increasing government spending. How much additional G would be needed, and what does this indicate about the multiplier?

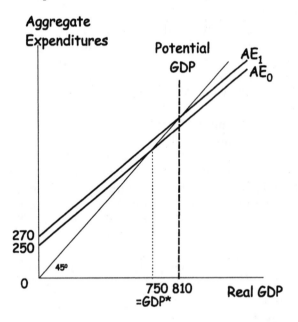

Discussion Questions

1. Define aggregate expenditures and explain why, in a market economy, aggregate expenditures determine the level of output and income.

2. Describe the relation between consumption and disposable income, and the relation between saving and disposable income; and then define the two average propensities and the two marginal propensities. Why does APC + APS always equal 1? Why does MPC + MPS always equal 1?

3. Determine how a change in each of the four non-income determinants will affect the consumption schedule and the saving schedule, and for each case explain concisely why consumption and saving change as you have indicated.

4. Explain: (a) when a business firm will or will not purchase additional capital goods; (b) how changes in the five non-interest-rate determinants of investment spending will affect the investment demand curve; (c) why investment spending tends to rise when the rate of interest falls; and (d) how changes in GDP might affect investment spending.

5. Why does the level of investment spending tend to fluctuate much more than the level of consumption spending?

6. What is meant by a leakage and by an injection? Which leakages and injections are considered in the different versions of the aggregate expenditures model? Why is the output at which leakages equals injections the equilibrium level of real GDP?

7. For investment, what is the distinction between the planned level and the actual level? Is the investment schedule planned or actual investment? What adjustment causes planned and actual investment to become equal?

8. What is the multiplier effect? Why is there such an effect, and what determines how large it will be? Why is the open economy multiplier smaller than the closed economy multiplier?

9. How does a change in the volume of exports and the volume of imports affect real GDP and the level of employment in an economy?

10. How would Canada's economy be affected by increased spending by the United States government to combat an American recession?

11. Explain what a recessionary gap and an inflationary gap mean. What economic conditions are present in the economy when each of these gaps exists? How is the size of each of these gaps measured?

12. What are the limitations of the aggregate expenditures model?

13. What aspects of classical macroeconomic thinking did J.M. Keynes disagree with, and why? How did his criticisms of classical economics affect the aggregate expenditures model?

Answers

Quick Quiz
1. (d) pp. 158-161
2. (b) pp. 161-162
3. (b) pp. 162-163
4. (c) pp. 165-167
5. (b) pp. 166-169
6. (a) pp. 166-169
7. (d) p. 176
8. (a) pp. 174-176
9. (a) pp. 173-176
10. (d) pp. 178-179
11. (b) p. 177
12. (c) pp. 179-180
13. (a) p. 181
14. (b) p. 182
15. (b) pp. 181-184
16. (d) pp. 187-188
17. (a) pp. 189-190
18. (d) pp. 189-190
19. (c) p. 191
20. (a) p. 191

Fill-in Questions
1. closed, purchases, taxes, personal, zero; consumption, investment,
2. excess, unemployed, aggregate, do not
3. consumption schedule, amount consumed
4. capital, return, interest
5. (a) acquisition, maintenance, and operating; (b) business; (c) technological; (d) capital goods on hand; (e) expectations
6. (a) expenditures, output; (b) consumption, planned investment; (c) 45-degree
7. (a) less, disinvestment, rise; (b) greater, investment, fall; (c) equal to, zero, neither rise nor fall
8. other countries, Canada
9. increase, decrease
10. less than, MPS + MPM
11. fall, full employment
12. Say's, supply, demand

True-False
1. T
2. F   224/240 = 0.93

3. F   S = 40
4. T   at GDP = 240, C > GDP
5. F   28/40 = 0.70
6. F   no, though MPC + MPS = 1, and APC + APS = 1
7. F   S decreases
8. T
9. F   real rate of interest must be below the expected rate of return
10. F   investment shifts to the right
11. F   actual GDP can be more or less than potential GDP
12. T
13. F   GDP will decrease by 25
14. T   our X and AE will increase as GDP rises in US
15. T   our products would now be relatively less expensive for American buyers
16. T
17. F   MPS = 1 - .3 = .7; multiplier = 1/(.7 + .2) = 1.11
18. F   the amount by which actual GDP falls short of potential GDP
19. T
20. T

Multiple-Choice

1. (d) we assume investment is independent of GDP
2. (a)
3. (d) because both MPC and MPS are positive
4. (b) 9/15 = 0.6
5. (c) .8 x 375 = 300; 375 – 300 = 75
6. (d) this is a movement along a C schedule, not a shift
7. (a) C2 is steeper than C1
8. (c) the intercept is 75, and between the two points for which values can be inferred, $\triangle C$ = 200 - 75 = 125, and $\triangle DI$ = 200 – 200 = 200, so MPC = 125/200 = 0.625
9. (a) 50/100 and 125/200
10. (b) the investment demand curve is downward-sloping
11. (d) the others cause investment demand to shift rightward, or cause a movement along the curve
12. (c) 440 + 60 = 500
13. (b) at GDP = 450, C = 400, so S = 50. Actual I = S = 50, so unplanned I = -10
14. (b) at GDP = 150, C = 125, and C + Ig = GDP
15. (b) where C + Ig = GDP
16. (a) output exceeds AE by 25
17. (b) there is excess demand

18. (d)
19. (d) Canadians and foreigners tend now to buy more Canadian produced goods and services
20. (d) imports rise and exports are unchanged
21. (a) the relative price change favours California fruits
22. (d) all of the others shift this schedule
23. (d) note the placement of the brackets
24. (a) MPC = 1 - MPS
25. (d) $S + M = Ig + X = 490$
26. (b) 1/(.20+.15) = 1/.35 = 2.86
27. (c) 2.86 x -35 = -100
28. (c) the aggregate expenditures schedule shifts down, intersecting the 45 degree line at a lower GDP level
29. (c) both are spending injections
30. (b) 977 + 3 = 980
31. (c) 993 + 7 = 1000
32. (d) (1000-980)/(7-3) = 20/4 = 5
33. (b) remember that $X_n = X - M$
34. (c) for $1 injected in spending on I_g or X, there is a $3 increase in GDP (e.g. (225-150)/(75-50) = 3)
35. (b) 130 - 50
36. (b) 130 x multiplier of 3 = 390
37. (a) actual GDP is below potential GDP by 10
38. (d) changes in the others would shift the intercept
39. (b)
40. (a)
41. (a) assuming that a larger percentage of expenditures now goes to imported goods
42. (b) because wages and prices are believed to be very flexible

Problems and Projects

1. (a) -40, -20, 0; (b) 1780; (c) 1700; (d) 80, 100, 0.80; 80, 100, 0.80; (e) 20, 100, 0.20; 20, 100, 0.20; (f) 1860, 40; (g)-0.027; (h) 1.013; (i) APC: 1.000, 0.989, 0.979, APS: 0, 0.011, 0.021; (j) falls, rises
2. (a) 4; (b) from one end of the C curve to the other, C rises by 9 while GDP rises by 15: 9/15 = 0.6; (c) 10, (d) -4; (e) 1 – MPC = 0.4; (f) 0; (g) see the next graph below; (h) C = 4 + 0.6 GDP; S = -4 + 0.4 GDP

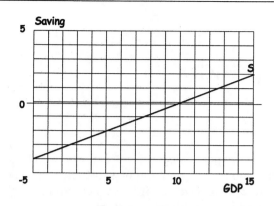

3. (a) spending rises before prices rise: C+, S-; (b) wealth effect: C-, S+; (c) movement along C and S schedules, but no shift: 0; (d) taxes are financed partly from consumption and partly from saving: C-, S-; (e) C-, S+

4. (a) 12%: none, 0; 11%: C, 3; 10%: C, D, 8; 9%: C, D, B, 18; 8%: C, D, B, A, 30; 7%: all, 38; (c) inverse; decrease.

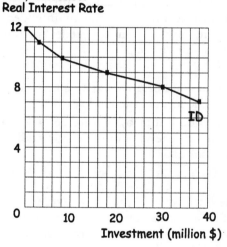

5. (a) - higher operating cost; (b) - lower after tax profitability in future; (c) – in short run, stock of capital on hand is high relative to what is needed; (d) - lower expected profitability in the short term; (e) + lower acquisitions costs; (f) - too much capital on hand in relation to needs in the short term

6. (a) C: 10, 50, 90, 130, 170, 210; S: -10, 0, 10, 20, 30, 40; I_g: 20 at all GDP values; C+I_g: 30, 70, 110, 150, 190, 230; UI = GDP – (C+I_g): -30, -20, -10, 0, 10, 20; GDP Change: +, +, +, equilibrium, -, -; (b) 150; C + I_g, planned investment; (c) 0.80, 0.20

7. Because the MPC = .6, MPS = .4, and the multiplier = 1/.4 = 2.5. Therefore, the total change in income must be 2.5 x 10 = 25. Hence, to fill the table, for each change in income, mul-

tiply by MPC to find the $\triangle C$ and by MPS to find $\triangle S$: $10, 6.00, 3.60, 2.16, 1.30, 1.94, 25.00; $\triangle C$: $6.00, 3.60, 2.16, 1.30, 0.78, 1.16, 15.00; $\triangle S$: $4.00, 2.40, 1.44, 0.86, 0.52, 0.77, 10.00

8. (a) 150, 225, 300, 375, 450, 525; (b) 300; (c) 175, 250, 325, 400, 475, 550; (d) 400; (e) 25, 100, 100, 25, 4

9. (a) 25, 75; (b) 75, 60, 15; (c) 60, 7.5; (d) 25, 15, 7.5, 47.5; (e) .475, .475, 2.11; (f) 2.11

10. (a) See the first table below; (b) $550 (c) $S_a+T+M_a = I_g+G+X$: $145=145 (d) inflationary gap of $100 (e) MPS = 0.2, MPM = 0.10; 1/(MPS+MPM) = 3.33 (f) $6; 6 x 3.33 = $20 (g) - 12 x 3.33 = decrease of $40 (h) inflationary gap of $80 (i) -80/3.33 = decrease by $24 (j) See second table below.

GDP	T	DI	Ca	Sa	Ig	X	Ma	Xna	G	AE
$400	50	350	$340	10	40	50	$40	10	55	445
450	50	400	380	20	40	50	45	5	55	480
500	50	450	420	30	40	50	50	0	55	515
550	50	500	460	40	40	50	55	-5	55	550
600	50	550	500	50	40	50	60	-10	55	585

GDP	T	DI	Ca	Sa	Ig	X	Ma	Xna	G	AE
$400	50	350	$340	10	46	38	$40	10	31	415
450	50	400	380	20	46	38	45	5	31	450
500	50	450	420	30	46	38	50	0	31	485
550	50	500	460	40	46	38	55	-5	31	520
600	50	550	500	50	46	38	60	-10	31	555

11. (a) - (net exports decrease); (b) + (net exports increase); (c) + (exports increase, and therefore net exports increase); (d) - (exports decrease, and therefore net exports decrease); (e) + (imports decrease and exports increase, and therefore net exports increase)

12. (a) recessionary gap, 810-750=60; (b) 270-250=20; multiplier = $\triangle$GDP/$\triangle$G = 60/20 = 3

Math Appendix

Overview

This appendix explains the mathematics behind the aggregate expenditures model. It describes the logic of how each of the components of aggregate expenditures is either a function of income or an autonomous parameter (constant amount). With all the component parts of aggregate expenditures are expressed in this way, we can then add them up to create the aggregate expenditures as a function of income. Using the knowledge that equilibrium income occurs where the amount of goods and services demanded equals the amount produced, or AE = GDP, we can set the aggregate expenditures function equal to income, and then solve for the unique equilibrium value of income. The appendix also shows the link between this algebraic presentation of the model and the graphical presentation.

Appendix Outline

◈ How is aggregate expenditures model expressed in algebraic form?

• Aggregate expenditures consists of several component parts of demand for goods and services
   o $AE = C + I + (X - M) + G$
• One part of consumption is constant or independent of income (therefore we call it autonomous, and label it a).
• The other part of consumption varies with disposable income according to the MPC (represented by b).
• Taxes on households have an autonomous or constant part (T_a) and variable portion depending on the tax rate (t). Income is represented by Y.
   o $C = a + b(Y - T_a - tY)$, or
   o $C = a - bT_a + b(1-t)Y$
• Planned investment is simply an autonomous amount: I_a.
• Government spending is autonomous: G_a.

• Net exports depend on exports which are autonomous, X_a, and imports, which are determined by the level of income according to the marginal propensity to import (m):
   o $M = mY$
• Substituting in all of the expressions for the different components of AE:
• $AE = a - bT_a + b(1-t)Y + I_a + G_a + X_a - mY$

⮕ The notation in this appendix is a bit different from that used in Chapter 7. The subscript "a" here stands for autonomous (that is, constant with respect to income). I means intended gross investment, and I_a simply reflects that this amount is autonomous.

◈ How is equilibrium income solved for in the algebraic form of the model?

• Find equilibrium by setting demand for output equal to the level of output produced: $AE = Y$.
• Then solve for Y:
$$Y = \frac{a - bT_a + I_a + G_a + X_a}{1 - [b(1 - t) - m]}$$
• The numerator of the above expression is the total of all autonomous parts of expenditure, A.
• The denominator is the rate of leakage, or withdrawal from domestic expenditures, W.
• Thus the equilibrium income, Y, can also be seen as:
   o $Y = A / W$
• This makes it clear that equilibrium income will be higher, *ceteris paribus,* the greater the level of any of the parts of autonomous expenditure, and the smaller the size of any of the leakage rates.
• The intercept of the AE curve on a graph is A. The slope is $(1 - W)$.

Quick Quiz
1. What is assumed about taxes in this appendix?
   (a)   there are no taxes
   (b)   taxes are strictly lump sum
   (c)   taxes are strictly proportional to income

(d) taxes have a lump sum portion and a portion induced by income

2. An autonomous expenditure is an expenditure that:
(a) will never change
(b) is independent of the level of income
(c) is dependent on the level of income
(d) none of the above

3. Which of the following does not affect the rate of withdrawals from spending (W)?
(a) marginal propensity to consume
(b) marginal tax rate
(c) marginal propensity to import
(d) they all affect W

Fill-In Questions

1. In this appendix, the subscript "a" signifies an amount that is _____.

2. W stands for the marginal propensity to _____, and A stands for _____.

True-False

Circle T if the statement is true, F if it is false.

1. A higher marginal tax rate will reduce disposable income at any given income level. **T F**

2. Equilibrium income is the ratio of autonomous expenditure to the marginal propensity to withdraw from domestic expenditure. **T F**

3. Disposable income, Y_d, is calculated as $Y - T$. **T F**

Multiple-Choice

Circle the letter that corresponds to the best answer.

Questions 1 and 2 use the following data.

Households spend $10 billion plus 90% of after tax income. Taxes equal $50 billion plus 10% of income.

1. If income is $400 billion, what is the total tax revenue for government?
(a) $10 billion
(b) $40 billion
(c) $50 billion
(d) $90 billion

2. If income is $400 billion, what is the level of consumption spending?
(a) 276
(b) 289
(c) 310
(d) 370

3. If autonomous consumption is 100, autonomous taxes are 50, the MPC is 0.7 and the marginal tax rate is 0.2, then which is correct?
(a) $C = 65 + .56Y$
(b) $C = 50 + .50Y$
(c) $C = 70 + .56Y$
(d) $C = 70 + .50Y$

4. Find the incorrect statement below. On the AE graph:
(a) the intercept is A
(b) the slope is W
(c) the slope is the marginal propensity to spend
(d) all of the statements are correct

5. The AE curve will become steeper as a result of an increase in:
(a) a
(b) b
(c) m
(d) t

6. The AE curve will down in a parallel fashion as a result of a drop in:
(a) a
(b) b
(c) m
(d) t

7. The AE curve has an intercept of 120 and a slope of 0.4. Then equilibrium GDP is:
(a) 48
(b) 72
(c) 200
(d) 300

Problems and Projects

1. Numerical Example: Finding Equilibrium in the Aggregate Expenditures Model

Assume the following data for the economy:

$C = 70 + .8Y_d$ $G_a = 60$
$T = 10 + .2Y$ $I_a = 50$
$M = .14Y$ $X_a = 40$

Identify the following values:
(a) marginal propensity to consume
(b) marginal propensity to import
(c) marginal tax rate
(d) autonomous consumption spending
(e) autonomous taxes

Derive expressions for the following:
(f) marginal propensity to spend
(g) marginal propensity to withdraw from domestic expenditures (W)
(h) total autonomous expenditures (A)

Solve for:
(i) equilibrium real GDP (Y)
(j) the change in equilibrium if one of the autonomous parts of consumption rises by 10.

Discussion Questions

1. Explain the assumptions made in this appendix regarding taxes.

2. What components of aggregate expenditures go into the level of autonomous expenditure?

3. What components of aggregate expenditures model determine marginal propensity to spend?

Answers

Quick Quiz
1. (d) p. 201
2. (b) p. 201
3. (d) p. 202

Fill-in Questions
1. autonomous
2. withdraw from domestic expenditures; autonomous expenditure

True-False
1. T   disposable means after-tax
2. T A/W
3. T

Multiple-Choice
1. (d) $50 + 0.10(400)$
2. (b) $10 + 0.90[400 - 50 - (0.10)(400)]$
3. (a) $100 + 0.7(Y - 50 - .2Y) = 100 + 0.7Y - 35 - 0.14Y = 65 + 0.56Y$
4. (b) the slope is $(1 - W)$
5. (b) a affects the intercept, and the other two change slope in the opposite direction
6. (a) a is the autonomous portion of C
7. (c) $A/W = 120/(1-0.4) = 200$

Problems and Projects
1. (a) 0.8; (b) 0.14; (c) 0.2; (d) 70; (e) 10; (f) $b(1-t) - m = 0.8(1-0.2) - 0.14 = 0.50$; (g) $1 - [b(1-t) - m] = 1 - 0.50 = 0.50$; (h) $a - bT_a + I_a + G_a + X_a = 70 - 0.8(10) + 50 + 60 + 40 = 212$; (i) $A/W = 212/0.5 = 424$; (j) $A' = 222$; $A'/W = 222/0.5 = 444$, so $\triangle Y = 20$.

Aggregate Demand and Aggregate Supply

Overview

This chapter introduces the aggregate demand-aggregate supply model. Unlike the aggregate expenditures model which holds the price level constant this model determines equilibrium levels of both real GDP and the price level.

The aggregate demand curve (AD) shows the amounts of real outputs that buyers collectively wish to purchase at each possible price level. Plotted on a price level vs. real output graph, AD is downsloping because less is demanded at higher price levels. Movements along a given AD curve are caused by three consequences of price changes: the real-balances effect, the interest-rate effect, and the foreign trade effect. The determinants of the AD curve (or aggregate demand shifters) are summarized in Figure 8-2, and include the factors that shift consumer spending, investment spending, government spending, and net export spending.

The short-run aggregate supply curve (AS) shows the level of real domestic output which will be produced at each price level, *if input prices remain fixed*. A rising price level implies greater profits for producers, and an incentive to produce and sell more output. But as output expands and full capacity is approached increasing shortages of inputs and inefficiencies in production raise the costs per unit of production and the selling prices. When the economy is far below capacity output, these problems are minor, so the AS curve is quite flat. But as output rises these problems become more severe, so the curve eventually becomes steeper, until it becomes nearly vertical as the economy nears its short-run full capacity output.

Equilibrium real domestic output and price level occur at the intersection of the AD and AS curves. The equilibrium values of real GDP and price level will change if anything happens to shift the AD curve or the AS curve. An increase in the AD curve will increase real GDP, but with a

small multiplier effect than in the aggregate expenditures model because some of the impact is absorbed in inflation. If AS increases, the market forces tend to increase real GDP and put down the price level.

In the short run nominal wages (and all input prices, in fact) are fixed. In the long run there is enough time for nominal wages and other input prices to respond fully to changes in the price level. Therefore, when the AD or AS shifts, the equilibrium real output will change in the short run, but in the long run the automatic adjustment of wages and prices will restore the economy to full employment. However, this process may be so slow that government may prefer to use fiscal and monetary policies in an effort to keep the economy at or near a non-inflationary, full-employment equilibrium. These policies are examined in the next few chapters.

Chapter Outline

8.1 Aggregate Demand

◈ What determines the shape of the AD curve?

◈ What factors shift the entire AD curve?

• Aggregate demand (AD) is the curve showing an inverse relationship between the total quantity of goods and services that will be purchased by households, firms, foreigners, and government and the price level.

• The AD curve is downward sloping for three reasons:

  o A higher price level reduces the purchasing power of financial assets, making asset holders feel less wealthy and causing them to reduce spending. This is the real-balance effect.

  o A higher price level causes people to demand more money to hold. With a fixed supply of money, the interest rate will rise, reducing interest-sensitive expenditures (by consumers and businesses). This is the interest-rate effect.

o A higher price level, when foreign prices are unchanged, will increase the relative price of goods produced in the domestic economy, reducing purchases of domestic output and increasing purchases of foreign output. This change in net export demand is the foreign trade effect.

• Whereas price changes cause movements along the AD curve, changes in spending due to other factors cause the AD curve to shift. An increase in AD is a rightward shift; a decrease in AD is a leftward shift.

• Consumption spending will increase if consumers experience:
o increases in wealth
o improved expectations
o reductions in indebtedness
o lower taxes.

• Investment spending (purchases of capital goods) will increase if businesses experience:
o lower interest rates
o improved expected returns due to better expected business conditions, improved technology, less excess capacity, or lower business taxes.

• Government spending will increase if government purchases more goods and services, assuming that tax collections and interest rates do not change as a result.

• Net export spending will increase if:
o the national incomes of our trading partners rise
o if our dollar depreciates and makes our goods relatively less expensive.

➲ Figures 8-2 and 8-5 are very useful to review for exams. They summarize the determinants of AD and AS, showing how these determinants shift the curves.

Quick Quiz

1. An increase in exports will cause:
   (a) a movement downward to the right along the AD curve
   (b) a movement upward to the left along the AD curve
   (c) a rightward shift of the AD curve
   (d) a leftward shift of the AD curve

2. The downward slope of the AD curve is the result of:

(a) the real-balance effect
(b) the interest-rate effect
(c) the foreign-trade effect
(d) all of the above effects

3. Which event will not shift the AD curve to the right?
   (a) an increase in the real interest rate
   (b) a drop in household indebtedness
   (c) an increase in government spending
   (d) an increase in expected returns on investment projects

8.2 Aggregate Supply

◈ What determines the shape of the AS curve in the long run and the short run?

◈ What factors shift the entire AS curve?

• The long run in macroeconomics is a period over which nominal wages and other resources prices fully adjust to price level changes. The short run is period too short for these adjustments to take place.

• The long-run aggregate supply curve (AS_{LR}) is vertical at the full-employment level of GDP. Given that wages and other resources prices adjust fully, producers earn the same level of real profit, and therefore wish to produce the same amount of real output, no matter what the price level is.

• The short-run aggregate supply (AS) curve shows the level of real domestic output that will be produced at each price level, holding constant the wage rate and other resource prices. Because resource prices are slow to adjust, higher price levels create higher real profits, giving firms the incentive to hire more resources and produce more output. Therefore, AS is upward-sloping.

• The steepness of AS depends on how per-unit production costs as capacity utilization changes. Consider the following scenarios when the price of output rises:
o When there is enough slack in the economy that output can expand without creating input shortages or production bottlenecks, there is no reason to raise prices when more is produced, so AS is relatively flat.
o When the economy is already at or beyond its potential GDP, resource shortages and production bottlenecks arise when firm try to produce more output.

These inefficiencies increase the per-unit cost of production, so the AS curve becomes steeper and steeper as real GDP rises.

• When per-unit production costs change for reasons other than a change in real output, firms collectively alter the amount of output they produce at each price level, so the AS curve shifts. The determinants of aggregate supply that shift the curve are discussed below. An increase (a decrease) in AS is a rightward (leftward) shift.

• Higher input prices increase per-unit production costs and decrease AS. Input prices could rise because of:

 o reduced availability of resources

 o depreciation of the domestic currency that raises the price of imported resources

 o increased market power of resource suppliers.

• An increase in the amount of output per unit of input means that productivity increases, and that AS increases. Note that productivity increase is the same as decrease in per-unit production costs.

• Increases in taxes, reductions in subsidies, or increased regulation of business will tend to raise per-unit costs of output and decrease the AS curve.

➲ Take note of the inverse relationship between productivity and per-unit cost of production.

➲ A common mistake when working with AS curves is to shift the curve in the wrong direction. If supply is increasing, the curve shifts rightward. It is easy to see how this leads to more output and lower prices.

Quick Quiz

4. The aggregate supply curve is vertical:

(a) in the short run

(b) when output prices have time to fully adjust

(c) when input prices have time to fully adjust

(d) when the unemployment rate is zero

5. An increase in the productivity of labour will in the short run:

(a) lower the per-unit cost of production

(b) shift the AS curve rightward

(c) increase the producers' profit margins

(d) all of the above

6. Which is not among the short run results of an increase in the price level due to a shift in AD?

(a) an increase in the real wage rate

(b) an increase in real output

(c) an increase in real profit margins

(d) an increase in employment

8.3 Equilibrium GDP and Changes in Equilibrium

◈ How are the equilibrium price level and real GDP level determined?

• The equilibrium real GDP and the equilibrium price level occur at the intersection of the AD and AS curves.

• At any price level above (below) the equilibrium, the amount of output produced is more than (less than) the amount demanded, so competition among sellers will drive the price level down (up) to equilibrium.

• An increase in aggregate demand leads to both increased output and demand-pull inflation. To the extent that inflation results, the increase in real output is smaller than the shift in the AD curve. The extent of the inflation depends on the steepness of the AS curve.

• A decrease in aggregate demand leads to a recession in which output and employment drop. However, no deflation accompanies the drop in output because product prices are inflexible in a downward direction. Reasons for this include the following:

 o wage contracts

 o efficiency wages

 o minimum wage laws

 o menu costs

 o fear of price wars

• A decrease in aggregate supply leads to a doubly bad result: falling real output and cyclical unemployment combined with cost-push inflation.

• An increase in aggregate supply driven by productivity increases will expand the economy's potential GDP and allow the economy to grow with less inflation than otherwise. Beginning in the late 1990s Canada experienced full employment, strong economic growth, and very low inflation. The underlying conditions that caused desirable combination of events can be understood with the AD-AS model.

• AD was growing, which alone would have increased real output and employment, but also the price level.

• However, productivity growth in the New Economy was also increasing the AS curve, further contributing to employment and output growth, and offsetting the inflationary effects of the AD shift.

Quick Quiz

7. In the short run, a sharp jump in energy prices will cause:
  (a) cost-push inflation and cyclical unemployment
  (b) demand-pull inflation and cyclical unemployment
  (c) inflation but no change in output
  (d) a drop in output but no change in the price level

8. Price inflexibility is a factor when:
  (a) aggregate demand increases
  (b) aggregate demand decreases
  (c) aggregate supply increases
  (d) aggregate supply decreases

9. Why was Canada's strong economic growth in the late 1990s not accompanied by much inflation?
  (a) prices were inflexible in the short run
  (b) the AS curve grew at the same time as the AD curve
  (c) wages and other resource prices were falling
  (d) there was no shift in the AD curve

8.4 From the Short Run to the Long Run

◈ How does the economy arrive at its long-run equilibrium?

• There are two reasons that nominal wages and other input prices remain fixed in the short run even if prices change:
  o Workers may not immediately realize the impact of price level changes on their real wages.
  o Collective agreements and other contracts fix nominal wages for a period of time, thus preventing immediate adjustment of

nominal wages in light of price level changes.

• Given enough time, nominal wages will adjust fully to whatever price level changes have occurred. At this point the long run is reached.

• Consider what happens in the short run if there is a price level change:
  o If the price level rises, but nominal wages are fixed, firms' profit margins rise since in nominal terms output prices have risen but input prices have not. Firms thus expand their output, hiring additional workers to do so. This pushes GDP beyond GDP_f and pushes the unemployment rate below its natural rate.
  o If the price level falls, but nominal wages are fixed, firms' profit margins drop because nominal output prices have fallen but nominal input prices have not. They cut production below GDP_f, laying off workers and pushing the unemployment rate up above its natural rate.

• The consequences of such price changes in the long run are as follows:
  o If initially the price level had risen in the short run, workers eventually realize that their real wages have fallen, and fixed-wage contracts come up for renewal. Therefore, the price increase will be matched by nominal wage increases, restoring real wages to their original level. This eliminates the unusually high profit margins that led employers to expand output and employment beyond their normal potential. GDP goes back the GDP_f and the unemployment rate returns to the natural rate.
  o If initially the price level had fallen in the short run, employers will eventually renegotiate nominal wages lower, restoring real wages to their original level. It this point their profit margins go back to normal, so they increase their output and hiring until GDP returns to GDP_f and unemployment returns to the natural rate.
  o Thus, whether the price level rises or falls in the short, the price level change has no long-run effect on real output, so the aggregate supply in the long run (AS_{LR}) is vertical at GDP_f.

Quick Quiz
10. Along the AS curve, which variable increases

as the price level falls:
  (a)   nominal wage rates
  (b)   employment
  (c)   real output
  (d)   real wage rates

11. Which variable is **not** constant at all points on an AS_{LR} curve:
  (a)   nominal wage rates
  (b)   employment
  (c)   real output
  (d)   real wage rates

12. When the economy is operating beyond its full-employment level of real GDP:
  (a)   there is pressure for nominal wages to rise
  (b)   there is pressure for real wages to fall
  (c)   unemployment is higher than its natural rate
  (d)   there is pressure for the price level to fall

8.5 Equilibrium Versus Full-Employment GDP

◈ Is equilibrium necessarily at full-employment GDP?

• Long-run equilibrium in the AD-AS model must be at the intersection of AD and AS (where demand for output and supply of output are equal), but it must also be on the vertical AS_{LR} curve (where nominal wages have adjusted to accommodate the price level and maintain the real wage). The AS_{LR} is vertical at the economy's full employment or potential GDP, and is consistent with the natural rate of unemployment.
• The equilibrium level of real GDP in the short run need not be at full employment: it could be higher or lower than that.
  o A recessionary gap is the amount by which equilibrium GDP falls short of full-employment GDP. In the absence of any policy action to combat the problem, prices and nominal wages will eventually fall until the economy returns to full-employment GDP, but this is likely to take an unacceptably long time.
  o An inflationary gap is the amount by which equilibrium GDP exceeds full-employment GDP. In the absence of any policy action, prices and nominal wages will rise far enough to reduce output until it returns to full-employment GDP. This

will add to the inflation, and will also take some time.
• For years, European unemployment rates have been above rates in Canada and the U.S. Competing theories view this high unemployment as the result of either: (a) high natural rate of unemployment, or (b) deficient aggregate demand.

Quick Quiz
13. Which statement is true?
  (a)   both short run and long run equilibrium must be at GDP_f
  (b)   long run equilibrium must be at GDP_f but short run equilibrium can be at a different GDP level
  (c)   short run equilibrium must be at GDP_f but long run equilibrium can be at a different GDP level
  (d)   neither short run nor long run equilibrium occurs at GDP_f

14. During an inflationary gap situations, responses in the labour market will include:
  (a)   more people enrolling in university
  (b)   increased rates of early retirement
  (c)   more workers working longer hours
  (d)   increased numbers of full-time homemakers

Terms and Concepts

aggregate demand-aggregate supply model
aggregate demand
real-balances effect
interest-rate effect
foreign trade effect
determinants of aggregate demand
long-run aggregate supply curve
short-run aggregate supply
determinants of aggregate supply
equilibrium price level
equilibrium real domestic output
efficiency wages
menu costs
long run
recessionary gap
inflationary gap

Fill-In Questions

1. In the AD-AS model the price level is _____, whereas in the aggregate expenditures model it is _____.

2. The AD curve shows the quantity of goods and services that will be _____ at various price _____. It slopes (upward, downward) _____ because of the _____, the _____, and the _____ effects.

3. (a) A change in one of the determinants of AD will cause a (movement along, shift of) _____ the AD curve.
(b) A change in the price will cause a (movement along, shift of) _____ the AD curve.

4. The AS curve shows the quantity of goods and services that will be _____ at various _____ levels. At all points along a given AS curve we assume that (input, output) _____ prices are constant.

5. The AS curve is _____ sloping because of the (increase, decrease) _____ in the per-unit costs of producing goods and services as output expands.

6. Along the long-run aggregate supply curve, prices and (real, nominal) _____ wages change, but _____ wages are constant, and therefore so are producers' _____ margins, the level of _____ of labour, and the level of real output.

7. The economy can reach a (short, long) _____ run equilibrium at an output level below potential GDP. Such a situation is termed a(n) _____ gap. Eventually the gap would be resolved automatically by (rising, falling) _____ prices and nominal wages.

True-False

Circle T if the statement is true, F if it is false.

1. A change in aggregate demand is caused by a change in the price level, other things equal. **T F**

2. A fall in the price level increases the real value of financial assets with fixed money value and, as a result, increases spending by the holders of these assets. **T F**

3. A fall in the price level reduces the demand for money, pushes interest rates upward, and decreases investment spending. **T F**

4. A rise in the price level of an economy (relative to foreign price levels) tends to increase that economy's net exports. **T F**

5. A decrease in the degree of excess capacity in the economy will retard the demand for new capital goods and therefore reduce AD. **T F**

6. The steepness of the AS curve depends on the degree of capacity utilization. **T F**

7. Lower prices for land, labour, or capital will tend to shift the AS to the left. **T F**

8. Productivity can be defined as the ratio of input divided by real output. **T F**

9. Increased government regulation tends to decrease the AS curve. **T F**

10. A decrease in AS is "doubly good" because it increases the real domestic output and prevents inflation. **T F**

11. Changes in the determinants of AS alter the per-unit production cost and shift AS. **T F**

12. An increase in productivity will shift the aggregate supply curve rightward. **T F**

13. A recessionary gap is the amount by which full-employment GDP falls short of actual GDP. **T F**

Multiple-Choice

Circle the letter that corresponds to the best answer.

1. When the price level rises:
(a) holders of financial assets with fixed money values increase their spending
(b) the demand for money falls
(c) interest rates rise and investment expenditures fall
(d) exports increase and imports fall

2. The downward slope of the AD curve is the result of:
(a)   the real-balance effect
(b)   the interest-rate effect
(c)   the foreign-trade effect
(d)   all of the above effects

3. Which of the following does not increase as a result of a decrease in the price level?
(a)   consumption
(b)   planned investment
(c)   net exports
(d)   government spending

4. The AS curve is the relationship between the:
(a)   price level and the real domestic output purchased
(b)   price level and the real domestic output produced
(c)   price level producers are willing to accept and the price level purchasers are willing to pay
(d)   real domestic output purchased and the real domestic output produced

5. The AS curve is upward sloping in the short run due to:
(a)   increased input prices as output rises
(b)   decreased input prices as output rises
(c)   rising per-unit production costs as output rises
(d)   a shortage of domestic resources

6. Which of the following is held constant when moving from one point on an AS curve to another point on the same curve?
(a)   the price level
(b)   the prices of inputs
(c)   the per unit cost of production
(d)   none of these are held constant

7. The AD curve will tend to be increased (shifted to the right) by:
(a)   a decrease in the price level
(b)   an increase in the price level
(c)   an increase in the excess capacity of factories
(d)   a depreciation in the Canadian dollar

8. An increase in business taxes will tend to:
(a)   decrease AD but not change AS
(b)   decrease AS but not change AD
(c)   decrease AD and AS

(d)   decrease AS and increase AD

9. An increase in AS will:
(a)   reduce the price level and real domestic output
(b)   reduce the price level and increase the real domestic output
(c)   increase the price level and real domestic output
(d)   reduce the price level and decrease the real domestic output

10. Why are nominal wages fixed in the short run, even when prices rise?
(a)   workers may not immediately be aware of the price increases
(b)   workers' wages may be fixed by contracts
(c)   both of the above
(d)   none of the above

11. If Parliament passed much stricter laws to control the air pollution from business, then this action would tend to:
(a)   increase per-unit production costs and shift the AS curve to the right
(b)   increase per-unit production costs and shift the AS curve to the left
(c)   increase per-unit production costs and shift the AD curve to the left
(d)   decrease per-unit production costs and shift the AS curve to the left

Suppose that real domestic output in an economy is 50, the quantity of inputs is 10, and the price of each input is $2. Answer questions 12 through 15 on the basis of this information.

12. The level of productivity in this economy is:
(a)   5
(b)   4
(c)   3
(d)   2

13. The per unit cost of production is:
(a) $0.40
(b) $0.50
(c) $0.75
(d) $1.00

14. If real domestic output in the economy rose to 60 units, then per-unit production costs would:
(a)   remain unchanged and AS would remain unchanged

(b)   increase and AS would decrease
(c)   decrease and AS would increase
(d)   decrease and AS would decrease

15. All else equal, if the price of each input increases from \$2 to \$4, productivity would:
(a)   decrease from \$4 to \$2 and AS would decrease
(b)   decrease from \$5 to \$3 and AS would decrease
(c)   increase from \$4 to \$2 and AS would increase
(d)   remain unchanged and AS would decrease

16. In the AD-AS model, an increase in the price level will:
(a)   shift the AD curve
(b)   shift the AS curve
(c)   shift both AD and AS curves
(d)   shift neither AD nor AS curve

17. When the economy is in deep recession, an increase in AD will:
(a)   increase the price level without affecting real output much
(b)   increase real output without affecting the price level much
(c)   substantially increase input prices
(d)   lead to widespread shortages of labour and raw materials

18. A decrease in the price of imported productive resources will:
(a)   expand output and lower the price level
(b)   expand output and raise the price level
(c)   contract output and lower the price level
(d)   contract output and raise the price level

Refer to the following graph to answer questions 19 through 21. Assume the economy begins with aggregate demand given by AD1 and short run aggregate supply by AS1.

19. Which is the current short-run equilibrium point?
(a)   *a*
(b)   *d*
(c)   *e*
(d)   *g*

20. Given the current short-run equilibrium point, where is the long-run equilibrium point that the economy would automatically move to, albeit slowly?
(a)   *d*
(b)   *e*
(c)   *f*
(d)   *g*

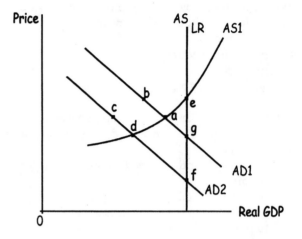

21. Beginning at the current short-run equilibrium point, a drop in aggregate demand to AD2 would cause the economy to shift in the short run to which point if the price level is downwardly inflexible?
(a)   *c*
(b)   *d*
(c)   *f*
(d)   *g*

Problems and Projects

1. Aggregate Demand and Aggregate Supply Equilibrium
The amounts of real output demanded and supplied at different price levels are given in the table below:
(a) Use this data to plot the AD and AS curves in the graph below.
(b) The short-run equilibrium price level is \$____, and the short-run equilibrium real GDP is \$____.
(c) Assuming that potential GDP is \$15, draw in the long-run aggregate supply curve (AS_LR) on the graph.
(d) At the short-run equilibrium in (b), there is a _____ gap of \$____.

Price level	Real GDP Supplied	Real GDP Demanded
25	1	16
50	8	14
75	12	12
100	15	10
125	17	8
150	18	6

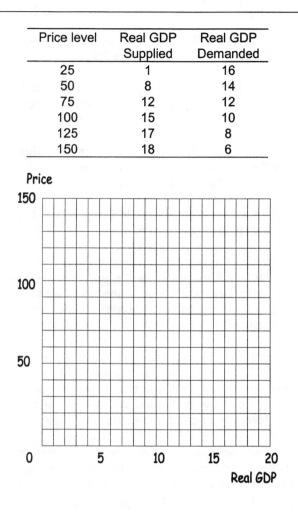

Price

2. Productivity, Per-Unit Costs and AS
The data below show relationships between the real GDP and the quantity of resource inputs needed to produce each level of output.

GDP	Input	Productivity (1)	(2)	Per-unit cost (3)	(4)	(5)
2500	500					
2400	400					
2100	300					
1600	200					

(a) In column (1) compute the level of productivity at each level of GDP.

(b) In column (2) compute the level of productivity if now there is a doubling in the quantity of inputs required to produce each level of output.

(c) In column (3) compute per-unit production cost at each level of output, if each unit of input costs $3, given the productivity in column (1).

(d) In column (4) compute the new per-unit production cost at each level of output given that input price is $3, given that there has been a doubling in the required quantity of inputs required to produce each level of output as shown in column (2). What happens to the AS curve if this situation occurs?

(e) In column (5), compute the new per-unit production cost at each level of output, given that input price is now $2 instead of $3, but the level of productivity stays as it was originally, as in column (1). What will happen to the AS curve if this situation occurs?

3. Shifts in AD and AS
For each event listed below, what is the most likely effect on Canada's: (1) aggregate demand; (2) aggregate supply; (3) the equilibrium price level, and; (4) equilibrium real GDP? Assume that all other things are equal, and that the AS curve is upward sloping. Use the following symbols to indicate the expected effects: I = increase; D = decrease; S = remains the same; and U = uncertain. (You are also encouraged to sketch out these situations on your own graphs.)

(a) A decrease in labour productivity:
        AD _____ AS _____ P _____ Q _____
(b) A drop in interest rates:
        AD _____ AS _____ P _____ Q _____
(c) Consumers' indebtedness increases to record high levels:
        AD _____ AS _____ P _____ Q _____
(d) Energy prices increase, raising production costs for businesses:
        AD _____ AS _____ P _____ Q _____
(e) The Canadian dollar appreciates:
        AD _____ AS _____ P _____ Q _____
(f) Personal income tax rates increase:
        AD _____ AS _____ P _____ Q _____
(g) Technological change improves productivity:
        AD _____ AS _____ P _____ Q _____

4. Real Wage and Nominal Wage Adjustment
Wimpyland produces nothing but hamburgers. The price level is therefore in $ per burger, nominal wages are in $, and real wages are in burgers. The initial nominal wage rate is $12. The current situation in Wimpyland is depicted by AS, AD_1, and AS_{LR} on the following graph.

(a) The short-run equilibrium price level is $_____ per burger, and the equilibrium output level is _____ burgers.

(b) Why is this equilibrium both a short-run equilibrium and a long-run equilibrium?

(c) In this equilibrium, the real wage rate is $____/$____ per burger = ____ burgers.

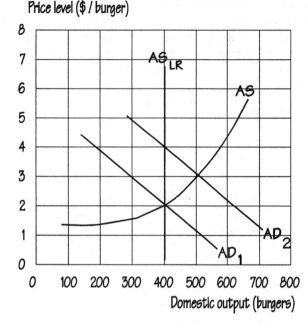

Price level ($ / burger)

Domestic output (burgers)

(d) If AD₁ shifts up to AD₂, the new short-run equilibrium price level is $____ per burger, and the output level is ____ burgers. There is a(n) _____ gap of 100 burgers.

(e) At this new short-run equilibrium, the real wage is $____ ÷ $____ per burger = ____ burgers. Therefore, the real wage is now (above, below) _____ its long-run equilibrium level.

(f) This disequilibrium will cause the AS curve to shift (rightward, leftward) _____ until a new long-run equilibrium is reached where the price level is $____ per burger, and the equilibrium output level is ____ burgers.

(g) At this new equilibrium, the real wage will have returned to ____ burgers. Given the new price level, this implies that the nominal wage must have risen to $____.

Discussion Questions

1. Define the AD and AS curves.

2. Explain why (a) the interest-rate effect, (b) the real-balance effect, and (c) the foreign-trade effect cause the AD curve to be downsloping.

3. What factors that affect investment spending would cause the AD curve to shift to the left?

What factors affecting consumption spending would move the AD curve to the left?

4. Why does the AS curve slope upward in the short run? What happens to per-unit costs of production as we move along the curve?

5. Explain how a change in input prices affects the AS curve. Define productivity and explain the effect on AS if productivity rises.

6. Explain the shape and location of the long-run aggregate supply curve.

7. How is the equilibrium real domestic output determined? Why will domestic producers reduce or expand their production when they find themselves producing more or less than the equilibrium output?

8. How are real domestic output and the price level affected when AD increases, and how do these effects depend on the slope of the AS curve? How are real domestic output and the price level affected when the AS decreases?

9. What are the characteristics of long-run equilibrium? What roles do the adjustments in nominal wages and real wages play in restoring the economy to a long-run equilibrium?

10. What is a recessionary gap, and an inflationary gap, and what economic conditions are present when each of these gaps exists? How is the size of each of these gaps measured? What changes in the economy would be needed to resolve an inflationary gap, or a recessionary gap?

Answers

Quick Quiz
1. (c) p. 209
2. (d) pp. 205-206
3. (a) p. 207
4. (c) p. 210
5. (d) pp. 213-214
6. (a) p. 215
7. (a) p. 219-220
8. (b) pp. 217-219
9. (b) pp. 220-221
10. (d) p. 222
11. (a) p. 223

12. (a) p. 223-224
13. (b) pp. 224-225
14. (c) p. 225

Fill-in Questions

1. variable, fixed
2. demanded (purchased), levels, downward, real-balance, interest-rate, foreign-trade
3. (a) shift of; (b) movement along
4. produced, price, input
5. upward, increase
6. nominal, real, profit, employment
7. short, recessionary, falling

True-False

1. F   price changes cause movements along AD, not shifts in AD
2. T   this is the real balance effect
3. F   interest rate will decrease and investment will increase
4. F   net exports will decrease
5. F   demand for capital is increased
6. T   as capital utilization increases, AS becomes steeper
7. F   AS increases, which is a rightward shift
8. F   output divided by input
9. T   by raising the cost per unit of production
10. F   an increase in AS would be "doubly good" for these reasons
11. T
12. T
13. F   actual GDP is less than full-employment GDP

Multiple-Choice

1. (c) all of the others are backwards
2. (d)
3. (d) all of the others depend on the price level
4. (b)
5. (c) as capacity utilization rises
6. (b)
7. (d) because net exports rise as goods from Canada drop in relative price
8. (b) per unit costs of production increase
9. (b)
10. (c)
11. (b)
12. (a) 50/10
13. (a) ($2 x 10)/50
14. (c)
15. (d) costs per unit increase, though productivity is constant

16. (d) change in price level causes movements along AD and AS
17. (b) AS is horizontal
18. (a) AS shifts rightward
19. (a) where AD1 = AS1
20. (d) as nominal wages eventually falls, AS1 would shift to down, or to the right
21. (a) point c has the same price level as the initial equilibrium, point a

Problems and Projects

1. (b) 75, 12; (d) recessionary, 3 (15-12)

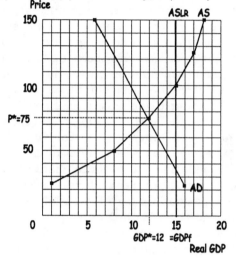

2. (a) 5, 6, 7, 8; (b) 2.5, 3, 3.5, 4; (c) 0.60, 0.50, 0.43, 0.38; (d) 1.20, 1.00, 0.86, 0.75; AS shifts leftward; (e) 0.40, 0.33, 0.29, 0.25; AS shifts rightward
3. (a) S, D, I, D; (b) I, S, I, I; (c) D, S, D, D; (d) S, D, I, D; (e) D, I, D, U; (f) D, S, D, D; (g) S, I, D, I
4. (a) 2, 400; (b) AS = AD = AS$_{LR}$; (c) 12, 2, 6; (d) 3, 500; inflationary; (e) 12, 3, 4; below; (f) leftward, 4, 400; (g) 6; 24

The Relationship of the Aggregate Expenditures Model to the AD-AS Model

Overview

This appendix shows how the flexible-price aggregate demand and aggregate supply model of Chapter 8 is related to the fixed-price aggregate expenditures model of Chapter 7. The specific connection is found in deriving the AD curve by varying the price level and observing the effect on the aggregate expenditures curve and the equilibrium level of real domestic output.

If, for example, the price level increases, this will decrease the level of aggregate expenditures (AE) through the interest-rate, real-balance, and foreign-trade effects. This is a downward shift in the AE schedule and it lowers equilibrium level of real domestic output. For each price level there is a unique position for the AE schedule and equilibrium real GDP. The AD curve plots all of the combinations of price level and real GDP level where the production of goods equals the demand for goods.

The AD curve is shifted by the same factors that shift the AE schedule. Holding the price level constant, any increase in the level of consumption, investment, government spending, or net exports, will shift the AE schedule upward, and the AD curve rightward.

From the aggregate expenditures model we are familiar with the multiplier effect whereby a shift in the AE leads to a larger increase in the equilibrium real GDP. Because of this multiplier effect, when the AE shifts vertically, the horizontal shift in the AD curve is a multiple of the AE shift.

Appendix Outline

◈ How is the aggregate demand curve derived from the aggregate expenditures model?

• The aggregate expenditures model is normally used as a fixed-price model, but for each distinct price level there is a separate aggregate expenditures (AE) schedule.

• On the graph, a change in price level shifts the AE schedule vertically due to the interest-rate, real-balance, and foreign-trade effects.
  o A rise in the price level will shift AE downward.
  o A drop in the price level will shift AE upward.
• A shift in the AE schedule due to a price level change will change the equilibrium level of real GDP.
  o If AE shifts up, real GDP increases.
  o If AE shifts down, real GDP decreases.
• The aggregate demand (AD) curve is a plot of all combinations of different price levels and the corresponding equilibrium real GDP levels.
• With price level on the vertical axis, and real GDP on the horizontal, AD is downward-sloping.

◈ How are shifts of the aggregate demand curve derived from the aggregate expenditures model?

• Any change in the determinants of the components of AE will horizontally shift the AD curve. The AD shift will be a multiple of the initial shift in expenditures due to the same multiplier effect discussed in Chapter 7.
  o An increase (decrease) in consumption, investment, government spending or net exports will shift the AE upward (downward) and the AD rightward (leftward).

➲ Remember that a price level change shifts the AE curve upwards or downwards, but causes only a movement along the AD curve.

➲ The size of the multiplier in the aggregate expenditures model dictates the extent of the horizontal shift in the AD curve when there a change in one of the determinants of expenditures. For example, if the multiplier is 3 and investment increases by $1 billion, the AD curve will shift rightward by $3 billion. In the AD-AS model the equilibrium GDP does not change by as much as this shift in the AD curve because there is also the AS curve to consider.

Quick Quiz

1. To derive the AD curve, we show how the AE schedule shifts to different positions as a result of changes in:
- (a) the price level
- (b) consumption spending
- (c) investment spending
- (d) net export spending

2. An upward shift in aggregate expenditures in the aggregate expenditure model shifts the AD curve to the:
- (a) right by the amount of the increase in aggregate expenditure
- (b) right by the amount of the increase in aggregate expenditure times the multiplier
- (c) left by the amount of the increase in aggregate expenditure
- (d) left by the amount of the increase in aggregate expenditure times the multiplier

Fill-In Questions

1. In the aggregate expenditure model, a price increase will shift the aggregate expenditure curve (up, down) _down_, and the equilibrium level of real GDP will (increase, decrease) _decrease_. This (direct, inverse) _direct how_ relationship between the price level and the amount of output demanded can be used to derive the _AD_ curve (or schedule).

2. Any event – except for a price change – that shifts the AE schedule upward will shift the (AD, AS) _AD_ curve to the (left, right) _right_ by (the same, a larger, a smaller) _the larger_ amount. This is the _multiplier_ effect.

3. The variables plotted on the axes of the AD curve are _price_ on the vertical, and _Rea GDP_ on the horizontal.

True-False

Circle T if the statement is true, F if it is false.

1. An increase in government purchases will shift the aggregate expenditures curve upwards, and shift AD leftward.   **T (F)**

2. If the AE schedule shifts up by $1 million, the AD curve will shift right by $1 million.   **T (F)**

3. The AE curve is used in the derivation of both the AD and AS curves.   **T (F)**

4. If the AD curve shifts $9 billion to the right when government spending rises by $2 billion, the aggregate expenditures model multiplier is 4.5.   **(T) F**

Multiple-Choice

Circle the letter that corresponds to the best answer.

1. In the aggregate expenditures model, a drop in the price level will lead to:
- (a) a lower aggregate expenditures curve and a lower multiplier
- (b) a higher aggregate expenditures curve and a higher multiplier
- (c) a lower aggregate expenditures curve and a lower equilibrium real output
- (d) a higher aggregate expenditures curve and a higher equilibrium real output

2. A decrease in the price level will shift the:
- (a) consumption, investment, and net exports curves downward
- (b) consumption, investment, and net exports curves upward
- (c) consumption and investment curves downward and the net exports curve upward
- (d) consumption and net exports curves upward, but the investment curve downward

3. A rise in prices will:
- (a) shift the AE curve down and shift the AD curve to the left
- (b) shift the AE curve down and shift the AD curve to the right
- (c) shift the AE curve up and shift the AD curve to the left
- (d) shift the AE curve down and not shift the AD curve

4. Which of the following will shift the AD curve to the right?
- (a) a decrease in investment spending

(b)   a decrease in government spending
(c)   a decrease in export spending
(d)   a decrease in import spending

5. If the multiplier is 2.5, a $2 billion increase in government spending will shift:
(a)   the AE schedule upward by $2 billion and the AD curve rightward by $2 billion
(b)   the AE schedule upward by $5 billion and the AD curve rightward by $5 billion
(c)   the AE schedule upward by $2 billion and the AD curve rightward by $5 billion
(d)   none of the above

6. The extent to which a $10 increase in government spending will shift the AD curve depends on what?
(a)   the marginal propensity to consume
(b)   the marginal propensity to import
(c)   both of the above
(d)   none of the above

Problems and Projects

1. Deriving the AD Curve From the Aggregate Expenditures Model
This question involves the derivation of a down-sloping AD curve from the aggregate expenditure model. Below are data for three versions of the AE schedule, one for each different price level.

GDP	AE₁ (P = 50)	AE₂ (P = 100)	AE₃ (P = 150)
0	6	4	2
4	8	6	4
8	10	8	6
12	12	10	8

(a)   In the upper panel of the graph plot the aggregate expenditure functions pertaining to three price levels: 50, 100, 150, and determine the equilibrium level of GDP that would correspond to each.
(b)   Use your findings in (a) to plot three combinations of price level and equilibrium GDP. Join these points to form the AD curve.

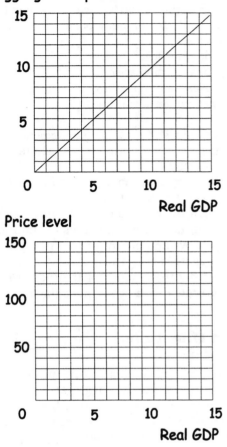

Aggregate Expenditures

Price level

Real GDP

2. Shifts in AD Caused by Shifts in AE
This question continues with the data from question 1.
(a)   Plot the new aggregate demand curve, AD', that results when investment spending increases by $1. (Hint: all three aggregate expenditures curves in the top panel shift upward by 1.)
(b)   Given the horizontal shift from AD to AD', the size of the multiplier for this economy is equal to _____.
(c)   The actual effective multiplier effect will be the value found in (b) if the AS curve is (horizontal, vertical, upward sloping) _____; it will be positive but smaller than this if the AS curve is _____; and it will be zero if the AS curve is _____.

Discussion Questions

1. Explain the difference between the AE schedule and the AD curve.

2. How is the AD curve derived from the aggregate expenditure model?

3. What determines how far the AD shifts when there is a change in one of the components of aggregate expenditures?

Answers

Quick Quiz
1. (a) pp. 231-232
2. (b) pp. 232-233

Fill-in Questions
1. down, decrease, inverse, AD
2. AD, right, a larger, multiplier
3. price level, real domestic output (GDP)

True-False
1. F   AD would shift rightward
2. F   AD would shift more than this because of the multiplier effect
3. F   the AS curve in no way depends on the AE schedule
4. T   4.5 x $2 billion

Multiple-Choice
1. (d)
2. (b) by the interest-rate, real-balance, and foreign trade effects
3. (d) this causes just a movement along AD
4. (d) because imports are deducted from net exports
5. (c) due to the multiplier effect: 2 x 2.5 = 5
6. (c) both MPC and MPM affect the multiplier

Problems and Projects
1. (a) At AE3 where P=150, GDP=AE at 4; at AE2 where P=100, GDP=AE at 8; at AE1 where P=50, GDP=AE at 12 (these are points a, b, c on the first panel of the following graph; (b) see the corresponding points a, b, c.
2. (a) See the graph where AE3', AE2' and AE1' result in AD'; (b) since $\triangle I_g$= 1 caused $\triangle$GDP* =2, multiplier = 2/1 = 2; (c) horizontal; upward sloping; vertical

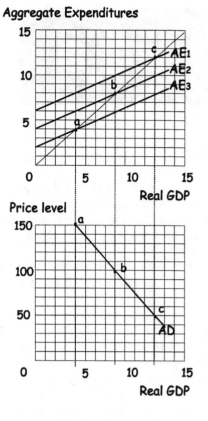

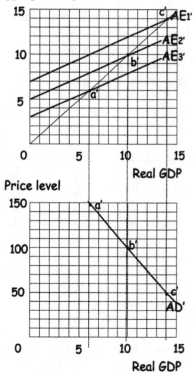

Chapter 9 Fiscal Policy

Overview

This chapter concerns fiscal policy, which is the federal government's use of its spending and taxation powers to help achieve full-employment GDP, price level stability, and a high rate of economic growth.

Fiscal policy can be discretionary or non-discretionary. Discretionary fiscal policy occurs when Parliament deliberately changes taxes and/or government spending. A recession calls for expansionary fiscal policy because AD is too low to produce equilibrium at full-employment GDP. To expand AD, the government should increase government spending, reduce taxes (to raise households' disposable incomes), or both. An inflationary gap calls for contractionary policy (lowering AD by cutting government spending, raising taxes, or both).

Non-discretionary fiscal policy does not involve deliberate government action when the economy moves away from full-employment. Instead, non-discretionary fiscal policy relies on built-in stabilizers that automatically increase government deficits during recessions and increase government surpluses during inflation. These changes occur automatically because taxes vary directly with GDP, and transfer payments are inversely related to GDP. Built-in stabilizers have the advantage of working immediately rather than waiting for Parliament's decisions, but they are not strong enough on their own to completely eliminate real GDP fluctuations.

How do we evaluate whether discretionary fiscal policy is contractionary, expansionary, or neutral at a given time? The government's actual budget won't tell us. Built-in stabilizers cause the actual budget to fluctuate whenever GDP does, even when the government has made no decision to change fiscal policy. Such illusions created by the built-in stabilizers forced economists to develop the "cyclically adjusted budget" to measure the budget balance at a standardized point: the full-employment level of real GDP. This budget measure changes only when there is a discretionary policy change.

There are problems with fiscal policy. Time lags produce delay, and political constraints often preempt or dissuade the federal government from taking the necessary policy actions. Increased government spending may crowd out private investment spending, thus offsetting some of the intended stimulus to aggregate expenditures. When the economy is in the upward sloping section of the aggregate supply curve, some of the impact of expansionary fiscal policy will be dissipated in inflation instead of raising real GDP and employment. Foreign trade makes it harder to know what fiscal policy to use because unpredictable AD disturbances abroad can be transmitted to Canada, and because the net export effect weakens the impact of fiscal policy.

These complications lead some economists to believe that discretionary fiscal policy is not helpful. The mainstream view, however, seems to be that fiscal policy can push the economy in the right general direction. And there is consensus on the importance of considering the long-run growth consequences of fiscal policy decisions.

Chapter Outline

9.1 Fiscal Policy and the AD-AS Model

◈ What is fiscal policy and what is it used for?

• Fiscal policy includes changes in government spending and taxation designed to achieve full employment and a stable price level.

• Since 1945 the Canadian government has used fiscal policy as a main tool of stabilization policy.

• Fiscal policy can be either discretionary or nondiscretionary. Discretionary fiscal policy is the deliberate manipulation of tax rates and government spending programs to offset cyclical fluctuations (recessionary and inflationary gaps).

    o Expansionary fiscal policy may be used when the economy has a recessionary gap. Such policy would entail an increase in government spending, a decrease in taxes, or a combination of both.

o Contractionary fiscal policy may be used to close an inflationary gap, and would involve decreased government spending, increased taxes, or a combination of both.

• Should the government choose not to use fiscal policy to close a gap, the economy will move back to full employment through the supply responses discussed in Chapter 8, but this may take an unacceptable length of time, especially in the case of a recessionary gap.

• Expansionary policy will move the government's budget toward a deficit, while contractionary policy tends to create a budget surplus.

• Whether government spending or taxes should be altered to reduce recession and inflation depends to a large extent upon whether an expansion or a contraction of the public sector is desired.

o (a) Some economists believe that government should do more to address social and infrastructure issues. In a recession, they would favour an increase in government spending (tending to make the public sector grow); in an inflationary period, they would prefer a tax increase (tending again to make the public sector grow).

o Other economists believe that government is too large. In a recession, they would favour a cut in taxes (making the public sector shrink); in an inflationary period, they would favour a cut in government spending (tending again to shrink the public sector).

➲ If you have studied Chapter 7, recall that multiplier effects exist when government changes fiscal policy by raising or lowering its expenditures or its tax collections.

Quick Quiz

1. To employ expansionary fiscal policy, the government may choose to:
- (a) raise tax rates
- (b) increase government spending
- (c) use a combination of higher tax rates and higher government spending
- (d) lower interest rates

2. The term "discretionary" used to describe fiscal policy refers to:

- (a) a deliberate decision to change policy
- (b) a slight, or minor, change in policy
- (c) a policy change that is not announced to the public
- (d) an automatic change the government's budget

3. An economist who believes the government is too large might argue that in an inflationary gap situation the best fiscal policy would be to:
- (a) raise tax rates
- (b) increase government spending
- (c) lower tax rates
- (d) decrease government spending

9.2 Built-In Stabilization

❖ What are built-in stabilizers and how do they work?

• Non-discretionary fiscal policy continually provides some built-in stability for the economy.

o Net tax revenues (tax receipts minus government transfers and subsidies) increase as the GDP rises and decrease as the GDP falls.

o The tax system serves as a built-in stabilizer of the economy by reducing purchasing power during an inflationary gap and expanding purchasing power during is a recessionary gap.

• As GDP increases, the average tax rates will increase in progressive systems, remain constant in proportional systems, and decrease in regressive tax systems, so there is more built-in stability with a more progressive tax system.

• Business cycles are reduced, but not totally eliminated, by built-in stabilizers.

• Built-in stabilizers cause the actual budget deficit or surplus to automatically fluctuate as GDP fluctuates. Therefore, movements in the actual budget deficit or surplus do not indicate whether government's fiscal policy has changed.

➲ Discretionary fiscal policy occurs when government deliberately chooses to change taxes or spending. Non-discretionary fiscal policy occurs when automatic stabilizers are at work. Using the analogy of your car, discretionary fiscal policy operates like brakes: unless you decide to step on the brake pedal, the brakes cannot slow you down. Non-discretionary fiscal policy operates like shock absorbers: they work automatically when you go over a bump, whether or not you noticed the bump, and without you taking any action.

• The cyclically adjusted budget is a better fiscal policy indicator than the actual budget because it measures what the federal budget deficit or surplus would be if the economy had achieved its full employment GDP level.

  o If the cyclically adjusted deficit as a percentage of GDP increases (decreases), then fiscal policy has become more expansionary (contractionary).

  o If the cyclically adjusted surplus as a percentage of GDP increases (decreases), then the stance of fiscal policy has become more contractionary (expansionary).

⮑ The cyclically adjusted deficit is the most difficult concept in this chapter. It may help to realize it is a hypothetical amount: what the government's budget **would be** if the economy was at full employment.

• A cyclical deficit occurs when the economy is operating below full employment and is computed as the difference between the actual budget deficit and the cyclically adjusted budget balance.

⮑ The cyclically adjusted deficit and the cyclical deficit are two different concepts.

• From 1991 through 1996, Canada consistently had substantial actual and cyclically adjusted budget deficits. Since then we have had budget surpluses – both actual and cyclically adjusted. The trend in the cyclically adjusted budget shows that fiscal policy became substantially more contractionary in the 1995 to 1997 period.

Quick Quiz
4. Automatic stabilizers:
  (a) are stronger if taxes are progressive
  (b) increase the government's budget deficit during inflation
  (c) decrease the government's budget deficit during recession
  (d) eliminate nearly all fluctuations in real GDP

5. The cyclically adjusted budget is also known as:
  (a) cyclical deficit
  (b) balanced budget
  (c) full-employment budget
  (d) zero deficit budget

6. We can conclude that fiscal policy has become more contractionary when:
  (a) the actual budget deficit shrinks
  (b) the actual budget deficit grows
  (c) the cyclically adjusted budget deficit shrinks
  (d) the cyclically adjusted budget deficit grows

9.3 Problems, Criticisms, and Complications

⬦ What are some of the problems with fiscal policy that limit its effectiveness?

• Timing problems create three lags: a recognition lag, an administrative lag, and an operational lag.

• Political considerations may lead government officials to make fiscal policy decisions that promote the government's re-election rather than economic stability. If so, there can be a "political business cycle."

• Fiscal policy may be weakened if the public expects policy initiatives to be reversed in the future. For example, a tax cut that the public believes will be short-lived will have minimal effects on consumption spending.

• Fiscal policy is the responsibility of the federal government, but the thrust of its policy may conflict with the thrust of budget decisions made by provincial and/or municipal governments.

• Expansionary fiscal policy may raise the interest rate and crowd out private spending, weakening the effect of the fiscal policy stimulus. The increased demand from the government is offset by decreased demand from the private sector. But this crowding-out effect may be small, especially during a severe recession, or if the Bank of Canada increases the supply of money to prevent interest rates from rising.

• The effect of expansionary fiscal policy will also be weakened when it results in a rise in the price level (inflation). The closer the economy is to full employment, the steeper the AS curve, and the greater is this concern.

• Other complications for fiscal policy arise because Canada is an open economy.

o We are vulnerable to demand shocks from abroad that could shift our exports in a way that offsets our domestic fiscal policy.

o When expansionary fiscal policy raises our interest rates, the Canadian dollar will appreciate against other currencies, decreasing the demand for our net exports, offsetting some of the fiscal stimulus. This net export effect is very similar to the crowding-out effect.

• In view of all of these complications in the use of fiscal policy, there is significant controversy over the use of discretionary fiscal policy.

o Some economists oppose the use of discretionary fiscal policy. They simply don't believe that it will work properly most of the time, and tend to favour the use of monetary policy instead.

o But most economists believe that discretionary fiscal policy can be helpful in moving the AD curve in the right general direction, though it is not possible to "fine tune" the economy.

o There is general agreement that fiscal policy proposals should be evaluated in terms of their impacts on productivity in the long run.

• Policy-makers monitor "leading indicators" to forecast fluctuations in real GDP. Since these variables have historically changed prior to GDP fluctuations, they provide advance warning.

Quick Quiz

7. Which is not among the lags involved in the use of fiscal policy?
(a) policy lag
(b) recognition lag
(c) administration lag
(d) operational lag

8. The ability of expansionary fiscal policy to boost equilibrium real GDP will be weakened by:
(a) inflation if the AS is horizontal
(b) the crowding-out effect if interest rate increases result
(c) the net export effect if our dollar depreciates
(d) all of the above

9. Economists generally agree that:
(a) fiscal policy is less powerful than monetary policy

(b) fiscal policy, if used properly, can eliminate most fluctuations in real GDP
(c) fiscal policy cannot reduce fluctuations in real GDP
(d) fiscal policy decisions should take into account how the policies will affect productivity growth in the long run

Terms and Concepts

fiscal policy	proportional tax
expansionary fiscal policy	regressive tax
budget deficit	cyclically adjusted budget
contractionary fiscal policy	cyclical deficit
budget surplus	political business cycle
built-in stabilizer	crowding-out effect
progressive tax	net export effect

Fill-In Questions

1. To increase real GDP during a recession, taxes should be (increased, decreased) _decreased_ and government spending should be _increased_. If fiscal policy is not used, the (AD, AS) _AD_ curve will (soon, eventually) _eventually_ shift to the right to close the gap.

2. If Parliament votes to increase tax revenues by raising income tax rates, it is using (discretionary, nondiscretionary) _dis_ fiscal policy, whereas when income tax revenues increase only because the GDP rises, this is _nondis_ fiscal policy.

3. A leading indicator is an economic variable that has traditionally reached its turning point (after, before) _____ the corresponding turns in the business cycle.

4. Those who favour growth in the public sector would, during a period of inflation, advocate a(n) (increase, decrease) _____ in government (spending, taxes) _____; and those who wish to contract the public sector during a recession would advocate a(n) _____ in _____.

5. Net taxes equal _____ minus _____ and _____.

6. When net tax revenues are directly related to the GDP the economy has some _____ stability because:
(a) when the GDP rises, tax revenues (increase, decrease) _____, helping to curb spending.
(b) when the GDP falls, tax revenues _____, helping to cushion the drop in spending.

7. The cyclically adjusted budget balance:
(a) indicates what the federal _____ would have been if the economy had operated at _____ during the year; and (b) tells us whether the fiscal policy has become more _____ or _____ during the year.

8. When the government employs an expansionary fiscal policy, it usually has a budget (surplus, deficit) _____ and normally (lends, borrows) _____ funds in the money market.
(a) This will (raise, lower) _____ interest rates in the economy and (contract, expand) _____ investment spending.
(b) This change in investment is called the _____ effect, and it tends to (weaken, strengthen) _____ the impact of the expansionary fiscal policy on real GDP and employment.

9. A contractionary fiscal policy will tend to (raise, lower) _____ the interest rate. In an open economy this will create capital (inflows, outflows) _____ that will lead to (appreciation, depreciation) _____ of the domestic currency. This currency value change will cause net exports to (increase, decrease) _____, which will (reinforce, offset) _____ the intended contraction in AD. This phenomenon is known as the _____ effect.

True-False

Circle T if the statement is true, F if it is false.

1. The main goal of fiscal policy is to stabilize the economy at full employment.   T F

2. A decrease in taxes will cause an upward shift in the consumption schedule and an increase in equilibrium GDP.   T F

3. Fiscal policy is contractionary whenever it results in an actual deficit on the government's budget.   T F

4. To stabilize the economy, the government should move their budget toward a surplus during the recession phase of the business cycle.   T F

5. Built-in stabilizers are not sufficiently strong to completely eliminate recession or inflation, but they can reduce the severity of a recession or of inflation.   T F

6. The cyclically adjusted budget balance compares government spending to the tax revenue that would be collected at full employment.   T F

7. Economists who see evidence of a political business cycle argue that the government tends to increase taxes and reduce expenditures before elections.   T F

8. If financing a deficit results in increased interest rates, investment spending will be reduced and the expansionary effect of the deficit on aggregate demand reduced.   T F

9. When a given increase in government spending is applied, the ultimate effect on real GDP is less if the AS curve is steeper.   T F

10. The current mainstream view among economists is that fiscal policy should be used for month-to-month stabilization of the economy.   T F

Multiple-Choice

Circle the letter that corresponds to the best answer.

1. Fiscal policy influences the level of economic activity by manipulating:
   (a)   the interest rate
   (b)   the money supply
   (c)   the foreign exchange rate
   (d)   government spending and tax rates

2. Contractionary fiscal policy is composed of:

(a) a reduction in government expenditure and the money supply or some combination of both

(b) an increase in government expenditure and taxes or some combination of both

(c) a reduction in government expenditure and increase in taxes or some combination of both

(d) a reduction in taxes and the money supply or some combination of both

3. If households are faced with increased taxes, they will pay these taxes:

(a) by reducing saving, so there is no effect on equilibrium output

(b) by reducing consumption, causing a drop in equilibrium output

(c) by reducing both consumption and saving, causing a drop in equilibrium output

(d) none of the above

4. In Canada, the idea that government should use fiscal policy to stabilize the economy arose as a result of:

(a) the Great Depression

(b) World War II

(c) stagflation of the 1970s

(d) the recession of the 1980s

5. If the government wishes to increase the level of real GDP, it might:

(a) reduce taxes

(b) reduce its purchases of goods and services

(c) reduce transfer payments

(d) reduce the size of the budget deficit

6. For the economy to have built-in stability, when real GDP falls:

(a) tax receipts and government transfer payments should fall

(b) tax receipts and government transfer payments should rise

(c) tax receipts should fall and government transfer payments should rise

(d) tax receipts should rise and government transfer payments should fall

7. A direct relation between taxes and real GDP:

(a) automatically produces budget surpluses during a recession

(b) makes it easier for discretionary fiscal policy to move the economy out of a recession and toward full employment

(c) makes it easier to maintain full employment in a growing economy

(d) reduces the effect of a change in planned investment spending on GDP and employment

8. Why does Canada's system of employment insurance work as an automatic stabilizer?

(a) approximately the same amount of employment insurance benefits are paid out each year

(b) the employment insurance system has the effect of stabilizing the unemployment rate

(c) employment insurance benefits paid out increase every year

(d) employment insurance benefits paid out increase during a recession

9. Which of the following is not an automatic stabilizer in the Canadian economy?

(a) GST

(b) CPP deductions

(c) income taxes

(d) all of these are automatic stabilizers

10. What type of tax system would produce the most built-in stability for the economy?

(a) proportional

(b) regressive

(c) progressive

(d) flat tax

11. The crowding-out effect of expansionary fiscal policy results from government borrowing that:

(a) increases interest rates and investment spending

(b) increases interest rates and decreases investment spending

(c) decreases interest rates and increases investment spending

(d) decreases interest rates and investment spending

12. Which of the following is not an example of a discretionary fiscal policy action?

(a) a new plan to spend $100 million on childbirth centres

(b) an increase in the number of people on welfare because of rising unemployment

(c)   a 10% cut in the rate of income tax
(d)   a change in the maximum benefits available under employment insurance

Use this diagram to answer questions 13 through 16:

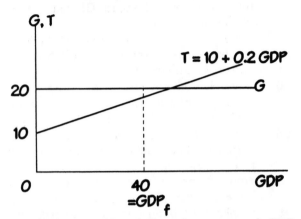

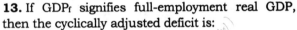

13. If GDP$_f$ signifies full-employment real GDP, then the cyclically adjusted deficit is:
(a)   0
(b)   2
(c)   4
(d)   6

14. If actual GDP is at 35, then the actual budget deficit or surplus will be:
(a)   a surplus of 1
(b)   a deficit of 1
(c)   a deficit of 3
(d)   a deficit of 5

15. If the government employs an expansionary fiscal policy by increasing government purchases by 2, and this moves equilibrium real GDP from 35 to 39, then:
(a)   the cyclically adjusted deficit rises by 2, and the actual deficit rises by 1.2
(b)   the cyclically adjusted deficit rises by 1.2, and the actual deficit drops by 0.8
(c)   the cyclically adjusted deficit falls by 2, and the actual deficit rises by 1.2
(d)   the cyclically adjusted deficit does not change, and the actual deficit rises by 1.2

16. If the T line had a steeper slope, there would be:
(a)   more built-in stability for the economy
(b)   less built-in stability for the economy
(c)   no change in the built-in stability in the economy

(d)   a need for more emphasis on discretionary fiscal policy

Questions 17 to 19 are based on this graph.

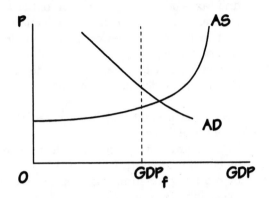

17. Given the current position of AD and AS, what is the situation in this economy?
(a)   there is an inflationary gap and contractionary fiscal policy is needed
(b)   there is an inflationary gap and expansionary fiscal policy is needed
(c)   there is a recessionary gap and contractionary fiscal policy is needed
(d)   there is a recessionary gap and expansionary fiscal policy is needed

18. In the neighbourhood of the current equilibrium, an expansionary fiscal policy will change:
(a)   the price level, but not output
(b)   output, but not the price level
(c)   both output and the price level
(d)   neither output nor the price level

19. If the government does not take any fiscal policy action, how will the economy shown in the graph adjust?
(a)   wages and input prices will eventually rise enough to shift the AS upward until it intersects AD at GDP$_f$
(b)   wages and input prices will eventually fall enough to shift the AS upward until it intersects AD at GDP$_f$
(c)   expenditures will eventually fall enough that AD will shift left until it intersects AS at GDP$_f$
(d)   none of the above

20. During the 1990s, Canada had a trend of:
(a)   decrease in the actual annual federal deficit

(b) increase in the cyclically adjusted annual deficit

(c) increasingly expansionary fiscal policy

(d) all of the above

21. The phenomenon where government generates an economic boom when an election is approaching, and a recession shortly after an election, is known as:

(a) stabilizing fiscal policy

(b) cyclically adjusted fiscal policy

(c) Keynesian economics

(d) a political business cycle

22. Once a fiscal policy action has been taken, the length of time it takes for the fiscal action to affect output, employment, or the price level is called the:

(a) administrative lag

(b) operational lag

(c) recognition lag

(d) fiscal lag

23. The length of time it takes for government to decide what policy to adopt to address a recessionary or inflationary gap is called the:

(a) administrative lag

(b) operational lag

(c) recognition lag

(d) fiscal lag

24. If there is an inflationary gap, those who favour smaller government would advocate that fiscal policy take the form of:

(a) increased taxes and government spending

(b) decreased taxes and government spending

(c) decreased government spending

(d) increased taxes

25. The crowding-out effect may be lessened if:

(a) the Bank of Canada increases the supply of money when government increases its borrowing

(b) the economy is already near full employment when government spending increases

(c) the profit expectations of businesses weaken when government spending increases

(d) all of the above

26. Suppose that the economies of Canada's trading partners improved substantially and at the same time Canada had adopted an expansionary fiscal policy. What would most likely happen in Canada?

(a) there would be a rise in net exports, a rise in aggregate demand, and the potential for inflation

(b) there would be a fall in interest rates, a rise in aggregate demand, and the potential for a recession

(c) there would be a rise in the incomes of trading partners, less demand for Canadian goods, and potential for a recession

(d) there would be a rise in the employment in other nations, a fall in net exports, and the potential for inflation

27. The effect of an expansionary fiscal policy on the real GDP of an economy with an upward sloping aggregate supply curve is lessened by:

(a) increases in aggregate supply

(b) the crowding-out effect

(c) increases in the price level

(d) both (b) and (c)

28. A change in the government's fiscal policy stance is best measured by changes in:

(a) equilibrium real GDP

(b) the actual deficit or surplus as a percentage of GDP

(c) the cyclical deficit or surplus as a percentage of GDP

(d) the cyclically adjusted deficit or surplus as a percentage of GDP

29. If expansionary fiscal policy is adopted in an open economy, the resulting increase in interest rates will tend to raise demand for the nation's currency, causing currency appreciation and reduction in the demand for the nation's exports. This is termed the:

(a) net export effect

(b) crowding-out effect

(c) exchange rate effect

(d) interest rate effect

30. Fiscal policy that benefits the economy in the short run may do damage in the long run by:

(a) producing more public infrastructure

(b) reducing the deficit

(c) increasing incentives to work

(d) reducing incentives to invest

Problems and Projects

1. Tax Progressivity
Columns A, B, and C show levels of taxes at different income levels, under three tax systems.

Income	A:_____	B:_____	C:_____
1000	200	200	100
2000	375	400	300
3000	525	600	600
4000	625	800	1000

(a) Indicate in the blanks whether each system is progressive, regressive, or proportional.
(b) In which system is there the greatest degree of built-in stability? _____ The least? _____

2. Evaluating Fiscal Policy
The next table shows a nation's fiscal situation in each of five different years. The budget amounts shown are measured in billions of $.

Year	1	2	3	4	5
Actual budget (surplus +, deficit -)	-40	-90	-60	-28	-50
Cyclically adjusted budget (surplus +, deficit -)	-20	-61	-60	-16	+4
GDP	600	630	660	630	600
Cyclically adjusted budget as % of GDP	-3.3	-9.7	-9.1	-2.5	+1.7
Direction of change in fiscal policy		___	___	___	___

(a) Starting with year 2, determine for each year whether fiscal policy became more expansionary (E), more contractionary (C), or neutral (N), as compared to the previous year.
(b) The full-employment GDP level in this economy is _____ and occurs in year _____.
(c) In which years was there a cyclical deficit, and what was the size of the cyclical deficit in each of those years? _____

3. Actual vs. Cyclically Adjusted Budget
The equation representing the economy's taxes (net of transfers) is $T = 20 + 0.25$ GDP. The level of government purchases is constant: $G = 90$. Full employment real GDP is 300, but the current equilibrium GDP is 260.
(a) Find the current actual deficit or surplus.
(b) Find the current cyclically adjusted budget balance.
(c) Find the current cyclical deficit or surplus.

4. Tax System and Built-In Stability
Using the model from Chapter 7, this question shows that an economy with a proportional tax system is more stable than an economy without taxes that vary with income. Assume the economy is closed. Initially assume no taxes or government spending. The consumption schedule is given by the equation: $C = 80 + 0.8Y$, and planned investment is constant at $I = 40$.
(a) Fill in the C and AE columns in the table below.
(b) The equilibrium output is Y = _____.

GDP = Y	C	I	I'	C+I = AE	C+I' = AE'
500	___	40	30	___	___
550	___	40	30	___	___
600	___	40	30	___	___
650	___	40	30	___	___
700	___	40	30	___	___

(c) Column I' shows a drop of 10 in investment spending. Fill in column AE' accordingly.
(d) After the drop in investment, the new equilibrium Y is _____.
(e) The multiplier in this model is = change in Y / initial change in spending = _____/_____ = _____.

Now we introduce a public sector. Taxes (T) are 10% of Y. The consumption function is as before, except the relevant income measure is disposable (after-tax) income (Y_d): $C = 80 + 0.80Y_d$. Government purchases are constant at 48. Again, investment is initially 40.
(f) Fill in the table below.
(g) The equilibrium GDP is _____.

Y	T	Yd	C	I	G	C+I+G = AE
500	___	___	___	40	48	___
550	___	___	___	40	48	___
600	___	___	___	40	48	___
650	___	___	___	40	48	___
700	___	___	___	40	48	___

(h) Suppose that planned investment drops by 14. Fill in the table below.

Y	T	Yd	C	I'	G	C+I+G = AE'
500	—	—	—	26	48	—
550	—	—	—	26	48	—
600	—	—	—	26	48	—
650	—	—	—	26	48	—
700	—	—	—	26	48	—

(i) After investment falls, equilibrium Y is now ____.

(j) The multiplier in this model is = change in Y / initial change in spending = ____/____ = ____.

(k) Because the multiplier is (larger, smaller) _____ in the economy with taxes that depend on income, this economy is (less, more) _____ stable in the face of shifts in expenditures.

Discussion Questions

1. What is meant by fiscal policy? When would expansionary (contractionary) fiscal policy be used? What options are open to the government when it applies expansionary (contractionary) fiscal policy?

2. What are the effects of different policy options on the federal budget?

3. Explain, for both a recession and an inflation, what kind of fiscal policy would be advocated (a) by those who prefer an expanded role for the public sector and (b) by those who wish to contract the influence of government in our lives.

4. What is the difference between discretionary and nondiscretionary fiscal policy? How do the built-in stabilizers work to reduce fluctuations in the economy?

5. Define progressive, proportional, and regressive tax systems. Explain which system leads to the most built-in stability for the economy.

6. How is the cyclically adjusted budget defined? For what purpose did economists define this measure? Under what circumstances will the cyclically adjusted deficit change, and under what circumstances will the actual deficit change?

7. Explain the three kinds of time lags involved in the use of fiscal policy. What problem is created by these lags?

8. How is the federal government's use of fiscal policy for stabilization purposes complicated by the fact that municipal and provincial governments also have large budgets and priorities of their own?

9. Explain how the following reduce the effectiveness of fiscal policy: (a) crowding-out effect, (b) inflation, and (c) net export effect.

10. Why does Canada's close trading relationship with the United States complicate the job of fiscal policy-makers in Canada?

11. What are the points of agreement and disagreement between economists on the question of how fiscal policy should be used?

Answers

Quick Quiz
1. (b) pp. 237-238
2. (a) p. 237
3. (d) pp. 239-240
4. (a) pp. 240-242
5. (c) p. 242
6. (c) pp. 242-243
7. (a) p. 245
8. (b) pp. 247-248
9. (d) p. 249

Fill-in Questions
1. decreased, increased, AS, eventually
2. discretionary, non-discretionary
3. before
4. increase, taxes; decrease, taxes
5. taxes, transfers, subsidies

6. built-in; (a) increase; (b) decrease
7. (a) budget balance, full employment GDP; (b) expansionary, contractionary
8. deficit, borrows; (a) raise, contract; (b) crowding-out, weaken
9. lower; outflows, depreciation, increase, offset, net export

True-False
1. T
2. T

3. F   whether contractionary or expansionary is judged by the change in the cyclically adjusted balance

4. F   towards a deficit

5. T   thus the term "stabilizers"

6. T

7. F   taxes decrease and expenditures rise

8. T   this is the crowding-out effect

9. T   the remainder of the effect is dissipated in inflation

10. F   monetary policy is probably better for this

Multiple-Choice

1. (d)

2. (c)   both will reduce AD

3. (c)   because both C and S depend on disposable (after-tax) income

4. (a)   prolonged unemployment led to Keynesian economic theory

5. (a)   in order to increase households' disposable income so that they can increase C

6. (c)   to increase disposable income and C

7. (d)   increased leakage means a smaller multiplier, and more built-in stability

8. (d)   thus replacing some of the household income lost when workers are laid off

9. (d)

10. (c)   proportionately more tax revenue is collected as GDP rises

11. (b)

12. (b)   all of the others require a deliberate action by the government; this one is automatic

13. (b)   at GDP$_f$: $20 - [10 + 0.2(40)] = 2$

14. (c) $20 - [10 + 0.2(35)] = 3$

15. (a) G rises by 2, but T rises by 0.8

16. (a)

17. (a)   AD = AD at GDP > GDPf

18. (c)   because AS is upward sloping

19. (a)

20. (a)   the cyclically adjusted balance moved toward surplus and policy became more contractionary

21. (d)

22. (b)

23. (a)

24. (c)   cutting spending would reduce the size of government; increasing taxes would increase the size of government

25. (a)   this would prevent interest rates from rising

26. (a)   the overall increase in AD would be too great

27. (d)

28. (d)

29. (a)

30. (d)   the others would be potential long-run benefits

Problems and Projects

1. (a) A: regressive (taxes as % of income falls as income rises); B: proportional (taxes as % of income rises); C: progressive (taxes remain constant % of income); (b) C; A

2. (a) judging by change in cyclically adjusted deficit as % of GDP: E, C, C, C; (b) 660; 3 (because in this year the actual budget balance and cyclically adjusted balance are equal); (c) there is a cyclical deficit whenever the actual deficit is bigger than the cyclically adjusted deficit (or the actual surplus is smaller than cyclically adjusted surplus): year 1= 20, year 2 = 29, year 4 = 12, year 5 = 54.

3. (a) $G - T = 90 - 85 = $ deficit of 5; (b) $G - T$ at full employment $= 90 - 95 = $ surplus of 5; (c) cyclical deficit of 10 (difference between cyclically adjusted and actual budget balance).

4. (a) C: 480, 520, 560, 600, 640; AE: 520, 560, 600, 640, 680; (b) 600 (where $Y = AE$); (c) AE': 510, 550, 590, 630, 670: (d) 550; (e) -50, -10, 5; (f) T: 50, 55, 60, 65, 70; Y_d: 450, 495, 540, 585, 630; C: 440, 476, 512, 548, 584; AE: 528, 564, 600, 636, 672; (g) 600; (h) T: 50, 55, 60, 65, 70; Y_d: 450, 495, 540, 585, 630; C: 440, 476, 512, 548, 584; AE': 514, 550, 586, 622, 658; (i) 550; (j) -50, -14, 3.57; (k) smaller; more

Chapter **10**

Deficits, Surpluses, and the Public Debt

Overview

After more than twenty consecutive years of deficits, the Canadian federal government has had a budget surplus each year since 1997. The past deficits have accumulated to create a public debt which stood at about $641 billion at the end of 2002. This debt has been caused by wars, recessions, and lack of political will. This chapter examines the economic impacts of deficits, surpluses, and the public debt.

A deficit occurs whenever the government's revenues fall short of their spending for the same period. A deficit adds to the total stock of the government's debt (public debt). A surplus exists if revenues exceed spending, and a surplus can be applied to reduce the debt.

There are three philosophies on how the government should manage its budget: annually balanced budgets; cyclically balanced budgets (by which the budget is balanced on average over the whole business cycle); and functional finance (by which fiscal policy is used to balance the economy, not the budget).

To get the best perspective on the debt, we examine: (1) the debt as a ratio to GDP; (2) Canada's debt situation compared to that of other major nations; (3) the burden of interest payments; and (4) the ownership of the debt. Considering all of these factors, Canada's debt situation has improved and is now manageable, despite the enormous amount. Two of the most common concerns – that Canada may become bankrupt, and that an enormous burden is being imposed on future generations – are shown to be false.

However, there are substantive issues with the debt, including the following: (1) increased inequality of incomes; (2) reduced incentives for work and production (because of higher taxes); (3) decreased standard of living when repayments must be made on external debt; and (4) crowding out of capital investment.

With government running surpluses for the past few years, the current debate concerns what to do with the surpluses. The basic options are: (1) pay off debt; (2) cut taxes; (3) increase public spending; or (4) a combination of these. Each alternative has merits, and people's preferences are likely to be influenced by their views on the relative value and efficiency of goods and services provided by government as compared to the private sector.

Chapter Outline

10.1 Deficits, Surpluses, and Debt: Definitions and Philosophies

◇ How are the terms deficit, surplus and debt defined?

◇ What are the different philosophies on how the government should manage its budget?

- Three definitions are key:
  o A budget deficit of a government is the amount by which its expenditures exceed its revenues in any year.
  o A budget surplus is the amount by which its revenues exceed expenditures in a year.
  o The public debt is the total accumulation of deficits and surpluses through time, and represents the total amount owed at a particular point in time.

➲ Media reports sometimes use the terms debt and deficit interchangeably. Don't make the same mistake. A deficit is a flow variable: so many dollars *per year*. A debt is a stock variable: so many dollars. The two are related: the larger the deficit flows the larger the stock of debt.

- If the government uses discretionary fiscal policy to combat recession or inflation, their budget will not usually be balanced. Three budgetary philosophies may be adopted by govern-

129

ment as they approach the trade-off between full-employment and budget balance.

- o The "annually balanced budget" philosophy requires government to balance expenditures and tax revenues each year. This strategy is pro-cyclical, meaning that the government's actions will intensify the business cycle. Some advocate this approach as a way to control undesirable expansion of the public sector.

- o In the "cyclically balanced budget" philosophy, government should run surpluses in boom years and deficits in recession years. The effect is counter-cyclical because the output swings in the business cycle are dampened by the government's actions. Ideally, over a period of years, surpluses will equal the deficits, so that the budget is balanced on average. This will not work so smoothly if upswings and downswings in the economy are not of equal magnitude and duration.

- o The "functional finance" philosophy requires government to choose fiscal policies that will achieve the goal of non-inflationary full employment, regardless of the effects upon the public debt.

Quick Quiz

1. One year government collects $250 billion in taxes and spends a total of $245 billion. Therefore:
- (a)   the deficit is $5 billion and the debt will increase by this amount
- (b)   the surplus is $5 billion and the debt will increase by this amount
- (c)   the deficit is $5 billion and the debt will decrease by this amount
- (d)   the surplus is $5 billion and the debt will decrease by this amount

2. Which budget philosophy depends on being able to predict how long periods of recessionary and inflationary gaps will last?
- (a)   annually balanced budget
- (b)   cyclically balanced budget
- (c)   functional finance
- (d)   all of the above

10.2   The Public Debt: Facts and Figures

◇ What is Canada's situation in terms of surpluses, deficits, and debt?

- The three principal reasons for Canada's debt are: (1) wars; (2) recessions; and (3) lack of political will to cut spending or to raise taxes.
- By 2002, the gross federal public debt was about $641 billion.
- To properly assess Canada's debt situation a number of aspects must be considered.

    - o The debt to GDP ratio is important because the nation's GDP is a measure of its ability to carry debt. Canada's debt as a percentage of GDP fell from the end of World War II until 1975. It then rose until the mid-1990s, and has fallen since. In 2002 the debt was 55.4% of GDP.

    - o Canada's total public debt to GDP ratio is one of the highest among major industrialized countries.

    - o Starting in the late 1970s, a mushrooming debt and higher interest rates pushed up the ratio of interest payments to GDP. This trend subsided in the 1990s as the debt to GDP ratio fell and lower inflation allowed for lower interest rates. In 2002 it was under 4%.

    - o About 8% of the public debt is held by the Bank of Canada and 92% by private households, companies, and financial institutions. More importantly, about 17% is held by foreigners.

⊃ The key measure of how the debt problem is evolving is the debt to GDP ratio. Inflation affects both the numerator and denominator, so it washes out of the ratio. The ratio also captures real output growth in the economy which improves our ability to "carry" the debt.

Quick Quiz

3. Canada's debt to GDP ratio:
- (a)   rises every year that we have a deficit
- (b)   is lower than most industrial countries'
- (c)   is reduced by economic growth
- (d)   all of the above

4. Canada's debt would be more likely to grow if:
- (a)   we experience a prolonged period of economic growth
- (b)   we have a budget surplus every year
- (c)   we avoid experiencing major recessions
- (d)   we become involved in a major war

10.3   False Concerns

◈ What are the common misconceptions about the problems created by budget deficits and public debt?

• Concerns that a large debt may bankrupt the government and pass the cost onto future generations are largely false.

• Debt does not threaten to bankrupt the federal government because:
   o It can refinance its debt by selling new bonds to raise money to pay off existing bonds as they come due.
   o It has the constitutional authority to levy and collect taxes.

• Deficit financing does not necessarily shift the burden of the debt to future generations.
   o About 83% of the debt is held by Canadians, so any repayment of principal or interest creates a transfer of wealth between Canadians, not a reduction of wealth for Canadians collectively.
   o Though a great deal of debt was incurred in World War II, the burden of the war was borne mainly by those whose standard of living was sharply reduced while the economy focused on producing military goods instead of consumer goods.
   o The burden imposed on future generations is lessened if the increase in government expenditures is for real or human capital or if the economy were initially operating at less than full employment (and the deficit stimulates an increase in investment demand).

➲ Whether, and how, the debt creates a burden on our society is the most interesting and controversial issue in the chapter. This section is worth studying especially carefully because some of the points are subtle, and they don't always match what you are told by politicians or the media.

Quick Quiz
5.   Which statement is true?
   (a)   that portion of Canada's debt owed to foreign citizens is no burden for Canadians
   (b)   Canadians today bear the burden of WWII because the government has never paid off the debt from the war
   (c)   interest payments paid by the Canadian government to Canadians who own the bonds is a burden for the nation

   (d)   most of Canada's debt is owed to Canadians

6.   There is minimal risk that the debt will bankrupt the federal government because:
   (a)   the government can raise taxes if necessary
   (b)   the government can continue to refinance the debt
   (c)   both (a) and (b)
   (d)   none of the above: the government is an significant risk of bankruptcy

10.4   Substantive Issues

◈ What are the substantive issues relating to deficits and public debt that we should be concerned about?

• The payment of interest on the debt probably increases the extent of income inequality.

• Economic growth slows down if the taxes levied to finance the debt reduce incentives to bear risks, to innovate, to invest, and to work.

• The 17% of Canadian bonds owned by foreigners represent claims on Canada's future GDP. That is, both debt repayment and interest payments require us to give up some of our output to foreigners instead of consuming it ourselves.

• Government borrowing to finance the debt tends to increase interest rates and reduce private investment spending. This "crowding-out effect" leaves future generations with a smaller stock of capital goods and a less productive economy. This concern is tempered by the fact that much government spending is on public investment that also improves the economy's productivity (e.g., roads, hospitals, airports). Moreover, there are often complementarities between public and private investments.

Quick Quiz
7.   How might a large debt impede economic growth?
   (a)   high tax rates to raise revenue for debt payments may reduce incentives to work, save, and invest
   (b)   the crowding-out effect may leave a larger capital stock for the future
   (c)   the debt may allow more schools and hospitals to be built
   (d)   all of the above

10.5   Deficits and Surpluses: 1990 to the Present

◇ What are the recent trends in our government's budget situation?

• From the mid-1970s to the mid-1990s, the federal government had a deficit every year, with the deficit hitting a high of $40 billion in 1993. This produced massive growth in the accumulated debt. Fiscal policy then turned to deficit elimination in order to promote a reverse crowding-out effect.

• Having turned the corner by eliminating deficits, the government now faces choices about what to do with the annual budgetary surplus. There are three main options (and combinations of these):

   o   Paying down the debt would create a reverse crowding-out effect, but there are questions about how significant this effect would be. There is also concern that reducing the stock of government securities in circulation might cause problems in financial markets.

   o   Cutting taxes (by reducing rates or increasing tax deductions and credits) could eventually stimulate economic growth, and (say some advocates) prevent undesirable growth of the public sector. This alternative may be inflationary if it expands the AD curve when we are already at or close to full employment.

   o   Increasing public expenditures would enable us to address various needs for public capital and social programs. This alternative may also be inflationary, and critics fear that additional government spending programs may quickly become institutionalized and difficult to scale back later.

• Lotteries are a significant, but controversial, source of revenues for governments. Some people consider lotteries to be a regressive tax preying on lower income individuals, and exposing people to serious problems of gambling addiction. Others do not consider lottery revenues to be taxes because buying lottery tickets is a voluntary choice. Given the need for public revenues, and the fact that consumers spend vast amounts on various forms of gambling, government might as well tap this revenue source.

Quick Quiz

8. What could government do with a surplus on its budget?
   (a)   pay off part of the debt
   (b)   reduce taxes to eliminate the surplus
   (c)   increase government spending
   (d)   all of the above are options

9. Paying down the public debt could help the economy by:
   (a)   raising interest rates
   (b)   attracting foreign capital inflows
   (c)   removing government bonds from the choices available in financial markets
   (d)   creating a reverse crowding-out effect

Terms and Concepts

public debt

annually balanced budget

cyclically balanced budget

functional finance

external public debt

public investments

Fill-In Questions

1. The budget deficit of the federal government in any year is equal to its (expenditures, revenues) _____ less its _____ in that year; and the public debt is equal to the sum of the federal government's past budget _____ less its budget _____.

2. An annually balanced budget is (pro-, counter-) _____ cyclical because when a recession sets in, tax revenues tend to (fall, rise) _____ so government must (cut, increase) _____ its spending to keep the budget balanced. This ends up (increasing, reducing) _____ AD at a time when the opposite is needed to stabilize the economy at full-employment output.

3. A cyclically balanced budget suggests that, to ensure full employment without inflation, the government should incur deficits during periods of _____ and surpluses during periods of _____, with the deficits and surpluses balancing out over the business cycle.

4. The principal causes of Canada's public debt are _____, _____, and lack of _____.

5. At the end of 2002 Canada's public debt was:

(a) about $____ billion and about ____% of the GDP;

(b) about ____% of this debt was held by foreigners, and about ____% was held by Canadians.

6. The possibility that the federal government will go bankrupt is a false issue because the government can retire maturing securities by _____ them; and it has the constitutional authority to _____ and _____ taxes.

7. A public debt – even if held internally – can burden future generations if the borrowing done to finance an increase in government expenditures (increases, decreases) _____ interest rates, _____ investment spending, and leaves future generations with a smaller stock of _____ goods.

(a) But if the increased government expenditures are financed by an increase in the taxes on personal income, the present generation will have fewer _____ goods and the burden of the increased government expenditures will be on the _____ generation.

(b) The burden on future generations of increased government expenditures financed by borrowing is reduced if the government expenditures pay for public _____.

True-False

Circle T if the statement is true, F if it is false.

1. The budget deficit in any year is equal to the amount by which the government's revenues exceed its expenditures.   **T F**

2. A budget surplus will reduce the public debt.   **T F**

3. A nation will not be able to use fiscal policy both to promote full employment and balance its budget annually.   **T F**

4. Proponents of functional finance argue that a balanced budget, whether it is balanced annually or over the business cycle, is less important than the objective of full employment without inflation.   **T F**

5. Canada's public debt is owed by the Canadian public to residents of foreign nations.   **T F**

6. Selling government securities to foreigners to finance increased expenditures by the government imposes a burden on future generations.   **T F**

7. The crowding-out effect of borrowing to finance an increase in government expenditures results from a rise in interest rates.   **T F**

8. Surpluses can produce a reverse crowding-out effect.   **T F**

9. If the government pays off its debt, investors would no longer have the option of holding Canada government bonds.   **T F**

10. Canada's public debt is higher than any other major industrialized country.   **T F**

11. If lottery revenues are considered a tax, then they are a progressive tax.   **T F**

Multiple-Choice

Circle the letter that corresponds to the best answer.

1. Canada's public debt is the sum of all previous:
- (a)   expenditures of the federal government
- (b)   budget deficits of the federal government
- (c)   budget deficits less the budget surpluses of the federal government
- (d)   none of the above

2. Which of the following would require cutting government expenditures and raising tax rates during a recession?
- (a)   an annually balanced budget policy
- (b)   functional finance
- (c)   a cyclically balanced budget policy
- (d)   a policy employing built-in stability

3. Which is the most likely consequence for a nation following a cyclically balanced budget philosophy, if that nation's recessions are of greater magnitude and longer duration than its booms?
- (a)   the nation will have a deficit every year
- (b)   the nation will have surpluses more often than deficits

(c)   the nation's surpluses will tend to be bigger than their deficits

(d)   the nation's debt will rise

4. Which is a true statement about the trends in Canada's debt situation since the late 1990s?

(a)   interest payments are growing as a percentage of GDP

(b)   interest payments are growing in absolute terms

(c)   the debt continues to increase in absolute terms

(d)   the debt is now falling as a percentage of GDP

5. The public debt cannot bankrupt the federal government because the federal government:

(a)   need not reduce the size of the debt

(b)   is able to refinance the debt

(c)   can levy and collect taxes to repay the debt and pay the interest on it

(d)   all of the above

6. Which one of the following is not a way for the government to finance its budget deficit?

(a)   sale of bonds to the Canadian public

(b)   sale of bonds to the Canadian central bank

(c)   sale of bonds to foreign investors

(d)   sale of common stock to Canadian investors

7. Canada's public debt is mainly held by:

(a)   the Bank of Canada

(b)   the Government of Canada

(c)   private households and financial institutions in Canada

(d)   foreign investors

8. Incurring internal debts to finance a war does not pass the cost of war on to future generations because:

(a)   the opportunity cost of the war is borne by the generation that fights it

(b)   the government need not pay interest on internally held debts

(c)   there is never a need for government to refinance the debt

(d)   war-time inflation reduces the relative size of the debt

9. If the government elects to pay down the public debt, what exactly would they do?

(a)   transfer money to foreign governments

(b)   send tax rebates to Canadian citizens

(c)   transfer money to the International Monetary Fund

(d)   buy back government bonds

10. Which of the following would be a consequence if the government pays off debt held by Canadians?

(a)   a reduction in the nation's productive capacity

(b)   a reduction in the nation's standard of living

(c)   a redistribution of the nation's wealth among its citizens

(d)   an increase in aggregate expenditures in the economy

11. Which of the following is a consequence of the public debt of Canada?

(a)   it increases incentives to work and invest

(b)   it transfers a portion of the Canadian output of goods and services to foreign nations

(c)   it reduces income inequality in Canada

(d)   it leads to greater saving at every level of disposable income

12. The crowding-out effect of government borrowing to finance an increase in expenditures:

(a)   increases the interest rate and reduces current private investment expenditures

(b)   decreases the interest rate and increases private investment expenditures

(c)   allows for an increase in government and private borrowing

(d)   places the burden of the debt on today's generation

13. The crowding-out effect of government borrowing to finance its increased expenditures is reduced:

(a)   when the economy is operating at or near full employment

(b)   when there are complementarities between public investments and private investments

(c)   when the interest rate is increased

(d)   all of the above

14. What is an argument against tax reductions as a way to dispose of a federal budget surplus?

(a) the surplus may be temporary, so taxes should not be reduced permanently
(b) tax reductions may be inflationary if the economy is already near full employment
(c) there may be important needs for increases in government spending
(d) all of the above

15. Which of the following strategies for disposing of a surplus might create a reverse crowding-out effect?
(a) increasing public expenditures
(b) cutting taxes
(c) paying off debt
(d) none of the above

Problems and Projects

1. Deficits and the Crowding-Out Effect

Columns (a) through (c) in the table show the investment demand schedule and the supply of loanable funds at various interest rates. Initially, government has a balanced budget.

(a) Interest rate	(b) Supply of loans	(c) Id	(d) Demand for loans
8	$45 billion	$24 billion	$____
7	42	28	____
6	39	32	____
5	36	36	____
4	33	40	____

(a) Find the equilibrium interest rate, and level of investment demand at this interest rate.
(b) Now the government has a budget deficit of $7 billion, which they will finance by selling bonds to the same lenders who finance investment by businesses. In column (d) show the new demand for loans (from government to finance the deficit, and businesses to finance investment).
(c) Find the new equilibrium interest rate, and the new amount of investment demand.
(d) How much investment spending has been crowded out by the government's deficit?

2. Budget Philosophies

Suppose that a nation's full-employment level of output is $500 billion per year. Over the course of a business cycle the nation's average output

would be $450 billion per year. Government spending has already been determined, and is a steady $100 billion per year.
(a) If the nation pursues a cyclically balanced budget, how much tax revenue should be collected per year (on average) and what tax rate would generate this much revenue? Revenue = $____ billion, Tax rate = ____%
(b) In order to have an annually balanced budget, how would taxes have to change from your result in (a)?
(c) If the government follows the functional finance philosophy, how would taxes have to change from your result in (a), again assuming government spending is held at $100 billion?

3. Deficits, Surpluses, and Debt

The table below shows data for four years for some country.
(a) Fill in the table assuming that: (1) taxes are 20% of GDP; (2) government annually pays 6% interest on the debt owing at the beginning of the year. Round to the nearest integer values.
(b) Since there is a deficit each year, the debt _____ each year.
(c) In years 1 and 2 there would be no deficit were it not for the _____ on debt from previous years.
(d) Though the debt increases each year, the country's debt situation improves in year _____ as measured by the _____.

Years	1	2	3	4
GDP ($)	1000	1100	1200	1300
Government purchases ($)	200	220	250	300
Tax revenues ($)	____	____	____	____
Interest on debt ($)	____	____	____	____
Debt at Jan 1 ($)	300	____	____	____
Deficit ($)	____	____	____	____
Debt at Dec 31 ($)	____	____	____	____
Debt at Dec 31 / GDP (%)	____	____	____	____

Discussion Questions

1. What is the difference between the government's budget deficit and the public debt?

2. Explain the three different budget philosophies, and explain whether each one tends to intensify or reduce the fluctuations of GDP during the business cycle.

3. How big is the public debt of Canada, absolutely and relatively? How large are the interest charges on the debt, absolutely and relatively? What has happened to the size of the debt and interest charges since 1926, between 1975 and 1997, and since 1997? Why did these changes occur?

4. Why should we not worry about the public debt bankrupting the federal government? Are the same arguments true for provincial government debts?

5. Explain the difference between an internally held and an externally held public debt. If the debt is internally held, government borrowing to finance a war does not pass all the cost of the war on to future generations. Why? Why does the portion of the public debt externally held impose a burden on the economy?

6. How does the public debt and the payment of interest on the debt affect the income distribution and incentives?

7. Under what conditions will deficits impose a burden on future generations? Why don't increases in government expenditures financed by increased personal taxes impose the same burden on future generations? What will lessen the burden of deficit financing on future generations?

8. What circumstances would help Canada to continue to have budget surpluses? What are the options for what should be done with the surpluses? What might be the consequences for you of each of these options?

9. What are the arguments for and against governments raising revenues from lotteries instead of regular taxes?

Answers

Quick Quiz
1. (d) p. 254
2. (b) pp. 254-255
3. (c) p. 257
4. (d) pp. 255-256
5. (d) pp. 259-260
6. (c) p. 259
7. (a) pp. 260-261
8. (d) pp. 263-264
9. (d) p. 263

Fill-in Questions
1. expenditures, revenues, deficits, surpluses
2. pro-, fall, cut, reducing
3. recession, inflation
4. wars, recessions, political will
5. (a) 641, 55; (b) 17, 83
6. refinancing, levy, collect
7. increases, decreases, capital; (a) consumer, present; (b) capital

True-False
1. F the amount by which expenditures exceed revenues
2. T debt increases when there is a deficit and decreases when there is a surplus
3. T an annually balanced budget is procyclical
4. T
5. F the debt is owed by the government to people who hold its bonds: mostly Canadians, though some foreigners
6. T foreigners acquire claims on some of the nation's future output
7. T investment falls when interest rates rise
8. T by causing interest rates to fall, investment will be increased
9. T these bonds are the government's main debt instrument
10. F several countries have larger debts, even on a debt to GDP ratio basis
11. F the lottery "tax" is regressive

Multiple-Choice
1. (c)
2. (a) which would tend to deepen the recession
3. (d) because deficits will occur more frequently than surpluses, and will usually be larger
4. (d)
5. (d)
6. (d) stocks are sold by corporations, not governments
7. (c) about 75% in 2002
8. (a)
9. (d) in simple terms, bonds are the government's "IOUs"
10. (c) the bonds are the liability of the government (and indirectly taxpayers at large), but are the assets of bondholders (most of whom are Canadians)

11. (b) to the extent that the debt is held externally
12. (a)
13. (b) these complementarities could increase private investment, offsetting the drop in private investment created by higher interest rates
14. (d)
15. (c) because this could reduce the interest rate

Problems and Projects
1. (a) at interest rate = 5%, supply of loans = investment demand; (b) 31, 35, 39, 43, 47; (c) at 6%, supply of loans = demand for loans; 32; (d) 36 − 32 = 4
2. (a) 100, 100/450 = 22; (b) higher in recession years, lower in inflation years; (c) lower taxes to expand AD to move GDP to full-employment
3. (a) see table; (b) increased; (c) interest; (d) 2, Debt/GDP ratio.

Years	1	2	3	4
GDP ($)	1000	1100	1200	1300
Government purchases ($)	200	220	250	300
Tax revenues ($)	200	220	240	260
Interest on debt ($)	18	19	20	22
Debt at Jan 1 ($)	300	318	337	367
Deficit ($)	18	19	30	62
Debt at Dec 31 ($)	318	337	367	429
Debt at Dec 31 / GDP (%)	32%	31%	31%	33%

Chapter 11 — Money and Banking

Overview

This chapter explains the nature and functions of money and the basic institutions in Canada's banking system. This information will prepare you for the later chapters on how banks can change the money supply, and how the Bank of Canada uses monetary policy.

Anything that performs the functions of money is considered to be money. Money serves, first and foremost, as a medium of exchange, but also as a unit of account and a store of value. Many different assets meet these criteria to varying degrees, so there are several definitions of the money supply. Most of the analysis in this text relies on M1, which is the narrowest definition. M1 includes currency (coins and paper money) outside chartered banks, and demand deposits (funds held in chequing accounts at chartered banks).

Perhaps surprisingly, our money supply is not backed by anything tangible: simply by the government's ability to keep the value of money fairly stable. So why does money have value? First, by social convention, we all accept money in exchange for goods and services (so these goods and services back the money, in a sense). Second, government has declared currency to be legal tender. Third, the value of money depends on its relative scarcity. Many historical episodes prove that when money suddenly becomes much too plentiful, prices rise and money loses its value. In cases of hyperinflation, people may cease to accept currency as a medium of exchange and revert to transacting business by barter, or substitute a more stable foreign currency.

Money's role as a medium of exchange creates the transactions demand for money, and its role as a store of value creates the asset demand for money. The transactions demand varies directly with nominal GDP, and the asset demand varies inversely with the rate of interest, so the total demand for money depends on these two variables in the same way. At the interest rate where the demand for money is equal to the supply of money, the money market is in equilibrium. A shift in the money supply will change the equilibrium. For example, if the money supply declines, there will be a shortage of money which people will try to make up by selling financial assets (bonds). The price of bonds will fall, and the interest rate on bonds will rise. Money market equilibrium is restored when the interest rate has increased enough that people are once again satisfied with their money balances relative to their holdings of bonds.

The chapter closes with a description of the Canadian banking system, an industry dominated by a few big players. Chartered banks try to maximize shareholder profits, mainly by lending at interest rates higher than the rates paid to depositors. The creation of money by the creation of new loans and deposits is the main banking activity of interest in macroeconomics, and is the subject of the next chapter.

Chapter Outline

11.1 The Definitions and Functions of Money

◈ What is money?

◈ What are the functions of money?

• Money is whatever performs the three basic functions of money
  o a medium of exchange
  o a standard of value
  o a store of value.

⮑ Money is not defined by its physical attributes; nor does something become money just because the government declares that it is. The public must accept it as a medium of exchange.

Quick Quiz

1. When you give a $20 bill to the cashier at a grocery store, you are using money as a:

(a) medium of exchange
(b) store of value
(c) unit of account
(d) token money

11.2   The Supply of Money

◈ What counts as part of the supply of money?

•   Historically, many different items have been used in different societies.

•   In Canada, currency (coins and paper money) outside the chartered banks and demand deposits (chequing account funds in chartered banks) constitute M1, which is the narrowest measure of the money supply.

   o   Coins are token money because their intrinsic value is below their face value.
   o   Paper currency is in the form of Bank of Canada notes.
   o   Demand deposits, which are bank-created money, account for about two-thirds of M1.

•   Certain other highly liquid financial assets are so easily converted into media of exchange that they are called near-monies, and are included in broader measures of the money supply such as M2, M2+ and M2++.

•   Credit cards are not included in the money supply. A credit card is a vehicle for gaining short term credit, not a method of making final payment. Use of credit cards does, however, allow individuals and businesses to hold less money than they would otherwise.

Quick Quiz

2. Which of the following is not included in M1?

(a) a $20 bill in your pocket
(b) a $20 bill in the vault at the Bank of Montreal
(c) $20 in a savings account at a credit union
(d) both (b) and (c)

3. Which statement is false?

(a) M1 is the broadest definition of the money supply
(b) coins represent a very small fraction of M1
(c) broader measures of the money supply are several times larger than M1

(d) near-monies are not included in M1

11.3   What "Backs" the Money Supply?

◈ What "backs" the money supply in Canada?

•   In Canada, money is debt owed by chartered banks (demand deposits) or the Bank of Canada (currency).

•   Currency has no significant intrinsic value, and cannot be redeemed for anything of tangible value.

•   Money has value only because people can exchange it for desirable goods and services. This occurs because of:

   o   social consensus that we accept money as payment;
   o   the government's designation of currency as legal tender (which makes currency fiat money);
   o   the relative scarcity of money.

•   The value of money is determined by its purchasing power in terms of real goods and services.

   o   The value of a dollar is inversely related to the price level.
   o   In a hyperinflation money can lose value so quickly that people become unwilling to hold money or to accept it as a medium of exchange. Then society reverts to barter or switches to a more stable money such as a foreign currency.

➲ Hyperinflation makes money nearly useless as a store of value (because money erodes in value), and a poor unit of account (because the prices of goods and services are constantly changing). These problems can be so severe that people seek other currencies, or even resort to barter. In other words, the money loses its status as the unquestioned medium of exchange.

Quick Quiz

4. If you ask the Bank of Canada to redeem a $20 bill, what will you receive?

(a) $20 worth of coins
(b) $20 worth of gold
(c) $20 worth of US currency
(d) possibly a fresh $20 bill, and definitely some strange looks

5. A 50% increase in the price level will have what effect on the value of a dollar?

(a)   it falls by 2%
(b)   it falls by 20%
(c)   it falls by 33%
(d)   it falls by 50%

11.4   The Demand for Money

◇ What are the components of money demand?

◇ What variables determine the amount of money demanded?

• The public (firms and households) has two motives for holding money.
   o The transactions demand stems from money's use as a medium of exchange. The higher nominal GDP is, the more transactions are made, and the greater the transactions demand for money.
   o The asset demand stems from money's function as a liquid store of value. The higher is the interest rate on bonds, the greater the opportunity cost of holding money, and the less the asset demand for money.
• The total demand for money is the horizontal sum found of the asset demand and the transactions demand. There is an inverse relation between the quantity of money the public wants to hold and the interest rate. Increases in nominal GDP shift the money demand curve to the right.
• The supply of money can be determined by the Bank of Canada, and does not vary with the interest rate.

Quick Quiz

6. The money the public holds to pay for groceries is included in:
   (a)   the transactions demand
   (b)   the asset demand
   (c)   the total demand
   (d)   both (a) and (c)

7. There is an asset demand for money because money is:
   (a)   a medium of exchange
   (b)   a standard of value
   (c)   a store of value
   (d)   a unit of account

8. If the interest rate rises, what will be among the consequences?
   (a)   a leftward shift in the total demand for money

(b)   a movement up to the left on the transactions demand for money
(c)   a movement up to the left on the asset demand for money
(d)   all of the above

11.5   Equilibrium in the Money Market

◇ How is the equilibrium interest rate determined in the money market?

• Equilibrium in the money market occurs at the interest rate where the downsloping money-demand curve and the vertical money-supply curve intersect.
• If the money supply declines, there will be a shortage of money. The public will then attempt to sell bonds and financial assets to restore their desired money balances. These transactions will decrease the prices of existing bonds and increase the interest rate. This interest rate adjustment continues until the amount of money demanded falls enough to match the fixed supply of money.
• If the money supply grows, there will be a surplus of money, Then the public will attempt to purchase bonds and other interest-bearing financial assets. This will drive up the prices of bonds, and drive down the interest rate. This continues until the interest rate is low enough to induce the public to willingly hold the amount of money that exists.

Quick Quiz

9. The equilibrium in the money market is found where:
   (a)   the demand for money equals the demand for bonds
   (b)   the demand for money equals the supply of money
   (c)   the interest rate on money equals the interest rate on bonds
   (d)   all of the above

10. If there is a surplus of money:
   (a)   people will attempt to sell bonds
   (b)   the interest rate will rise
   (c)   there is a shortage of bonds
   (d)   the supply of money will decrease

11.6   The Canadian Financial System

◇ What are the main structural characteristics

of Canada's financial system?

• Chartered banks are privately-owned firms that Parliamentary has granted charters to operate as banks.

• There are numerous banks in Canada, but about 90% of deposits are held by the six largest chartered banks.

• In recent years banks have expanded their activities, often through mergers and acquisitions. Many now offer services previously provided only by trust companies or stock brokerages.

• The banks perform the two essential functions of holding deposits and making loans. They strive to make profits for shareholders by making as many loans as prudently possible, and by charging higher interest rates on loans than they pay on deposits.

• In addition to chartered banks, financial intermediaries include trust companies, loan companies, credit unions, *caisses populaires*, and insurance companies. All of these institutions act as intermediaries by accepting deposits from savers and lending to investors.

• The Canadian Payments Association provides an inter-bank cheque clearing system between the chartered banks and near-banks.

Quick Quiz

11. The main goal of a chartered bank is to:
(a) create deposit money
(b) lend money
(c) raise interest rates
(d) maximize profits

12. The functions of chartered banks include all but which of the following:
(a) accept deposits
(b) lend money
(c) clear cheques through the CPA
(d) determine monetary policy for Canada

11.7   Recent Developments in Money and Banking

◈ What are the key recent developments in money and banking?

• The banking industry is undergoing many changes as a result of competition, globalization of financial markets, and technological progress:
  o Banks are offering new products (different kinds of deposit accounts and loans)

and expanded services (more branches, ABMs);
  o Banks are competing more than ever in international markets for both deposit, loan, and credit card customers;
  o Electronic transactions, including internet banking, are now commonplace, and other innovations in how the public makes payments (such as smart cards) seem likely to gain popularity.

Quick Quiz

13. Stored-value cards:
(a) are not yet in use in Canada
(b) function the same way as credit cards
(c) are predicted to replace cash by the year 2010
(d) are used by some retailers and mass transit companies

Terms and Concepts

medium of exchange
unit of account
store of value
M1
demand deposit
token money
Bank of Canada notes
near-monies
M2
M2+
legal tender

transactions demand for money
asset demand for money
total demand for money
money market
chartered bank
prime rate
financial intermediary
electronic transactions

Fill-In Questions

1. Three functions of money are
(a) _medium of exchange_
(b) _store of value_
(c) _unit of account_.

2. The supply of money, M1, in Canada consists of currency (_coin_ and _paper_) outside chartered banks and _dem dep_ in chartered banks.

3. Near-monies are highly _liquid_ financial assets that do not directly function as a medium of _exchg_ but can be readily converted in _current_ or _demand_ deposits. Near-monies (are, are not) _____ counted in the M1 measure of the money supply.

4. Paper money is the debt of the _Canadian ba_. and demand deposits are the debts of _chartered_

5. Money has value because it can be exchanged for _____. Its value varies (directly, inversely) _____ with changes in the _____ level.

6. The total demand for money is the sum of:
(a) the _____ demand, which relates to money's function as a medium of exchange, and which depends (directly, inversely) _____ upon the _____;
(b) and the _____ demand, which relates to money's function as a store of value, and which depends _____ upon the _____.

True-False

Circle T if the statement is true, F if it is false.

1. All money in Canada is issued by the Bank of Canada or the federal government.   **T F**

2. Money, by providing a convenient way to exchange goods and services, promotes specialization.   **T F**

3. Money serves as a store of value when it is used for measuring the worth of goods.   **T F**

4. Currency includes both coins and paper money.   **T F**

5. A loonie is "token money" because its face value is less than its intrinsic value.   **T F**

6. Canadian paper money can be converted into gold at a rate fixed by the government.   **T F**

7. The most inclusive measure of money discussed in the chapter is M1.   **T F**

8. The fastest growing part of the Canadian money supply is credit card money.   **T F**

9. If money is to have a fairly stable value, its supply must be limited relative to the demand for it.   **T F**

10. If the price level triples, the value of one unit of currency will be only one-third of what it was previously.   **T F**

11. An increase in the equilibrium GDP will shift the money demand curve to the left and increase the equilibrium interest rate.   **T F**

12. A surplus of money will cause bond prices to rise.   **T F**

13. Hyperinflation can cause money to fall out of use.   **T F**

14. The Royal Bank of Canada is one of the ten largest banks in the world.   **T F**

15. The Canadian government has established rules under which banks may merge.   **T F**

Multiple-Choice

Circle the letter that corresponds to the best answer.

1. Which of the following has been used as money?
(a)   circular stones
(b)   furs
(c)   cigarettes
(d)   all of the above

2. Which of the following is not one of the functions of money?
(a)   a factor of production
(b)   a medium of exchange
(c)   a store of value
(d)   a unit of account

3. Which of the following best expresses how the use of money benefits our society?
(a)   money is intrinsically valuable
(b)   money creates wealth by generating interest income
(c)   money creates wealth by facilitating specialization
(d)   the larger the money supply the larger the economy's output

4. Which of the following makes up the biggest share of Canada's M1 money supply?
- (a) coins
- (b) paper money
- (c) term and notice deposits
- (d) demand deposits

5. Demand deposits are money because they are:
- (a) legal tender
- (b) fiat money
- (c) accepted as a medium of exchange
- (d) fully guaranteed by the chartered banks

6. The supply of money, M1, consists of the debts of:
- (a) the federal government
- (b) the Bank of Canada
- (c) chartered banks
- (d) the Bank of Canada and chartered banks

7. Which of the following best describes the "backing" of money in Canada?
- (a) the gold bullion stored in the Bank of Canada's vaults
- (b) the belief of holders of money that it can be exchanged for desirable goods and services
- (c) the willingness of banks and the government to surrender something of value in exchange for money
- (d) the faith and confidence of the public in the ability of government to pay its debts

8. Bank of Canada notes are:
- (a) "backed" by gold
- (b) counted as part of the money supply when held by the chartered banks
- (c) legal tender in Canada
- (d) circulating assets of the Bank of Canada

9. Whenever a person withdraws $100 cash from a demand deposit at a chartered bank, the M1 money supply has:
- (a) increased
- (b) decreased
- (c) stayed the same
- (d) not enough information provided to tell

10. If a person closes her personal chequing account at the Bank of Montreal and deposits the balance in her personal chequing account at Vancouver City Savings Credit Union, then:
- (a) M1 falls, M2 falls, and M2+ rises

- (b) M1 is unchanged, M2 rises, and M2+ rises
- (c) M1 falls, M2 is unchanged, and M2+ rises
- (d) M1 falls, M2 falls, M2+ is unchanged

11. Pre-1967 dimes and quarters with high silver content have nearly disappeared from circulation, whereas pre-1967 pennies and nickels still circulate. Why?
- (a) the quarters and dimes wore out
- (b) the token value of quarters and dimes exceeds the intrinsic value
- (c) more pennies and nickels were issued to begin with
- (d) the intrinsic value of quarters and dimes exceeds the token value

12. The purchasing power of money decreases whenever:
- (a) the unemployment rate rises
- (b) the GDP price index falls
- (c) the Consumer Price Index rises
- (d) the interest rate falls

13. There is an asset demand for money because money is:
- (a) a medium of exchange
- (b) a standard of value
- (c) a store of value
- (d) a standard of deferred payment

14. The transactions demand for money:
- (a) varies directly with nominal GDP
- (b) varies inversely with nominal GDP
- (c) varies directly with the interest rate
- (d) varies inversely with the interest rate

15. The total demand for money would shift to the left as a result of:
- (a) an increase in the interest rate
- (b) a decline in nominal GDP
- (c) a decrease in the interest rate
- (d) an increase in nominal GDP

16. The equilibrium interest rate is determined by:
- (a) the demand for money and the level of nominal GDP
- (b) the transactions demand for money and the supply of money
- (c) the total demand for money and the supply of money

(d)   the demand for money and the demand for bonds

17. An increase in the interest rate would increase:
(a)   the opportunity cost of holding money
(b)   the transactions demand for money
(c)   the asset demand for money
(d)   the price of bonds

18. Suppose the transactions demand for money is equal to 10% of the nominal GDP, the supply of money is $45 billion, and the asset demand for money is as shown in the following table. If nominal GDP is $300 billion, the equilibrium interest rate is:
(a)   14%
(b)   13%
(c)   12%
(d)   11%

Interest Rate (%)	Asset Demand (billions)
14	$10
13	15
12	20
11	25

19. Given the data in Question 18, what change in the money supply would be needed to lower the interest rate by 1%?
(a) $5 billion increase
(b) $5 billion decrease
(c) $10 billion increase
(d) $10 billion decrease

20. Which of the following statements is true?
(a)   bond prices and the interest rates are directly related
(b)   a lower interest rate shifts the aggregate demand curve to the left
(c)   the supply of money is directly related to the interest rate
(d)   bond prices and interest rates are inversely related

21. A bond that pays a fixed interest payment of $100 per year falls in price from $1,000 to $800. What happens to the interest rate on the bond?
(a)   increase by 1.25 percent per year
(b)   decrease by 1.25 percent per year
(c)   increase by 2.50 percent per year
(d)   decrease by 2.50 percent per year

22. Which of the following is **not** an example of a financial intermediary?
(a)   a credit union
(b)   a caisse populaire
(c)   a trust company
(d)   the Bank of Canada

23. The Canadian Payments Association:
(a)   represents the Canadian chartered banks in discussions with the government
(b)   helps restructure loans for individuals and institutions that are unable to repay borrowings from the banks
(c)   operates the inter-bank cheque clearing system
(d)   determines the prices to be charged for different banking services

24. The prime rate of interest is:
(a)   the interest rate paid on Canada Savings Bonds
(b)   the interest rate on Government of Canada bonds
(c)   the interest rate charged by the chartered banks to their best customers
(d)   the interest rate charged by the chartered banks for home mortgages

25. Which is not among the "Four Pillars" of the Canadian financial system?
(a)   insurance companies
(b)   banks
(c)   securities dealers
(d)   Bank of Canada

26. When banks work on the "fractional reserve system" it means that:
(a)   they pay only a small interest rate to their depositors
(b)   a fraction of their borrowers default on their bank loans
(c)   they keep only a small fraction of deposits to meet cash withdrawals
(d)   they lend out only a small fraction of the funds deposited with them

27. Many transactions in Russia now occur in American dollars rather than in rubles because:
(a)   Russians now support capitalism
(b)   there is a severe shortage of rubles
(c)   there is an oversupply of dollars
(d)   the value of the dollar is much more stable than the ruble

Problems and Projects

1. Money Definitions
With the information given below, determine M1, M2 and M2+.

Currency outside banks:	$ 39
Currency at chartered banks:	17
Demand deposits at chartered banks:	60
Non-personal notice deposits at chartered banks:	205
Personal savings deposits at chartered banks:	112
Deposits at trust and mortgage companies, credit unions, and *caisses populaires:*	240

M1 = $____ ; M2 = $____ ; M2+ = $____

2. Inflation and the Value of Money
Complete the following table showing the relationship between the percentage change in the price level and the percentage change in the value of money. Calculate to one decimal place.

Change in the Price Level	Change in the Value of Money
(a) Rise by:	
5%	- ____ %
10%	- ____ %
20%	- ____ %
(b) Fall by:	
5%	+ ____ %
10%	+ ____ %
20%	+ ____ %

3. The Terminology of Money
Match the term on the left with the appropriate description on the right.

(a) paper money	(1) demand deposits
(b) token money	(2) declared by government to be legal tender
(c) near money	(3) readily convertible into medium of exchange
(d) chequebook money	(4) intrinsic value is less than face value

4. What Counts as Money?
Which money supply measure(s) include each of the following items? For each, check off as many as apply. If an item is not included in any of the money supply measures, indicate "none."

	M1	M2	M2+	none
(a) Currency in your pocket	☐	☐	☐	☐
(b) A savings deposit in a credit union	☐	☐	☐	☐
(c) Currency in the vault of a bank	☐	☐	☐	☐
(d) A savings account in a bank	☐	☐	☐	☐
(e) Money market mutual funds	☐	☐	☐	☐
(f) A Canada Savings bond	☐	☐	☐	☐

5. Demand for Money and the Money Market
The transactions demand for money (D_t) is a constant 150. The asset demand (D_a) depends on the interest rate (i) as given by: $D_a = 200 - 25i$.
(a) On the graph below, plot the curves for D_t, D_a, and the total demand for money (D_m).
(b) Assuming the money supply is 250, plot S_m.
(c) What is the equilibrium interest rate?
(d) At an interest rate of 6%, would there be an excess supply or excess demand for money, and of what amount?

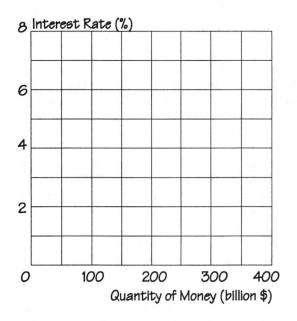

Discussion Questions

1. How would you define money? Why are credit cards not counted as money?

2. At the University of B.C., plastic tokens redeemable for beer at the student pub were routinely accepted instead of currency in card games in the student residences. To what extent were these tokens considered to be money, and why did they function as such?

3. What are the components of M1? What are some examples of near-monies?

4. Suppose that you spend the summer working on a grain farm to earn money for school. Why would you rather be paid in money instead of in grain of equivalent market value? In responding, consider the three functions of money.

5. What "backs" the money used in Canada? What determines the value of money?

6. Why do you think that cigarettes came to be used as money in World War II prisoner-of-war camps?

7. Explain the relationship between the value of money and the price level. If prices are rising rapidly, what happens to the usefulness of currency in serving the three functions of money?

8. For what two reasons do people wish to hold money? How are these two reasons related to the functions of money?

9. Explain the determinants of the two demands for money. Explain how changes in these determinants will affect the amount of money people want to hold.

10. Explain how the demand for money and the supply of money determine the interest rate. Explain how the money market adjusts if there is a shortage or a surplus of money.

11. Describe the relationship between the changes in the interest rate and changes in the price of existing bonds.

12. What roles do financial intermediaries play in a modern economy? How are chartered banks different from other financial intermediaries and how are they similar? Where do you have your "bank" account; at a chartered bank, or at a near bank? Why did you choose that one?

13. Banks are firms that seek to maximize profits for their shareholders. How do they go about doing this? What risks are there to the public?

14. Should the government permit mergers between chartered banks that already have large market shares in the Canadian banking industry?

15. How is the rise in electronic transactions changing the public's use of currency and cheques? How are these new payment mechanisms different from credit cards?

Answers

Quick Quiz
1. (a) p. 271
2. (b) p. 271
3. (a) pp. 272-273
4. (d) p. 275
5. (c) p. 276
6. (a) p. 277
7. (c) p. 277
8. (c) pp. 277-278
9. (b) p. 279
10. (c) p. 279
11. (d) p. 283
12. (d) p. 281
13. (d) p. 285

Fill-in Questions
1. (a) medium of exchange; (b) unit of account; (c) store of value
2. coins, paper money, demand deposits
3. liquid, exchange, currency, demand, are not
4. Bank of Canada, chartered banks
5. goods and services, inversely, price
6. (a) transactions, directly, nominal GDP; (b) asset, inversely, interest rate

True-False
1. F   chartered banks are responsible for issuing chequing deposits
2. T   without money, exchange would be by the inefficient barter system
3. F   this is its "unit of account" role
4. T
5. F   its face value exceeds its intrinsic value (the worth of the metal)
6. F   in Canada paper money is not redeemable into anything at all

7. F   this measure is the narrowest (least inclusive)

8. F   credit cards are not money

9. T

10. T

11. F   money demand shifts right, leading to an interest rate increase

12. T   a surplus of money means a shortage of bonds

13. T   causing society to resort to barter

14. F   no Canadian bank is among the 10 largest in the world

15. T   and thereby prevented some proposed mergers

Multiple-Choice

1. (d) in different times and societies

2. (a)

3. (c) a specialized economy is not viable without the means for efficient exchange of goods and services

4. (d) in other words, chequing accounts at banks

5. (c)

6. (d)

7. (b) this social confidence is vitally important

8. (c) though not backed by anything tangible, they are the debts of the Bank of Canada

9. (c) currency has increased $100, and demand deposits have decreased $100, so the total is unchanged

10. (d) M1 and M2 fall because they only include chartered bank deposits; M2+ is unchanged because the total deposits are unchanged (despite the transfer)

11. (d) so these coins were presumably melted down

12. (c)

13. (c)

14. (a)

15. (b) due to the transactions demand component

16. (c)

17. (a)

18. (b) transactions demand = 30, so asset demand must = 15 in order for total demand = supply = 45.

19. (b)

20. (d)

21. (c)   100/1000 = 10%; 100/800 = 12.5%

22. (d) the Bank of Canada does not deal with the general public

23. (c) for both chartered banks and certain other financial institutions

24. (c)

25. (d)

26. (c) implications of this are discussed in the next chapter

27. (d)

Problems and Projects

1. M1 = 99; M2 = 416; M2+ = 656 (note that currency at chartered banks is not included in any money supply definition)

2. (a) 4.8, 9.1, 16.7; (b) 5.3, 11.1, 25.0

3. (a)(2); (b)(4); (c)(3); (d)(1)

4. (a) M1, M2, M2+; (b) M2+; (c) none; (d) M2, M2+; (e) M2+; (f) none

5. (c)   4%; (d) excess supply = 250 – 200 = 50

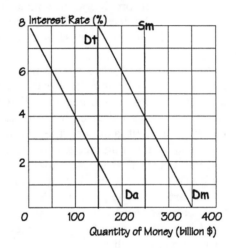

Chapter 12   How Banks Create Money

Overview

Chapter 11 showed that demand deposits at chartered banks are money. This chapter explains how chartered banks can create these deposits – and thereby create money! The principles behind this seemingly mysterious process are laid bare by the brief history of goldsmiths. Goldsmiths evolved from providers of simple safekeeping services to lenders who could issue paper money based on the gold stored in their vaults.

To explain banking operations we use a simple balance sheet, showing how each action changes assets and liabilities. Accounts listed on the left side of a firm's balance sheet are its assets, and on the right side are the claims on those assets: liabilities and net worth. Accounting principles dictate that assets must equal liabilities plus net worth. The balance sheet for Canadian chartered banks (see Table 11-2) shows that loans represent the majority of bank assets, and various kinds of deposits represent the majority of bank liabilities.

Whenever a bank has excess reserves it can create new deposits. The money creation process is explained in two scenarios: a single chartered bank, and the banking system (all banks as a group). The key difference is that the money-creating ability of the banking system as a whole is subject to a multiplier effect because the system as a whole does not lose reserves, whereas the money-creating ability of a single bank is not, because the bank must account for loss of reserves to other banks in the system.

The equilibrium level of deposits in the banking system is achieved through banks balancing the conflicting goals of profit and liquidity. Banks wish to create loans (and buy securities) in order to earn interest, but they also want to have enough liquidity (e.g., cash reserves) to be able to meet obligations to depositors. When a bank temporarily has excess reserves it may compromise by lending those funds to another bank on a day-to-day basis at the overnight loans rate.

Chapter Outline

12.1 Chartered Banks and the Creation of Money

⬦ How do chartered banks create (or destroy) money?

• The balance sheet of a chartered bank is a statement of its assets and claims on assets at a specific time. Claims on assets consist of claims by non-owners (liabilities) and claims by owners (net worth). Always, assets must equal liabilities plus net worth.

⮕ A balance sheet must balance. A bank's assets are either claimed by owners (net worth) or by non-owners (liabilities). Assets = liabilities + net worth. Use this principle to check both your calculations and your intuition when you work with balance sheets.

• Medieval goldsmiths operated like modern banks.
   o Traders deposited gold with a goldsmith in exchange for receipts which began to circulate in place of gold; in effect, the receipts became paper money.
   o Eventually goldsmiths realized that little of the gold deposited with them was ever withdrawn, so they began to create interest-earning loans by creating additional gold receipts.
   o Once loans were created, even though the receipts (paper money) could be redeemed for gold, these receipts were only fractionally backed by gold. Thus, there was always some risk of a bank panic.
   o Goldsmiths' receipts (and gold in their vaults) are analogous to chartered banks' demand deposits (and cash reserves).

⮑ The story of the goldsmith is superbly instructive because the scenario is easily understood and closely analogous to today's banking system, which seems much more difficult to understand.

• By seeing how the balance sheet of the chartered bank is affected by various transactions, one can understand how a single chartered bank in a multi-bank system can create money.
  o Initial transactions in the formation of a bank include capitalization by sale of shares, acquisition of property, and the acceptance of initial deposits from customers.
  o The chartered bank desires to keep some cash reserves for depositor withdrawals (usually as vault cash), and for cheque clearing (usually as deposits at the Bank of Canada). These reserves are referred to as desired reserves.
  o When a cheque is drawn against an account in one bank and deposited to an account at a second bank, the first bank loses reserves and deposits, and the second bank gains reserves and deposits.
• There are several key points about reserves.
  o Desired reserves are usually a percentage of deposits; this can be expressed as the desired reserve ratio.
  o Actual reserves of vault cash and deposits at the Bank of Canada may not equal desired reserves.
  o Excess reserves equal actual reserves less desired reserves.
  o Money creation depends upon the presence of excess reserves.
  o The Bank of Canada (as we learn more about in the next chapter) can influence the lending ability of chartered banks changing the amount of excess reserves.
• The next transactions are crucial for understanding money creation and destruction.
  o When a single bank extends loans or buys securities, it increases its own deposit liabilities (and, therefore, the supply of money) by the amount of the loan or security purchase. But the bank will lend or buy securities in an amount no more than its excess reserves because it anticipates a loss of reserves to other banks.
  o When a single bank receives loan payments or sells securities, its deposit li-

abilities decrease (and the money supply shrinks) by the same amount.
  o A bank balances its desire for profits (from interest earned on loans and securities) with its desire for liquidity or safety (which it achieves by having reserves). A bank may compromise somewhat when it temporarily has excess reserves by lending these funds to another bank at the overnight loans rate.

⮑ A chartered bank is "loaned up" (in equilibrium) when it has zero excess reserves, because then it has precisely balanced the conflicting goals of profit and liquidity. If we know a bank's desired reserve ratio, we can determine how many reserves a bank will desire for a given level of deposits, or we can determine how many deposits a bank can support with a given level of actual reserves.

⮑ In working with balance sheets, it is easy to confuse two different concepts of "balance." Since assets must always equal liabilities + net worth, the accounts will always balance, but this does not imply balance in the sense of equilibrium. That is, the bank is not necessarily satisfied with its present ratio of reserves to demand deposits just because its balance sheet is balanced.

Quick Quiz

1. Which is a liability for a chartered bank?
  (a) property
  (b) demand deposits
  (c) reserves
  (d) loans

2. A chartered bank creates money when it:
  (a) sells shares to investors
  (b) accepts deposits
  (c) deposits reserves at the Bank of Canada
  (d) creates loans

3. A chartered bank's assets and liabilities will both increase when the bank:
  (a) cashes a cheque against one of its customers' deposit accounts
  (b) spends reserves to buy government securities
  (c) receives loan repayments from borrowers
  (d) creates new loans that are deposited to borrowers' accounts

12.2   The Banking System: Multiple-Deposit Expansion

◈ How can the chartered banking system create money by a multiple of its excess reserves?

• The banking system taken as a whole can create an amount of new loans and deposit money greater than its excess reserves.

• Even though no single bank ever lends an amount greater than its excess reserves, the banking system as a whole **can** because, unlike a single bank, it does not lose reserves because a cheque written against one bank is deposited in another bank in the system. Accordingly reserves lost by one bank are gained by another.

• The banking system reaches equilibrium when it is "loaned up" such that actual reserves equal desired reserves.

Quick Quiz

4. The multiple-deposit expansion described in this section is possible because:
  (a)   each bank can lend more than its excess reserves
  (b)   one bank's lost reserves are gained by other banks
  (c)   people who take out loans are assumed to withdraw the loans in cash
  (d)   all of the above

5. Banks G and H have a desired reserve ratio of 10%. Bank G lends Mr. X $1000, which he transfers by cheque to Mrs. Y to pay for a horse. Mrs. Y deposits the cheque in Bank H. What will Bank H do as a result?
  (a)   create new loans of $900
  (b)   create new loans of $1000
  (c)   call in $900 worth of existing loans
  (d)   call in $1000 worth of existing loans

12.3   The Monetary Multiplier

◈ What is the monetary multiplier and how is it calculated?

• The monetary multiplier is equal to the reciprocal of the desired reserve ratio; the maximum expansion of demand deposits is equal to the excess reserves in the system times the monetary multiplier.

• The multiplier process applies to money destruction as well as money creation.

• Less new money will be created than the monetary multiplier suggests if there are leakages because borrowers choose to have addi-

tional currency or if bankers choose to have excess reserves.

• If bankers lend the maximum during periods of prosperity and less than the maximum during recessions, they add to the instability of the economy. To reduce the instability, the Bank of Canada must use monetary policy tools to control the money supply in a countercyclical way.

Quick Quiz

6. If chartered banks all have a desired reserve ratio of 8%, the monetary multiplier is:
  (a)   0.08
  (b)   0.125
  (c)   8.0
  (d)   12.5

7. One day while moving furniture, the staff at Alpha Bank find $100 behind a desk. This represents excess reserves. If all banks have a desired reserve ratio of 5%, the result will be the creation of new loans and deposits equal to:
  (a) $100 at Alpha Bank and a total of $1900 by all other banks combined
  (b) $100 at Alpha Bank and a total of $2000 by all other banks combined
  (c) $2000 at Alpha Bank and none by any other banks
  (d) $2000 at Alpha Bank and $2000 more by all other banks combined

8. The money-creating potential of reserves in the banking systems potentially is limited by:
  (a)   the banks' desire to hold reserves
  (b)   the public's desire to hold more cash
  (c)   the inability of banks to find suitable borrowers
  (d)   all of the above

Terms and Concepts

balance sheet
fractional reserve
vault cash
desired reserves
desired reserve ratio

excess reserves
actual reserves
liquidity
overnight loans rate
monetary multiplier

Fill-In Questions

1. Medieval goldsmiths issued receipts that could be redeemed for _____ but were also used as a medium of exchange. Therefore these receipts served as _____. Much like modern banks, the medieval goldsmiths operated on a _____ reserve system. Under such a system, banks (or medieval goldsmiths) are able to _____ money.

2. A bank _____ can occur when many depositors lose confidence in banks and decide to _____ large amounts of deposits.

3. Banks hold vault cash to meet the needs of depositors who wish to _____ cash.

4. The goal of _____ motivates banks to keep their reserves to a minimum, while the goal of _____ motivates banks to hold a prudent amount of reserves.

5. When a cheque is drawn upon bank X, deposited in bank Y, and cleared, the reserves of bank X are (increased, decreased, not changed) _____ and the reserves of bank Y are _____; deposits in bank X are _____, and deposits in bank Y are _____.

6. When a chartered bank sells a $2,000 government bond to a securities dealer, the supply of money (increases, decreases) _____ by $_____.

7. The banking system can make loans (or buy securities) and create money in an amount equal to its excess reserves multiplied by the _____. Its lending potential per dollar of excess reserves is greater than the lending potential of a single bank because it does not lose _____ to other banks.

8. If the desired reserve ratio is 5%, the banking system is $6 million short of reserves, and the banking system is unable to increase its reserves, the banking system must _____ the money supply by $_____. This can be accomplished by customers making _____ payments totalling this amount, or by banks selling this amount of _____ to the public. In either case, we assume that payments would be made by writing _____ that would result in (an increase, a decrease) _____ in the banks' _____ liabilities.

True-False

Circle T if the statement is true, F if it is false.

1. A chartered bank's assets plus its net worth equal the bank's liabilities. **T F**

2. Goldsmiths increased the money supply when they made loans and issued paper receipts that were not fully backed by gold in their vaults. **T F**

3. Chartered banks hold their reserves either as deposits in the Bank of Canada or as government bonds in their own vaults. **T F**

4. If the office owned by a bank increases in value, this will increase the bank's assets and bank owners' net worth. **T F**

5. A goldsmith might experience a bank panic if customers began to doubt whether the goldsmith would be able to redeem gold receipts. **T F**

6. An increase in a bank's deposit liabilities will increase the bank's desired reserve ratio. **T F**

7. The actual reserves of a chartered bank equal excess reserves plus desired reserves. **T F**

8. A cheque for $1,000 drawn on bank X by a depositor and deposited in bank Y will increase the excess reserves of bank Y by $1,000. **T F**

9. When a borrower repays a loan of $500, either in cash or by cheque, the supply of money is reduced by $500. **T F**

10. The monetary multiplier effect is reduced if the public wishes to hold more currency when their deposit balances increase. **T F**

11. The monetary multiplier is also known as the demand-deposit multiplier. **T F**

12. A chartered bank seeks both profits and liquidity, but these are conflicting goals. **T F**

Multiple-Choice

Circle the letter that corresponds to the best answer.

1. The fundamental balance identity is:
   (a)   assets = liabilities - net worth
   (b)   assets = liabilities + net worth
   (c)   assets = liabilities
   (d)   assets + liabilities = net worth

2. On a bank's balance sheet, loans are recorded as:
   (a)   part of net worth
   (b)   an asset
   (c)   a liability
   (d)   none of the above

3. The entry on the balance sheet of a bank that counts as part of the money supply is:
   (a)   cash held by the bank
   (b)   bank loans
   (c)   reserves held at the central bank
   (d)   demand deposits

4. On a bank's balance sheet, the entry for capital stock represents:
   (a)   cash reserves
   (b)   bank loans
   (c)   owners' equity
   (d)   government securities

5. The goldsmiths became bankers when:
   (a)   they accepted deposits of gold for safe storage
   (b)   they issued receipts for the gold stored with them
   (c)   their receipts for deposited gold were used as paper money
   (d)   they issued paper money in excess of the amount of gold stored with them

6. The immediate effect when cash is deposited in a deposit account in a chartered bank is:
   (a)   a decrease in the money supply
   (b)   an increase in the money supply
   (c)   no change in the composition of the money supply
   (d)   a change in the composition of the money supply

7. A chartered bank has actual reserves of $2,000 and deposit liabilities of $30,000; the de-sired reserve ratio is 5%. Excess reserves of the bank are:
   (a) $500
   (b) $0
   (c)   minus $1,000
   (d) $1,500

8. The basic reason that a chartered bank chooses to hold reserves is:
   (a)   to protect the chartered bank against losses from unpaid loans
   (b)   to maximize the bank's interest income
   (c)   to meet the Bank of Canada's regulations
   (d)   to provide liquidity for the chartered bank and protect it against a "run" on the bank

9. A depositor places $1,000 in cash in a char-tered bank, which has a desired reserve ratio of 5%. As a result, the reserves and excess reserves of the bank have been increased, respectively, by:
   (a) $1,000 and $50
   (b) $1,000 and $950
   (c) $1,000 and $1,000
   (d) $500 and $500

10. A chartered bank has no excess reserves, but then a depositor places $600 in cash in the bank, and the bank adds the $600 to its reserves. The bank then loans $300 to a borrower. The net effect is that the money supply has:
    (a)   not been affected
    (b)   increased by $300
    (c)   increased by $600
    (d)   increased by $900

11. A chartered bank has excess reserves of $500 and desires a reserve ratio of 10%; it grants a loan of $1,000. If the borrower writes a cheque for $1,000, which is deposited in another chartered bank, the first bank will be short of reserves, after the cheque has been cleared, in the amount of:
    (a) $100
    (b) $700
    (c) $500
    (d) $1,000

12. A chartered bank sells a $1,000 government security to a broker. The broker pays for the bond in cash, which the bank puts in its vault. Strictly by this transaction alone, the money supply has:
    (a)   not been affected
    (b)   decreased by $1,000
    (c)   increased by $1,000

(d) increased by $1,000 multiplied by the monetary multiplier

13. If the desired reserve ratio were 4%, the value of the monetary multiplier would be:
(a) 16
(b) 20
(c) 24
(d) 25

14. A chartered bank has deposit liabilities of $100,000, reserves of $37,000, and a desired reserve ratio of 25%. The amount by which a single chartered bank and the amount by which the banking system can increase loans are, respectively:
(a) $12,000 and $48,000
(b) $17,000 and $68,000
(c) $12,000 and $60,000
(d) $17,000 and $85,000

15. By making new loans of $7,000 the banking system eliminates its excess reserves of $700, and becomes "loaned up." The desired reserve ratio for this banking system must be:
(a) 5%
(b) 6.25%
(c) 8%
(d) 10%

16. The chartered banking system finds that its desired reserve ratio has risen from 5% to 6.25%, with the result that it is $100 million short of reserves. If it is unable to obtain any additional reserves, it must decrease its money supply by:
(a) $100 million
(b) $125 million
(c) $1,600 million
(d) $2,000 million

17. The money-creating potential of the banking system is reduced when:
(a) bankers choose to have excess reserves
(b) borrowers choose to hold none of the funds they have borrowed in currency
(c) bankers borrow from the Bank of Canada
(d) banks reduce their loan interest rates

18. The excess reserves held by banks tend to:
(a) rise during periods of prosperity
(b) fall during periods of recession
(c) rise during periods of recession

(d) fall when interest rates in the economy fall

19. Unless controlled, the money supply will:
(a) fall during periods of prosperity
(b) rise during periods of recession
(c) change in a fashion that reinforces cyclical fluctuations in the economy
(d) change in a fashion that counters cyclical fluctuations in the economy

Use the following balance sheet for the Maple Leaf Bank for questions 20 through 22. Assume the desired reserve ratio is 20%.

Assets		Liabilities and Net Worth	
Reserves	$50,000	Demand deposits	$150,000
Loans	70,000	Capital stock	100,000
Securities	30,000		
Property	100,000		

20. Maple Leaf Bank has excess reserves of:
(a) $10,000
(b) $20,000
(c) $30,000
(d) -$20,000

21. Maple Leaf Bank can safely expand its loans by a maximum of:
(a) $50,000
(b) $40,000
(c) $30,000
(d) $20,000

22. If the original bank balance sheet was for the chartered banking system, rather than just for Maple Leaf Bank, loans and deposits could have been expanded by a maximum of:
(a) $50,000
(b) $100,000
(c) $150,000
(d) $200,000

23. The overnight loans rate is:
(a) the interest rate on short term cash advances on credit cards
(b) the interest rate banks charge one another for short term loans of cash reserves
(c) the interest rate the Bank of Canada charges banks
(d) the percentage of cash reserves which chartered banks are willing to lend out

24. A bank is said to be "loaned up" when:
- (a)   it has no excess reserves
- (b)   it can find no more willing borrowers to take out new loans
- (c)   when all of its assets are invested in loans
- (d)   when all of its loans have been repaid

Questions 25 and 26 are based on the following consolidated balance sheet for the banking system. All figures are in billions. The desired reserve ratio is 12.5%.

Assets		Liabilities and Net Worth	
Reserves	$20	Demand deposits	$200
Loans	95	Capital stock	120
Securities	120		
Property	85		

25. This banking system will have to contract deposits by how much?
- (a) $5 billion
- (b) $20 billion
- (c) $25 billion
- (d) $40 billion

26. The required contraction of deposits could be accomplished by:
- (a)   calling in loans
- (b)   buying government securities
- (c)   reducing reserves
- (d)   any of the above

27. The formula for the monetary multiplier is given by $m = 1/R$, where R stands for:
- (a)   excess reserves
- (b)   the desired reserve ratio
- (c)   the marginal propensity to save
- (d)   the interest rate

28. The maximum deposit expansion for the whole banking system is found by multiplying the volume of excess reserves by:
- (a)   the desired reserve ratio
- (b)   1 minus the desired reserve ratio
- (c)   the monetary multiplier
- (d)   the reciprocal of the interest rate

Problems and Projects

1. Classifying Bank Assets and Liabilities
Indicate whether each item following would be listed under the assets (A) or under the liabilities + net worth (L) of a bank's balance sheet.

- (a)   A government bond held by the bank   ___
- (b)   A mortgage loan to a homeowner   ___
- (c)   The computer owned by the bank   ___
- (d)   Demand deposits   ___
- (e)   Cash held in a bank vault   ___
- (f)   A government deposit held in the bank   ___
- (g)   Reserves held at the Bank of Canada   ___
- (h)   Common stock issued by the bank   ___

2. Banking Transactions on the Balance Sheet
Following is the simplified balance sheet of a chartered bank. Assume that the figures given show the bank's situation prior to each of the following four transactions. Fill in the blanks in each column to show the balance sheet effects of the corresponding transaction. For each transaction, start from the "initial" figures.

	Initial	(a)	(b)	(c)	(d)
Assets					
Reserves	$100	$___	$___	$___	$___
Loans	700	___	___	___	___
Securities	200	___	___	___	___
Liabilities					
& net worth					
Deposits	900	___	___	___	___
Capital	100	100	100	100	100

(a) A cheque for $50 is written by a depositor of the bank, and given to a person who deposits it in another bank, and then cleared.

(b) The bank loans $40 to a customer, and deposits the $40 into the customer's account.

(c) A cheque for $60 drawn on another bank is deposited in this bank and cleared.

(d) The bank sells $100 of government bonds to the Bank of Canada.

3. Deposit Creation by a Single Bank
In the table below are four balance sheets for a single chartered bank [columns (1)-(4)]. The desired reserve ratio is 20%.

(a) In the opening situation shown in column (1), compute the following amounts: desired reserves = $____, excess reserves = $____, and new loans that can be extended = $____

(b) Fill in column (2) showing the bank's new balance sheet after the bank has extended the maximum amount of new loans, and has deposited the funds in borrowers' deposit accounts.

(c) Fill in column (3) showing the bank's new balance sheet after the borrowers have spent the funds just borrowed, assuming that they do so by writing cheques to people who are customers of other banks.

(d) Given the situation shown in column (3), confirm that the bank is "loaned up" and incapable of further expansion deposits and loans.

	(1)	(2)	(3)
Assets			
Reserves	$50	$____	$____
Loans	100	____	____
Securities	50	____	____
Liabilities & net worth			
Deposits	175	____	____
Capital	25	____	____

4. Monetary Multiplier

Suppose that banks desire a 4% reserve ratio.

(a) What is the size of the monetary multiplier?

____

(b) What is the maximum amount of new loans and deposits that a single bank could create if they had $1 of excess reserves? $____

(c) What is the maximum amount of new loans and deposits that the whole banking system could create if one bank had $1 of excess reserves? $____

(d) How many excess reserves would have to exist in the banking system to make possible the creation of $75 of new loans and deposit money? $____

5. Deposit Creation by a Banking System

Following is the simplified consolidated balance sheet for all chartered banks in the economy. Assume that the figures given show the bank's assets and liabilities prior to each of the following three transactions, and that the desired reserve ratio is 5%. For each of the three transactions ((a), (b), and (c)), start with the figures in the "initial" column.

(a) The public deposits $5 in cash in the banks, and the banks keep the cash in their vaults. Fill in column 1. Fill in column 2 on the assumption that the banking system extends the maximum amount of new loans.

(b) The banking system sells $8 worth of securities to the Bank of Canada in exchange for new reserves. Complete column 3. Assuming the system extends the maximum amount of loans that it can, fill in column 4.

(c) The Bank of Canada sells $1 worth of securities to the chartered banks. Complete column 5. Complete column 6 showing the condition of the banks after they have contracted their loans by the amount necessary to meet the desired reserve ratio.

	initial	(1)	(2)	(3)	(4)	(5)	(6)
Assets:							
Reserves	$25	$__	$__	$__	$__	$__	$__
Loans	425	__	__	__	__	__	__
Securities	100	__	__	__	__	__	__
Liabilities & net worth							
Deposits	500	__	__	__	__	__	__
Capital	50	50	50	50	50	50	50

6. Cheque Clearing

Imagine a banking system with only three chartered banks: the Bank of Charlottetown, Newfoundland Marine Bank, and the Moncton Bank. Through the Canadian Payments Association, the three banks settle claims against one another as follows:

Charlottetown depositors wrote cheques to Newfoundland depositors = $20

Charlottetown depositors wrote cheques to Moncton depositors = $80

Newfoundland depositors wrote cheques to Charlottetown depositors = $50

Newfoundland depositors wrote cheques to Moncton depositors = $60

Moncton depositors wrote cheques to Charlottetown depositors = $30

Moncton depositors wrote cheques to Newfoundland depositors = $70.

(a) How much do the inter-bank clearing settlements increase or decrease each bank's reserves: Bank of Charlottetown: $____; Newfoundland Marine Bank: $____; Moncton Bank: $____

(b) How much will each bank expand or contract their deposits (and loan or security holdings), assuming the maximum effects?

Bank of Charlottetown: $____
Newfoundland Marine Bank: $____
Moncton Bank: $____

(c) Ultimately, what is the net effect on the money supply of this shuffling of reserves among the three banks? $_____

Discussion Questions

1. List and explain each category of assets and liabilities in the simplified balance sheet of a bank.

2. How did the early goldsmiths come to issue paper money and then become bankers? Explain the difference between 100% and a fractional reserve system of banking, and why the latter system is subject to bank panics and may require public regulation.

3. Chartered banks seek both profits and liquidity. Why are the two objectives in conflict?

4. Why does it work for banks to hold only fractional reserves? What might be some reasons that the desired reserve ratio might change from time to time?

5. Why does the granting of a loan by a chartered bank increase the supply of money? Why does the repayment of a loan decrease the money supply?

6. The owner of a ski shop writes a cheque on his account in a Banff bank and sends it to one of his suppliers, who deposits it in a different bank in Calgary. How does the Calgary bank obtain payment from the Banff bank? How are the reserves of the two banks affected?

7. Why is a single bank able to loan safely an amount equal to only its excess reserves, while the banking system as a whole can extend loans and expand the money supply by an amount that is a multiple of the system's excess reserves? How does such a multiple expansion of deposits (that is, money) take place?

8. What are two reasons why the potential expansion of the money supply – as according to the monetary multiplier – may not be fully achieved?

9. Why is there a "need for monetary control" in the Canadian economy?

10. Why is there a need for deposit insurance?

Answers

Quick Quiz
1. (b) p. 292
2. (d) pp. 294-295
3. (d) p. 295
4. (b) pp. 298-300
5. (a) pp. 298-300
6. (d) p. 300
7. (a) p. 300
8. (d) pp. 301-302

Fill-in Questions
1. gold, money, fractional, create
2. panic (failure), withdraw
3. withdraw
4. profitability, liquidity
5. decreased, increased, decreased, increased
6. decreases, 2,000
7. monetary multiplier, reserves
8. decrease, 120 million, loan, securities, cheques, decrease, deposit

True-False
1. F   assets = liabilities + net worth
2. T
3. F   government bonds are not considered reserves; only cash and deposits at the Bank of Canada qualify
4. F
5. T
6. F   this would increase the amount of actual and desired reserves, but not the desired reserve ratio
7. T
8. F   Bank Y will have excess reserves but only $1,000 less whatever the desired reserves are for the added $1,000 in deposits
9. T   either currency in circulation or demand deposits decrease by $500
10. T   currency drain is a leakage from the monetary multiplier
11. T
12. T

Multiple-Choice
1. (b)
2. (b)   the loans are owed to the bank
3. (d)
4. (c)   the owners' claims on the firm's assets

5. (d) this represents fractional reserve banking

6. (d) the total money supply does not change, but the composition (deposits vs. currency) does

7. (a) 30,000 x .05 = 1,500; 2,000 – 1,500 = 500

8. (d) they must be able to meet depositors' demands for withdrawals

9. (b) because $50 of the $1,000 is desired reserves against the new deposit

10. (b) the initial deposit had no net effect on the money supply, but the loan increases it

11. (c) the bank loses $1,000 in reserves

12. (b) currency in circulation has decreased by $1,000

13. (d) 1/.04 = 25

14. (a) R = 25%, so the monetary multiplier is 4

15. (d) if excess reserves can be turned into 10 times as much in new loans and deposits

16. (c) 1/.0625 = 16

17. (a) excess reserves are a leakage from the multiplier process

18. (c) because there are less qualified borrowers

19. (c) this procyclical tendency creates a need for monetary control by the Bank of Canada

20. (b) 150,000 x .20 = 30,000; 50,000 – 30,000

21. (d) the amount of their excess reserves

22. (b) excess reserves x monetary multiplier

23. (b)

24. (a) its actual reserve ratio = its desired reserve ratio

25. (d) shortage of reserves x monetary multiplier

26. (a) borrowers will use up demand deposits to make loan payments

27. (b)

28. (c)

Problems and Projects

1. (a) A; (b) A; (c) A; (d) L; (e) A; (f) L; (g) A; (h) L

2.

	(a)	(b)	(c)	(d)
Assets:				
Reserves	50	100	160	200
Loans	700	740	700	700
Securities	200	200	200	100
Liabilities and net worth:				
Deposits	850	940	960	900

3. (a) 35, 15, 15; (b) entries down column (2): 50, 115, 50, 190, 25; (c) entries down column (3): 35, 115, 50, 175, 25; (d) Deposits = 175, and Reserves = 35 = 20% of 175.

4. (a) 25; (b) 1; (c) 25; (d) 3

5.

	(1)	(2)	(3)	(4)	(5)	(6)
Assets:						
Reserves	$30	$30	$33	$33	$24	$24
Loans	425	520	425	585	425	405
Securities	100	100	92	92	101	101
Liabilities and net worth:						
Deposits	505	600	500	660	500	480

6. (a) Charlottetown pays $50 to Moncton, and receives $30 from Newfoundland = net reserve decrease of $20; Newfoundland pays $30 to Charlottetown, and receives $10 from Moncton = net reserve decrease of $20; Moncton: receives $50 from Charlottetown, and pays $10 to Newfoundland = net reserve increase of $40;

(b) Charlottetown: contract by $20; Newfoundland: contract by $20; Moncton: expand by $40;

(c) No change, since the banking system as a whole experiences neither loss nor gain of reserves.

Chapter 13

The Bank of Canada and Monetary Policy

Overview

This, the last of three chapters on money and banking, explains how the Bank of Canada uses monetary policy — the control of the money supply — to fight macroeconomic fluctuations and attain full employment GDP without inflation.

The Bank of Canada has five functions: (1) acting as a "bankers' bank" when chartered banks need to borrow extra reserves; (2) issuing paper currency; (3) acting as fiscal agent for the federal government; (4) supervising the chartered banks; and (5) regulating the supply of money. The last one is the most important from a macroeconomic standpoint, and is the focus of the chapter.

The central bank implements monetary policy by influencing short-term interest rates. By changing the reserves of chartered banks the Bank of Canada induces chartered banks to change the level of deposits. The two main instruments for this are open-market operations and government deposit switching. In open-market operations the Bank of Canada buys or sells securities in the open market. For example, to expand the money supply the Bank of Canada will buy securities, paying for them by creating deposits at the Bank of Canada. These newly created deposits are reserves for the chartered banks, and enable them to make new loans and deposits that expand the money supply. If the Bank of Canada switches some of the government's deposits from itself to chartered banks, the result will be the same. A third method of influencing the money supply is to change the bank rate — the interest rate that the Bank of Canada charges chartered banks for advances of reserves. Since 1996 the bank rate has been based on the upper limit of its operating band for the overnight loans rate.

The cause-effect chain from money supply changes to changes in employment, output, and inflation is called the transmission mechanism.

Consider the case of an expansionary monetary policy. When chartered banks get new excess reserves they will create new deposit money, leading to a surplus of money and shortage of bonds. As people try to buy more bonds, bond prices rise and interest rates fall. Lower interest rates stimulate investment spending, causing AD to expand, and the equilibrium levels of employment, output, and prices to rise. The Bank of Canada signals tighter or easier monetary policy by announcing changes in the target overnight lending rate.

As with fiscal policy, the effectiveness of monetary policy is subject to several complications. There are time lags, but less so for monetary policy than fiscal policy. Monetary policy is weakened if fluctuations in the velocity of money's circulation weaken the link between AD and the money supply. Monetary policy is more effective for stemming inflationary pressures than for pulling the economy out of recession. Whether the Bank of Canada's approach of announcing inflation targets is helpful is debatable.

Linkages between Canada and foreign economies also pose complications. Expansionary monetary policy will lower domestic interest rates, and thereby reduce capital inflows. Less financial investment from abroad means less demand for the Canadian dollar, so the dollar will depreciate, boosting our net exports. This net export effect reinforces the demand stimulus intended by the expansionary monetary policy but may also work against achieving a balance of trade.

Chapter Outline

13.1 Functions of the Bank of Canada

◈ What are the main functions of the Bank of Canada?

- The Bank of Canada has five functions:

- to serve as the "bankers' bank," settling payment balances among chartered banks and lending them reserves if needed
- to supply paper currency to the economy;
- to act as fiscal agent for the federal government;
- to supervise chartered banks;
- to regulate the supply of money to help the economy enjoy high rates of economic growth with stable prices.

• To understand how monetary policy works, it is necessary to understand the assets and liabilities on the balance sheet of the Bank of Canada.

- The main assets are Government of Canada securities (bonds and Treasury bills), and advances (normally very short-term loans) to chartered banks.
- The main liabilities are bank notes in circulation (currency), reserve deposits of chartered banks, and Government of Canada deposits.

Quick Quiz

1. Which of its functions deals with the Bank of Canada's main policy-setting responsibility?
(a) issuer of currency
(b) supervisor of chartered banks
(c) fiscal agent
(d) money supply regulator

2. When the Bank of Canada manages the marketing of the federal government's bonds, which function is it fulfilling?
(a) issuer of currency
(b) bankers' bank
(c) fiscal agent
(d) money supply regulator

3. The vast majority of the Bank of Canada's liabilities consist of:
(a) Treasury bills
(b) Government of Canada securities
(c) advances to chartered banks
(d) notes in circulation

13.2 Goals and Tools of Monetary Policy

◇ What are the goals and tools of monetary policy?

• The objective of monetary policy is to keep inflation low, stable and predictable to help moderate the business cycle and move the economy closer to full employment and sustained economic growth.

• The Bank of Canada currently has an inflation target of 1 to 3 percent annually.

• To achieve its goals the Bank of Canada manipulates the level of chartered banks' excess reserves, inducing the banks to change their levels of deposits. This changes the money supply.

• The Bank of Canada implements monetary policy through its influence on short-term interest rates and by altering chartered bank reserves. For this task it has three instruments:

- open-market operations, through which the Bank of Canada buys and sells government securities;
- government deposit switching, through which the Bank of Canada switches Government of Canada bank deposits between itself and the chartered banks;
- bank rate changes, through which the Bank of Canada makes it more or less attractive for chartered banks to borrow reserves.

• In a recession the Bank of Canada will pursue an easy money policy to stimulate aggregate demand. The policy choices available are:

- through open-market operations, to buy securities, which increases chartered banks' reserves;
- to switch government deposits to the chartered banks, which increases chartered banks' reserves;
- to lower the bank rate, which increases the willingness of chartered banks to borrow reserves short term from the Bank of Canada.

• During an inflationary gap the Bank of Canada will follow a tight money policy to restrain aggregate demand. The policy options are:

- through open-market operations to sell government securities, causing the chartered banks to give up reserves.
- to switch government deposits away from chartered banks, along with the reserves.
- to raise the bank rate, discouraging chartered banks from borrowing as many reserves.

• As "lender of last resort" the Bank of Canada occasionally makes short-term loans of reserves to chartered banks. The interest rate on such loans is the bank rate. When the Bank of Canada lends and borrows in the overnight loans market, it affects the availability of reserves and the chartered banks' ability to create deposits.

• Of the three policy instruments open-market operations is the most important. The Bank of Canada uses switching of government deposits relatively rarely and bank rate changes are more of a signaling device.

Quick Quiz

4. Open-market operations refers to actions by the Bank of Canada to:
 (a) buy or sell bonds
 (b) raise or lower the bank rate
 (c) make loans to the public
 (d) switch government deposits to or from it-self

5. The Bank of Canada is applying easy money policy when it:
 (a) sells bonds
 (b) switches government deposits to the chartered banks
 (c) raises the bank rate
 (d) none of the above

6. How does the Bank of Canada signal to financial markets when it is tightening monetary policy?
 (a) it raises the bank rate
 (b) it buys Government of Canada securities
 (c) to provides more advances to chartered banks
 (d) it reduces the amount of notes in circulation

13.3   Monetary Policy, Real GDP, and Price Level

◈ What is the transmission mechanism by which monetary policy affects real GDP and the price level?

• The cause-effect chain from monetary policy changes to changes in equilibrium GDP and price level is known as the transmission mechanism, and is summarized as follows:
 o In the money market the demand curve and the supply curve determine the equilibrium interest rate.
 o The investment-demand curve and the equilibrium rate of interest determine planned investment.

 o Planned investment helps determine the level of the aggregate demand curve (and the aggregate expenditures curve).
 o The intersection of aggregate supply and aggregate demand determines the equilibrium GDP and price level.

• In the case of a recessionary gap, the Bank of Canada adopts an easy money policy. It increases the money supply, causing the interest rate to fall and investment spending to increase, thereby increasing real GDP by a multiple of the increase in investment.

• In the case of an inflationary gap, the Bank of Canada adopts a tight money policy. It decreases the money supply, causing the interest rate to rise and investment spending to decrease, thereby reducing inflation.

• As with fiscal policy, the impact of a particular monetary policy will depend on the aggregate supply conditions. The flatter the AS is, the greater is the effect of a change in the money supply on real GDP and the smaller is the effect on the price level. If there is no monetary policy (or fiscal policy) action when there is a recessionary or inflationary gap, the short-run aggregate supply curve will eventually shift to close the gap.

• In Canada today monetary policy is a more important stabilization policy than fiscal policy. Compared to fiscal policy it works more quickly and flexibly, and is much less subject to political pressure.

• Since 1996 the bank rate has been set at 1/2% above the prevailing overnight loans rate in the money market. The Bank of Canada publicizes a target range for the overnight loans rate.

• The Bank of Canada does not set the overnight rate or prime rate; both are set by the market interaction between borrowers and lenders. However, by altering the availability of reserves the Bank of Canada can influence these interest rates.

• The Bank of Canada typically conducts open-market operations by buying and selling Government of Canada securities in the overnight loans market through "special purchase and resale agreements" (SPRA).

• Throughout much of the last decade the Bank of Canada has been able to follow expansionary monetary policy with few interruptions, and has been successful in maintaining quite strong economic growth while also keeping inflation well within the Bank of Canada's target range.

➲ The transmission mechanism is crucial. Be sure that you can explain it thoroughly, and that you can draw the three graphs that illustrate all of the linkages: the money market graph, the investment-demand graph, and the aggregate supply and aggregate demand graph.

Quick Quiz

7. Suppose the Bank of Canada implements a tight money policy. Which of the following would not be one of the events in the transmission mechanism?
(a)   excess reserves decrease
(b)   money supply falls
(c)   interest rate rises
(d)   investment spending increases

8. An easy money policy will produce results including:
(a)   increasing price level
(b)   increasing interest rate
(c)   decreased excess reserves
(d)   decreased money supply

9. Which statement best describes the Bank of Canada's influence in the overnight lending market?
(a)   the Bank of Canada influences interest rates by influencing the level of reserves
(b)   the Bank of Canada has no influence over the overnight lending rate
(c)   the Bank of Canada sets the prime rate
(d)   the Bank of Canada sets the overnight lending rate

13.4   Problems and Complications

◈ What limitations and complications does monetary policy face in the real world?

•   Monetary policy is hindered by a recognition lag and an operational lag.
•   There is a stable relationship between aggregate demand and the supply of money only if the velocity of money's circulation is stable. Fluctuations in velocity may counteract the intended impact of monetary policy.
•   Monetary policy is prone to a cyclical asymmetry in that it is more effective in slowing expansions and controlling inflations than in stimulating the economy when in recession.

•   Some economists credit much of the Bank of Canada's recent successes to their current policy of setting and announcing inflation targets (currently 1% to 3% per year). The increased transparency and accountability may have helped to convince the public to adopt expectations of low inflation. Others credit the success with underlying economic conditions and would actually prefer the Bank of Canada to take a more active role in the economy.

Quick Quiz

10. Which lag is a more serious problem for fiscal policy than for money policy?
(a)   recognition lag
(b)   decision lag
(c)   operational lag
(d)   legislation lag

11. The issue of cyclical asymmetry has to do with the Bank of Canada's ability to:
(a)   increase reserves vs. decrease reserves
(b)   increase interest rates vs. decrease interest rates
(c)   increase AD vs. decrease AD
(d)   sell bonds vs. buy bonds

13.5   Monetary Policy and the International Economy

◈ How do linkages with the international economy affect the operation of monetary policy?

•   Expansionary monetary policy will decrease Canadian interest rates, thereby decreasing the amount of capital inflows from abroad. Demand for the Canadian dollar will fall, and the dollar will depreciate, causing increased demand for Canada's exports, and decreased demand for imports. In summary, this net export effort will reinforce the expansionary effect on AD of an expansionary monetary policy.
•   A widely held economic goal is that Canada should balance its exports and imports. A monetary policy appropriate for alleviating a domestic stabilization problem could either complement or conflict with the goal of balanced trade.
•   To sum up the models presented in Chapters 6 through 13, the equilibrium levels of real GDP, employment, and prices are determined by aggregate supply and aggregate demand.

o There are four expenditure components of AD: consumption, planned investment, government, and net exports.

o The three major determinants of AS are: input prices, productivity, and legal-institutional environment.

o Fiscal, monetary, or other government policies may effect either AD or AS, and thereby influence the level of real GDP, employment and prices.

• John Taylor proposes an alternative to central banks taking either a passive, rules-based approach or an activist, discretionary approach to fight business cycles. The Taylor rule would require the central bank to apply a certain monetary policy change whenever the GDP rises above potential, or the inflation rate rises above its target. The central bank would still retain authority to override the rule.

➲ Figure 13-4 is an excellent tool for preparing for the final exam. It is a comprehensive diagram of all of the macroeconomic models and theories from previous chapters.

Quick Quiz

12. When the Bank of Canada applies a tight money policy, which is not part of the resulting net export effect?
  (a) rising interest rates
  (b) increased foreign demand for our dollars
  (c) depreciation of our dollar
  (d) drop in net exports

13. Suppose the nation desires full employment and price stability, and desires a balance of trade. In which situation would an easy money policy be appropriate in terms of both goals?
  (a) inflationary gap and trade deficit
  (b) inflationary gap and trade surplus
  (c) recessionary gap and trade deficit
  (d) recessionary gap and trade surplus

Terms and Concepts

monetary policy	overnight lending rate
open-market opera- tions	easy money policy
	tight money policy
government deposit switching	velocity of money
	cyclical asymmetry
bank rate	deflation
operating band	inflation targeting

Fill-In Questions

1. The objective of monetary policy in Canada is to help achieve and maintain a _____, _____ level of total output. The institution responsible for these monetary policies is the _____.

2. As fiscal agent for the federal government, the Bank of Canada helps the government collect _____, and administers the sale and redemption of government _____.

3. In open-market operations, the Bank of Canada buys and sells _____ in the open market in order to change the level of chartered banks' _____, and therefore influence the amount of new _____ that chartered banks can create.

4. If the Bank of Canada sells $10 million in government bonds to the public, who pays for them by cheque, and the desired reserve ratio is 5%, the supply of money is immediately reduced by $_____, the reserves of the chartered banks are immediately reduced by $_____, and the excess reserves of the banks are immediately reduced by $_____. But if these bonds are sold to the chartered banks instead, the supply of money is immediately reduced by $_____, the reserves of the banks are immediately reduced by $_____, and the excess reserves of the banks are immediately reduced by $_____. In either case, the final net effect on the money supply will be a reduction of $_____ if the maximum money multiplier effects take place.

5. Suppose that the Bank of Canada buys government securities in the open market. Complete the chain of effects by indicating increase (+) or decrease (-) in each case:
  (a) chartered bank reserves   ☐
  (b) chartered bank deposit liabilities ☐
  (c) money supply   ☐
  (d) interest rate   ☐
  (e) planned investment   ☐
  (f) aggregate demand   ☐
  (g) price level and real GDP level   ☐

6. Beginning from an equilibrium in the money market, a decrease in the supply of money will cause a (surplus, shortage) _____ of money, and a _____ of bonds and other interest-

bearing assets. This causes the prices of bonds to be bid (down, up) _____, and interest rates to (fall, rise) _____. This in turn, would cause investment spending, aggregate demand, and output to _____. This action by the Bank of Canada would be considered a(n) _____ monetary policy.

7. Expansionary monetary policy will push interest rates (down, up) _____, which in turn (increases, decreases) _____ the demand for the domestic currency. Therefore, the currency will (appreciate, depreciate) _____, leading net exports to (increase, decrease) _____. This net export effect (reinforces, counteracts) _____ the intended expansionary effect of the monetary policy.

True-False

Circle T if the statement is true, F if it is false.

1. Paper currency is among the main assets of the Bank of Canada. **T F**

2. Chartered banks' deposits held at the Bank of Canada are assets for the chartered banks and liabilities for the Bank of Canada. **T F**

3. The Bank of Canada's policies are determined by the federal Minister of Finance. **T F**

4. When the Bank of Canada sells bonds in the open market, the price of these bonds falls. **T F**

5. As the "lender of last resort," the Bank of Canada makes short-term loans of cash reserves to chartered banks. **T F**

6. If the Bank of Canada wished to follow a contractionary monetary policy, it would seek to reduce the reserves of the chartered banks. **T F**

7. The major instrument of monetary policy is changes in the prime rate of interest. **T F**

8. When the Bank of Canada switches government deposits from itself to the chartered banks, the reserves of the chartered banks will be decreased. **T F**

9. Monetary policy is more effective in fighting recession than it is in curbing inflation. **T F**

10. It is generally agreed that fiscal policy is more effective than monetary policy in controlling the business cycle because fiscal policy is more flexible. **T F**

11. When the Bank of Canada enters into a special purchase and resale agreement (SPRA) it intends to put downward pressure on short-term interest rates. **T F**

12. If no monetary policy or fiscal policy is used to close an inflationary gap, the AS curve will eventually shift leftward to close the gap. **T F**

13. Monetary policy is weakened if the velocity of money's circulation decreases when the money supply is expanded. **T F**

14. When the AS curve is very steep, expansionary monetary policy has more impact on real GDP than on prices. **T F**

15. If the economy has a trade surplus and a recessionary gap, an expansionary monetary policy is compatible with both the domestic stabilization goal and the balance of trade goal. **T F**

Multiple-Choice

Circle the letter that corresponds to the best answer.

1. The agency directly responsible for monetary policy in Canada is:
(a) the Canadian Bankers' Association
(b) the Bank of Canada
(c) the Parliament of Canada
(d) the Department of Finance

2. The largest single asset on the Bank of Canada's balance sheet is:
(a) government securities
(b) loans
(c) notes in circulation
(d) chartered banks' deposits

3. All of the following are functions of the Bank of Canada with the exception of:
(a) acting as fiscal agent of the government

(b)   holding deposits of the chartered banks
(c)   regulating the supply of money
(d)   determining the prime rate of interest

4. Open-market operations refer to:
(a)   the buying and selling of government bonds by the Bank of Canada
(b)   the buying and selling of government bonds by the chartered banks
(c)   the buying and selling of stocks and bonds by the Bank of Canada
(d)   the shifting of government deposits to and from the chartered banks by the Bank of Canada.

5. Which of the following is not one of the tools of monetary policy used by the Bank of Canada?
(a)   switching of government deposits
(b)   open-market operations
(c)   setting the bank rate
(d)   setting the required reserve ratio

6. Which of the following acts would not change the money supply in the same direction as the other three?
(a)   the Bank of Canada sells bonds to chartered banks
(b)   the Bank of Canada raises the bank rate
(c)   the Bank of Canada shifts government deposits to the chartered banks
(d)   the Bank of Canada sells bonds to the public

7. If the Bank of Canada sells $20 million in government securities to chartered banks who have a desired reserve ratio of 10%, then the potential change on the money supply is:
(a)   an increase of $20 million
(b)   an increase of $200 million
(c)   a decrease of $20 million
(d)   a decrease of $200 million

8. In the transmission mechanism between changes in the excess reserves of chartered banks and the resulting changes in real GDP and prices:
(a)   an increase in excess reserves will decrease the money supply
(b)   a decrease in the money supply will increase the rate of interest
(c)   an increase in the rate of interest will increase aggregate demand
(d)   an increase in aggregate expenditures will decrease real GDP and prices

9. To contract the money supply, the Bank of Canada could:
(a)   buy bonds or switch government deposits away from chartered banks
(b)   sell bonds or switch government deposits away from chartered banks
(c)   buy bonds or switch government deposits into chartered banks
(d)   sell bonds or switch government deposits into chartered banks

10. If the Bank of Canada decides to buy government bonds, the demand for government bonds will:
(a)   decrease, bond prices will decrease, and the interest rate will decrease
(b)   increase, bond prices will increase, and the interest rate will decrease
(c)   increase, bond prices will increase, and the interest rate will increase
(d)   decrease, bond prices will increase, and the interest rate will decrease

11. Compared to fiscal policy, monetary policy is:
(a)   more subject to political interference
(b)   more direct in its effects on aggregate demand
(c)   used less frequently
(d)   more quickly altered

12. An expansionary monetary policy:
(a)   reduces the supply of money, increases the interest rate, reduces investment, and reduces the equilibrium GDP
(b)   increases the money supply, reduces the rate of interest, increases investment, and reduces the equilibrium GDP
(c)   reduces the money supply, reduces the rate of interest, increases investment, and increases the equilibrium GDP
(d)   increases the money supply, reduces the interest rate, increases investment, and increases the equilibrium GDP

13. The transmission mechanism through which monetary policy affects aggregate demand is primarily through:
(a)   consumption spending
(b)   investment spending
(c)   government spending
(d)   net exports

14. At the time the text was written, the Bank of Canada's inflation target range was:
- (a)   -1% to 1% per year
- (b)   0% to 2% per year
- (c)   1% to 3% per year
- (d)   2% to 4% per year

15. Suppose there is a recessionary gap which the Bank of Canada attacks with a policy of easy money. The policy effort may be ineffective if:
- (a)   the velocity of money slows down
- (b)   the investment demand curve shifts left due to dismal prospects for businesses
- (c)   households are unwilling to take out more loans, or use loans to retire existing debt
- (d)   any of the above

16. Which statement regarding the overnight lending rate is false?
- (a)   the Bank of Canada sets an operating band for the overnight rate
- (b)   changes in the overnight rate generally signal that the Bank of Canada is moving to tighter or easier monetary policy
- (c)   the Bank of Canada directly dictates the overnight rate
- (d)   the Bank of Canada influences the over-night rate by buying or selling bonds

17. SPRA stands for:
- (a)   special purchase and resale agreement
- (b)   social policy research action
- (c)   special projects research agency
- (d)   special political redemption agreement

18. The bank rate is currently set:
- (a)   at the upper limit of the Bank of Canada's operating band for the overnight rate
- (b)   ¼ percentage point above the yield on Treasury bills, set after a weekly auction
- (c)   halfway between the prime rate and the overnight lending rate
- (d)   ¼ percentage point above the overnight lending rate

19. When Canada's money supply expands, the net export effect:
- (a)   increases AD, because the interest rate falls, causing depreciation of the dollar
- (b)   increases AD, because the interest rate falls, causing appreciation of the dollar
- (c)   decreases AD, because the interest rate falls, causing depreciation of the dollar
- (d)   decreases AD, because the interest rate rises, causing appreciation of the dollar

20. In which situation would a tight money policy help to resolve both the domestic stabilization problem and the balance of trade problem?
- (a)   inflationary gap and trade surplus
- (b)   inflationary gap and trade deficit
- (c)   recessionary gap and trade surplus
- (d)   recessionary gap and trade deficit

21. The phrase "pushing versus pulling on a string" is used in reference to:
- (a)   the difference between buying and selling bonds
- (b)   the cyclical asymmetry of monetary policy
- (c)   the effectiveness of fiscal policy compared to monetary policy
- (d)   the lags in the use of monetary policy

22. By the Taylor rule, the Bank of Canada should:
- (a)   raise the overnight rate if GDP rises 1% above potential GDP
- (b)   raise the overnight rate if inflation rises by 1% above its target rate
- (c)   both of the above
- (d)   allow the money supply to grow by a steady percentage every year

Problems and Projects

1. Open-Market Operations

The consolidated balance sheet of the chartered banks and the balance sheet of the Bank of Canada are shown below. The chartered banks have a desired reserve ratio of 10%.

(a) Initially, demand deposits are $____ and the currency in circulation is $____, so the money supply is $____.

(b) Suppose that the Bank of Canada conducts open-market operations by purchasing $10 in government securities directly from chartered banks. In the (b) columns of the two balance sheets show the immediate results prior to the chartered banks making any adjustments to restore their desired reserve ratio.

(c) The money supply immediately after the open-market operation is $____.

(d) In the (d) columns, show the balance sheet entries after the chartered banks create as many new loans and deposits as they can, consistent with their desired reserve ratio.

(e) The money supply after this is $_____.

(f) Since an increase of $____ in bank reserves increased the money supply by $___, the monetary multiplier in this case is _____.

CHARTERED BANKS		(b)	(d)
Assets			
Reserves	$50	____	____
Government Securities	100	____	____
Loans	350	____	____
Liabilities			
Demand deposits	500	____	____

BANK OF CANADA		(b)	(d)
Assets			
Government Securities	$300	____	____
Liabilities			
Reserves of banks	50	____	____
Government deposits	100	____	____
Bank of Canada Notes	150	____	____

2. Open-Market Operations and Government Deposit Switching

Below are balance sheets for the Bank of Canada and chartered banks. Now the Bank of Canada wants chartered bank reserves cut by $5.

(a) In the (a) columns show how this could be accomplished by an open-market operation.

CHARTERED BANKS		(a)	(b)
Assets			
Reserves	$25	____	____
Government Securities	50	____	____
Loans	250	____	____
Liabilities			
Demand deposits	325	____	____

BANK OF CANADA		(a)	(b)
Assets			
Government Securities	$80	____	____
Liabilities			
Reserves of banks	25	____	____
Government deposits	15	____	____
Bank of Canada Notes	40	____	____

(b) In the (b) columns show how this could be accomplished by switching government deposits. For this part start with the original data.

3. Monetary Policy and the Transmission Mechanism

The two graphs following show the money market and the investment demand curve for the economy.

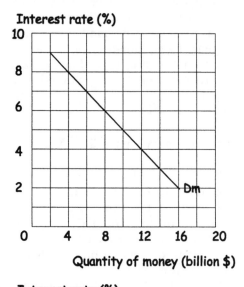

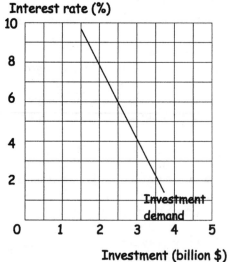

(a) Assuming the current money supply is $8 billion, graph the money supply curve (S_{m0}).

(b) The equilibrium interest rate is _____%.

(c) The level of planned investment at the equilibrium interest rate is $_____ billion.

(d) If the Bank of Canada increases the money supply by $4 billion, Graph the new money supply (S_{m1}).

(e) Now there will be a (shortage, surplus) _____ of $___ billion unless the interest rate changes.

(f) The new equilibrium interest rate is ___%.

(g) The new level of investment demand is $____ billion.

(h) If the expenditures multiplier in this situation is 3, the money supply increase will shift the AD curve (leftward, rightward) ____ by $__ billion.

Discussion Questions

1. Define monetary policy and state its basic objective.

2. Describe the five main functions of the Bank of Canada.

3. What are the principal assets and liabilities of the Bank of Canada?

4. What are the two main instruments of monetary control available to the Bank of Canada, and how do they work?

5. Using open-market operations, what would the Bank of Canada do to contract the money supply? Or to expand it?

6. Use a simplified balance sheet of the chartered banking system to explain the effect on reserves of switching government deposits between the Bank of Canada and the chartered banks.

7. Why does a change in the bank rate end up affecting interest rates and the money supply? How does the Bank of Canada set the bank rate?

8. Use a set of three graphs to explain what determines: (a) the equilibrium interest rate; (b) planned investment; and (c) the equilibrium GDP. Now employ these graphs to show the effects of a cut in the money supply on equilibrium GDP.

9. What are the strengths and shortcomings of monetary policy?

10. Why is monetary policy more effective in controlling inflation than in reducing unemployment?

11. Explain the net export effect caused by monetary policy.

12. Distinguish between fiscal and monetary policy and explain how each may be used to achieve reasonably full employment and relatively stable prices.

Answers

Quick Quiz
1. (d) p. 307
2. (c) p. 307
3. (b) p. 308
4. (a) pp. 310-314
5. (b) p. 314
6. (a) pp. 314-315
7. (d) pp. 317-319
8. (a) pp. 317-319
9. (a) pp. 314-315
10. (b) p. 322
11. (c) pp. 323-324
12. (c) p. 325
13. (c) pp. 325-328

Fill-in Questions
1. full-employment, non-inflationary, Bank of Canada
2. taxes, bonds
3. bonds, reserves, money (or deposits)
4. 10 million, 10 million, 9.5 million, 0, 10 million, 10 million, 200 million (10 million x (1/.05))
5. (a) +, (b) +, (c) +, (d) -, (e) +, (f) +, (g) +
6. shortage, surplus, down, rise, asset, equal
7. down, decreases, depreciate, increase; reinforces

True-False
1. F   currency is a liability for the Bank of Canada
2. T
3. F   the Bank of Canada is largely independent of the federal government
4. T   and the interest rate on them rises
5. T   not often, but when necessary
6. T   which would lead to a multiple contraction of deposit money
7. F   the Bank of Canada does not control the prime rate
8. F   the reserves would be increased, and most of the added reserves would be excess
9. F   the opposite is true

10. F fiscal policy is less flexible than monetary policy

11. T the Bank of Canada is expanding the reserves available to the chartered banks

12. T with emphasis on the word "eventually"

13. T as people substitute quickly between near-monies and other financial assets

14. F it has almost all of its effect on price level since the economy is already at or beyond normal capacity

15. F the net export effect would tend to increase the size of the trade surplus

Multiple-Choice

1. (b)

2. (a) bonds and Treasury bills

3. (d) this is determined by chartered banks and other lending institutions

4. (a)

5. (d) the Bank of Canada cannot manipulate this ratio

6. (c) this action is expansionary while all of the others are contractionary

7. (d) reserves fall 20 million; multiplier is 10

8. (b)

9. (b) both actions reduce reserves

10. (b)

11. (d) it affects AD more indirectly, but can be changed quickly without a long political process, so it is used often

12. (d)

13. (b) investment spending responds to interest rate changes

14. (c)

15. (d) the first two offset the monetary stimulus and third weakens a link in the transmission mechanism

16. (c)

17. (a)

18. (a)

19. (a) which would stimulate net exports

20. (a) interest rate would rise, the currency appreciate, and net exports fall (reducing AD and the trade surplus)

21. (b) monetary policy is more effective against inflationary gaps

22. (c) thus it is a rule, but one that responds to changing circumstances

Problems and Projects

1. (a) $500, $150, $650; (b) Chartered banks: $60, 90, 350, 500; Bank of Canada: $310, 60, 100, 150; (c) $650; (d) Chartered banks: $60, 90, 450, 600; Bank of Canada: $310, 60, 100, 150; (e) $750; (f) 10, 100, 10

2. (a) Chartered banks: $20, 55, 250, 325; Bank of Canada: $75, 20, 15, 40; (b) Chartered banks: $20, 50, 250, 320; Bank of Canada: $80, 20, 20, 40

3. (a) see graph; (b) 6; (c) $I_0 = 2.5$; (d) see graph; (e) surplus, 4; (f) 4; (g) $I_1 = 3$; (h) rightward, 1.5 (0.5×3)

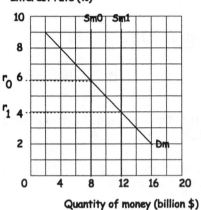

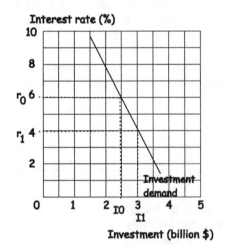

Chapter 14

Long-Run Macroeconomic Adjustments

Overview

Keynes shifted the focus of macroeconomics onto questions of short-run equilibrium. Much of the more recent work in macroeconomics has focused on longer run issues, particularly the long-run aggregate supply and the inflation-unemployment relationship. These topics are addressed in this chapter.

In a situation of demand-pull inflation the economy can temporarily exceed its potential real GDP, but labour market adjustments will eventually restore real wages and return the economy to its long-run equilibrium at potential GDP. When the economy experiences cost-push inflation the real output drops below the potential level, posing a dilemma for policy-makers. They can wait for market forces to close the recessionary gap, but it may be a very long wait. Otherwise they can use expansionary fiscal or monetary policy, but this will push prices yet higher, risking setting off an inflationary spiral of nominal wage increases followed by price increases. In a recession stemming from falling demand, output drops below potential but will eventually recover when prices and nominal wages fall far enough. Here the key question is how long the process will take.

These three cases support three generalizations about the long-run outcomes in the AD-AS model: (1) there is normally a short-run tradeoff between inflation and unemployment; (2) AS shocks can cause both higher inflation and higher unemployment; and (3) there is no significant lasting tradeoff between inflation and unemployment. The chapter then examines each of these generalizations.

Data from the 1960s led economists to believe there was a trade-off between inflation and unemployment (the original Phillips curve model). Policy-makers thought that they could choose any inflation and unemployment combination on the Phillips curve. For example, unemployment could be cut by tolerating higher inflation. Stagflation in the 1970s showed that such a trade-off existed only if economic shocks were limited to shifts in the aggregate demand. Economists needed to begin paying more attention to the supply side of the economy.

Stagflation was caused by adverse supply shocks that shifted the AS curve to the left and shifted the Phillips curve outward to points with higher unemployment and inflation. There was still a Phillips curve showing a trade-off, but a short-run tradeoff that shifts up or down as inflation expectations change. In the long-run there is no tradeoff, so the long-run Phillips curve is vertical at the full-employment GDP. In other words, in the long run the economy tends towards a natural rate of unemployment regardless of the level of inflation. Expectations are central to the process: when market participants react to their expectations about inflation, there is no lasting Phillips curve tradeoff.

Supply-side economists emphasize that AS determinants have important effects on inflation, real output, and economic growth. Taxation is their key concern. They argue that cutting marginal tax rates would substantially increase incentives to work, save, and invest, and thereby increase aggregate supply. A famous and controversial element of supply-side economics is the Laffer curve.

Chapter Outline

14.1 Applying the Long-Run AD-AS Model

✑ How does the long-run AD-AS model explain inflation, recessions, and unemployment?

• If the economy begins at full employment, demand-pull inflation occurs when AD increases.

 o The short-run impact is an expansion in output and an increase in the price level.

Because nominal wages are fixed over this period, real wages drop.

o When workers' contracts expire, and when they realize that their real wages have fallen, workers demand and get higher nominal wages. This shifts the AS curve leftward until the inflationary gap is closed and the economy is back at full-employment equilibrium where real wages are restored to their original level.

o Demand-pull inflation produces a lasting price level increase and a temporary real output increase.

• If the economy begins at full employment, cost-push inflation occurs when per-unit production costs rise, and AS decreases.

o The short-run impact is a drop in output and an increase in the price level.

o If no government stabilization policy is used, input prices will eventually fall, shifting the AS back to the right until a long-run equilibrium is restored at full-employment output. This will be a very slow process, meaning a prolonged recession.

o If government uses an expansionary monetary or fiscal policy, the AD curve could be increased to meet the new AS curve at full-employment. However, this would drive prices even higher, and might ignite an inflationary spiral of further increases in wages and prices.

• Starting from full employment, a recession that stems from falling expenditures will decrease the AD curve.

o The short-run impact is a drop in output and in the price level. Because nominal wages are fixed, real wages rise, leading to employment losses.

o Eventually nominal wages will fall to restore the previous real wage, employment, and output levels. This economy is likely to endure a prolonged recession before this adjustment process is complete.

➲ The role of real and nominal wages is crucial in the explanation of how the economy moves away from the natural rate of unemployment, and then returns to the natural rate. Since decisions by workers and employers are ultimately based on real wages, price level changes must ultimately be matched by nominal wage changes in order to keep real wages in equilibrium.

Quick Quiz
1. Demand-pull inflation causes:
   (a) higher prices in the short run only
   (b) higher prices in the long run only
   (c) higher prices in the short run and the long run
   (d) higher prices in the short run but prices stabilize in the long run

2. Cost-push inflation is caused by shifts in:
   (a) AD
   (b) AS
   (c) AD or AS
   (d) AD and AS

3. In the absence of fiscal or monetary policy, a recession will end eventually because of adjustments that begin with changes in:
   (a) nominal wage rates
   (b) prices
   (c) employment
   (d) output

14.2   The Inflation-Unemployment Relationship

✧ What is the relationship between inflation and unemployment in the short run?

• From the analysis of the three scenarios above, we conclude that the long-run AD-AS model supports three generalizations:

o Under normal circumstances, there is a short-run tradeoff between inflation and unemployment.

o AS shocks can cause both higher inflation rates and higher unemployment rates.

o There is no significant tradeoff between inflation and unemployment over longer periods.

• If AS is upward sloping, the greater the rate of increase in AD the greater is the rate of increase in the price level and in real output, and the lower is the rate of unemployment.

o This inverse relationship between the inflation rate and the unemployment rate is called the Phillips curve.

o According to the Phillips curve theory, fiscal and monetary policy can be used to manage AD and to target a combination of inflation and unemployment along this curve.

- o Data from the 1960s showed this inverse relationship between unemployment and inflation rates for many countries, including Canada.

• The 1970s and 1980s changed our understanding of the Phillips curve because Canada experienced "stagflation": higher rates of inflation **and** unemployment.

- o A series of adverse supply shocks (especially a quadrupling of oil prices) decreased AS, and increased both inflation and unemployment in Canada.
- o Various factors helped stop stagflation in the 1980s. Unemployment and inflation both decreased (instead of moving in opposite directions as predicted by the Phillips curve theory).
- o This experience suggests that the Phillips curve is not a stable relationship and cannot be used as the basis for economic policy. Instead, there seems to be a short-run tradeoff, but one that shifts. Supply shocks shifted the short-run Phillips curve rightward between 1971 and 1982, and other events shifted it leftward between 1983 and 1989.

Quick Quiz

4. The Phillips curve graph plots:
   (a) price level on the vertical axis and unemployment on the horizontal axis
   (b) inflation rate on the vertical axis and unemployment rate on the horizontal axis
   (c) inflation rate on the vertical axis and unemployment on the horizontal axis
   (d) price level on the horizontal axis and unemployment rate on the vertical axis

5. What events in the 1970s began to distort the usual inflation-unemployment relationship?
   (a) fiscal policy changes
   (b) monetary policy changes
   (c) technology changes
   (d) oil price shocks

6. The demise of stagflation in the 1980s resulted from several contributing factors. Which was not among those factors?
   (a) slower rates of nominal wage increase due to high unemployment
   (b) increased foreign competition held prices

down in some basic industries
   (c) deregulation in some industries led to wage givebacks
   (d) decreases in government spending led to large layoffs in the government sector

14.3 The Long-Run Phillips Curve

◈ What is the relationship between inflation and unemployment in the long run?

• The data since the 1960s shows that in the long run the natural rate of unemployment can exist with any rate of inflation. Therefore, the long-run Phillips curve is vertical at the natural rate of unemployment. The processes behind this involve the expectations of inflation and how the economy adjusts when the inflation rate is not what was expected.

- o Starting from full employment, with a certain expected rate of inflation, nominal wages will be set to increase at the same rate as prices, thus maintaining the real wage.
- o If inflation turns out to be higher than expected, firms enjoy higher than normal profit margins, because of lower than normal real wages. Accordingly, they hire more workers and produce more output. Unemployment drops below the natural rate. The result is higher inflation and lower unemployment: the Phillips curve tradeoff!
- o The higher inflation rate is soon factored into nominal wage expectations, and real wage rates return to normal. Profit margins also return to normal, and so does the level of unemployment. Now unemployment is back to its natural rate, and the inflation rate is higher than before, so the short-run Phillips curve has shifted upward.
- o The process is repeated if government tries again to reduce unemployment, and the inflation rate accelerates as the short-run Phillips curve shifts upward. Expansionary policies generate accelerating inflation rather than lower unemployment.
- o If the inflation begins to fall because AD is grows slower than expected, then nominal wages will rise faster than inflation. This drives up the real wages, eroding profit margins and provoking layoffs. So lower than expected inflation leads to

a temporary increase in the unemployment rate.

- o In the long run, the Phillips curve is stable only as a vertical line at the natural rate of unemployment. There is no trade-off between unemployment and inflation.

⮑ This chapter shows how real world experience can change prevailing economic theories. Actual inflation and unemployment from the late 1960s through the early 1980s dramatically changed theories of the Phillips curve. There was a drastic shift in the mainstream opinion among economists on the unemployment-inflation relationship.

Quick Quiz

7. The long-run Phillips curve is:
- (a) downward-sloping
- (b) upward-sloping
- (c) vertical
- (d) horizontal

8. A given short-run Phillips curve will intersect the long-run Phillips curve at the point where:
- (a) the actual inflation rate equals the expected inflation rate
- (b) the actual inflation rate equals zero
- (c) the expected inflation rate equals zero
- (d) the unemployment rate equals zero

9. The long-run Phillips curve will shift if there is a change in:
- (a) the actual inflation rate
- (b) the expected inflation rate
- (c) the natural rate of unemployment
- (d) the actual rate of unemployment

14.4   Taxation and Aggregate Supply

◈ How does taxation affect aggregate supply?

- According to supply-side economists, it is critical that policy-makers be mindful of the effects of shifts in the aggregate supply.
  - o Supply-siders argue that lower marginal income tax rates would increase incentives to work, save, and invest, thereby increasing the economy's productivity. This would shift both short-run and long-run AS curves to the right.
- The Laffer curve suggests that lower tax rates are compatible with constant or even larger tax

revenues. If tax rates are cut, enough output and taxable income could be generated to increase the total tax revenue. Reduced tax avoidance and tax evasion would also result.

- Critics of supply-side economics and the Laffer curve question whether tax cuts would create such benefits for aggregate supply because:
  - o The effects on incentives are small or uncertain.
  - o Tax cuts would cause AD to increase, creating inflationary pressure.
  - o Tax revenues will only increase if the economy is on the right section of the Laffer curve, and there is no evidence that it is.

Quick Quiz

10. Higher marginal income tax rates give individuals more incentive to:
- (a) supply labour
- (b) save
- (c) invest
- (d) consumer leisure

11. On which part of the Laffer curve will a cut in the marginal tax rate increase the total revenue collected by the government?
- (a) the upper part
- (b) the lower part
- (c) everywhere on the curve
- (d) only at one specific point on the curve

Terms and Concepts

Phillips Curve
stagflation
aggregate supply
  shocks

supply-side economics
Laffer Curve

Fill-In Questions

1. Demand-pull inflation is initiated by a shift to the (right, left) _____ of the (AD, AS) _____ curve. This will (decrease, increase) _____ the price level and temporarily _____ real output. As a consequence, the (short-run, long-run) _____ aggregate supply curve will shift left because of a rise in (real, nominal) _____ wages, producing a (lower, higher) _____ price level at the original level of real output. Eventually equilibrium is restored at the _____ level of output.

2. Cost-push inflation starts with a shift to the (right, left) _____ of the (AD, AS) _____ curve. Thus the price level will (increase, decrease) _____ and real output will temporarily _____. If government takes no action to counter the cost-push inflation, the resulting recession will _____ nominal wages, and shift the _____ curve back to its original position. If the government tries to counter the cost-push inflation and recession with an expansionary monetary or fiscal policy, the price level will move (back down, even higher) _____.

3. According to the traditional Phillips curve theory accepted in the 1960s, the policy dilemma faced by government policy-makers is that:
(a) to have full employment we must also have _____, and to have stable prices we must tolerate _____;
(b) to reduce the unemployment rate, the rate of inflation must (increase, decrease) _____; and to reduce the rate of inflation the unemployment rate must _____.

4. The expectation of inflation by workers and employers leads to (higher, lower) _____ nominal wage rates and in turn to a (rise, fall) _____ in per-unit production costs, to a(n) (increase, decrease) _____ in AS, to a (higher, lower) _____ price level, and to a _____ rate of unemployment in the economy.

5. If inflation is lower than expected, and (real, nominal) _____ wage rates are temporarily fixed by labour contracts, then the (real, nominal) _____ wage will be (higher, lower) _____ than usual, causing profit margins to be (higher, lower) _____ than usual. Therefore, firms (hire, layoff) _____ workers, causing the unemployment rate to be (above, below) _____ the natural rate.

6. The _____ Curve is a relationship between the tax rate and tax _____. Supply-side economists believe that (higher, lower) _____ tax rates will increase tax _____. They also argue that lower tax rates will shift the (AD, AS) _____ to the right.

True-False

Circle T if the statement is true, F if it is false.

1. When aggregate supply is constant, higher rates of inflation are accompanied by higher rates of unemployment. **T F**

2. According to the original Phillips curve theory, the rate of inflation increases as the level of unemployment decreases. **T F**

3. Stagflation refers to a situation in which both the price level and the unemployment rate are falling. **T F**

4. The stagflation of the 1970s and early 1980s was mainly due to a series of demand shocks. **T F**

5. Both inflationary expectations and increasing labour productivity can shift the aggregate supply curve leftward and cause stagflation. **T F**

6. Expectations of inflation induce workers to demand a higher nominal wage and their employers to pay them higher nominal wages. **T F**

7. When the nominal wage rate increases at a rate greater than the rate at which the productivity of labour increases, unit labour costs will rise. **T F**

8. A change in the level of expected inflation will cause the economy to move to a different point on a given short-run Phillips curve. **T F**

9. According to the long-run Phillips curve theory, the economy's natural rate of unemployment can be achieved only if the rate of inflation is zero. **T F**

10. When the actual rate of inflation is higher than the expected rate, the unemployment rate will fall. **T F**

11. The long-run AS is vertical at the GDP level corresponding to the natural rate of unemployment. **T F**

12. Demand-pull inflation will increase the price level and real output in the short run; but, in the long run, only the price level will increase.   **T F**

13. An inflationary spiral is likely to result from the use of stabilization policies to maintain full employment when the economy is experiencing cost-push inflation.   **T F**

14. The Laffer curve proves that tax cuts would enable our government to collect more tax revenue.   **T F**

Multiple-Choice

Circle the letter that corresponds to the best answer.

1. As long as AS remains constant and the economy operates along the upward sloping portion of AS, the greater the increase in AD:
   (a) the greater is the increase in the price level
   (b) the greater is the increase in the unemployment rate
   (c) the smaller is the increase in real output
   (d) the smaller is the increase in employment

2. The conventional Phillips curve:
   (a) shows the inverse relation between the rate of increase in the price level and the unemployment rate
   (b) indicates that it is possible for the economy to achieve full employment and stable prices
   (c) indicates that prices do not rise until full employment has been achieved
   (d) slopes upward from left to right

3. The stabilization policy dilemma illustrated by a Phillips curve is the mutual inconsistency of:
   (a) more employment and price stability
   (b) a higher unemployment rate and price stability
   (c) inflation and more employment
   (d) inflation and a lower unemployment rate

4. Stagflation is characterized by:
   (a) rising inflation and rising government deficits
   (b) rising unemployment and rising government deficits
   (c) rising taxes and rising government deficits
   (d) rising inflation and rising unemployment

5. Which of the following was a supply-side shock that affected Canada during the 1970s and early 1980s?
   (a) the imposition of wage and price controls
   (b) the appreciation of the dollar
   (c) the fall in the price charged by OPEC nations for oil
   (d) worldwide agricultural shortfalls

6. If productivity of labour rises by 2% and nominal wage rates rise 5%, the percentage change in unit labour costs is:
   (a) 1%
   (b) 3%
   (c) 7%
   (d) 10%

7. Which of the following factors contributed to the demise of stagflation in the 1983-1988 period?
   (a) lessening of foreign competition
   (b) strengthening OPEC's monopoly power
   (c) a recession caused by tight money policy
   (d) increased regulation of transportation industries

8. Our current theories of the Phillips curve suggest that the economy is stable only in the:
   (a) short run at the natural rate of unemployment
   (b) short run at the natural rate of inflation
   (c) long run at the natural rate of unemployment
   (d) long run at the natural rate of inflation

9. An inflationary spiral is particularly a risk if:
   (a) there is cost-push inflation and government counters the recession with expansionary policy
   (b) there is demand-pull inflation and government counters the inflation with contractionary policy
   (c) there is cost-push inflation and government takes no policy action to counter the recession
   (d) there is demand-pull inflation and government takes no policy action to counter the inflation

10. Which of the following is an example of an adverse supply shock?
(a)   falling oil prices
(b)   mass crop failures
(c)   productivity growth from computerization
(d)   appreciation of the domestic currency

11. When the actual inflation rate falls below the expected inflation rate:
(a)   real wages rise temporarily
(b)   profit margins fall temporarily
(c)   layoffs occur and unemployment temporarily exceeds the natural rate
(d)   all of the above

12. In the short run, demand-pull inflation:
(a)   is caused by a downward shift in the Phillips curve
(b)   is the result of a decrease in AD
(c)   produces an increase in real output
(d)   is caused by rising wage rates

13. In the long run, demand-pull inflation will:
(a)   decrease the unemployment rate
(b)   decrease the level of nominal wages
(c)   increase the level of prices
(d)   increase real national output

14. The short-run Phillips curve will shift down if:
(a)   actual inflation decreases
(b)   expected inflation decreases
(c)   unemployment goes down
(d)   any of the above

15. Supply-side economists would argue for fighting stagflation with a policy of:
(a)   tax cuts
(b)   government regulation
(c)   government spending
(d)   monetary policy

16. What benefits would supply-side economists expect to see from a cut in the marginal tax rate on personal incomes:
(a)   an increase in labour force participation
(b)   an increase in personal saving
(c)   an increase in investment
(d)   all of the above

17. The Laffer curve is a relationship between:
(a)   the rate of inflation and the rate of unemployment

(b)   the rate of inflation and the rate of employment
(c)   the tax rate and the budget deficit
(d)   the tax rate and tax revenue

18. Which of the following is a criticism of the Laffer curve as an argument for tax cuts?
(a)   tax cuts have large effects on incentives to work, save and invest
(b)   tax cuts reinforce inflation
(c)   tax cuts will generate more tax revenue
(d)   none of the above

19. Oil price increases in 2000 seemed to be less inflationary than oil price increases in the 1970s and 1980s. Which of the following is not among the possible reasons?
(a)   in 2000 the Bank of Canada is more adept at maintaining price stability through monetary policy
(b)   in 2000 favourable supply-side changes were taking place at the same time as the oil price increases
(c)   in 2000 goods that are energy intensive to make and transport make up a much lower share of GDP
(d)   in 2000 the Bank of Canada accommodated the oil price increases with expansionary monetary policy

Problems and Projects

1. Phillips Curve
Below is a traditional Phillips curve.

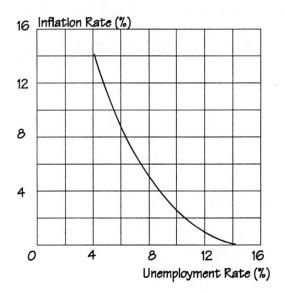

(a) At full employment (8% unemployment), the price level would rise by _____ % each year.

(b) If the price level were stable (increasing by 0% per year), the unemployment rate would be _____%.

(c) Which of the combinations along the Phillips curve would you choose for the economy? Why would you select this combination?

2. AD and AS Adjustments in the Long Run

Following is a graph of the AD-AS model. Assume that the economy is initially in equilibrium at AD1 and AS1. The price level will be _____ and the real domestic output will be _____.

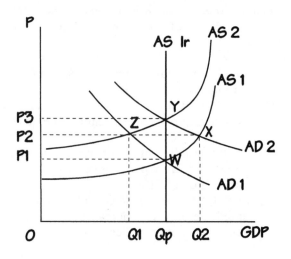

(a) If there is demand-pull inflation, then:

(1) in the short run, the new equilibrium is at point _____, with the price level at _____ and real output at _____;

(2) in the long run, nominal wages will rise so the aggregate supply curve will shift from _____ to _____. The equilibrium will be at point _____ with the price level at _____ and real output at _____; and so the increase in aggregate demand has only moved the economy along its _____ curve.

(b) Now assume that the economy is initially in equilibrium at point W, where AD1 and AS1 intersect. If there is cost-push inflation, then:

(1) in the short run, the new equilibrium is at point _____, with the price level at _____ and real output at _____.

(2) if government tries to counter the cost-push inflation with expansionary monetary and fiscal policy, then AD shifts from _____ to _____, with the price level becoming _____ and real output _____. This policy has a trap because the price level has shifted from _____ to _____ and the new level of inflation might shift _____ leftward.

(3) if government does not counter the cost-push inflation, the price level will eventually move to _____ and real output to _____ as the recession reduces nominal wages and shifts the AS curve from _____ to _____.

3. The Long-Run Phillips Curve

The next graph shows short-and long-run Phillips curves.

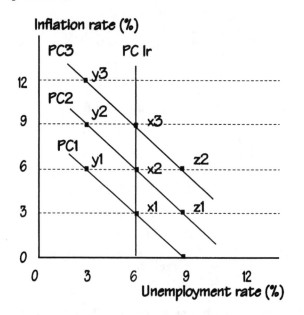

(a) The economy is initially at point X1, with nominal wages currently being set on the expectation that a 3% rate of inflation will continue.

(1) If government uses expansionary fiscal or monetary policy to cut unemployment from 6% to 3%, the actual rate of inflation will move to _____%. The higher prices will lift firms' profits and they will hire more workers; thus moving the economy temporarily to point _____.

(2) If workers now demand and receive higher wages to compensate for the loss of purchasing power from higher than expected inflation, then business profits will fall from previous levels and firms will reduce employment. Therefore, employment will move from point _____ to point _____ on the graph. The short-run Phillips curve has shifted from _____ to _____.

(3) If government again tries to stimulate AD with monetary or fiscal policy to reduce the unemployment rate from 6% to 3%, then prices will rise before nominal wages, and output and employment will increase, causing a move from point _____ to point _____.

(4) But when workers get nominal wage increases, profits fall, and unemployment moves from point _____ at _____% to point _____ at _____%. The short-run Phillips curve has now shifted from _____ to _____.

(5) The long-run Phillips curve is the line _____.

(b) Suppose now the economy begins at point X3, with expected and actual inflation at 9% and unemployment rate at 6%.

(1) If AD decreases because of a recession and if the actual rate of inflation should fall to 6%, below the expected rate of 9%, business profits will fall and the unemployment rate will rise to 9% as shown by the movement from point X3 to point _____.

(2) If firms and workers now expect inflation to be 6%, then nominal wages will fall, profits will rise, and the economy will move from point _____ to point _____. The short-run Phillips curve will shift from _____ to _____.

(3) If this process is repeated, the long-run Phillips curve will be traced as line _____.

4. Taxation

The table below shows the level of real GDP the economy would achieve at various different marginal income tax rates.

Tax Rate	Level of GDP ($ billions)	Tax Revenue ($ billions)
20%	4,500	_____
30%	4,000	_____
40%	3,500	_____
50%	3,100	_____
60%	2,500	_____
70%	2,000	_____

(a) Fill in the blank column for tax revenues at each tax rate.

(b) The data in this example supports the supply-siders' policy advice only for tax rates above _____%. At any tax rates lower than this, tax revenue will (fall, rise) _____ if the tax rate is cut.

Discussion Questions

1. Describe the process of demand-pull inflation in the short run and in the long run. How does demand-pull inflation affect the AS curve?

2. Define cost-push inflation and describe how it comes about. How does the economy adjust to cost-push inflation in the short run? In the long run? What dilemma does cost-push inflation pose for macroeconomic policy-makers?

3. How does the economy recover in the long-run from a recession if: (a) the government uses no expansionary policy, and (b) the government uses expansionary policy when the recession is diagnosed?

4. What is a Phillips curve? Explain how a Phillips curve with a negative slope may be derived by holding AS constant and increasing AD.

5. What is the stabilization policy dilemma illustrated by the traditional Phillips curve? Does the manipulation of AD through monetary and fiscal policy shift the Phillips curve or cause a movement along the Phillips curve?

6. Over what period(s) of Canada's history was our experience consistent with the conventional Phillips curve explanation?

7. What supply-side shocks brought stagflation to the Canadian economy during the 1970s and early 1980s? How did these shocks affect aggregate supply and the short-run Phillips curve? What factors contributed to stagflation's demise during the 1983-88 period?

8. What causes the short-run Phillips curve to shift? What does the long-run Phillips curve look like, and why?

9. Supply-side economists believe that there are significant tax and transfer payment disincentives in the economy. What are they, and what policies are suggested?

10. Draw a Laffer curve. Explain the economic implications of the curve according to supply-side economists. Outline three criticisms of the ideas expressed by the Laffer curve.

Answers

Quick Quiz
1. (c) pp. 335-336
2. (b) pp. 336-337

3. (a) pp. 335-337
4. (b) p. 340
5. (d) pp. 340-341
6. (d) p. 341
7. (c) p. 343
8. (a) pp. 343-344
9. (c) pp. 343-345
10. (d) pp. 345-346
11. (a) pp. 346-347

Fill-in Questions

1. right, AD, increase, increase, short-run, nominal, higher, full-employment
2. left, AS, increase, decrease, decrease, AS, even higher
3. (a) inflation, unemployment; (b) increase, increase
4. higher, rise, decrease, higher, higher
5. nominal, real, higher, lower, lay off, above
6. Laffer, revenues, lower, revenues, AS

True-False

1. F   with AS fixed, higher inflation must be due to a rightward shift in AD; this would also imply lower unemployment
2. T   there is a tradeoff between the two in this view
3. F   both price level and unemployment are rising
4. F   supply shocks were the main reason
5. F   true for inflationary expectations, but false for productivity increases
6. T   thus maintaining real wage levels if nominal wage increases match price level increases
7. T   the two factors offset one another, so the AS will shift in the direction of the stronger effect
8. F   the short-run Phillips curve shifts (e.g. upwards if expected inflation rises)
9. F   this unemployment rate is compatible with any rate of inflation
10. T   because real wages fall and profit margins improve, firms hire more workers
11. T
12. T   the inflationary gap will eventually be resolved, returning the economy to full-employment GDP
13. T
14. F   it's possible, depending on which section of the Laffer curve we are currently on

Multiple-Choice

1. (a)   AD shifts right against a static AS
2. (a)

3. (a)
4. (d)
5. (d)   decreased productivity in food production
6. (b)   5% - 2%
7. (c)   this took much inflationary pressure out of wages, etc.
8. (c)
9. (a)   the leftward AS shift is countered by a rightward AD shift, perhaps triggering another leftward AS shift
10. (b)
11. (d)   because nominal wages were based on the (higher) expected inflation
12. (b)
13. (c)   prices (and nominal wages) will rise; there is no permanent effect on real output or unemployment
14. (b)
15. (a)   to increase the AS curve
16. (d)
17. (d)
18. (b)   by increasing disposable income, tax cuts are likely to cause AD to shift rightward
19. (a)   accommodating the oil price increases would have fed the inflation

Problems and Projects

1. (a) 5 (b) 14 (c) (it's your choice)
2. P1, Qp (a) (1) X, P2, Q2 (2) AS1, AS2; Y, P3, Qp, ASlr; (b) (1) Z, P2, Q1 (2) AD1, AD2, P3, Qp; P2, P3, AS (3) P1, Qp, AS2, AS1
3. (a) (1) 6, Y1 (2) Y1, X2; PC1, PC2, (3) X2, Y2 (4) Y2, 3, X3, 6, PC2, PC3 (5) PClr; (b) (1) Z2 (2) Z2, X2,,PC3, PC2, (3) PClr
4. (a) 900, 1200, 1400, 1550, 1500, 1400; (b) 50, fall

Chapter 15 Economic Growth

Overview

In the 20th century economic growth radically increased the standard of living for Canadians. As we face the ongoing challenge of producing enough goods to raise the standard of living for an ever expanding population, it is important to understand the sources and consequences of growth.

There are six main ingredients in economic growth. Four supply factors determine the output potential of the economy: increases or improvements in: (1) the quantity and quality of natural resources; (2) the quantity and quality of human resources; (3) the stock of capital goods; and (4) production technology. These factors are often rolled into one equation showing real GDP calculated as the product of worker-hours and labour productivity. Whether the economy's full potential is reached depends upon the demand factor, and the efficiency factor. Economic growth requires that the production possibilities curve shift outward, but there must also be enough demand, and efficient use of the resources, in order for the expanded potential to be realized. Or, from the perspective of the aggregate demand-aggregate supply model, growth requires shifts in both the AS_{LR} and AD curves.

Since 1926 Canada's real GDP has grown an average rate of 4% per year, and our per capita real GDP has grown an average of 2.1% per year. Growth was very weak in the early 1990s, but recovered at the end of the decade. What accounts for Canada's growth? We have more labour and capital, and the productivity of these inputs has increased. The chapter shows that these factors can be traced back to a number of root causes.

In the long run, labour productivity determines the average real wage rate per hour of work. The dominant source of recent growth is the New Economy – the explosion of investment and entrepreneurial activity stemming from innovations with the microchip and information technology. This activity occurs in existing industries (with established firms implementing new technologies to reduce costs and improve products) and in start-up firms that have emerged strictly because of the new technologies.

The productivity growth generated by the New Economy means that our long-run aggregate supply curve is increasing faster, generating significant macroeconomic benefits in terms of reduced inflation and unemployment pressures.

It is unclear whether there really is a sustainable New Economy, or simply a temporary boom. The economy is unlikely to continue growing so fast without inflationary pressures setting in. Whether growth is desirable and sustainable is also a serious question. The arguments on both sides are presented.

Chapter Outline

15.1   The Ingredients of Economic Growth

◈ What are the main ingredients of economic growth?

• Economic growth has six main ingredients.
• Four of these factors relate to the economy's production possibilities:
  o increases in quantity and quality of natural resources
  o increases in quantity and quality of human resources
  o increases in supply of capital goods
  o improvement in technology
• Fifth is the demand factor; there must be adequate growth in aggregate demand to purchase all of the output that is produced.
• Sixth, there must be economic efficiency in production: both productive efficiency (goods be produced in the least costly way) and allocative efficiency (resources used to produce goods that maximize society's well-being).

Quick Quiz
1. Which statement best describes the nature of the ingredients of growth?

(a)   growth depends strictly on the supply of resources

(b)   growth depends strictly on the techno-logical improvements

(c)   growth depends strictly on the level of ag-gregate demand

(d)   growth depends on the interaction of supply and demand factors

2. If China experiences a 6% increase in worker-hours along with a 2% improvement in produc-tivity then China's real GDP should increase by:
(a)   2%
(b)   3%
(c)   4%
(d)   8%

➲ The rate of economic growth depends on the rate of increase in the quantity and the quality of inputs, and on changes in technology (which rep-resent our "know how" for turning inputs into outputs). However, these factors merely increase the potential output of the economy. For growth to occur, actual output must increase. That re-quires growth in demand as well as growth in supply.

➲ Figure 15-2 is a nifty summary of how to think about the ingredients of growth. The focus is on labour. Real GDP is defined as the amount of labour employed times the productivity of la-bour. In this view, changes in capital, technology, education programs, etc. all impact real GDP through their effect on labour productivity.

15.2   Production Possibilities Analysis

◈ How can the production possibilities curve model and the AD-AS model be used to ana-lyse aspects of economic growth?

•   Economic growth shifts the production pos-sibilities curve outward because of improvement in supply factors that increase real output by increasing labour inputs or by increasing the productivity of labour.
•   Two useful equations related to this are:
o   Real GDP = worker-hours × labour pro-ductivity
o   %△Real GDP = %△worker-hours + %△productivity

•   Efficiency and demand factors must also co-operate; otherwise the growth in the production possibilities curve will not generate growth.
•   In the AD-AS model supply factors that con-tribute to economic growth shift the long-run ag-gregate supply curve to the right. If the economy is faced with downward price and wage inflexibil-ity, growth cannot be achieved unless the aggre-gate demand curve also increases.

➲ As always when working with production possibilities curves, it is important to note the difference between a shift of the curve (changing potential output) and a change of the production point (changing the actual level of output).

Quick Quiz
3. A rightward shift in the production possibili-ties curve could be generated by:
(a)   a drop in the labour force participation rate
(b)   a decrease in the stock of capital goods
(c)   a decrease in cyclical unemployment
(d)   an improvement in the physical health of the labour force

4. An increase in the AS_{LR} curve is most likely to produce economic growth if:
(a)   the AD curve also increases
(b)   the AD curve remains stable
(c)   the AD curve decreases
(d)   none of the above because no matter what happens to AD, an increase in AS_{LR} represents growth

15.3   Canadian Economic Growth

◈ What has Canada's economic growth record been over recent decades?
•   Since 1950 the Canadian real GDP has grown at an average rate of about 4% per year, and about 2.1% per year on a per capita basis.
•   Our growth was especially strong in the 1950s and 1960s, then slowed down. The slow-down continued through the 1970s, 1980s, and early 1990s, but some improvement occurred at the end of the 1990s.

Quick Quiz
5. Canada's economic growth in the second half of the 20th century:
(a)   was quite steady

(b)   averaged about 4% per year in real GDP per capita

(c)   ceased completely in the 1980s and 1990s.

(d)   was strongest at the beginning of this period

15.4   Accounting for Growth in Canada

◈ What have been the sources of growth in Canada?

• Canada's output growth in the latter part of the 20th century was much greater than can be accounted for simply by increases in the amounts of labour and capital. Specifically, between 1961 and 2000, growth in labour accounted for 30% of GDP growth, and growth in capital accounted for 36%, leaving a residual of about 33% of growth.

• The two basic factors account for this residual of 33% are shifting of labour from low-productivity occupations to high-productivity occupations, and increases in multi-factor productivity, which is the overall efficiency with which resources are used in production.

• The following specific factors have contributed to real growth in the Canadian economy:

   o   labour force growth due to immigration and increased labour force participation by women have more than offset the effects of the falling birth rate;

   o   technological advances (including innovative production techniques, new managerial methods, and forms of business organization) have rapid and profound;

   o   capital accumulation through business investment in plant and equipment, and government investment in infrastructure;

   o   human capital accumulation through investment in education and training of workers;

   o   economies of scale from growing size of markets and firms;

   o   improved resource allocation through industrial restructuring, lessening of labour market discrimination, freer international trade;

   o   a very favourable social-cultural-political environment.

Quick Quiz

6. Improved levels of education among Canadian workers have contributed to which portion of Canada's real GDP growth?

(a)   the share attributable to growth in labour

(b)   the share attributable to growth in capital

(c)   the share attributable to growth in multi-factor productivity

(d)   none of the above

7. Multi-factor productivity would be enhanced by:

(a)   increased number of workers in the labour force

(b)   increased capital stock

(c)   more efficient ways of organizing businesses

(d)   all of the above

15.5   The Productivity Speedup: A New Economy?

◈ Has faster productivity growth in recent years been created by the emergence of a "new economy"?

• Resurgence in the second half of the 1990s in Canada's rate of growth in labour productivity has led to the theory that Canada has achieved a New Economy with a higher trend in productivity growth and real GDP growth.

• There are several reasons for the productivity speedup in the New Economy:

   o   The invention of the microchip, and its application to countless industrial, commercial and household uses, created an explosion of entrepreneurial and investment activity. The information technology industry is the best example.

   o   The new technology has given birth to many start-up firms, many of which enjoy increasing returns and economies of scale because: (1) they can use more specialized inputs; (2) they can spread fixed development costs over more units as production increases; (3) many of their products can be consumed simultaneously by many consumers; (4) many of their products create network effects for consumers; and (5) operations are made more efficient through learning-by-doing especially while firms are very new.

   o   There has been heightened global competition in many markets. Many multilateral trade blocs and other initiatives have contributed.

• The acceleration in productivity increases due to the New Economy has macroeconomic implications.

   o The AS_{LR} is shifting rightward faster, increasing our full-employment GDP level. Growth in the affected sectors of the economy produces less inflationary pressure because increasing returns are common, and because of global competition.

   o The natural rate of unemployment has fallen.

   o Government revenue from income taxes has grown quickly, enabling the federal government to cease running deficits every year.

• Some people believe that the New Economy will turn out to have been a temporary boom, and like the old economy in that capacity constraints will be met – sooner or later – and that traditional inflationary pressures are inevitable if the growth continues much longer.

Quick Quiz

8. The rise of what is known as the New Economy is associated more than anything else with:
   (a) falling levels of government spending and tax rates
   (b) the North American Free Trade Agreement
   (c) the development of microchip and information technology
   (d) the increased labour force participation of women

9. The macroeconomic consequences of the New Economy include all but which one of the following?
   (a) reduction in inflationary pressures
   (b) increased government tax revenues
   (c) increase in the natural rate of unemployment
   (d) more rapid economic growth

15.6   Is Growth Sustainable and Desirable?

◇ What are the pros and cons of economic growth?

• Economists usually assume that growth is desirable and sustainable, but both of these assumptions are debatable.

• Opponents of economic growth contend that it pollutes the environment, creates poor-quality, alienating jobs, does little or nothing to solve social problems such as poverty or crime, and while providing more goods and services, it does not provide a better life.

• Advocates of growth argue that it results in a higher standard of living and lessens the burden of scarcity, thereby giving us the resources to fight social problems, clean up pollution, improve working conditions, etc. They argue that many problems are falsely blamed on growth, and that growth is actually sustainable.

Quick Quiz

10. Which viewpoint would be associated with the advocates of economic growth?
   (a) most pollution problems arise where common property exists
   (b) most jobs today are more unpleasant than in the past but pay higher wages
   (c) the best way to reduce poverty is to use redistribution policies more aggressively
   (d) supplies of most natural resources are being depleted

Terms and Concepts

supply factor	New Economy
demand factor	information
efficiency factor	technology
labour productivity	start-up firm
labour force participation rate	increasing returns
	network effects
infrastructure	learning-by-doing
economies of scale	

Fill-In Questions

1. Assume that an economy has a GDP of $800 billion. If the growth rate is 4%, GDP will increase by $_____ billion in one year; but if the rate of growth is only 2%, the year's increase in GDP will be $_____ billion. A two percentage point difference in the growth rate results in a $_____ billion difference in the year's increase in GDP. At a constant annual growth rate of 4%, real GDP will double in _____ years, whereas at a

growth rate of 2%, it will take _____ years for real GDP to double. (Hint: recall the rule of 70).

2. Graphically, economic growth can be shown as a _____ shift of the production possibilities curve or as a combined shift to the right of the _____ and _____ curves.

3. The four supply factors in economic growth are:
(a) increases in _____
(b) increases in _____
(c) increases in _____
(d) improvements in _____
The other two factors are the _____ factor and the _____ factor.

4. The real GDP of any economy in any year is equal to the _____ of labour employed multiplied by the _____ of labour.
(a) The former is measured by the number of _____.
(b) The latter is measured as _____ per _____.

5. In Canada between 1961 and 2000 about (1/3, 2/3) _____ of the economic growth was due to use of more inputs, and the remaining _____ was due to increase in _____.

True-False

Circle T if the statement is true, F if it is false.

1. An economy that expands its productive capacity will not realize its potential economic growth unless there is full employment of resources and full production.   **T F**

2. The efficiency factor in economic growth incorporates issues of productive efficiency and allocative efficiency.   **T F**

3. Real GDP has tended to increase more rapidly than per capita GDP in Canada.   **T F**

4. The growth rate in Canada's real GDP fell throughout the 1990s.   **T F**

5. A decline in the rate of increase of population may cause a decline in the rate of growth of real GDP, but may also raise the growth rate of real GDP per capita, especially if a larger percentage of the population is able to find employment.   **T F**

6. Multifactor productivity measures the change in output not accounted for by changes in the quantity of inputs.   **T F**

7. More often than not, technological progress requires the economy to invest in new machinery and equipment.   **T F**

8. The Canadian social, cultural, and political environment has, in general, worked to slow Canadian economic growth.   **T F**

9. Increases in labour productivity can, at least in the Canadian economy, be taken largely for grant-ed, because the rate of increase has been nearly constant for much more than half a century.   **T F**

10. Critics of economic growth point to the negative consequences for the nature of work and the number of meaningful jobs in the economy.   **T F**

11. A telephone system is an example of a good that has network effects in consumption, meaning that one user's value increases the more other users there are.   **T F**

Multiple-Choice

Circle the letter that corresponds to the best answer.

1. If the real GDP of a nation increases from $2,000 billion to $2,100 billion in one year, the rate of growth of real GDP during that year would be:
(a)   0.5%
(b)   5%
(c)   10%
(d)   50%

2. Over the course of a decade a nation experiences a 12% increase in real GDP. During the same decade the number of worker-hours supplied in this economy shrank by 4%. What else must have happened?

(a)   the labour supply grew by 16%
(b)   labour productivity grew by 16%
(c)   technology grew by 8%
(d)   population shrank by 8%

3. Suppose an economy has a GDP of $700 billion and a steady annual growth rate of 5%. Over a two-year period, GDP will increase by:
(a) $14 billion
(b) $35 billion
(c) $70 billion
(d) $71.75 billion

The labour input in hours worked and the real GDP for a hypothetical economy are given in the table below. Use the data to answer questions 4 and 5.

Year	Hours Worked (Millions)	Real GDP (Billion $)
1990	150	30.0
1995	156	31.2
2000	160	32.4

4. From 1990 to 2000 the total growth in GDP was:
(a)   8%
(b)   2.4%
(c)   4%
(d)   none of the above

5. Labour productivity was highest in:
(a)   1990
(b)   1995
(c)   2000
(d)   labour productivity was constant

6. An outward shift of the entire production possibilities curve of an economy is most likely caused by:
(a)   supply factors
(b)   demand factors
(c)   allocative factors
(d)   efficiency factors

7. If a nation is presently operating at a point that lies inside its current production possibilities curve, the most likely reason is:
(a)   supply and environmental factors
(b)   demand and efficiency factors
(c)   increased labour productivity
(d)   increased total factor productivity

8. Which of the following is not a supply factor in economic growth?
(a)   an expansion in purchasing power
(b)   an increase in the economy's stock of capital goods
(c)   more natural resources
(d)   technological improvements

9. That Canada's real GDP growth has been accompanied by inflation is a sign that:
(a)   AD and AS_{LR} have increased equally
(b)   AD has increased relative to AS_{LR}
(c)   AD has increased less than AS_{LR}
(d)   AD has increased but the AS_{LR} curve has decreased

10. Which of the following is an accurate statement about the relationship between technological advance and investment spending?
(a)   technological advances usually spur spending on new capital goods
(b)   technological advances are not related to investment spending
(c)   technological advances reduce the need for spending on new capital goods
(d)   spending on technology and on capital goods are usually substitutes

11. Which types of capital contribute to economic growth?
(a)   private capital such as factories
(b)   public capital such as highways
(c)   both private and public capital
(d)   only financial capital

12. Concerns about the quality of Canadian education arise from:
(a)   the fact that a smaller percentage of our population is attending college or university
(b)   the fact that more students are attending college instead of university
(c)   decreases in government expenditures on post-secondary education
(d)   deterioration in the performance of Canadian students on standardized achievement tests

13. Which of the following has contributed to improved resource allocation in the Canadian economy?
(a)   decline of discrimination against women in labour markets

(b)   freer international trade
(c)   the shift of labour out of the agricultural sector
(d)   all of the above

14. Canada enjoys a social-cultural-political environment that is on the whole very favourable for growth. Which of the following does not contribute to this favourable environment?
(a)   few taboos against work, production, and material progress
(b)   strong personal and corporate incentives encouraging growth
(c)   a stable rule of law and enforcement of contracts
(d)   some social programs give incentives not to work

15. Increasing returns are common in information technology industries because of:
(a)   network effects
(b)   high fixed development costs
(c)   products can be simultaneously consumed by many consumers
(d)   all of the above

16. Which of the following goods is a prime example of simultaneous consumption?
(a)   recorded music
(b)   apples
(c)   haircuts
(d)   automobiles

17. How has expansion in the New Economy helped drive down the natural rate of unemployment?
(a)   start-ups hired large numbers of unemployed people already trained for the high-tech sector
(b)   many high-tech firms have been willing to hire and then train workers
(c)   information technology has improved the flow of information between workers and employers, reducing frictional unemployment
(d)   both (b) and (c)

18. Which is not among the reasons that skeptics doubt whether the "miracle" of the New Economy will endure?
(a)   several other productivity booms have lasted a few years and then petered out

(b)   even this sector will eventually reach capacity constraints if it grows long enough
(c)   business cycles are likely to occur, even around a higher trend of productivity growth
(d)   the New Economy has not actually raised our productivity so far

19. Which of the following is not a part of the case against economic growth?
(a)   growth produces pollution
(b)   growth impedes the increased production of consumer goods
(c)   growth prevents the attainment of a better life
(d)   growth is not needed to provide us with the means of solving domestic social problems

20. Which of the following is not a part of the case in favour of economic growth?
(a)   growth lessens the scarcity problem
(b)   growth lessens the extent of anxiety and insecurity
(c)   growth is not the primary reason for pollution and environmental degradation
(d)   growth is the only practical way to reduce poverty

21. The fact that natural resource prices have not generally risen is presented as an argument in support of the view that:
(a)   growth is beneficial
(b)   growth is sustainable
(c)   growth allows us to escape the laws of economics
(d)   all of the above

Problems and Projects

1. Labour Productivity and Growth
The next table shows the quantity of labour (in hours) and the productivity of labour (in real GDP per hour) in a hypothetical economy in three different years.
(a) Compute the economy's real GDP in each of the three years and enter them in the table.
(b) Between years 1 and 2, the quantity of labour remained constant; but
(1) labour productivity increased by ____%; and, therefore,
(2) real GDP increased by ____%.

(c) Between years 2 and 3, labour productivity remained constant; but
1) the quantity of labour increased by ____%; and, therefore,
(2) real GDP increased by ____%.

Year	Quantity of Labour	Productivity of Labour	Real GDP
1	1000	$100	$____
2	1000	105	____
3	1100	105	____

(d) Between years 1 and 3,
(1) real GDP increased by ____%; and
(2) this rate of increase is approximately equal to the sum of the rates of increase in the _____ and the _____ of labour.

2.   The New Economy and Network Effects
An information technology company has developed a videoconferencing service for corporate subscribers. The service is able to connect only subscribers who join this particular service. The provider pays the initial development cost of $1,000,000 and a variable cost of $20,000 per subscriber. The value of the service to customers rises the more other subscribers are connected. This is reflected in the price schedule in the following table.

Subscribers	10	100	200
Development Cost	$____	$____	$____
Variable Cost	____	____	____
Total Cost	____	____	____
ATC	____	____	____
Price	$5000	$15000	$25000
Total Revenue	____	____	____
Profit	____	____	____

(a) Calculate and fill in the remaining values.
(b) That the videoconferencing provider experiences economies of scales is shown by the (rising, falling) _____ values for the _____ variable as the number of subscribers increases.
(c) That videoconferencing services are subject to network effects is shown by the (rising, falling) _____ values for the _____ variable as the number of subscribers increases.
(d) In order to break even the firm needs at least ____ subscribers.
(e) Why would increasing demand for this service not be likely to contribute to inflation?

Discussion Questions

1. How does economic growth affect the production possibilities curve? What demand and efficiency assumptions are necessary to achieve maximum productive potential?

2. Describe how economic growth can be illustrated in an aggregate demand-aggregate supply model.

3. What are the six basic ingredients of economic growth? What is the essential difference between the supply factors and the other two factors?

4. What is Canada's record on economic growth? During what periods did our economy grow particularly quickly or slowly?

5. What is the relationship between the annual real GDP, the quantity of labour employed, and the productivity of labour? What factors affect the productivity of labour?

6. What is the relationship between investment and the stock of capital? What is the connection between increases in the capital stock and the rate of economic growth?

7. If the quantity of the labour and capital inputs stayed constant from year to year what productivity measure would indicate how quickly production is growing? How much has this source of productivity contributed to Canada's economic growth since 1961?

8. What is the nature of the New Economy, and what are the reasons that businesses in this sector tend to have increasing returns?

9. Why, or under what conditions, would growth stemming from the New Economy be less inflationary than growth stemming from traditional industries such as manufacturing? Again, relative to growth in traditional sectors, why might growth in the New Economy lower the natural rate of unemployment?

10. What are the arguments for and against the desirability and the sustainability of economic growth in Canada?

Answers

Quick Quiz
1. (d) p. 352
2. (d) p. 354
3. (d) pp. 353-354
4. (a) pp. 355-356
5. (d) p. 357
6. (c) pp. 358-360
7. (c) p. 361
8. (c) pp. 362-363
9. (c) pp. 365-366
10. (a) p. 368

Fill-in Questions
1. 32, 16, 16, approx. 18, 35
2. rightward, AD, AS_{LR}
3. (a) quantity and quality of natural resources; (b) quantity and quality of human resources; (c) the supply or stock of capital goods; (d) technology; demand, efficiency
4. quantity, productivity; (a) worker hours; (b) output, worker hour
5. 2/3, 1/3, multifactor productivity

True-False
1. T
2. T
3. T   population increases has diluted the per capita real GDP growth rate to some extent
4. F   the growth rate recovered at the end of the 1990s
5. T
6. T
7. T
8. F   these factor improve the general productivity of our economy, thus improved our growth rate
9. F   this component of growth has fluctuated significantly
10. T
11. T

Multiple-Choice
1. (b) 100/2,000
2. (b) 16 + (-4) = 12
3. (d) 5% of 700 + 5% of (700 + 5% of 700)
4. (a) 2.4/30
5. (c) real GDP/hours worked = .2025 in 2000
6. (a) such as more labour or other resources
7. (b) insufficient AD
8. (a) this is a demand factor
9. (b) whether long-run AS has increased or not, AD has increased more

10. (a) e.g., the internet has necessitated huge spending on computers, fibre optics networks, etc.
11. (c) like factory machinery, better roads and hospitals improve society's productivity
12. (d) some example results are shown in the chapter
13. (d)
14. (d)
15. (d)
16. (a) any number of people can simultaneously listen to copies of the same piece of music
17. (d) the natural rate depends on both frictional and structural unemployment
18. (d) activity in the New Economy has raised productivity significantly
19. (b) economic growth leads to increased production of consumer goods
20. (b) unfortunately, problems of anxiety and insecurity may well worsen in a dynamic growing economy
21. (b) were natural resources becoming depleted, one would expect to see ongoing price rises on these commodities, but we haven't seen this happen

Problems and Projects
1. (a) 100,000, 105,000, 115,500; (b) (1) 5, (2) 5; (c) (1) 10, (2) 10; (d) (1) 15.5, (2) quantity, productivity
2. (a) Development: $1.0 million all entries; Variable Cost: $0.2 million, 2.0 million, 4.0 million; Total Cost: $1.2 million, 3.0 million, 5,0 million; ATC: $120,000/subscriber, 30,000, 25,000; Total Revenue: $50,000, 1.5 million, 5.0 million; $-1.15 million; -1.50 million; 0; (b) falling, ATC; (c) rising, price; (d) 200; (e) increasing returns

International Trade

Overview

This chapter builds on Chapter 4 which introduced Canada's connections with the global economy. After reviewing the key facts about world trade, the chapter examines the theory of comparative advantage. This theory demonstrates that both nations in an export-import relationship can gain. This explains why Canada and many other nations specialize and trade so extensively.

So why do we benefit from trade? Given that economic resources (natural, human, and capital) are distributed unevenly between nations, some nations are well-suited to producing labour-intensive goods while others are well-suited to capital-intensive goods. The theory of comparative advantage predicts that each nation will specialize in producing those goods for which they have the lower opportunity cost. Production according to this principle will maximize the total output of goods. Then, through exports and imports, each nation will end up able to consume larger quantities than they could without free trade.

The standard supply and demand model can be adapted to find export supply and import demand curves. If the price in Canada is above (below) the world price, Canada will sell exports (demand imports) equal to our domestic surplus (shortage). In a two-country model, the world price for a product is found where one country's export supply curve intersects the other country's import demand curve.

Despite the strong case for specialization and free trade according to comparative advantage, virtually all nations engage in protectionism by erecting barriers to free trade: tariffs, quotas, and other restrictions on imports. Thus, the chapter looks at: (1) what techniques nations use to limit imports; (2) the economic impacts of trade barriers; and (3) the arguments in favour of protectionism. Though it is easy to understand why certain groups desire protection from competition with foreign producers, protectionism is costly to a nation overall. The final section describes several multilateral trade agreements and free-trade zones: the General Agreement on Trade and Tariffs (GATT), the World Trade Organization (WTO), the European Union (EU), and the North American Free Trade Agreement (NAFTA).

Chapter Outline

16.1 Canada and International Linkages

◈ What are the key facts and patterns concerning Canada's trade with other nations?

•   International trade is vital to the Canadian economy. We import and export goods and services, capital and labour, information and technology, and money.

•   Canada is more trade dependent than most nations; exports are 40% of Canadian GDP.

•   Canada's principal commodity exports are machinery and equipment, and automotive products. Our main imports are the same kinds of goods.

•   Most of Canada's trade is with other industrialized nations, particularly the United States.

Quick Quiz

1. Which statement is most descriptive of Canada's international trade?

(a)   most nations are more dependent on international trade than Canada is

(b)   more than three-quarters of Canada's exports are sold to the United States

(c)   Canada imports quite different types of goods than she exports

(d)   trade as a percentage of Canada's GDP has remained quite stable for several decades

2. The causes of the rapid growth in trade world-wide include:

(a)   improved communications technology

(b)   decreases in transportation costs
(c)   decreases in tariffs
(d)   all of the above

16.2   The Economic Basis for Trade

◇ Why are production specialization and trade beneficial?

- Specialization and trade between nations are advantageous because:
  - o Nations differ in their endowments of natural, human, and capital resources.
  - o Efficient production of different products requires different technologies and combinations of resources.
  - o Products are differentiated, and people may prefer certain imported goods over domestically produced varieties of the same good.

- The basis for trade is the principle of comparative advantage. It states that the allocation of resources is most efficient, and total output is maximized, when each good is produced where its opportunity cost is lowest. A simple hypothetical example illustrates comparative advantage and the gains from trade.
  - o Suppose the world has only two nations, each able to produce two different commodities and having straight-line production possibilities curves with different slopes. That is, each country has a constant but different opportunity cost of producing each good.
  - o Given that their opportunity costs differ, each nation has a comparative advantage in the production of one of the two goods. For the world to use its resources economically, each nation must specialize according to their comparative advantage.
  - o The ratio at which one product is traded for another is called the "terms of trade" and must be between the opportunity cost ratios of the two nations in order for trade to be mutually beneficial.
  - o If so, each nation shares in the gains from trade because specialization permits a greater total output from the same resources and a better allocation of the world's resources.
  - o If cost ratios in the two nations are not constant, specialization may not be complete.

  - o If opportunity cost ratios do not differ, there is no basis for mutually beneficial trade.
- In addition to improving efficiency and expanding output, free trade has side-benefits. It promotes competition and deters monopoly, and offers consumers a wider range of product choices. By linking national interests it may also lead to more cooperation and less conflict between nations.

➲ Spend time working numerical examples of the comparative advantage model. This is a very important model, but it can be tricky to master.

Quick Quiz

3. Mrs. Black can mow a lawn in 2 hours or weed a garden in 1 hour. Torben can mow a lawn in 3 hours or weed a garden in 2 hours. Who has the comparative advantage in each activity?
   (a)   Mrs. Black in weeding, Torben in mowing
   (b)   Mrs. Black in mowing, Torben in weeding
   (c)   Mrs. Black in both weeding and mowing
   (d)   Torben in both weeding and mowing

4. In Vietnam one worker can produce in a day 12 units of rice or 3 units of textiles. In Bangladesh one worker can produce 6 units of rice or 2 units of textiles. Where is the comparative advantage for each good?
   (a)   Vietnam in rice and Bangladesh in textiles
   (b)   Vietnam in textiles and Bangladesh in rice
   (c)   Vietnam in rice and textiles
   (d)   Bangladesh in rice and textiles

5. Based on the data in question 4, mutually beneficial trade between these countries would be possible if the terms of trade were:
   (a)   between 3 and 4 units of rice per unit of textiles
   (b)   between 6 and 12 units of rice per unit of textiles
   (c)   between 4 and 9 units of rice per unit of textiles
   (d)   mutually beneficial trade is impossible at any price

16.3   Supply and Demand Analysis of Exports and Imports

◇ How can the supply and demand model be

adapted to analyse exports and imports?

• Supply and demand analysis can show how the equilibrium price and quantity of exports and imports for a product are determined in trade between two nations.

• Each nation has a domestic demand and a domestic supply. In the absence of international trade, the intersections of these curves establish the domestic price in each nation.

• If there is trade, the export supply curve shows how much domestic producers are willing to sell abroad at each world price above the domestic (no-trade) equilibrium price. The import demand curve shows how much consumers are willing to buy from abroad at each world price below the domestic equilibrium price.

• In a two country model, the equilibrium world price and world levels of exports and imports are determined where one nation's import demand curve intersects the other nation's export supply curve.

Quick Quiz

6. As the world price of steel rises relative to Canada's domestic price:
(a)   Canadian steel exports rise
(b)   Canadian steel imports rise
(c)   Canadian steel exports and imports rise
(d)   Canadian steel exports and imports fall

7. Szenland's domestic supply and demand schedules for coal are:
    Price   10 9   8   7   6
    Qd   20 24 28 32 36
    Qs   34 31 28 25 22
Given this, if Szenland can trade internationally:
(a)   Szenland will export coal at any price below 8
(b)   Szenland's export supply curve exists at any price greater than or equal to 7
(c)   Szenland's import demand curve exists at any price below 8
(d)   Szenland will import at any price below 9

16.4   Trade Barriers

◈ Why do nations impose trade barriers?

◈ How do trade barriers work and what effects do they have on a nation's economic well-being?

• Nations restrict international trade by imposing various types of trade barriers:

o   tariffs
o   import quotas
o   non-tariff barriers
o   voluntary export restrictions.

• The imposition of a tariff on a good imported from abroad has both direct and indirect effects on an economy.

o   The tariff increases the domestic price of the good, reduces its domestic consumption, expands its domestic production, decreases foreign production, and transfers income from domestic consumers to producers and the government.

o   The tariff also reduces the income of foreign producers and the ability of foreign nations to purchase goods and services in the nation imposing the tariff. Export industries in the nation imposing the tariff suffer a loss of sales, and must cut production and release resources, despite their efficiency (as proven by their comparative advantage).

• An import quota is a legal limit on the amount of a product that may be imported each year. Its direct and indirect effects are similar to those of a tariff, except that what would otherwise be tariff revenue for the government ends up as revenue for foreign producers.

• Special-interest groups within nations benefit from protection and persuade their governments to erect trade barriers, but costs to consumers exceed the benefits to workers and shareholders, so the economy experiences a net cost.

➲ To understand why tariffs exist, even if the costs to consumers exceed the benefits to domestic producers, consider the following questions. Do you know whether or not Canada has a tariff on shoelaces, and if so, what is it? If you were a Canadian manufacturer of shoelaces, do you think that you would know more about the tariff? Why?

Quick Quiz

8. If Canada imposes a new tariff on imported hockey sticks, the effects would include:
(a)   increased employment in Canada's hockey stick manufacturing industry
(b)   lower prices for hockey sticks sold in Canada
(c)   increased imports of foreign-made hockey sticks
(d)   increased overall efficiency of the Cana-

dian economy

9. Why might the government favour a tariff on hockey sticks over a quota on the number of imported hockey sticks?
- (a) the tariff has better employment effects for Canada
- (b) the tariff has less impact on consumer prices
- (c) other countries would be less opposed to a tariff
- (d) a tariff generates revenue for the Canadian government

10. Which is an accurate statement about the usual effects of tariffs?
- (a) the cost to consumers is less than the extra tax revenue for government
- (b) the cost to consumers is less than the benefits for the domestic producers
- (c) the cost to consumers is less than the sum of the government revenue and the benefits to domestic producers
- (d) the cost to consumers exceeds all benefits for government and the domestic producers

16.5 The Case for Protection: A Critical Review

◇ What are the usual arguments for protectionism (against free trade)?

• The political-military self-sufficiency argument for protectionism has some validity, but is problematic because it is difficult to say which industry is "vital" to national security and therefore must be protected. It may be more efficient economically to provide a direct subsidy to strategic industries.

• Trade barriers are often implemented to protect jobs at home but, for several reasons, this strategy often fails:
- o Imports may eliminate some jobs, but they create others; therefore, imports may change the composition of employment, not the overall level of employment;
- o There is a fallacy of composition problem: it is impossible for all nations to restrict imports, yet still maintain their exports. Trade barriers can be viewed as "beggar thy neighbour" policies;
- o Other nations are likely to retaliate with their own tariffs and quotas, leading to

reduced national output and employment; and
- o Barriers reduce the efficiency of resource allocation by shielding domestic industries from competition.

• Tariffs are sometimes advocated as devices to help diversify, and thereby stabilize, the economy. The Canadian economy is already quite diversified, so this justification has no merit here. In less-developed nations this strategy could create grave economic costs by pushing nations to produce contrary to comparative advantage.

• It is alleged that infant industries need protection until they are strong enough to compete. However, it is difficult to determine which industries might prosper with such protection, and protectionism tends to persist long after it is needed. Once again, direct subsidies may be more economically efficient.

• As instruments of strategic trade policy, tariffs may give domestic producers an advantage over foreign competitors, allowing them to grow more rapidly and achieve greater economies of scale. The protected firms can then dominate world markets because of lower costs. In other words, the goal is to acquire a comparative advantage that would not otherwise exist. This strategy, however, tends to provoke retaliatory trade barriers by other nations.

• Sometimes protection is sought against the "dumping" of foreign goods at a price below cost. Dumping is a legitimate concern and is restricted under Canadian trade law; but proven cases of dumping are so rare that the problem does not justify widespread tariff protection. Often, what is alleged to be dumping may actually be the result of comparative advantage on behalf of foreign producers.

• Protection is sometimes sought to shield Canadian workers from cheap foreign labour. In fact these differences in labour costs are the very basis for mutually beneficial trade. If low-wage countries cannot export labour-intensive goods to high-wage nations, their living standards – and ours – will be lower.

• In summary, there are many arguments for protectionism, but most are fallacious or based on half-truths. The only arguments that are valid, under certain conditions, are the infant-industry and military-sufficiency arguments, but both are subject to abuse.

• Historical evidence suggests that free trade promotes prosperity and growth in the world.

Quick Quiz

11. Which statement is correct?
   (a)   tariffs are the most efficient way to promote self-sufficiency in industries vital to the national interest
   (b)   most infant industries quickly outgrow the need for tariff protection
   (c)   tariffs are an effective policy for increasing a nation's overall level of employment
   (d)   the imposition of tariffs often provokes retaliatory tariffs from other nations

12. If American book publishers sell books in Canada at below their cost of production they are likely engaging in:
   (a)   strategic trade policy
   (b)   dumping
   (c)   development of an infant industry
   (d)   pursuit of national security

16.6   Multilateral Trade Agreements and Free-Trade Zones

◈ How do the WTO and other arrangements work to promote international trade?

•   The inefficiencies of trade protectionism motivate nations to work together for freer trade.

•   In 1947, Canada and 22 other nations signed the General Agreement on Trade and Tariffs (GATT) based on the principles of equal, non-discriminatory trade among signatory nations, reduction of tariffs, and elimination of quotas. Several rounds of GATT negotiations have taken place since, resulting in much lower levels of protection today.

•   The World Trade Organization (WTO) arose as an outgrowth of the Uruguay Round of GATT negotiations in 1993. The WTO has approximately 145 member countries who have agreed to trade liberalizations including: tariff reductions, rules to promote trade in services, reductions in agricultural subsidies, protections for property in intellectual property. The WTO has been heavily protested by groups concerned about globalization, environmental degradation, loss of sovereignty, etc.

•   The European Union (EU) is the most important example of a "free-trade zone." With 15 member nations in 2003, and numerous others applying for membership, the EU is an increasingly influential trade bloc. One of its most significant accomplishments is the establishment of a common currency (the euro) that most member states have agreed to use.

•   The North American Free Agreement (NAFTA) is a trade bloc consisting of Canada, the United States, and Mexico. It was formed in 1993 as an extension of the Free Trade Agreement between Canada and the U.S.

Quick Quiz

13. The goals of the GATT include all but which one of the following?
   (a)   elimination of tariffs
   (b)   elimination of quotas
   (c)   improved intellectual property rights
   (d)   establishment of a common currency

14. Canada is a member of:
   (a)   NAFTA
   (b)   WTO
   (c)   GATT
   (d)   all of the above

Terms and Concepts

multinational corporation
labour-intensive goods
land-intensive goods
capital-intensive goods
absolute advantage
cost ratio
comparative advantage
trading possibilities line
gains from trade
world price
domestic price
export supply curve
import demand curve
equilibrium world price
tariff
revenue tariff
protective tariff

import quota
non-tariff barriers
voluntary export restriction (VER)
strategic trade policy
dumping
most-favoured-nation clause
General Agreement on Trade and Tariffs (GATT)
World Trade Organization (WTO)
European Union (EU)
trade bloc
euro
North American Free Trade Agreement (NAFTA)

Fill-In Questions

1. A nation with relatively low wages will tend to produce and export goods that are (capital, labour) _____ -intensive to produce.

2. Nations tend to trade among themselves because the distribution of economic resources among them is (even, uneven) _____ and because the efficient production of various goods and services necessitates (the same, different) _____ technologies or combinations of resources.

3. If the opportunity cost of one banana in country X is four hats, while in country Y the opportunity cost of one banana is three hats:
(a) hats are relatively (more, less) _____ expensive in country X and bananas relatively _____ expensive;
(b) hats are relatively _____ expensive in country Y and bananas relatively _____ expensive;
(c) X has a comparative advantage and should specialize in the production of _____ and Y has a comparative advantage and should specialize in the production of _____.
(d) When X and Y specialize and trade, the terms of trade will be somewhere between _____ and _____ hats for each banana; and will depend upon world _____ and _____ for hats and bananas.
(e) If the terms of trade turn out to be 3.5 hats for one banana, the cost of obtaining one hat has been decreased from _____ to _____ bananas in Y, and the cost of one banana has been decreased from _____ to _____ hats in X.
(f) This international specialization will not be complete if the cost of producing either good (increases, decreases, remains constant) _____ as a nation produces more of it.

4. The basic argument for free trade is that it results in a better _____ of resources and a higher _____ of living.

5. The barriers to international trade include _____, _____ quotas, _____ barriers, and _____ restrictions.

6. When Canada imposes a tariff on a good that is imported from abroad,
(a) the price of that good in Canada will (increase, decrease) _____;
(b) the total amount purchased of that good in Canada will _____;
(c) the output of:
(1) Canadian producers of the good will _____;

(2) foreign producers of the good will _____;
(d) the ability of foreigners to buy goods from Canada will _____, and, as a result, output and employment in Canadian industries that export will _____.

7. List the six main arguments that protectionists use to justify trade barriers.
(a) _____
(b) _____
(c) _____
(d) _____
(e) _____
(f) _____

True-False

Circle T if the statement is true, F if it is false.

The following data represent the intercepts on straight-line production possibilities curves for Adanac and Zatelba. Use the data to answer true-false questions 1 through 6 and multiple-choice questions 4 and 5.

ADANAC		
Butter	0	20
Cloth	40	0

ZATELBA		
Butter	0	60
Cloth	60	0

1. In Adanac the opportunity cost of one unit of cloth is 1/4 unit of butter. T F

2. In Adanac the opportunity cost of butter is constant. T F

3. In Zatelba the opportunity cost of one unit of cloth is one unit of butter. T F

4. Adanac has the comparative advantage in the production of cloth. T F

5. Zatelba has the comparative advantage in the production of both goods. T F

6. With specialization and trade, the trading possibilities line of both nations would move outside their production possibilities curves. T F

7. International trade tends to increase the efficiency of allocation of the world's resources and leads to a greater world output of goods.   **T F**

8. A tariff on coffee in Canada is an example of a protective tariff.   **T F**

9. When Canada levies an import tariff, some groups in Canada gain and others lose.   **T F**

10. Direct subsidies to vital industries would be more effective than tariffs as a means to ensure military self-sufficiency.   **T F**

11. An import quota specifies the minimum price that can be charged for an imported good.   **T F**

12. The economic consequences of tariffs and import quotas are identical.   **T F**

13. One-crop economies may be able to make themselves more stable and diversified by imposing tariffs on goods imported from abroad; but these tariffs are apt also to lower the standard of living in these economies.   **T F**

14. The only argument for tariffs that has strong economic justification is the argument of increasing domestic employment.   **T F**

15. If A and B are the only nations that produce and consume figs, and there is free trade between the two nations, an increase in the supply of figs in B will lower the price of figs in B and in A. **T F**

16. Canada's standard of living would increase if we stopped importing goods produced in countries with very low wages.   **T F**

17. A policy of free trade was a contributing factor in Great Britain's industrialization and rapid growth in the mid-nineteenth century.   **T F**

18. The basic goal of the WTO is liberalization of world trade.   **T F**

Multiple-Choice

Circle the letter that corresponds to the best answer.

1. Nations would not need to engage in trade if:

(a)   all products were produced from the same combinations of resources
(b)   world resources were evenly distributed among nations
(c)   consumers had no preference for imported brands over domestic brands of goods
(d)   all of the above

2. Country A has a comparative advantage over country B in the production of sofas:
(a)   when sofas are produced in both countries and wages are lower in country A
(b)   when country A has an absolute advantage in the production of sofas
(c)   when the opportunity cost of sofas is lower in country A than in country B
(d)   when the opportunity cost of sofas is lower in country B than in country A

3. If country B has a comparative advantage over country A in the production of steel, then:
(a)   country B has an absolute advantage in the production of steel
(b)   the production of steel in country B uses fewer resources than in country A
(c)   the opportunity cost of producing steel is less in country B than in country A
(d)   inputs are more efficient in country B than in country A

Use the tables preceding true-false question 1 to answer the following two questions.

4. If Adanac and Zatelba engage in trade, the terms of trade will be:
(a)   between one and two units of butter for one unit of cloth
(b)   between 1/2 and one unit of butter for one unit of cloth
(c)   between three and four units of butter for one unit of cloth
(d)   between 1/8 and 1/4 unit of butter for one unit of cloth.

5. If, after trade starts, the exchange ratio was 1 cloth for 1/2 butter, the gains from trade would:
(a)   all go to Adanac
(b)   all go to Zatelba
(c)   be equally distributed between Adanac and Zatelba
(d)   be captured by the larger of the two countries

6. The terms of trade:
  (a)   are the reciprocal of the exchange rate
  (b)   measure the number of units of imports obtained per unit of export
  (c)   are given by the reciprocal of the foreign trade multiplier
  (d)   improve whenever the exchange rate depreciates

7. What does economic growth have in common with specialization and trade according to the principle of comparative advantage?
  (a)   both cause a nation's production possibilities curve to shift outward
  (b)   both permit a nation to consume combinations of goods that would otherwise not have been available
  (c)   both change the slope or steepness of the production possibilities curve
  (d)   both expand the supply of available resources

8. In the trade model, changing the assumption of constant costs to one of increasing costs results in:
  (a)   the principle of comparative advantage no longer holding
  (b)   only one of two trading partners gaining from trade
  (c)   a tendency towards incomplete specialization
  (d)   trade flows being greater than in the constant cost model

9. Suppose that only three nations trade in the world market for molybdenum. At the current world price, nation A wants to import 3 million tons, nation B wants to export 2 million tons, and nation C wants to export 4 million tons. What can be inferred about the current world price?
  (a)   it is below the equilibrium world price
  (b)   it is above equilibrium world price
  (c)   it is the equilibrium world price
  (d)   it could the equilibrium but we don't have enough information to be certain

10. Which one of the following is a characteristic of tariffs?
  (a)   they legally prohibit the importation of goods from abroad
  (b)   they specify the maximum amounts of specific commodities that may be imported during a given period of time
  (c)   they often protect domestic producers from foreign competition
  (d)   they enable nations to reduce their exports and increase their imports during periods of depression

11. The motive for a nation to erect barriers to the importation of goods and services is to:
  (a)   improve economic efficiency in that nation
  (b)   protect and benefit special-interest groups in that nation
  (c)   reduce the prices of the goods and services produced in that nation
  (d)   expand the export of goods and services to foreign nations

12. Which of the following is the likely result of Canada employing tariffs to protect its high wages and standard of living from cheap foreign labour?
  (a)   a decrease in the productivity of Canadian workers
  (b)   an increase in Canadian exports
  (c)   a rise in the Canadian real GDP
  (d)   an improved standard of living for workers in low-wage country

13. Which of the following is a likely result of imposing tariffs to increase domestic employment?
  (a)   a short-run increase in domestic employment
  (b)   retaliatory increases in the tariffs of foreign nations
  (c)   a long-run decline in exports
  (d)   all of the above

14. Which of the following is not true of tariffs established to support an infant industry?
  (a)   such tariffs tend to remain in place long after the industry has matured
  (b)   it is difficult for government to determine which infant industries have potential to benefit from such a tariff
  (c)   such tariffs may not be the best way to achieve the goal: direct subsidies might be more effective
  (d)   all of the above are true

Answer the next four questions (15 through 18) on the basis of the following diagram, where *Sd* and *Dd* are the domestic supply and demand for a product and Pw is the world price of that product.

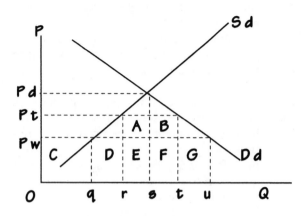

15. In a closed economy (without international trade), the equilibrium price would be:
(a)   *OPd*; but in an open economy, the equilibrium price will be *OPt*
(b)   *OPd*; but in an open economy, the equilibrium price will be *OPw*
(c)   *OPd*; but in an open economy, the equilibrium price will be *OPd*
(d)   *OPd*; but in an open economy, the equilibrium price will be *OPt*

16. If there were free trade in this economy and no tariffs, the total revenue going to the foreign producers is represented by:
(a)   area C
(b)   areas A and B combined
(c)   areas A, B, E, and F combined
(d)   areas D, E, F, and G combined

17. If a tariff was imposed in the amount of *PwPt* per unit imported, then domestic producers would supply:
(a)   *0q* units and foreign producers would supply *qu* units
(b)   *0s* units and foreign producers would supply *su* units
(c)   *0r* units and foreign producers would supply *rt* units
(d)   *0t* units and foreign producers would supply *tu* units

18. Given a per unit tariff in the amount of P_wP_t, the amount of the tariff revenue paid by consumers of this product is represented by:
(a)   area A
(b)   area B
(c)   areas A and B combined
(d)   areas D, E, F, and G combined

19. A tariff introduced to protect the Canadian clothing industry would create:
(a)   gains for shareholders, workers and consumers of the Canadian clothing industry
(b)   gains for shareholders and workers that exceed the costs to consumers
(c)   costs to consumers that exceed the gains for shareholders and workers
(d)   costs to shareholders, workers and consumers

20. In Canada, a tariff on which good would be considered a revenue tariff (as opposed to a protective tariff)?
(a)   wheat
(b)   potatoes
(c)   coffee
(d)   apples

21. An example of a non-tariff barrier is:
(a)   unreasonable labelling standards for food products imported from Brazil
(b)   a quota on imported French wine
(c)   voluntary export restriction by Toyota
(d)   an export subsidy for Canadian book publishers

22. If Japanese manufacturers dump VCRs in Canada, they are:
(a)   selling VCRs in Canada at a price less than the cost of production
(b)   selling VCRs in Canada at a price less than the price in Japan
(c)   selling VCRs in Canada at a price that is less than the price in Japan plus shipping cost
(d)   selling VCRs in Canada that were produced in a foreign government-owned establishment

23. Which group would be unlikely to be in support of a Canadian tariff on foreign-recorded CDs?
(a)   artists recording in Canada
(b)   owners of recording studios in Canada
(c)   employees in recording studios in Canada
(d)   music retail stores in Canada

24. Strategic trade policy is a variant of which argument in favour of tariffs?
(a)   infant-industry
(b)   diversification for stability
(c)   protection against dumping
(d)   increased domestic employment

25. Which of the following is not among the initiatives of the World Trade Organization?
 (a) reductions in tariffs worldwide
 (b) rules to promote trade in services
 (c) protections for intellectual property rights
 (d) sanctions against nations who violate human rights

26. The common currency used by most nations in the European Union is the:
 (a) pound
 (b) deutschmark
 (c) dollar
 (d) euro

Problems and Projects

1. Comparative Advantage: Cloth and Wine

Assume that labour is the only input for making cloth and wine. In England it takes six hours of labour to produce one unit of cloth and four hours to produce one unit of wine. There are a total of 60 hours of labour available in the English economy. In Canada it takes 2.5 hours to produce one unit of cloth and two hours to produce one unit of wine. There are a total of 30 labour hours available in Canada.

(a) Construct the production possibilities graphs for cloth and wine in England and Canada.
(b) What does Canada have a comparative advantage in producing?
(c) If trade takes place, what should Canada produce, export, and import?
(d) Suppose that the number of labour hours available in England increases to 120. What does Canada now have a comparative advantage in producing?
(e) If trade takes place, what should Canada produce, export, and import?

2. Comparative Advantage: Wheat and Copper

Below are the production possibilities curves for Canada and Chile. Suppose these two nations do not currently engage in international trade or specialization, and suppose that points A and a show the combinations of wheat and copper they now produce and consume.

(a) The fact that the curves are straight lines indicates that the cost ratios in the two nations are (changing, constant) _____.

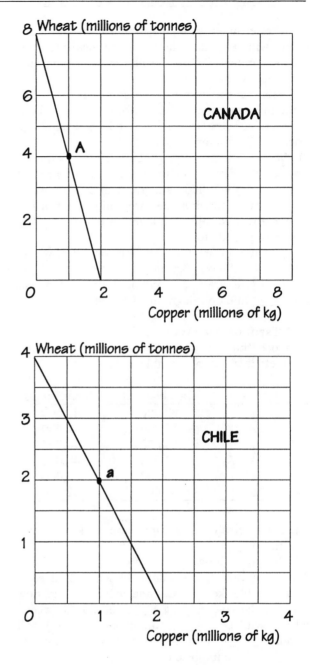

(b) Examination of the two curves reveals that the cost ratio in
(1) Canada is _____ million tonnes of wheat for one million kilograms of copper.
(2) Chile is _____ million tonnes of wheat for one million kilograms of copper.
(c) If these two nations were to specialize and trade wheat for copper,
(1) Canada would specialize in producing _____ (Why?);
(2) Chile would specialize in producing _____.

(d) The terms of trade, if specialization and trade occur, will be greater than two and less than four million tonnes of wheat for one million kilograms of copper. Why?

(e) Assume the terms of trade turn out to be three million tonnes of wheat for one million kilograms of copper. Draw in the trading possibilities lines for Canada and Chile.

(f) With these trading possibilities lines, suppose Canada decides to consume five million tonnes of wheat and one million kilograms of copper, while Chile decides to consume three million tonnes of wheat and one million kilograms of copper. The gains from trade to:

    (1) Canada are _____ million tonnes of wheat and _____ million kilograms of copper.

    (2) Chile are _____ million tonnes of wheat and _____ million kilograms of copper.

3. A Tariff on Blankets

Suppose that the Canadian demand for woven blankets is given in the table.

Price	Canadian Qd	Canadian Qs
21	62,000	42,000
22	59,000	44,000
23	56,000	46,000
24	53,000	48,000
25	50,000	50,000
26	47,000	52,000

(a) The domestic equilibrium price is $_____, and quantity is _____.

(b) Suppose Canada can now import blankets. Foreign suppliers are willing to sell at $22 each as many blankets as Canada will buy. The new price in Canada will be $_____, and quantity consumed with be _____. Canadian producers will supply _____ and the remaining quantity of _____ will be imported.

(c) If the Canadian government imposes an import tariff of $1 per blanket, the new price in Canada will be $_____, and quantity consumed with be _____. Canadian producers will supply _____ and the remaining quantity of _____ will be imported. The government will collect tariff revenue of $_____.

(d) Of the following groups, who gains from the tariff, and who loses: Canadian blanket consumers, Canadian blanket producers, foreign blanket producers?

4. Export Supply, Import Demand, and World Equilibrium

The following table shows demand and supply for wine in Italy and France.

(a) If there is no trade, the price in Italy would be $_____, and the price in France would be $_____.

(b) Use the data to generate export supply and import demand schedules for each nation, and plot these in the graph below.

(c) When the two nations trade, the equilibrium price in both nations will be $_____.

(d) In equilibrium: Italy produces _____ units, consumes _____ units, and (exports, imports) _____ the difference. France produces _____ units, consumes _____ units, and (exports, imports) _____ the rest.

Price	Italy		France	
	Qd	Qs	Qd	Qs
$8	2	10	4	8
7	3	9	5	7
6	4	8	6	6
5	5	7	7	5
4	6	6	8	4
3	7	5	9	3

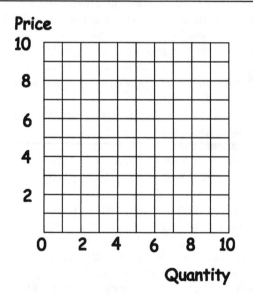

Discussion Questions

1. Why do nations specialize in certain products and export their surplus production of these goods at the same time that they are importing other goods? Why not reallocate their resources to producing on their own the goods and services that they wish to consume?

2. What three facts provide the basis for trade among nations?

3. Explain: (a) the theory of comparative advantage; (b) what is meant by and what determines the terms of trade; (c) the gains from the trade.

4. What motivates nations to erect barriers to the importation of goods from abroad, and what types of barriers do they erect?

5. Suppose Canada were to increase the tariff on wine imported from Europe (and elsewhere). How would this affect the following:
(a) the price of wines in Canada;
(b) the total amount of wine sold each year in Canada;
(c) output and employment in the European wine industry;
(d) production and employment in the Canadian wine industry;
(e) European incomes obtained by selling wine in Canada;
(f) the European demand for goods produced in Canada;
(g) the production and employment in those Canadian industries that export goods to Europe;
(h) the standard of living in Canada and Europe;
(i) the allocation of resources in Canada;
(j) the allocation of Europe's resources?

6. What is the "case for protection"? How valid and pertinent to Canada is each of the six basic arguments for protection?

7. If it is true that trade barriers impose greater costs on consumers than the benefits conferred on businesses and workers, why have trade barriers been so prevalent throughout our history?

8. What is the WTO, and what does this organization seek to achieve?

Answers

Quick Quiz
1. (b) pp. 376-378
2. (d) pp. 378-379
3. (a) pp. 381-383
4. (a) pp. 381-383
5. (a) pp. 384-386

6. (a) pp. 390-391
7. (c) p. 389
8. (a) pp. 392-395
9. (d) pp. 392-395
10. (d) p. 395
11. (d) pp. 395-399
12. (b) p. 398
13. (d) pp. 400-401
14. (d) pp. 400-402

Fill-in Questions
1. labour
2. uneven, different
3. (a) less, more; (b) more, less; (c) hats, bananas; (d) 3, 4, demand, supply; (e) 1/3, 2/7, 4, 3.5; (f) increases
4. allocation, standard
5. tariffs, import, non-tariff, voluntary export
6. (a) increase; (b) decrease; (c) (1) increase, (2) decrease; (d) decrease, decrease
7. (a) military self-sufficiency; (b) infant industry; (c) increase domestic employment; (d) diversification for stability; (e) cheap foreign labour; (f) protection against dumping

True-False
1. F   1/2 unit of butter
2. T   straight line PPCs
3. T
4. T   1/2 butter is lower than 1 butter
5. F   with only two goods one country cannot have a comparative advantage in both goods
6. T   onto their trading lines
7. T
8. F   we don't grow coffee, so no domestic jobs
9. T   e.g., consumers lose and producers gain
10. T
11. F   quota is a maximum amount that may be imported
12. F   a tariff generates government revenue; a quota does not
13. T   diversification goes against comparative advantage
14. F
15. T
16. F   our standard of living would deteriorate
17. T
18. T

Multiple-Choice
1. (d) if any of the three conditions hold, there is reason to trade
2. (c) comparative advantage is defined in terms of relative opportunity costs

3. (c) as for the previous question

4. (b) between the opportunity cost ratios of the two producers

5. (b) because the terms of trade simply match Adanac's opportunity costs along their PPC

6. (b)

7. (b) growth by shifting the PPC, and specialization and trade by creating a trading line outside the PPC

8. (c) specialization occurs only until the opportunity cost has reached the terms of trade

9. (b) exports (2+4) exceed imports (3), implying an excess supply at the current price, tending to push price down

10. (c) typically, though some tariffs are exclusively revenue tariffs

11. (b) typically

12. (a) we make ourselves worse off by using some workers in industries where we do not have comparative advantage

13. (d)

14. (d) unfortunately!

15. (b)

16. (d) they sell quantity qu at a price of Pw

17. (c)

18. (c) $PtPw$ x import quantity (rt)

19. (c)

20. (c) because we don't produce coffee; we do produce the other goods

21. (a)

22. (a)

23. (d) stores sell predominantly music recorded elsewhere, so would lose sales; the other groups would gain income

24. (a) the idea is to create a comparative advantage where one would not otherwise exist

25. (d) the others are stated goals of the WTO

26. (d)

Problems and Projects

1. (a) endpoints: England: 60 hrs/6 hrs per cloth = 10 cloth; 60 hrs/4 hrs per wine = 15 wine; Canada: 30/2.5 = 12, 30/2 = 15 – see graphs below; (b) cloth; (c) cloth, cloth, wine; (d) still cloth since the opportunity cost ratio comparison has not changed (England's PPC expands but its slope is unchanged); (e) cloth, cloth, wine

2. (a) constant; (b) (1) 4, (2) 2; (c) (1) wheat; because its cost of producing 1 wheat is only 0.25 copper, compared to Chile's cost of 0.50 copper, (2) copper; (d) one of the two nations would be unwilling to trade if the terms of trade were outside this range; (e) see graphs below; (f) by com-

paring before specialization and trade point "A" and "a" with after specialization and trade "T" and "t": (1) 1, 0, (2) 1, 0

graphs for problem 1:

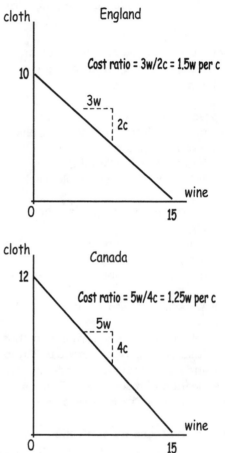

3. (a) 25, 50,000; (b) 22, 59,000, 44,000, 15,000; (c) 23, 56,000, 46,000, 10,000, 10,000; (d) Canadian consumers lose (price rises from $22 to $23); Canadian producers gain (from the same price increase, and increase of their sales from 44,000 to 46,000); foreign producers lose (sales fall from 15,000 to 10,000)

4. (a) 4, 6 (where Qd=Qs); (b) see table and graph below; (c) 5; (d) Nation 1 produces 7, consumes 5, exports 2; Nation 2 produces 5, consumes 7, imports 2

Price	Italy		France	
	import	export	import	export
$8	0	8	0	4
7	0	6	0	2
6	0	4	0	0
5	0	2	2	0
4	0	0	4	0
3	2	0	6	0

graphs for problem 2:

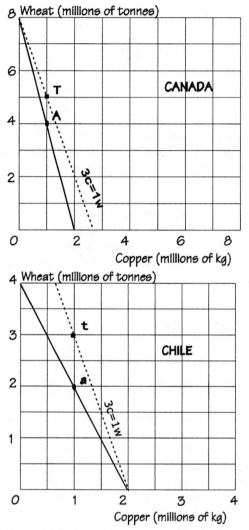

graph for problem 4:

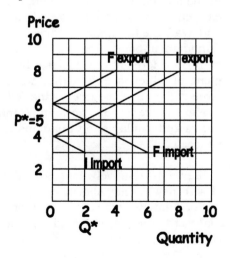

Chapter 17

Exchange Rates and the Balance of Payments

Overview

This chapter is about the financial side of the international trade discussed in Chapter 16. The main topics are: (1) how nations using different currencies are able to trade with each other; (2) how transactions with non-residents are recorded in the balance of payments accounts; (3) how to interpret various balance of payments accounts and terminology; (4) how foreign exchange rates are determined in flexible rate and fixed rate systems; and (5) a brief outline of different exchange rate systems that have been used in recent times.

To facilitate transactions of goods, services, or financial assets between people in different countries, there must be a mechanism for them to exchange their respective currencies. The foreign exchange market serves this function. The price in one money for a unit of another money is called the foreign exchange rate (or rate of exchange). Canada's exchange rate for any foreign currency is determined by the demand for and the supply of that currency. Exports from Canada create a demand for Canadian dollars (and a supply of foreign currency). Canadian imports create a supply of Canadian dollars (and a demand for foreign currency).

A nation summarizes its transactions with the rest of the world in its balance of payments: a record of how it obtained foreign money during the year and what it did with this foreign money. Of course, all foreign money obtained was used for some purpose — it did not evaporate — and consequently the balance of payments always balances. However, individual accounts (current account and capital account) need not balance.

A balance of payments deficit (surplus) exists when the receipts of foreign money are less (greater) than the payments of foreign money and the nation's official international reserves are reduced (expanded). The discussion of these topics is linked with explanations of exchange-rate determination under flexible rate and fixed rate systems. How balance of payments deficits or surpluses are resolved depends on the type of exchange rate system in effect. This difference is an important element to consider in weighing the advantages and disadvantages of fixed versus flexible rates.

In the twentieth century three main exchange-rate systems were used: the gold standard and the Bretton Woods system (both fixed exchange-rate systems), and the current managed floating rate system.

Chapter Outline

17.1 Financing International Trade

◈ How are import and export transactions financed?

• International trade differs from domestic trade because each nation uses a different currency. The problem is resolved with foreign exchange markets where money used by one nation can be traded for another nation's money.

  o Canadian exports create a foreign demand for dollars, the fulfillment of which increases the supply of foreign currency in the foreign exchange market. More foreign currency is now in Canadian banks and available to Canadian buyers.

  o Canadian imports create a domestic demand for foreign currencies, the fulfillment of which requires that we supply more dollars in the currency market. Less foreign currency is now in Canadian banks and available to Canadians to purchase.

➲ This chapter is relatively long and difficult, and filled with new terms. Allocate your time accordingly. Fortunately, some of the new terms are just special words used in international economics for economic concepts already familiar to you.

Quick Quiz

1. A transaction that creates a demand for dollars will simultaneously give rise to:
    (a) a demand for foreign currency
    (b) a supply of foreign currency
    (c) a supply of dollars
    (d) none of the above

2. A decision by a Canadian to purchase a rare Elvis album from a dealer in London, England leads to:
    (a) an increase in the demand for pounds and a decrease in the demand for dollars
    (b) an increase in the demand for pounds and an increase in the supply of dollars
    (c) a decrease in the supply of dollars and an increase in the supply of pounds
    (d) a decrease in the demand for dollars and an increase in the supply of dollars

17.2 The Balance of Payments

◇ How are different types of transactions classified in the balance of payments accounts?

◇ What is the connection between a nation's balance of payments and its official international reserves?

• A nation's balance of payments is an annual record of all transactions between its residents and residents of all other nations.

• The current account records trade in goods and services.
    o Credits are: merchandise exports, exports of services, receipts of investment income, and receipts of transfers.
    o Debits are: merchandise imports, imports of services, payments of investment income, and transfers paid out.
    o The trade balance is equal to the difference between the exports and imports of goods. A "favourable" trade balance exists if exports exceed imports.
    o The balance on current account is equal to the balance on goods and services plus the balance on investment income and transfers.

• The capital account records the nation's trade in real and financial assets.
    o Credits are sales of assets.
    o Debits are purchases of assets.

    o The capital account balance is a surplus (deficit) if sales are greater (less) than purchases.

• The current and capital accounts are interrelated. A nation with a current account deficit can finance the deficit by borrowing or selling assets abroad (incurring a capital account surplus), and a nation with a current account surplus can lend or buy assets abroad (incurring a capital account deficit).

• The official settlement account refers to the movement of official international reserves. When Canada has a net surplus on its current and capital accounts combined, our reserves of foreign currency will increase, showing in the balance of payments as a negative value on the official settlements account. When our current and capital accounts combine for a deficit, we will have used up some international reserves, and the official settlements account will show a positive value.

• Whenever the balance of payments is said to be in surplus or deficit, this refers to the net surplus or deficit before including the official settlements account. Canada has a balance of payments surplus (deficit) when the current and capital account combined balance is positive (negative) and the official reserves increase (decrease).

• A balance of payments deficit is not necessarily bad (nor is a surplus necessarily good). However, a persistent balance of payments deficit is undesirable because the nation's official international reserves are limited, and if they are exhausted the nation may be forced to take painful macroeconomic adjustments to correct the deficit.

• These points can be illustrated using Canadian 2002 data shown in Table 17-1. We had a current account surplus of $17.3 billion, so we were able to lend or buy assets abroad to the extent of this excess of current account inpayments over outpayments. The capital account deficit of $6.6 billion reflects the net outflow of investment from Canada. Overall, there was a net inflow of foreign currency equal to $10.7 billion (+$17.3 - $6.6), and this was added to our official reserves. It was recorded as -$10.7 billion on the official settlements account.

⮕ Capital flows can be tricky to classify as debits or credits. To keep this straight, think of merchandise trade. When Canada exports a satellite dish, money comes in from abroad so that is a credit for Canada. Similarly, when Canada exports a government bond, or the title deed to an office building in Brampton, or shares in Nortel, money comes in from abroad so that is also a credit for Canada.

➲ Be careful with the sign (+ or -) when referring to the official settlement balance. The correct sign is counterintuitive for most people.

Quick Quiz

3. Canadian wheat exports to Asia count in Canada's balance of payments as:
(a)   a current account credit (or inpayment)
(b)   a current account debit (or outpayment)
(c)   a capital account credit (or inpayment)
(d)   a capital account debit (or outpayment)

4. Sales of Canadian real capital or financial assets to foreigners:
(a)   push the capital account in the direction of a deficit
(b)   result in an inpayment of foreign currencies
(c)   uses up Canada's inventories of foreign currencies
(d)   none of the above

5. If the current account has a deficit of $8 billion and the capital account a surplus of $5 billion, then:
(a)   there is a favourable balance of trade
(b)   there is a balance of payments surplus
(c)   the official settlement account will show a positive number
(d)   there is a gain of official international reserves

17.3   Foreign Exchange Markets: Flexible Exchange Rates

◈ How does a flexible-exchange rate system work?

◈ How does a flexible-exchange rate system affect the domestic economy?

• With flexible rates, the demand for and the supply of foreign exchange determine exchange rates. The exchange rate for a currency is the price of that currency in terms of our dollars, and the equilibrium rate is found where the quantity

demanded of that money is equal to the quantity supplied.

• A change in the demand or supply of foreign money will cause the exchange rate for that money to rise or fall. When the dollar price of one unit of a foreign currency rises (falls), it is said that the dollar has depreciated (appreciated) and that the foreign money has appreciated (depreciated).

• Changes in the demand for or supply of a foreign currency are caused by changes in:
   o   tastes
   o   relative incomes
   o   relative price levels
   o   relative interest rates
   o   speculation

• The flexible-exchange rate system has the huge advantage of providing an automatic adjustment mechanism for payments imbalances. A balance of payments deficit (surplus), will cause a nation's currency to depreciate (appreciate). This will make foreign goods and services more (less) expensive, decrease (increase) imports, make a nation's goods and services less (more) expensive for foreigners to buy, and increase (decrease) its exports. These adjustments correct the nation's payments deficit (surplus).

• Flexible exchange rates have three disadvantages:
   o   currency fluctuations create uncertainties for international traders and discourage trade;
   o   exchange rate changes change the terms of trade;
   o   exchange rate fluctuations can destabilize economies (by creating inflation or unemployment).

➲ The terms depreciate and appreciate can be confusing. To depreciate means to decrease in exchange value (and appreciate means to increase). If country A's currency depreciates, the amount of country B's currency that a unit of A's currency will exchange for will decrease. If 1 dollar first bought 10 pesos, and later bought only 8 pesos, the dollar has depreciated.

Quick Quiz

6. If the rouble-dollar exchange rate moves from 20 roubles per dollar to 22 roubles per dollar, then:
(a)   the price of buying a certain number of dollars has fallen
(b)   the rouble has appreciated

(c)   the dollar has depreciated
(d)   the price of buying a certain number of roubles has fallen

7. The Canadian dollar would depreciate against the South Korean won if:
(a)   Koreans begin buying real estate in the Maritimes
(b)   the Bank of Canada tightens monetary policy, pushing up our interest rates
(c)   a recession in Korea reduces their purchases of Canadian minerals and forest products
(d)   Korean-built cars gain popularity with Canadian consumers

8. Which of the following does not shift either the supply curve or the demand curve for a nation's currency?
(a)   a change in the exchange rate
(b)   a change in the nation's interest rates
(c)   a change in the nation's GDP
(d)   a change in the nation's price level

17.4   Fixed Exchange Rates

◇ How does a fixed exchange-rate system work?

• When a nation elects to fix (or "peg") its exchange rate at a certain level, its government must somehow prevent the surpluses (or shortages) of their currency in the foreign exchange market that result from balance of payments deficits (or surpluses). There are several ways to do this:
   o   With currency intervention a government can stabilize the exchange rate by selling (buying) foreign money in exchange for its own money when there is a shortage (surplus) of the foreign money.
   o   With trade policies (such as import tariffs and quotas, and export subsidies) a nation with a payments deficit can discourage imports and encourage exports. Such tactics reduce the volume of trade and hamper efficient resource allocation.
   o   With exchange controls a nation can deal with a payments deficit by requiring exporters who earn foreign exchange to sell it to the government. The government then rations available foreign exchange among importers to ensure that imports are not too high compared to exports.

   o   Using domestic stabilization policies (monetary and fiscal policies) a nation with a balance of payments deficit can reduce its national income and price level to stimulate net exports, and raise interest rates to attract capital inflows.

Quick Quiz
9. The Bank of Canada's reserves of foreign currency:
(a)   are decreased when Canada has a balance of payments surplus
(b)   are essentially infinite
(c)   consist mainly of gold
(d)   will run out if Canada has persistent and sizable balance of payments deficits

10. To maintain a fixed exchange rate in the face of a significant and ongoing balance of payments deficit, a nation may choose to:
(a)   increase government spending
(b)   lower interest rates
(c)   devalue their currency
(d)   put tariffs on imports and subsidies on exports

11. Exchange controls are intended to serve as a means of:
(a)   avoiding currency appreciation
(b)   controlling the quantity of outpayments made by the nation's citizens
(c)   controlling the quantity of inpayments received by the nation's citizens
(d)   creating a black market for foreign exchange

17.5   International Exchange Rate Systems

◇ What exchange rate systems have been used in the past and what system is used today by most countries?

• In recent times major trading nations have employed three different exchange-rate systems.
• From 1879 to 1934 the gold standard system kept exchange rates fairly stable. A nation was on the gold standard when it:
   o   defined its currency in terms of a quantity of gold;
   o   maintained a fixed relationship between its stock of gold and its money supply, and;
   o   allowed gold to be freely exported and imported.

- Because each currency had a fixed gold value, and gold could flow freely between countries, currencies also had fixed values (exchange rates) in terms of one another.
- When a nation with a balance of payments deficit (surplus) began to lose (gain) gold, its money supply would shrink (grow). This would raise (lower) interest rates and reduce (expand) aggregate demand, domestic output, employment, and prices in that country; and the payments deficit (surplus) would be eliminated.
- The relative stability of exchange rates under the gold standard encouraged trade and automatically corrected payments imbalances. However, it required a nation to tolerate unpleasant domestic adjustments such as recession and inflation, because they had no independent control over their own money supply.
- During the Great Depression of the 1930s, many nations abandoned the gold standard, devaluing their currencies in hopes of selling more exports and boosting their employment and output.
- From 1944 until 1971 most nations used an adjustable-peg system known as the Bretton Woods system. The International Monetary Fund (IMF) was created to manage this system that kept exchange rates relatively stable.
  - The system required each IMF member nation to define its currency in terms of gold or US dollars. This established fixed exchange rates.
  - Each nation committed to use their international reserve, when necessary to maintain their fixed exchange rate.
  - Each nation could acquire reserves for protecting their exchange rates by selling foreign currencies, selling gold, or borrowing on a short-term basis from the IMF.
  - A nation experiencing a fundamental imbalance (persistent and sizable balance of payments deficit) was permitted to address the problem by orderly devaluation of its currency (increasing its defined gold or dollar equivalent).
- Gold and US dollars came to be regarded as international reserves. Other nations accumulated vast quantities of US dollars, as the United States ran continual balance of payments deficits. Because US gold reserves were limited, it eventually became unlikely that the United States would be able to maintain free convertibility of dollars into

gold at $35 per ounce. The United States suspended convertibility of the dollar in 1971, ending the Bretton Woods system, and beginning the era of floating exchange rates.
- Exchange rates today are managed by individual nations to avoid short-term fluctuations. Rates are allowed to float in the long term to correct fundamental payments imbalances. There is a loose agreement between major nations on this system. This new system of managed floating exchange rates is favoured by some and criticized by others.
- Many people blame fluctuations in exchange rates on speculators who try to profit from buying and selling currencies. Speculative "bubbles" certainly can occur, where expectations temporarily become self-fulfilling and an exchange rate moves for no good economic reason, but such cases are rare. Typically, speculation has two beneficial effects:
  - Speculators help to lessen rate fluctuations by buying currencies that are low (thus raising their value) and selling currencies that are high (thus dropping their value).
  - Speculators absorb some of the risk that most international traders want to avoid. They do this by participating in currency futures markets where traders wanting to avoid risk can "hedge" against adverse fluctuations.

Quick Quiz
12. Under the gold standard, a nation with a balance of payments surplus would experience:
   (a)   gold inflows
   (b)   money supply contraction
   (c)   interest rate increases
   (d)   all of the above

13. Under the Bretton Woods system:
   (a)   gold and U.S. dollars functioned as international reserves
   (b)   the United States experienced balance of payments deficits
   (c)   doubt arose over the ability of the United States to continue to convert U.S. dollars into gold at the guaranteed rate of $35 per ounce
   (d)   all of the above

14. Canada's current exchange rate system is best described as:

(a) the gold standard
(b) a flexible exchange-rate system
(c) a fixed-exchange rate system
(d) a managed floating exchange-rate system

Terms and Concepts

foreign exchange market
balance of payments
current account
balance on goods and services
trade surplus
trade deficit
capital account
official international reserves
balance of payments deficit
balance of payments surplus
exchange rate

flexible or floating exchange-rate system
fixed-exchange rate system
depreciation
appreciation
purchasing power parity theory
currency intervention
exchange control
gold standard
devaluation
Bretton Woods System
International Monetary Fund
managed floating exchange rates

Fill-In Questions

1. The rate of exchange for the French franc is the number of (francs, dollars) _____ that a Canadian must pay to obtain one (franc, dollar) _____.

2. When the rate of exchange for 1 Euro is 1.339 Canadian dollars, the rate of exchange for the Canadian dollar is _____ Euros.

3. (a) Canadian exports create a (demand for, supply of) _____ foreign money and generate a _____ dollars;
(b) Canadian imports create a _____ foreign money and generate a _____ dollars.

4. A balance of payments transaction that earns foreign exchange for a nation is a (debit, credit) _____ and is shown with a (+, -) _____ sign. In contrast, a transaction that uses up foreign exchange is a _____ and is shown with a _____ sign.

5. The capital account records the capital inflows and capital outflows of a nation.

(a) Capital inflows are the expenditures made (in that nation, abroad) _____ for _____ and _____ assets by residents of (that nation, other nations) _____; and capital outflows are the expenditures made _____ by residents of _____ for _____ and _____ assets.
(b) A nation has a capital account surplus when its capital inflows are (greater, less) _____ than its outflows.

6. A nation may:
(a) finance a current account deficit by (buying, selling) _____ assets or by (borrowing, lending) _____ abroad; and
(b) use a current account surplus to (buy, sell) _____ assets or to (borrow, lend) _____ abroad.

7. (a) The official international reserves of a nation are the quantities of _____ owned by its _____ bank.
(b) In the official settlements balance, if Canada has an entry with a + (plus) sign, this indicates that the Bank of Canada has (bought, sold) _____ foreign exchange reserves.
(c) Thus a + (plus) on the official settlements balance means Canada has had a balance of payments (surplus, deficit) _____; and a - (minus) sign would mean Canada has had a payments _____.

8. If our dollar is floating freely, so the Bank of Canada (is, is not) _____ intervening in the foreign exchange market, and Canada is tending towards a balance of payments deficit:
(a) our dollar will (appreciate, depreciate) _____; and
(b) this change in the exchange rate will cause our imports to (increase, decrease) _____, our exports to _____, and the size of our payments deficit will _____.

9. To fix or "peg" the rate of exchange for the euro when:
(a) the Canadian dollar is appreciating against the euro, Canada would (buy, sell) _____ euros in exchange for dollars;
(b) the Canadian dollar is depreciating against the euro, Canada would _____ euros in exchange for dollars.

10. A nation on the gold standard: (1) defines its money in terms of _____; (2) maintains a fixed relationship between its _____ supply and gold _____; and (3) allows gold to be freely _____ from and _____ into the nation.

11. When the gold standard was in effect:
(a) exchange rates were relatively (stable, unstable) _____;
(b) but when a nation had a payments deficit, gold flowed (into, out of) _____ the nation, its money supply and price level (increased, decreased) _____, and its interest rates _____. Thus, its payments deficit (rose, fell) _____, but it suffered (inflation, recession) _____.

12. The Bretton Woods system was designed to bring about a modified fixed exchange rate system; and, to accomplish this, it employed the _____ system of exchange rates. Under this system:
(a) each member nation defined its monetary unit in terms of _____ or _____;
(b) each member nation stabilized the exchange rate for its currency and prevented it from rising by (buying, selling) _____ foreign currency, by (buying, selling) _____ gold, or by (borrowing from, lending to) _____ the International Monetary Fund;
(c) a nation with a fundamental payments deficit could (devalue, revalue) _____ its currency;
(d) it was hoped that exchange rates in the short run would be (stable, flexible) _____ enough to promote international trade and in the long run would be _____ enough to correct balance of payments imbalances.

True-False

Circle T if the statement is true, F if it is false.

1. The importation of goods by Canadians creates a supply of dollars in the foreign exchange market. **T F**

2. A country will have a favourable balance of trade whenever the value of exported goods is greater than the value of imported goods. **T F**

3. If a resident of Germany buys a cottage on Salt Spring Island, this counts as a credit on Canada's capital account, and a debit on Germany's capital account. **T F**

4. If the current account balance is $5 billion and the official settlements balance is -$4 billion, the capital account must be in a deficit of $1 billion. **T F**

5. A nation with a balance of payments deficit is losing official international reserves. **T F**

6. If Canadian $1.35 = US $1.00, then it must also be that US $0.65 = Canadian $1.00. **T F**

7. In a system of managed floating exchange rates, the central bank sometimes intervenes in the foreign exchange market. **T F**

8. The quantity demanded of US dollars is downsloping because foreigners purchase greater quantities of American goods, and so require more US dollars, as the US dollar becomes less expensive in foreign currency terms. **T F**

9. When the Bank of Canada buys US dollars, it is putting upward pressure on the international value of the Canadian dollar. **T F**

10. If Canada wishes to fix (or "peg") the value of the Canadian dollar in terms of the US dollar, the Bank of Canada must sell US dollars (in exchange for Canadian dollars) when the Canadian dollar is tending to depreciate. **T F**

11. Under the gold standard, if 1 franc is convertible for 5 grains of gold, and 1 pound is convertible for 15 grains of gold, then there will be a fixed exchange rate of 3 francs per 1 pound. **T F**

12. In the Bretton Woods system, a nation was permitted to devalue its currency by as much as 10% in order to address a fundamental balance of payments deficit. **T F**

13. A basic problem with the Bretton Woods system was its inability to bring about the changes in exchange rates needed to correct persistent payments deficits and surpluses. **T F**

14. The adjustable-peg system was intended to keep exchange rates nearly fixed, but also to avoid painful macroeconomic adjustments. **T F**

Multiple-Choice

Circle the letter that corresponds to the best answer.

1. If a Canadian could buy 25,000 British pounds for $100,000, the rate of exchange for the pound would be:
(a) $40
(b) $25
(c) $4
(d) $0.25

2. There is an increased demand for foreign currency (increased supply of Canadian dollars) when Canadians:
(a) pay for goods and services imported from abroad
(b) make payments of interest and dividends to foreign countries on their investments in Canada
(c) make real and financial investments abroad
(d) all of the above

3. A nation's balance on the current account is equal to its:
(a) exports less its imports of merchandise (goods)
(b) exports less its imports of goods and services
(c) exports less its imports of goods and services plus its net investment income and net transfers
(d) exports less its imports of goods, services, and capital

4. Capital flows into Canada include the purchase by foreign residents of:
(a) a factory building owned by Canadians
(b) shares of stock owned by Canadians
(c) bonds owned by Canadians
(d) all of the above

5. A Canadian current account deficit may be financed by:
(a) borrowing abroad
(b) selling real assets to foreigners

(c) selling financial assets to foreigners
(d) any of the above

6. If Canada's official settlements balance is zero, and Canada has a capital account surplus, it must also have a:
(a) current account surplus
(b) current account deficit
(c) balance of payments surplus
(d) balance of payments deficit

7. A nation may be able to correct or eliminate a persistent balance of payments deficit by:
(a) lowering the barriers on imported goods
(b) reducing the international value of its currency
(c) expanding its national income
(d) reducing its official international reserves

8. If exchange rates float freely, the exchange rate for any currency is determined by:
(a) the demand for it
(b) the supply of it
(c) the demand for and the supply of it
(d) the official reserves that "back" it

9. Under a floating exchange rate system, an increase in Canadian interest rates relative to US interest will:
(a) appreciate the Canadian dollar relative to the US dollar
(b) depreciate the Canadian dollar relative to the US dollar
(c) raise the price of US goods in Canadian dollars
(d) appreciate the US dollar relative to the Canadian dollar

10. If a Canadian province finances a deficit by borrowing abroad:
(a) Canadian interest rates will rise
(b) the Canadian dollar will depreciate
(c) the Canadian dollar will appreciate
(d) there will be an outflow of capital from Canada

11. If a nation had a balance of payments surplus and a floating exchange rate:
(a) its currency would appreciate, its exports would increase, and its imports would decrease

(b)   its currency would appreciate, its exports would decrease, and its imports would increase

(c)   its currency would depreciate, its exports would increase, and its imports would decrease

(d)   its currency would depreciate, its exports would decrease, and its imports would increase

Questions 12 and 13 are based on this graph. Assume that the only nations are Canada and Britain, and their currencies are the dollar and the pound.

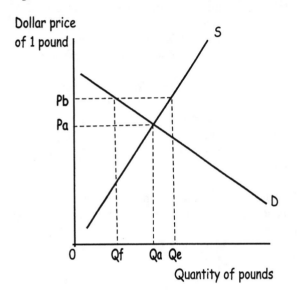

12. Which statement is false?
(a)   a change in the exchange rate from *Pa* to *Pb* represents a depreciation of the dollar relative to the pound
(b)   the exchange rate could move from *Pa* to *Pb* if the demand for pounds increases
(c)   the exchange rate could move from *Pa* to *Pb* if the supply of pounds decreases
(d)   given the current *S* and *D* curves, if the exchange rate were *Pb* there would be a balance of payments deficit for Canada.

13. If the exchange rate is at *Pb*, then what is Britain's balance of payments?
(a)   a deficit of *Qe* – *Qf* pounds
(b)   a surplus of *Qe* – *Qa* pounds
(c)   a deficit of *Qe* – *Qa* pounds
(d)   a surplus of *Qe* – *Qf* pounds

14. If exchange rates are flexible, which of the following would increase the Canadian dollar price of the Swedish krona?
(a)   a rate of inflation greater in Sweden than in Canada
(b)   real interest-rate decreases greater in Sweden than in Canada
(c)   national income increases slower in Sweden than in Canada
(d)   expectations that the price of the krona will be lower in the future

15. According to the theory of purchasing power parity, if a given basket of goods costs $40 in Canada, and 3,600 yen in Japan, then the exchange rate should move towards:
(a) $1 = 1 yen
(b) $1 = 90 yen
(c) $90 = 1 yen
(d)   none of the above

16. Which of the following would be one of the results of using flexible exchange rates to correct a nation's balance of payments surplus?
(a)   the nation's terms of trade with other nations would be worsened
(b)   the currency will depreciate
(c)   if the nation were at full employment, the decrease in exports and the increase in imports would be inflationary
(d)   exporters in the nation would find their sales abroad had decreased

17. Disadvantages of a floating exchange rate system include all of the following except:
(a)   uncertainty over future exchange rates
(b)   instability in the macroeconomy caused by changing exchange rates
(c)   decline in the terms of trade that accompany a currency depreciation
(d)   an automatic adjustment mechanism for balance of payments problems

18. A nation with fixed exchange rates and a payments surplus might attempt to resolve the surplus by employing:
(a)   import quotas
(b)   higher tariffs
(c)   subsidies on items the nation exports
(d)   none of the above

19. Which one of the following was not among the conditions a nation was required to meet to operate under the gold standard?
- (a)   use only gold as a medium of exchange
- (b)   maintain a fixed relationship between its gold stock and its money supply
- (c)   allow gold to be freely exported from and imported into the nation
- (d)   define its monetary unit in terms of a fixed quantity of gold

20. If the nations of the world were on the gold standard and one nation had a balance of payments surplus:
- (a)   foreign-exchange rates in that nation would rise toward the gold import point
- (b)   gold would tend to be imported into that nation
- (c)   the level of prices in that nation would tend to fall
- (d)   employment in that nation would tend to fall

21. Under the gold standard, a nation with a balance of payments deficit would experience all but one of the following. Which one?
- (a)   gold would flow out of the nation
- (b)   the nation's money supply would contract
- (c)   interest rates in the nation would fall
- (d)   real domestic output, employment, and prices in the nation would decline

22. Which of the following was the principal disadvantage of the gold standard?
- (a)   unstable foreign-exchange rates
- (b)   persistent payments imbalances
- (c)   the uncertainties and decreased trade that resulted from the depreciation of gold
- (d)   domestic macroeconomic adjustments experienced by a nation with a payments imbalance

23. Which of the following was not among the elements of the adjustable-peg system of foreign exchange rates?
- (a)   each nation defined its monetary unit in terms of gold or dollars
- (b)   nations bought and sold their own currencies to stabilize exchange rates
- (c)   nations were allowed to devalue their currencies when faced with persistent payments deficits

- (d)   the deposit by all nations of their international reserves with the IMF

24. With the demise of the Bretton Wood systems, the United States "floated" the dollar. This meant that:
- (a)   the value of the dollar was to be determined by the demand for and the supply of the dollar
- (b)   the dollar price of gold was to be increased
- (c)   the price of the dollar was to be set by international agreement
- (d)   the gold content of the dollar was to be reduced

25. Canada's current exchange-rate system is not *exactly* like any of the following, but which does it most closely resemble?
- (a)   gold standard
- (b)   flexible exchange-rate system
- (c)   fixed exchange-rate system
- (d)   currency union

26. A system of managed floating exchange rates:
- (a)   allows nations to stabilize exchange rates in the short term
- (b)   requires nations to stabilize exchange rates in the long term
- (c)   entails stable exchange rates in both the short and long term
- (d)   none of the above

27. Floating exchange rates:
- (a)   tend to correct payments imbalances
- (b)   reduce the uncertainties and risks associated with international trade
- (c)   increase the world's need for official international reserves
- (d)   tend to expand the volume of world trade

28. Exchange controls are subject to all of the following problems, except which one?
- (a)   distortions of trade patters
- (b)   favouritism towards some importers over others
- (c)   black markets where foreign exchange is sold at illegal exchange rates
- (d)   loss of control of the nation's money supply

29. Which of the following is an *incorrect* statement about currency speculators?

(a)   speculators' activity sometimes cause excess currency volatility

(b)   speculators' activity generally lessens exchange rate fluctuations

(c)   speculators in currency futures markets absorb some of the risk that others do not want to bear

(d)   on balance, speculators' activity is detrimental to international trade

Problems and Projects

1. Financing International Trade

1.   A Canadian exporter sells $3 million worth of wheat to an importer in Colombia. If the exchange rate for the Colombian peso is $0.02 (two cents), the wheat has a total value of 150 million pesos.

(a) There are two ways the import firm might pay for the wheat. One way is to write a cheque for 150 million pesos drawn on its bank in Bogota and send it to the Canadian exporter.

(1) The Canadian exporter would then sell the cheque to its bank in Regina where its demand deposit would increase by $_____ million.

(2) This Regina bank branch sells the cheque for 150 million pesos to its main branch, that is, the head office branch of the bank that keeps an account in the Bogota bank. The Regina bank's account in the main branch increases by _____ million (dollars, pesos) _____; and the main branch's account in the Bogota bank increases by _____ million (pesos, dollars) _____.

(b) The second way for the importer to pay is to buy from its bank in Bogota a draft on a Canadian bank for $3 million, pay for this draft by writing a cheque for 150 million pesos drawn on the Bogota bank, and send the cheque to the Canadian exporter.

(1) The Canadian exporter would then deposit the draft in its account in the Regina bank and its demand deposit account there would increase by $_____ million.

(2) The Regina bank collects the amount of the draft from the Canadian bank on which it is drawn through the clearinghouse. The account at the Bank of Canada of the bank of which the Regina branch forms a part increases by $_____ million; and the account of the bank on which the draft was drawn decreases by $_____ million.

(c) Regardless of the method employed by the Colombian importer to pay for the wheat,

(1) the export of the wheat created a (demand for, supply of) _____ dollars and a _____ pesos;

(2) the number of dollars owned by the Canadian exporter has (increased, decreased) _____ and the number of pesos owned by the Colombian importer has _____.

2. Current Account, Capital Account and the Official Settlements Account

Canada has a current account surplus of $27 billion, and a capital account deficit of $23 billion.

(a) Canada has a balance of payments (deficit, surplus) _____ of $____ billion.

(b) Accordingly, the official settlements balance would show an entry of $____ billion. (Hint: specify the sign + or -)

(c) This entry means that Canada has (gained, lost) _____ this amount of foreign reserves.

3. Balance of Payments Accounts

(a) Fill in the blanks in the table below showing a nation's data for 2004.

Current Account	
Merchandise exports	50
Merchandise imports	-32
Balance of trade	—
Exports of services	22
Imports of services	-13
Balance on goods and services	—
Net investment income	-11
Net transfers	4
Current account balance	—
Capital Account	
Net change in foreign investment in Canada (capital inflow)	7
Net change in Canadian investment abroad (capital outflow)	-12
Capital account balance	—
Official Settlements Account	—
Official international reserves	—
Balance of Payments	—

(b) Does the nation have a balance of payments deficit or surplus in 2004?

(c) Has the nation acquired or sold foreign exchange reserves in 2004?

(d) If the exchange rate was completely flexible, would the nation's currency have appreciated or depreciated in 2004?

4. The Market for British Pounds

Below are the supply and demand schedules for the British pound.

Qs of Pounds	Price per Pound ($)	Qd of Pounds
400	5.00	100
360	4.50	200
300	4.00	300
286	3.50	400
267	3.00	500
240	2.50	600
200	2.00	700

(a) Assume that exchange rates are flexible.
(1) The rate of exchange for the pound will be $_____ per pound.
(2) The rate of exchange for the dollar will be _____ pounds per dollar.
(3) How many pounds will be purchased in the market? _____
(4) How many dollars will be purchased in the market? _____
(b) If the Bank of Canada wished to fix or "peg" the price of the pound at $5.00, it would have to (buy, sell) _____ (how many) _____ pounds for $_____.

5. Appreciation and Depreciation in a Flexible Exchange-Rate Market

The exchange rate between the Canadian dollar and the US dollar is floating. What effect, if any, is each of the events below likely to have on the exchange rate, other things being equal? In the blanks, indicate "A" for appreciation of Canada's $, "D" for depreciation, and "N" for no change.
(a) ___ Canadian corporations make large payments to American bondholders.
(b) ___ The rate of inflation in Canada increases relative to the US inflation rate.
(c) ___ The Bank of Canada purchases Canadian dollars with US dollars to build its foreign exchange reserves.
(d) ___ The US enters the recovery stage of the business cycle, while Canada remains mired in recession.
(e) ___ The province of Ontario finances its deficit by borrowing in New York.
(f) ___ Interest rates fall in Canada and remain constant in the United States.
(g) ___ Falling unit labour costs in Canada increase the competitiveness of Canadian exports in the US market.
(h) ___ An American-owned firm reinvests in Canada profits that are earned in Canada.
(i) ___ Speculators anticipate a depreciation of the Canadian dollar relative to the US dollar.
(j) ___ The demand by Americans for Canadian-produced forest products diminishes sharply due to trade disputes.

Discussion Questions

1. What are foreign exchange and the foreign exchange rate? Who are the demanders and suppliers of a particular foreign exchange, say, the French franc? Why is a buyer (demander) in the foreign exchange markets always a seller (supplier) also?

2. What does a nation's balance of payments summarize? What are the principal sections of a nation's balance of payments?

3. How does a nation finance a balance of payments deficit and what does it do with a balance of payments surplus?

4. Is it good or bad for a nation to have a balance of payments deficit or surplus?

5. What types of events cause the exchange rate for a foreign currency to appreciate or depreciate? How will each of these events affect the exchange rate for a nation's currency?

6. How can floating exchange rates eliminate balance of payments deficits and surpluses? What are the problems associated with this method of correcting payments imbalances?

7. How may a nation employ its foreign exchange reserves to fix or "peg" foreign-exchange rates? Be precise. How does a nation obtain or acquire these official international reserves?

8. How can foreign exchange controls be used to overcome a payments deficit? Why do such exchange controls necessarily involve the rationing of foreign exchange?

9. If exchange rates are fixed, what kind of domestic macroeconomic adjustments are required to eliminate a payments deficit? To eliminate a payments surplus?

10. How did the gold standard operate? How did the gold standard correct payments imbalances? What were the disadvantages of this method of eliminating payments deficits and surpluses?

11. What is the "critical difference" between the adjustment necessary to correct payments deficits and surpluses under the gold standard and those necessary when exchange rates are flexible? How did this difference lead to the demise of the gold standard during the 1930s?

12. Explain: (a) why the IMF was established, and what the objectives of the adjustable-peg (or Bretton Woods) system were; (b) how the system worked, and how it stabilized exchange rates in the short run; and (c) how the system could allow long-run exchange rate adjustments.

13. What was the role of the US dollar under the Bretton Woods system? Why was the dollar used by nations as an international money, and how could they acquire additional dollars?

14. Explain how the managed floating system of exchange rates works. When are exchange rates managed, and when are they allowed to float?

15. Explain the arguments of the proponents and the critics of the managed floating system.

16. How does speculation affect the currency markets, and therefore international trade?

Answers

Quick Quiz

1. (b) pp. 408-409
2. (b) pp. 408-409
3. (a) p. 409
4. (b) p. 411
5. (a) p. 412
6. (d) p. 415
7. (c) pp. 415-417
8. (a) p. 417
9. (d) pp. 419-420
10. (d) p. 420
11. (b) p. 420
12. (a) pp. 421-422
13. (d) pp. 423-424
14. (d) pp. 424-425

Fill-in Questions

1. dollars, franc
2. 0.747
3. (a) supply of, demand for; (b) demand for, supply of
4. (a) credit, +; (b) debit, -
5. (a) in that nation, real, financial, other nations, abroad, that nation, real, financial; (b) greater
6. (a) selling, borrowing; (b) buy, lend
7. (a) foreign monies, central; (b) sold; (c) deficit, surplus
8. is not; (a) depreciate; (b) decrease, increase, decrease
9. (a) buy; (b) sell
10. (1) gold; (2) money, stock; (3) exported, imported
11. (a) stable; (b) out of, decreased, rose, fell, recession
12. adjustable-peg; (a) gold, US dollars; (b) selling, selling, borrowing from; (c) devalue; (d) stable, flexible

True-False

1. T so we can buy foreign currency to pay for imports
2. T
3. T the German buyer transfers money to Canadian seller
4. T the three accounts must add to zero
5. T
6. F it is a reciprocal relationship: 1/1.35 =0.74
7. T
8. T this is an application of the law of demand
9. F no, because it must also be selling C$
10. T they will then be buying some C$ off the market
11. T because 3 francs and 1 pound are worth an equal amount of gold
12. T
13. T
14. T the painful adjustments would be a consequence of rigidly fixed rates

Multiple-Choice

1. (c) 100,000/25,000

2. (d) in all cases Canadians need to make payments abroad
3. (c)
4. (d) in all cases foreigners make payments to Canadians
5. (d) all would produce additional credits on the capital account
6. (b) of exactly the same magnitude as the capital account surplus
7. (b) this will stimulate export demand (more credits) and cut import demand (less debits)
8. (c)
9. (a) capital flows into Canada, causing a demand for C$, as people try to take advantage of favourable returns on Canadian financial assets
10. (c) a capital inflow creates more demand for C$
11. (b) the appreciation changes the relative prices of domestic and foreign goods
12. (d) the excess supply of pounds indicates a deficit for Britain, and surplus for Canada
13. (a) the deficit is equal to the quantity supplied less the quantity demanded
14. (c) our import demand grows faster than Sweden's, so our Swedish net exports rise, creating stronger demand for the krona
15. (c) 3600/40
16 (d) because this country's goods become relatively more expensive
17. (d) this is the key advantage of such a system
18. (d) all of the measures suggested would work in the right way to resolve a deficit, not a surplus
19. (a) in fact under the modern gold standard most countries made no use of gold as money
20. (b) and its money supply, employment, and price level would all tend to rise
21. (c) with the money supply shrinking the interest rate would rise
22. (d) monetary policy could not be used for domestic stabilization
23. (a) this describes a fixed-exchange rate system
24. (a) breaking the link to gold
25. (b) a managed float
26. (a) intervention in the short term can smooth out some fluctuations
27. (a) automatically
28. (d)
29. (d) on balance, speculation is helpful

Problems and Projects
1. (a) (1) 3, (2) 3, dollars, 150, pesos; (b) (1) 3, (2) 3, 3; (c) (1) demand for, supply of, (2) increased, decreased
2. (a) surplus, 4; (b) -4; (c) gained
3. (a) see below; (b) 20 + (-5) = 15 = surplus; (c) -15 implies acquisition of 15 in foreign reserves; (d) appreciated since balance of payments surplus = excess demand for the currency.

Current Account

Merchandise exports	50	
Merchandise imports	-32	
Balance of trade		18
Exports of services	22	
Imports of services	-13	
Balance on goods and services		27
Net investment income	-11	
Net transfers	4	
Current account balance		20

Capital Account

Net change in foreign investment in Canada (capital inflow)	7	
Net change in Canadian investment abroad (capital outflow)	-12	
Capital account balance		-5

Official Settlements Account

Official international reserves	-15
Balance of Payments	0

4. (a) (1) 4.00, (2) 0.25, (3) 300, (4) 300 x 4 = 1200; (b) buy, 300, 1500 (5.00 x 300)
5. (a) D, (b) D, (c) A, (d) A, (e) A, (f) D, (g) A, (h) N, (i) D, (j) D

Answers to the Key Questions

Chapter 1

1-4 (*Key Question*) Use the economic perspective to explain why someone who is normally a light eater at a standard restaurant may become somewhat of a glutton at a buffet-style restaurant which charges a single price for all you can eat.

This behaviour can be explained in terms of marginal costs and marginal benefits. At a standard restaurant, items are priced individually—they have a positive marginal cost. If you order more, it will cost you more. You order until the marginal benefit from the extra food no longer exceeds the marginal cost. At a buffet you pay a flat fee no matter how much you eat. Once the fee is paid, additional food items have a zero marginal cost. You therefore continue to eat until your marginal benefit becomes zero.

1-8 (*Key Question*) Explain in detail the interrelationships between economic facts, theory, and policy. Critically evaluate this statement: "The trouble with economic theory is that it is not practical. It is detached from the real world."

Economic theory consists of factually supported generalizations about economic behaviour that can be used to formulate economic policies. Economic theory enables policymakers to formulate economic policies that are relevant to real-world goals and problems that are based upon carefully observed facts.

1-10 (*Key Question*) Indicate whether each of the following statements applies to microeconomics or macroeconomics:
(a), (d), and (f) are macro; (b), (c), and (e) are micro.

1-11 (*Key Question*) Identify each of the following as either a positive or a normative statement:
a. The high temperature today was 30 degrees.
b. It was too hot today.

c. Other things being equal, higher interest rates reduce the total amount of borrowing.
d. Interest rates are too high.
(a) and (c) are positive; (b) and (d) are normative.

1-12 (*Key Question*) Explain and give an illustration of (a) the fallacy of composition; and (b) the "after this, therefore because of this" fallacy. Why are cause-and-effect relationships difficult to isolate in the social sciences?
(a) The fallacy of composition is the mistake of believing that something true for an individual part is necessarily true for the whole. Example: A single auto producer can increase its profits by lowering its price and taking business away from its competitors. But matched price cuts by all auto manufacturers will not necessarily yield higher industry profits.
(b) The "after this, therefore because of this" fallacy is incorrectly reasoning that when one event precedes another, the first even necessarily caused the second. Example: Interest rates rise, followed by an increase in the rate of inflation, leading to the erroneous conclusion that the rise in interest rates caused the inflation. Actually higher interest rates slow inflation. Cause-and-effect relationships are difficult to isolate because "other things" are continually changing.

Chapter 1 - Appendix

A1-2 (*Key Appendix Question*) Indicate how each of the following might affect the data shown in Table A1- 2 and Figure A1-2 of this appendix:
a. IU's athletic director schedules higher-quality opponents.
b. An NBA team locates in the city where IU plays.
c. IU contracts to have all its home games televised.

(a) More tickets are bought at each price; the line shifts to the right.
(b) Fewer tickets are bought at each price, the line shifts to the left.
(c) Fewer tickets are bought at each price, the line shifts to the left.

A1-3 (Key Appendix Question) The following table contains data on the relationship between saving and income. Rearrange these data into a meaningful order and graph them on the accompanying grid. What is the slope of the line? The vertical intercept? Interpret the meaning of both the slope and the intercept. Write the equation which represents this line. What would you predict saving to be at the $12,500 level of income?

Income (per year)	Saving (per year)
$15,000	$1,000
0	-500
10,000	500
5,000	0
20,000	1,500

Income column: $0; $5,000; $10,000, $15,000; $20,000. Saving column: $-500; 0; $500; $1,000; $1,500. Slope = 0.1 (= $1,000 - $500)/($15,000 - $10,000). Vertical intercept = $-500. The slope shows the amount saving will increase for every $1 increase in income; the intercept shows the amount of saving (dissaving) occurring when income is zero. Equation: $S = \$-500 + 0.1Y$ (where S is saving and Y is income). Saving will be $750 at the $12,500 income level.

A1-7 (Key Appendix Question) The accompanying graph shows curve XX' and tangents at points A, B, and C. Calculate the slope of the curve at these three points.

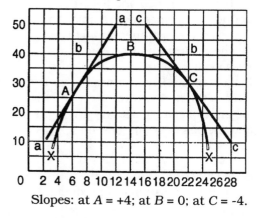

Slopes: at A = +4; at B = 0; at C = -4.

Chapter 2

2-4 (Key Graph) Classify the following Microsoft factors of production as labour, land, capital, or entrepreneurial ability: code writers for software; Bill Gates; production facility for Window CD-ROMs; "campus" on which Microsoft buildings sit; grounds crew at Microsoft campus; Microsoft corporate jet.

Labour: code writers, grounds crew; land: campus; capital: CD production facility, corporate jet; entrepreneurial ability: Bill Gates.

2-5 (Key Question) Distinguish between full employment and full production as they relate to production possibilities analysis. Distinguish between productive efficiency and allocative efficiency. Give an illustration of achieving productive efficiency, but not allocative efficiency.

Full employment occurs when all available resources are utilized; full production means that all employed resources are used to provide the maximum possible satisfaction of material wants. Both are required for an economy to be producing on the production possibilities curve. An economy that is employing all available resources but which allocates labour to unproductive tasks will operate inside the curve. Likewise, putting resources to their most productive uses but failing to employ all resources will result in an economy producing inside the curve.

Allocative efficiency means that resources are being used to produce the goods and services most wanted by society. The economy is then located at the optimal point on its production possibilities curve where marginal benefit equals marginal cost for each good. Productive efficiency means the least costly production techniques are being used to produce wanted goods and services. Examples: manual typewriters produced using the least-cost techniques but for which there is no demand; cigarettes produced using least-cost techniques but for which there are "bads" created that are not accounted for by the market.

2-6 (Key Question) Here is a production possibilities table for war goods and civilian goods:

Type of Production	Production Alternatives				
	A	B	C	D	E
Automobiles	0	2	4	6	8
Rockets	30	27	21	12	0

a. Show these data graphically. Upon what specific assumptions is this production possibilities curve based?

b. If the economy is at point C, what is the cost of one more automobile? One more rocket? Explain how this curve reflects increasing opportunity costs.

c. What must the economy do to operate at some point on the production possibilities curve?

(a) See curve EDCBA. The assumptions are full employment and productive efficiency, fixed supplies of factors, and fixed technology.

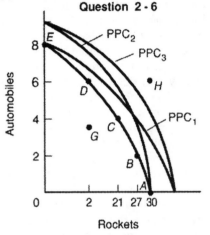

Question 2 - 6

(b) 4.5 rockets; .33 automobiles, as determined from the table. Increasing opportunity costs are

reflected in the concave-from-the-origin shape of the curve. This means the economy must give up larger and larger amounts of rockets to get constant added amounts of automobiles—and vice versa.

(c) It must obtain full employment and productive efficiency.

2-9   (Key Question) Specify and explain the shapes of the marginal-benefit and marginal-cost curves and use these curves to determine the optimal allocation of resources to a particular product. If current output is such that marginal cost exceeds marginal benefit, should more or less resources be allocated to this product? Explain.

The marginal benefit curve is downward sloping, MB falls as more of a product is consumed because additional units of a good yield less satisfaction than previous units. The marginal cost curve is upward sloping, MC increases as more of

a product is produced since additional units require the use of increasingly unsuitable factor. The optimal amount of a particular product occurs where MB equals MC. If MC exceeds MB, fewer resources should be allocated to this use. The resources are more valuable in some alternative use (as reflected in the higher MC) than in this use (as reflected in the lower MB).

2-10 (Key Question) Label point G inside the production possibilities curve you have drawn for question 6. What does it indicate? Label point H outside the curve. What does this point indicate? What must occur before the economy can attain the level of production indicated by point H?

G indicated unemployment, productive inefficiency, or both. H is at present unattainable. Economic growth—through more inputs, better inputs, improved technology—must be achieved to attain H.

2-11 (Key Question) Referring again to question 6, suppose improvement occurs in the technology of producing rockets but not in the production of automobiles. Draw the new production possibilities curve. Now assume that a technological advance occurs in producing automobiles but not in producing rockets. Draw the new production possibilities curve. Now draw a production possibilities curve that reflects technological improvement in the production of both products.

See the graph for question 2-6. PPC$_1$ shows improved rocket technology. PPC$_2$ shows improved auto technology. PPC$_3$ shows improved technology in producing both products.

Chapter 3

3-2   (Key Question) What effect will each of the following have on the demand for product B?

a. Product B becomes more fashionable.

b. The price of substitute product C falls.

c. Income declines and product B is an inferior good.

d. Consumers anticipate the price of B will be lower in the near future.

e. The price of complementary product D falls.

Demand increases in (a), (c), and (e); decreases in (b) and (d).

3-5   (Key Question) What effect will each of the following have on the supply of product B?

a. A technological advance in the methods of producing B.

b. A decline in the number of firms in industry B.

c. An increase in the price of factors required in the production of B.

d. The expectation that the equilibrium price of B will be lower in the future than it is currently.

e. A decline in the price of product A, a good whose production requires substantially the same techniques as does the production of B.

f. The levying of a specific sales tax upon B.

g. The granting of a 50-cent per unit subsidy for each unit of B produced.

Supply increases in (a), (d), (e), and (g); decreases in (b), (c), and (f).

3-7 (Key Question) Suppose the total demand for wheat and the total supply of wheat per month in the Kansas City grain market are as follows:

Thousands of bushels demanded	Price per bushel	Thousand of bushels supplied	Surplus (+) or shortage (-)
85	$3.40	72	____
80	3.70	73	____
75	4.00	75	____
70	4.30	77	____
65	4.60	79	____
60	4.90	81	____

a. What will be the market or equilibrium price? What is the equilibrium quantity? Using the surplus-shortage column, explain why your answers are correct.

b. Graph the demand for wheat and the supply of wheat. Be sure to label the axes of your graph correctly. Label equilibrium price "P" and the equilibrium quantity "Q."

c. Why will $3.40 not be the equilibrium price in this market? Why not $4.90? "Surpluses drive prices up; shortages drive them down." Do you agree?

d. Now suppose that the government establishes a ceiling price of, say, $3.70 for wheat. Explain carefully the effects of this ceiling price. Demonstrate your answer graphically. What might prompt the government to establish a ceiling price?

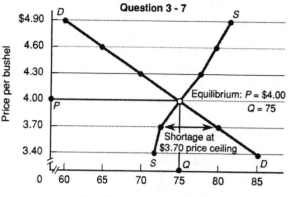

Question 3 - 7

Quantity (thousands) of bushels

Data from top to bottom: -13; -7; 0; +7; +14; and +21.

(a) P_e = $4.00; Q_e = 75,000. Equilibrium occurs where there is neither a shortage nor surplus of wheat. At the immediately lower price of $3.70, there is a shortage of 7,000 bushels. At the immediately higher price of $4.30, there is a surplus of 7,000 bushels. (See Graph top of next page.

(b) Quantity (thousands) of bushels.

(c) Because at $3.40 there will be a 13,000 bushel shortage which will drive price up. Because at $4.90 there will be a 21,000 bushel surplus which will drive the price down. Quotation is incorrect; just the opposite is true.

[d] A $3.70 ceiling causes a persistent shortage. This product may be a necessity and the government is concerned that some consumers might not being able to afford it.

3-8 (Key Question) How will each of the following changes in demand and/or supply affect equilibrium price and equilibrium quantity in a competitive market; that is do price and quantity rise, fall, remain unchanged, or are the answers indeterminate, depending on the magnitudes of the shifts in supply and demand? You should rely on a supply and demand diagram to verify answers.

a. Supply decreases and demand remains constant.

b. Demand decreases and supply remains constant.

c. Supply increases and demand is constant.

d. Demand increases and supply increases.

e. Demand increases and supply is constant.

f. Supply increases and demand decreases.

g. Demand increases and supply decreases.

h.   Demand decreases and supply decreases.
(a) Price up; quantity down;
(b) Price down; quantity down;
(c) Price down; quantity up;
(d) Price indeterminate; quantity up;
(e) Price up; quantity up;
(f) Price down; quantity indeterminate;
(g) Price up, quantity indeterminate;
(h) Price indeterminate and quantity down.

3-12 (Key Question) What do economists mean when they say that "price floors and ceilings stifle the rationing function of prices and distort resource allocation?"

Price floors can lead to surpluses and price ceilings can lead to shortages, thus stifling the rationing function of prices, and leading to a distortion of resource allocation.

Chapter 4

4-9 (Key Question) Some large hardware stores such as Canadian Tire boast of carrying as many as 20,000 different products in each store. What motivated the producers of those products—everything from screwdrivers to ladders to water heaters—to make them and offer them for sale? How did producers decide on the best combinations of factors to use? Who made these factors available, and why? Who decides whether these particular hardware products should continue to get produced and offered for sale?

The quest for profit led firms to produce these goods. Producers looked for and found the least-cost combination of factors in producing their output. Factor suppliers, seeking income, made these factors available. Consumers, through their dollar votes, ultimately decide on what will continue to be produced.

4-12 (Key Question) What are the two characteristics of public goods? Explain the significance of each for public provision as opposed to private provision. What is the free-rider problem as it relates to public goods?

Public goods are non-rival (one person's consumption does not prevent consumption by another) and non-excludable (once the goods are produced nobody—including free riders—can be excluded from the goods' benefits). If goods are non-rival, there is less incentive for private firms to produce them – those purchasing the good could simply allow others their

the good could simply allow others their use without compensation. Similarly, if goods are non-excludable, private firms are unlikely to produce them as the potential for profit is low. The free-rider problem occurs when people benefit from the public good without contributing to the cost (tax revenue proportionate to the benefit received).

4-13 (Key Question) Draw a production possibilities curve with public goods on the vertical axis and private goods on the horizontal axis. Assuming the economy is initially operating on the curve, indicate the means by which the production of public goods might be increased. How might output of public goods be increased if the economy is initially functioning at a point inside the curve?

On the curve, the only way to obtain more public goods is to reduce the production of private goods (from C to B).

An economy operating inside the curve can expand the production of public goods without sacrificing private goods (say, from A to B) by making use of unemployed resources.

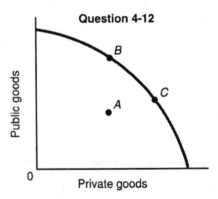

Question 4-12

4-16 (Key Question) The following are production possibilities tables for South Korea and Canada. Assume that before specialization and trade the optimal product mix for South Korea is alternative B and for Canada alternative D.

Product	South Korea's production possibilities					
	A	B	C	D	E	F
Radios (in 1000s)	30	24	18	12	6	0
Chemicals (tons)	0	6	12	18	24	30
Product	Canada's production possibilities					
	R	S	T	U	V	W
Radios (in 1000s)	10	8	6	4	2	0
Chemicals (tons)	0	4	8	12	16	20

a. Are comparative cost conditions such that the two areas should specialize? If so, what product should each produce?

b. What is the total gain in radio and chemical output which results from this specialization?

c. What are the limits of the terms of trade? Suppose actual terms of trade are 1 unit of radios for 1-1/2 units of chemicals and that 4 units of radios are exchanged for 6 units of chemicals. What are the gains from specialization and trade for each area?

d. Can you conclude from this illustration that specialization according to comparative advantage results in more efficient use of world resources? Explain.

(a) Yes, because the opportunity cost of radios is less (1R = 1C) in South Korea than in Canada (1R = 2C). South Korea should produce radios and Canada should produce chemicals.

(b) If they specialize, Canada can produce 20 tons of chemicals and South Korea can produce 30,000 radios. Before specialization South Korea produced alternative B and Canada alternative U for a total of 28,000 radios (24,000 + 4,000) and 18 tons of chemicals (6 tons + 12 tons). The gain is 2,000 radios and 2 tons of chemicals.

(c) The limits of the terms of trade are determined by the comparative cost conditions in each country before trade: 1R = 1C in South Korea and 1R = 2C in Canada. The terms of trade must be somewhere between these two ratios for trade to occur.

If the terms of trade are 1R = 1-1/2C, South Korea would end up with 26,000 radios (= 30,000 - 4,000) and 6 tons of chemicals. Canada would have 4,000 radios and 14 tons of chemicals (= 20 - 6). South Korea has gained 2,000 radios. Canada has gained 2 tons of chemicals.

(d) Yes, the world is obtaining more output from its fixed resources.

Chapter 5

5-3 (*Key Question*) Why do national income accountants include only final goods in measuring total output GDP in a particular year? Why don't they include the value of stocks and bonds bought and sold? Why don't they include the value of used furniture?

They are excluded because the dollar value of final goods includes the dollar value of intermediate goods. If intermediate goods were counted, then multiple counting would occur. The value of steel (intermediate good) used in autos is included in the price of the auto (the final product).

This value is not included in GDP because such sales and purchases simply transfer the ownership of existing assets; such sales and purchases are not themselves (economic) investment and thus should not be counted as production of final goods and services.

Used furniture was produced in some previous year; it was counted as GDP then. Its resale does not measure new production.

5.8 (*Key Question*) Following is a list of domestic output and national income figures for a given year. All figures are in billions. Calculate GDP by both the expenditure and income methods. The answers derived by each approach should be the same.

Personal consumption expenditures	$120
Capital consumption allowances (depreciation)	20
Interest and miscellaneous investment income	10
Net income of farms and unincorporated business	17
Net exports	+2
Profits of corporation and government enterprises before taxes	42
Wages, salaries, and supplementary labour income	113
Indirect business taxes (less subsidies)	11
Government current purchases of goods and services	40
Net investment (net capital formation)	30
Taxes less subsidies on factors of production	10

GDP = $212

5-9 Using the following national income accounting data, compute (a) GDP, (b) GNP, (c) NDP, (d) NNI, (e) PI, (f) DI. All figures are in billions.

Wages, salaries, and supplementary labour income	$194.2
Canadian exports of goods and services	17.8
Capital consumption allowances	11.8
Government current purchases of goods and services	59.4
Indirect taxes less subsidies	14.4
Net investment (net capital formation)	52.1
Government transfer payments	13.9
Canadian imports of goods and services	16-5
Personal taxes	40.5
Personal consumption expenditures	219.1
Net investments from non-residents	2.2
Undistributed corporate profits	10

(a) GDP= $343.7; (b) GNP = $341.5; (c) NDP = $329.7; (d) NNI = $315.3; (e) (PI) = $319.2; (f) DI = $278.7

5-11 (Key Question) Suppose that in 1984 the total output in a single-good economy was 7,000 buckets of chicken. Also suppose that in 1984 each bucket of chicken was priced at $10. Finally, assume that in 1992 the price per bucket of chicken was $16 and that 22,000 buckets were purchased. Determine the GDP price index for 1984, using 1992 as the base year. By what percentage did the price level, as measured by this index, rise between 1984 and 1992? Use the two methods listed in Table 5-7 to determine real GDP for 1984 and 1992.

Price index for 1984 = 62.5; 60 percent; real GDP for 1984 = $112,000 and real GDP for 1992 = $352,000.

5-13 (Key Question) The following table shows nominal GDP and an appropriate price index for a group of selected years. Compute real GDP. Indicate in each calculation whether you are inflating or deflating the nominal GDP data.

Year	Nominal GDP, billions	GDP deflator (1997= 100)	Real GDP billions
1929	$6.1	8.6	$_____
1933	3.5	7.0	$_____
1962	44.8	17.6	$_____
1974	173.9	32.8	$_____
1984	449.6	71.8	$_____
1994	770.9	102.4	$_____
2002	1154.9	107.5	$_____

Values for real GDP, top to bottom of the column: $70.9(inflating); $50.0 (inflating); $254.4 (inflating); $ (inflating); $530.2 (inflating); $626.2 (inflating); $809.8(inflating);$1074.3(deflating).

Chapter 6

6-2 (Key Question) Suppose an economy's real GDP is $30,000 in year 1 and $31,200 in year 2. What is the growth rate of its real GDP? Assume that population was 100 in year 1 and 102 in year 2. What is the growth rate of GDP per capita?

Growth rate of real GDP = 4 percent (= $31,200 - $30,000)/$30,000). GDP per capita in year 1 = $300 (= $30,000/100). GDP per capita in year 2 = $305.88 (= $31,200/102). Growth rate of GDP per capita is 1.96 percent = ($305.88 – $300)/300).

6-4 (Key Question) What are the four major phases of the business cycle? How long do business cycles last? How do seasonal variations and secular trends complicate measurement of the business cycle? Why does the business cycle affect output and employment in durable goods industries more severely than in industries producing nondurables?

The four phases of a typical business cycle, starting at the bottom, are trough, recovery, peak, and recession. As seen in Figure 6-1, the length of a complete cycle varies from about 2 to 3 years to as long as 15 years.

Normally there is a pre-Christmas spurt in production and sales and a January slackening. This normal seasonal variation does not signal boom or recession. From decade to decade, the long-term trend (the secular trend) of the Canadian economy has been upward. A period of no GDP growth thus does not mean that all is normal but that the economy is operating below its trend growth of output.

Because durable goods last, consumers can postpone buying replacements. This happens when people are worried about a recession and whether there will be a paycheque next month. And firms will soon stop producing what people are not buying. Durable goods industries therefore suffer large output declines during recessions. In contrast, consumers cannot long postpone the buying of non-durables such as food; therefore recessions only slightly reduce nondurable output.

6-6   (Key Question) Use the following data to calculate (a) the size of the labour force and (b) the official unemployment rate: total population, 500; population under 15 years of age or institutionalized, 120; not in labour force, 150; unemployed, 23; part-time workers looking for full-time jobs, 10.

Labour force = 230 [= 500 - (120 + 150)]; Official unemployment rate = 10% [= (23/230) × 100].

6-8   (Key Question) Assume that in a particular year the natural rate of unemployment is 5 percent and the actual rate of unemployment is 9 percent. Use Okun's law to determine the size of the GDP gap in percentage-point terms. If the nominal GDP is $500 billion in that year, how much output is being foregone because of cyclical unemployment?

GDP gap = 8 percent [= (9 – 5) × 2]; forgone output = $40 billion (= 8% of $500 billion).

6-11   (Key Question) If the price index was 110 last year and is 121 this year, what was this year's rate of inflation? What is the "rule of 70"? How long would it take for the price level to double if inflation persisted at (a) 2, (b) 5, and (c) 10 percent per year?

This year's rate of inflation is 10% or [(121 – 110)/110] × 100.

Dividing 70 by the annual percentage rate of increase of any variable (for instance, the rate of inflation or population growth) will give the approximate number of years for doubling of the variable.

(a) 35 years (= 70/2);
(b) 14 years (=70/5);
(c) 7 years (=70/10).

Chapter 7

7-5   (Key Question) Complete the table below.

Level of output and income (GDP = DI)	Consumption	Saving	APC	APS	MPC	MPS
$240	$ _____	$ –4	_____	_____	_____	_____
260	$ _____	0	_____	_____	_____	_____
280	$ _____	4	_____	_____	_____	_____
300	$ _____	8	_____	_____	_____	_____
320	$ _____	12	_____	_____	_____	_____
340	$ _____	16	_____	_____	_____	_____
360	$ _____	20	_____	_____	_____	_____
380	$ _____	24	_____	_____	_____	_____
400	$ _____	28	_____	_____	_____	_____

a. Show the consumption and saving schedules graphically.
b. Locate the break-even level of income. How is it possible for households to dissave at very low income levels?
c. If the proportion of total income consumed decreases and the proportion saved increases as income rises, explain both verbally and graphically how the MPC and MPS can be constant at various levels of income.

Data for completing the table (top to bottom). Consumption: $244; $260; $276; $292; $308; $324; $340; $356; $372. APC: 1.02; 1.00; .99; .97; .96; .95; .94; .94; .93. APS: -.02; .00; .01; .03; .04; .05; .06; .06; .07. MPC: .8 throughout. MPS: .20 throughout.

(a) See the graphs.
(b) Break-even income = $260. Households dissave borrowing or using past savings.

(c) Technically, the APC diminishes and the APS increases because the consumption and saving schedules have positive and negative vertical intercepts respectively. (Appendix to Chapter 1). MPC and MPS measure *changes* in consumption and saving as income changes; they are the *slopes* of the consumption and saving schedules. For straight-line consumption and saving schedules, these slopes do not change as the level of income changes; the slopes and thus the MPC and MPS remain constant.

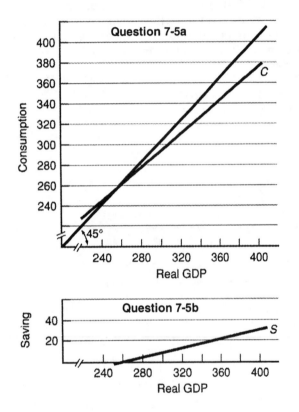

7-7 (*Key Question*) Suppose a handbill publisher can buy a new duplicating machine for $500 and that the duplicator has a 1-year life. The machine is expected to contribute $550 to the year's net revenue. What is the expected rate of return? If the real interest rate at which funds can be borrowed to purchase the machine is 8 percent, will the publisher choose to invest in the machine? Explain.

The expected rate of return is 10% ($50 expected profit/$500 cost of machine). The $50 expected profit comes from the net revenue of $550 less the $500 cost of the machine.

If the real interest rate is 8%, the publisher will invest in the machine as the expected profit (marginal benefit) from the investment exceeds the cost of borrowing the funds (marginal cost).

7-8 (*Key Question*) Assume there are no investment projects in the economy that yield an expected rate of return of 25 percent or more. But suppose there are $10 billion of investment projects yielding an expected rate of return of between 20 and 25 percent; another $10 billion yielding between 15 and 20 percent; another $10 billion between 10 and 15 percent; and so forth. Cumulate these data and present them graphically, putting the expected rate of net return on the vertical axis and the amount of investment on the horizontal axis. What will be the equilibrium level of aggregate investment if the real interest rate is (a) 15 percent, (b) 10 percent, and (c) 5 percent? Explain why this curve is the investment-demand curve.

See the graph below. Aggregate investment: (a) $20 billion; (b) $30 billion; (c) $40 billion. This is the investment-demand curve because we have applied the rule of undertaking all investment up to the point where the expected rate of return, r, equals the interest rate, i.

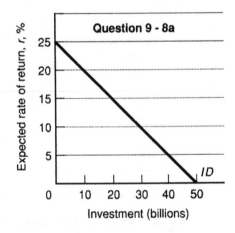

7-10 (*Key Question*) Assuming the level of investment is $16 billion and independent of the level of total output, complete the following table and determine the equilibrium levels of output and employment that this private, closed economy would provide. What are the sizes of the MPC and MPS?

Possible levels of employment (millions)	Real domestic output (GDP=DI) (billions)	Consumption (billions)	Saving (billions)
40	$240	$244	$ _____
45	260	260	$ _____
50	280	276	$ _____
55	300	292	$ _____
60	320	308	$ _____
65	340	324	$ _____
70	360	340	$ _____
75	380	356	$ _____
80	400	372	$ _____

Saving data for completing the table (top to bottom): $-4; $0; $4; $8; $12; $16; $20; $24; $28.

Equilibrium GDP = $340 billion, determined where (1) aggregate expenditures equal GDP (C of $324 billion + I of $16 billion = GDP of $340 billion); or (2) where planned I = S (I of $16 billion = S of $16 billion). Equilibrium level of employment = 65 million; MCP = .8; MPS = .2.

7-11 **(Key Question)** Using the consumption and saving data given in question 10, and assuming the level of investment is $16 billion, what are the levels of saving and planned investment at the $380 billion level of domestic output? What are the levels of saving and actual investment? What are saving and planned investment at the $300 billion level of domestic output? What are the levels of saving and actual investment? Use the concept of unintended investment to explain adjustments toward equilibrium from both the $380 and $300 billion levels of domestic output.

At the $380 billion level of GDP, saving = $24 billion; planned investment = $16 billion (from the question). This deficiency of $8 billion of planned investment causes an unplanned $8 billion *increase* in inventories. Actual investment is $24 billion (= $16 billion of planned investment *plus* $8 billion of unplanned inventory investment), matching the $24 billion of actual saving.

At the $300 billion level of GDP, saving = $8 billion; planned investment = $16 billion (from the question). This excess of $8 billion of planned investment causes an unplanned $8 billion *de-*cline in inventories. Actual investment is $8 billion (= $16 billion of planned investment *minus* $8 billion of unplanned inventory disinvestment) matching the actual of $8 billion.

When unplanned investments in inventories occur, as at the $380 billion level of GDP, businesses revise their production plans downward and GDP falls. When unintended disinvestments in inventories occur, as at the $300 billion level of GDP, businesses revise their production plans upward and GDP rises. Equilibrium GDP—in this case, $340 billion—occurs where planned investment equals saving.

7-16 **(Key Question)** What is the multiplier effect? What relationship does the MPC bear to the size of the multiplier? The MPS? What will the multiplier be when the MPS is 0, .4, .6, and 1? When the MPC is 1, .90, .67, .50, and 0? How much of a change in GDP will result if businesses increase their level of investment by $8 billion and the MPC in the economy is .80? If the MPC is .67? Explain the difference between the simple and the complex multiplier.

The multiplier effect is the magnified increase in equilibrium GDP that occurs when any component of aggregate expenditures changes. The greater the MPC (the smaller the MPS), the greater the multiplier.

MPS = 0, multiplier = infinity; MPS = .4, multiplier = 2.5; MPS = .6, multiplier = 1.67; MPS = 1, multiplier = 1.

MPC = .8: Change in GDP = $40 billion (= $8 billion ∞ multiplier of 5); MPC = .67: Change in GDP = $24 billion ($8 billion ∞ multiplier of 3). The simple multiplier takes account of only the leak-

age of saving. The complex multiplier also takes account of leakages of taxes and imports, making the complex multiplier less than the simple multiplier.

7-19 (**Key Question**) The data in columns 1 and 2 of the table below are for a private closed economy

(1) Real domestic output (GDP=DI) billions	(2) Aggregate expenditures private closed economy, billions	(3) Exports, billions	(4) Imports, billions	(5) Net exports, private economy	(6) Aggregate expenditures, open billions
$200	$240	$20	$30	$ ____	$ ____
$250	$280	$20	$30	$ ____	$ ____
$300	$320	$20	$30	$ ____	$ ____
$350	$360	$20	$30	$ ____	$ ____
$400	$400	$20	$30	$ ____	$ ____
$450	$440	$20	$30	$ ____	$ ____
$500	$480	$20	$30	$ ____	$ ____
$550	$520	$20	$30	$ ____	$ ____

a. Use columns 1 and 2 to determine the equilibrium GDP for this hypothetical economy.

b. Now open this economy for international trade by including the export and import figures of columns 3 and 4. Calculate net exports and determine the equilibrium GDP for the open economy. Explain why equilibrium GDP differs from the closed economy.

c. Given the original $20 billion level of exports, what would be the equilibrium GDP if imports were $10 billion greater at each level of GDP?

d. What is the size of the multiplier in these examples?

(a) Equilibrium GDP for closed economy = $400 billion.

(b) Net export data for column 5 (top to bottom); $-10 billion in each space. Aggregate expenditure data for column 6 (top to bottom): $230; $270; $310; $350; $390; $430; $470; $510. Equilibrium GDP for the open economy is $350 billion, $50 billion below the $400 billion equilibrium GDP for the closed economy. The $-10 billion of net exports is a leakage which reduces equilibrium GDP by $50 billion.

(c) Imports = $40 billion: Aggregate expenditures in the private open economy would fall by $10 billion at each GDP level and the new equilibrium GDP would be $300 billion.

(d) Since every rise of $50 billion in GDP increases aggregate expenditures by $40 billion, the MPC is .8 and so the multiplier is 5.

7-22 (**Key Question**) Refer to columns 1 and 6 of the tabular data for question 19. Incorporate government into the table by assuming that it plans to tax and spend $20 billion at each possible level of GDP. Also assume that all taxes are personal taxes and that government spending does not induce a shift in the private aggregate expenditures schedule. Compute and explain the changes in equilibrium GDP caused by the addition of government.

Before G is added, open private sector equilibrium will be at 350. The addition of government expenditures of G to our analysis raises the aggregate expenditures $(C + I_g + X_n + G)$ schedule and increases the equilibrium level of GDP as would an increase in C, 1_g, or X_n. Note that changes in government spending are subject to the multiplier effect. Government spending supplements private investment and export spending $(I_g + X + G)$, increasing the equilibrium GDP to 450.

The addition of $20 billion of government expenditures and $20 billion of personal taxes increases equilibrium GDP from $350 to $370 billion. The $20 billion increase in G *raises* equilibrium GDP by $100 billion (= $20 billion x the multiplier of 5); the $20 billion increase in T *reduces* consumption by $16 billion at every level. (= $20 billion x the MPC of .8). This $16 billion decline in turn reduces equilibrium GDP by $80 billion ($16 billion x multiplier of 5). The net change from including balanced government spending and taxes is $20 billion (= $100 billion - $80 billion).

7-23 (*Key Question*) Refer to the accompanying table in answering the questions which follow:

(1) Possible levels of employment, millions	(2) Real domestic output, billions	(2) Real domestic output, billions
90	$500	$520
100	550	560
110	600	600
120	650	640
130	700	680

a. If full employment in this economy is 130 million, will there be an inflationary or recessionary gap? What will be the consequence of this gap? By how much would aggregate expenditures in column 3 have to change at each level of GDP to eliminate the inflationary or recessionary gap? Explain.

b. Will there be an inflationary or recessionary gap if the full-employment level of output is $500 billion? Explain the consequences. By how much would aggregate expenditures in column 3 have to change at each level of

GDP to eliminate the inflationary or recessionary gap? Explain.

c. Assuming that investment, net exports, and government expenditures do not change with changes in real GDP, what are the sizes of the MPC, the MPS, and the multiplier?

(a) A recessionary gap. Equilibrium GDP is $600 billion, while full employment GDP is $700 billion. Employment will be 20 million less than at full employment. Aggregate expenditures would have to increase by $20 billion (= $700 billion -$680 billion) at each level of GDP to eliminate the recessionary gap.

(b) An inflationary gap. Aggregate expenditures will be excessive, causing demand-pull inflation. Aggregate expenditures would have to *fall* by $20 billion (= $520 billion -$500 billion) at each level of GDP to eliminate the inflationary gap.

(c) MPC = .8 (= $40 billion/$50 billion); MPS = .2 (= 1 -.8); multiplier = 5 (= 1/.2).

Chapter 8

8-4   (*Key Question*) Suppose that aggregate demand and the short run supply for a hypothetical economy are as shown below:

Amount of real domestic output demanded, billions	Price level (price index)	Amount of real domestic output supplied, billions
$100	300	$400
200	250	400
300	200	300
400	150	200
500	150	100

a. Use these sets of data to graph the aggregate demand and supply curves. What will be the equilibrium price level and level of real domestic output in this hypothetical economy? Is the equilibrium real output also the absolute full-capacity real output? Explain.

b. Why will a price level of 150 not be an equilibrium price level in this economy? Why not 250?

c. Suppose that buyers desire to purchase $200 billion of extra real domestic output at each price level. What factors might cause this change in aggregate demand? What is the new equilibrium price level and level of real output?

(a) See the graph. Equilibrium price level = 200. Equilibrium real output = $300 billion. No, the full-capacity level of GDP is $400 billion, where the AS curve becomes vertical

(b) At a price level of 150, real GDP supplied is a maximum of $200 billion, less than the real GDP demanded of $400 billion. The shortage of real output will drive the price level up. At a price level of 250, real GDP supplied is $400 billion, which is more than the real GDP demanded of $200 billion. The surplus of real output will drive down the price level. Equilibrium occurs at the price level at which AS and AD intersect.

(c) See the graph. Increases in consumer, investment, government, or net export spending might shift the AD curve rightward. New equilibrium price level = 250. New equilibrium GDP = $400 billion.

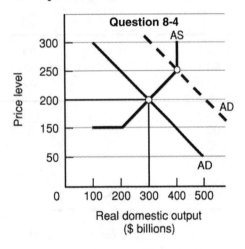

Question 8-4

8-5 **(Key Question)** Suppose that the hypothetical economy in question 3 had the following relationship between its real domestic output and the input quantities necessary for producing that level of output:

a. What is the level of productivity in this economy?

b. What is the per unit cost of production if the price of each input is $2?

c. Assume that the input price increases from $2 to $3 with no accompanying change in productivity. What is the new per unit cost of production? In what direction did the $1 increase in input price push the aggregate supply curve? What effect would this shift in aggregate supply have upon the price level and the level of real output?

d. Suppose that the increase in input price had not occurred but instead that productivity had increased by 100 percent. What would be the new per unit cost of production? What effect would this change in per unit production cost have on the aggregate supply curve? What effect would this shift in aggregate supply have on the price level and the level of real output?

Input quantity	Real domestic output
150.0	400
112.5	300
75.0	200

(a) Productivity = 2.67 (= 300 / 112.5).

(b) Per unit cost of production = $.75 (= $2 × 112.5 / 300).

(c) New per unit production cost = $.75 (= $2 × 112.5 / 300). The AS curve would shift leftward. The price level would rise and real output would decrease.

(d) New per unit cost of production = $0.375 (= $2 × 112.5 / 300). AS curve shifts to the right; price level declines and real output increases.

8-6 **(Key Question)** What effects would each of the following have on aggregate demand or aggregate supply? In each case use a diagram to show the expected effects on the equilibrium price level and level of real output. Assume that all other things remain constant.

a. A widespread fear of depression on the part of consumers.

b. A $2 increase in the excise tax on a pack of cigarettes.

c. A reduction in interest rates at each price level.

d. A major increase in Federal spending for health care.

e. The expectation of rapid inflation.

f. The complete disintegration of OPEC, causing oil prices to fall by one-half.

g. A 10 percent reduction in personal income tax rates.

h. A sizable increase in labor productivity (with no change in nominal wages).

i. A 12 percent increase in nominal wages (with no change in productivity).

j. Depreciation in the international value of the dollar.

(a) AD curve left, output down, and price level down.

(b) AS curve left, output down, and price level up.

(c) AD curve right, output and price level up.

(d) AD curve right, output and price level up (any real improvements in health care resulting from the spending would eventually increase productivity and shift AS right).

(e) AD curve right, output and price level up.

(f) AS curve right, output up and price level down.

(g) AD curve right, output and price level up.

(h) AS curve right, output up and price level down.

(i) AS curve left, output down and price level up.

(j) AD curve right (increased net exports); AS curve left (higher input prices)

8-7 (Key Question) Other things equal, what effect will each of the following have on the equilibrium price level and level of real output:

a. An increase in aggregate demand in the steep portion of the aggregate supply curve.

b. An increase in aggregate supply with no change in aggregate demand (assume that prices and wages are flexible upward and downward).

c. Equal increases in aggregate demand and aggregate supply.

d. A reduction in aggregate demand in the flat portion of the aggregate supply curve.

e. An increase in aggregate demand and a decrease in aggregate supply.

(a) Price level rises rapidly and little change in real output.

(b) Price level drops and real output increases.

(c) Price level falls slowly and real output falls rapidly.

(d) Price level does not change, but real output declines.

(e) Price level increases, but the change in real output is indeterminate.

8-12 (Key Question) Suppose the full employment level of real output (Q) for a hypothetical economy is $250 and the price level (P) initially is 100. Use the short-run aggregate supply schedules below to answer the questions which follow:

$AS(P=_{100})$		$AS(P=_{125})$		$AS(P=_{75})$	
P	Q	P	Q	P	Q
125	280	125	250	125	310
100	250	100	220	100	280
75	220	75	190	75	250

a. What will be the level of real output in the *short run* if the price level unexpectedly rises from 100 to 125 because of an increase in aggregate demand? What if the price level falls unexpectedly from 100 to 75 because of a decrease in aggregate demand? Explain each situation, using numbers from the table.

b. What will be the level of real output in the long run when the price level rises from 100 to 125? When it falls from 100 to 75? Explain each situation.

c. Show the circumstances described in parts a and b on graph paper, and derive the long-run aggregate supply curve.

(a) $280; $220. When the price level rises from 100 to 125 [in aggregate supply schedule $AS(P_{100})$], producers experience higher prices for their products. Because nominal wages are constant, profits rise and producers increase output to $Q = $280. When the price level decreases from 100 to 75, profits decline and producers adjust their output to $Q = $75. These are short-run responses to changes in the price level.

(b) $250; $250. In the long run, a rise in the price level to 125 leads to nominal wage increases. The $AS(P_{100})$ schedule changes to $AS(P_{125})$ and Q returns to $250, now at a price level of 125. In the long run, a decrease in price level to 75 leads to lower nominal wages, yielding aggregate supply schedule $AS(P_{75})$. Equilibrium Q returns to $250, now at a price level of 75.

(c) Graphically, the explanation is identical to Figure 9-10. Short-run AS: $P_1 = 100$; $P_2 = 125$; $P_3 = 75$; and $Q_1 = $250; $Q_2 = $280; and $Q_3 = $220. Long-run aggregate supply = $Q_1 = $250 at each of the three price levels.

8-13 (**Key Question**) Use graphical analysis to show how each of the following would affect the economy first in the short run and then in the long run. Assume that Canada is initially operating at its full-employment level of output, that prices and wages are eventually flexible both upward and downward, and that there is no counteracting fiscal or monetary policy.

   a. Because of a war abroad, the oil supply to Canada is disrupted, sending oil prices rocketing upward.
   b. Construction spending on new homes rises dramatically, greatly increasing total Canadian investment spending.
   c. Economic recession occurs abroad, significantly reducing foreign purchases of Canadian exports.

(a) See Figure 8-13 in the chapter, less AD₂. Short run: The aggregate supply curve shifts to the left, the price level rises, and real output declines. Long run: The aggregate supply curve shifts back rightward (due to declining nominal wages), the price level falls, and real output increases.

(b) See Figure 8-13. Short run: The aggregate demand curve shifts to the right, and both the price level and real output increase. Long run: The aggregate supply curve shifts to the left (due to higher nominal wages), the price level rises, and real output declines.

(c) See Figure 8-13. Short run: The aggregate demand curve shifts to the left, both the price level and real output decline. Long run: The aggregate supply curve shifts to the right, the price level falls further, and real output increases.

Chapter 9

9-1 (**Key Question**) What are government's fiscal policy options for an inflationary gap caused by demand-pull inflation? Use the aggregate demand–aggregate supply model to show the impact of these policies on the price level. Which of these fiscal policy options do you think a "conservative" economist might favour? A "liberal" economist?

Reduce government spending, increase taxes, or some combination of both. See Figure 9-2. If the price level is flexible downward, it will fall. In the real world, the goal is to reduce inflation—to keep prices from rising so rapidly—not to reduce the price level. A "conservative" economist might favour cuts in government spending, since this would reduce the size of government. A "liberal" economist might favour a tax hike; it would preserve government spending programs.

9-5 (**Key Question**) Define the "cyclically adjusted budget," explain its significance, and state why it may differ from the "actual budget." Suppose the full-employment, non-inflationary level of real output is GDP₃ (not GDP₂) in the economy depicted in Figure 9-3. If the economy is operating at GDP₂ instead of GDP₃, what is the status of its cyclically budget? Of its current fiscal policy? What change in fiscal policy would you recommend? How would you accomplish that in terms of the G and T lines in the figure?

The cyclically adjusted budget (also called the full employment budget) measures what the federal deficit or surplus would be if the economy reached full-employment level of GDP with existing tax and spending policies. If the cyclically adjusted budget is balanced, then the government is engaging in neither expansionary nor contractionary policy, even if, for example, a deficit automatically results when GDP declines. The "actual" budget is the deficit or surplus that results when revenues and expenditures occur over a year if the economy is not operating at full-employment.

Looking at Figure 9-3, if full-employment GDP level was GDP₃, then the cyclically adjusted budget is contractionary since a surplus would exist. Even though the "actual" budget has no deficit at GDP₂, fiscal policy is contractionary. To move the economy to full-employment, government should cut taxes or increase spending. You would raise the G line or lower the T line or a combination of each until they intersect at GDP₃.

9-7 (**Key Question**) Briefly state and evaluate the problem of time lags in enacting and applying fiscal policy. Explain the notion of a political business cycle. What is the crowding out effect and why is it relevant to fiscal policy? In what respect is the net export effect similar to the crowding-out effect? Do you think people increase their saving in anticipation of the future higher taxes they believe will follow government's use of expansionary fiscal policy?

It takes time to ascertain the direction in which the economy is moving (recognition lag); to get a fiscal policy enacted into law (administrative lag); and for the policy to have its full effect on the economy (operational lag). Meanwhile, other factors may change, rendering inappropriate a particular fiscal policy. Nevertheless, discretionary fiscal policy is a valuable tool in preventing severe recession or severe demand-pull inflation.

A political business cycle is the concept that politicians are more interested in re-election than in stabilizing the economy. Before the election, they enact tax cuts and spending increases to please voters, even though this may fuel inflation. After the election, they apply the brakes to restrain inflation; the economy will slow and unemployment will rise. In this view the political process creates economic instability.

The crowding out effect is the reduction in investment spending caused by the increase in interest rates arising from an increase in government spending, financed by borrowing. The increase in G was designed to increase AD but the resulting increase in interest rates may decrease I. Thus the impact of the expansionary fiscal policy may be reduced.

The next export effect also arises from the higher interest rates accompanying expansionary fiscal policy. The higher interest rates make Canadian bonds more attractive to foreign buyers. The inflow of foreign currency to buy dollars to purchase the bonds drives up the international value of the dollar, making imports less expensive for Canada, and Canadian exports more expensive for people abroad. Net exports from Canada decline, and like the crowding out effect, diminish the expansionary fiscal policy.

Chapter 10

10-1 (Key Question) Assess the leeway for using fiscal policy as a stabilization device under (a) an annually balanced budget, (b) a cyclically balanced budget, and (c) functional finance.

(a) There is practically no potential for using fiscal policy as a stabilization tool under an annually balanced budget. In an economic downturn, tax revenues fall. To keep the budget in balance, fiscal policy would require the government to reduce its spending or increase its tax rates, adding to the deficiency in spending and accelerating the downturn. If the economy were booming

and tax revenues were mounting, to keep the budget balanced fiscal policy would have to increase government spending or reduce taxes, thus adding to the already excessive demand and accelerating the inflationary pressures. An annually balanced budget would intensify cyclical ups and downs.

(b) A cyclically balanced budget would be countercyclical, as it should be, since it would bolster demand by lowering taxes and increasing government spending during a recession and restrain demand by raising taxes and reducing government spending during an inflationary boom. However, because boom and bust are not always of equal intensity and duration, budget surpluses during the upswing need not automatically match budget deficits during the downswing. Requiring the budget to be balanced over the cycle may necessitate inappropriate changes in tax rates or levels of government expenditures.

(c) Functional finance pays no attention to the balance of deficits and surpluses annually or over the cycle. What counts is the maintenance of a non-inflationary full-employment level of spending. Balancing the economy is what counts, not the budget.

10-3 (Key Question) What are the two main ways the size of the public debt is measured? Distinguish between refinancing the debt and retiring the debt. How does an internally held public debt differ from an externally held public debt? Contrast the effects of retiring an internally held debt and retiring an externally held debt.

Two ways of measuring the public debt: (1) measure its absolute dollar size; or (2) measure its size as a percentage of GDP.

Refinancing the public debt simply means rolling over outstanding debt—selling "new" bonds to retire maturing bonds. Retiring the debt means purchasing bonds back from those who hold them or paying the bonds off at maturity.

An internally held debt is one in which the bondholders live in the nation having the debt; an externally held debt is one in which the bondholders are citizens of other nations. Paying off an internally held debt would involve buying back government bonds. This could present a problem of income distribution because holders of the government bonds generally have higher incomes than the average taxpayer. But paying off an internally held debt would not burden the economy as a whole—the money used to pay off the debt would stay within the domestic economy. In paying off an externally held debt, people abroad could use the proceeds of the bonds sales to buy products or other assets from Canada. However, the dollars gained could be simply exchanged for foreign currency and brought back to their home country. This reduces Canadian foreign reserves holdings and may lower the dollar exchange rate.

10-7 (Key Question) Trace the cause-and-effect chain through which financing and refinancing of the public debt might affect real interest rates, private investment, the stock of capital, and economic growth. How might investment in public capital and complementarities between public and private capital alter the outcome of the cause-effect chain?

Cause and effect chain: Government borrowing to finance the debt competes with private borrowing and drives up the interest rate; the higher interest rate causes a decline in private capital and economic growth slows.

However, if public investment complements private investment, private borrowers may be willing to pay higher rates for positive growth opportunities. Productivity and economic growth could rise.

Chapter 11

11-3 (Key Question) What are the components of the $M1$ money supply? What is the most important component of the $M1$ money supply? Why is the face value of a coin greater than its intrinsic value? Distinguish between $M2$ and $M2+$. What are near-monies? Of what significance are they? What arguments can you make for including savings deposits in a definition of money?

$M1$ = currency (in circulation) + demand deposits. The largest component of $M1$ is demand deposits. If the face value of a coin were not greater than its intrinsic (metallic) value, people would remove coins from circulation and sell them for their metallic content. $M2$ = $M1$ + personal and business savings deposits requiring notice before

withdrawl. $M2+$ = $M2$ + deposits non-bank deposit taking institutions (trust and mortgage loan companies, and deposits at *caisses populaires* and credit unions), plus money market mutual funds, and individual aanuities at life insurance companies.

Near-monies represent wealth; the more wealth people have, the more they are likely to spend out of current income. Also, the fact that near-monies are liquid adds to potential economic instability. People may cash in their near-monies and spend the proceeds while the monetary authorities are trying to stem inflation by reducing the money supply. Finally, near-monies can complicate monetary policy because $M1$, $M2$, and $M2+$ do not always change in the same direction.

The argument for including non-chequable savings deposits in a definition of money is that saving deposits can quickly be transferred to a chequing account or withdrawn as cash and spent.

11-5 (Key Question) Suppose the price level and value of the dollar in year 1 are 1.0 and $1.00, respectively. If the price level rises to 1.25 in year 2, what is the new value of the dollar? If instead the price level had fallen to .50, what would have been the value of the dollar? What generalization can you draw from your answer?

In the first case, the value of the dollar (in year 2, relative to year 1) is $.80 (= 1/1.25); in the second case the value is $2 (= 1/.50). Generalization: the price level and the value of the dollar are inversely related.

11-6 (Key Question) What is the basic determinant of (a) the transactions demand and (b) the asset demand for money? Explain how these two demands might be combined graphically to determine total money demand. How is the equilibrium interest rate in the money market determined? How might (a) the expanded use of credit cards, (b) a shortening of worker pay periods, and (c) an increase in nominal GDP each independently affect the transactions demand for money and the equilibrium interest rate?

(a) The level of nominal GDP. The higher this level, the greater the amount of money demanded for transactions. (b) The interest rate. The higher the interest rate, the smaller the amount of money demanded as an asset.

On a graph measuring the interest rate vertically and the amount of money demanded horizontally, the two demand-for-money curves can be summed horizontally to get the total demand for money. This total demand shows the total amount of money demanded at each interest rate. The equilibrium interest rate is determined at the intersection of the total demand for money curve and the supply of money curve.

(a) Expanded use of credit cards: transaction demand for money declines; total demand for money declines; interest rate falls. (b) Shortening of worker pay periods: transaction demand for money declines; total demand for money declines; interest rate falls. (c) Increase in nominal GDP: transaction demand for money increases; total demand for money increases; interest rate rises.

Chapter 12

12-2 (Key Question) Why do chartered banks hold reserves? Explain why reserves are assets to chartered banks but liabilities to the Bank of Canada. What are excess reserves? How do you calculate the amount of excess reserves held by a bank? What is their significance?

Reserves are assets to chartered banks in that they are cash that belongs to these banks: either cash with which the bank started operations, or profits, or money deposited in the bank by its customers and for which the bank has created in exchange a deposit liability. Excess reserves are cash owned by a chartered bank over and above what it desires to hold as its cash reserves to meet its customers' demand. Excess reserves may safely be lent by the chartered bank; when they are, the money supply increases by the amount of the loan.

12-4 (Key Question) "When a chartered bank makes loans, it creates money; when loans are repaid, money is destroyed." Explain.

Banks create or add to chequing, or demand, account balances when they make loans; these demand deposits are part of the money supply. People pay off loans by writing cheques. Demand deposits fall, meaning the money supply drops. Money is "destroyed."

12-8 (Key Question) Suppose the Yukon Bank has the following simplified balance sheet. The reserve ratio is 6.25 percent.

	Assets				Liabilities and net worth		
		(1)	(2)			(1)	(2)
Reserves	$22,000	___	___	Demand deposits $100,000		___	___
Securities	38,000	___	___				
Loans	40,000	___	___				
		___	___				

a. What is the maximum amount of new loans that this bank can make? Show in column 1 how the bank's balance sheet will appear after the bank has loaned this additional amount.

b. By how much has the supply of money changed? Explain.

c. How will the bank's balance sheet appear after cheques drawn for the entire amount of the new loans have been cleared against this bank? Show this new balance sheet in column 2.

d. Answer questions a, b, and c on the assumption that the reserve ratio is 10 percent.

Assets		(1)	(2)	Liabilities and net worth		(1)	(2)
Reserves	$22,000	$22,000	$ 6,250	Demand deposits	$100,000	$115,750	$100,000
Securities	$38,000	$38,000	$38,000				
Loans	$40,000	$55,750	$55,750				

Desired reserves are 6.25% of $100,000 = $6,250.
Actual reserves = $22,000
Desired reserves = $ 6,250
Excess reserves = $15,750

(a) The maximum amount of new loans the bank may make is $15,750. The new balance sheet is shown in column 1 above.

(b) The money supply has increased by $15,750, since this is the amount by which demand deposits have increased, and demand deposits are part of the money supply.

(c) After cheques are drawn for the entire amount of the loan and cleared against this bank, its balance sheet will appear as column 2 above.

(d) Desired reserves are now $10,000 (-10% of $100,000). Excess reserves are now $12,000 ($22,000 - $10,000), which this bank may safely lend. When it does so, the money supply increases by $12,000.
Questions (a) and (b) are answered below, with the change in the desired reserve ratio factored in.

Assets		(1)	(2)	Liabilities and net worth		(1)	(2)
Reserves	$22,000	$22,000	$10,000	Demand deposits	$100,000	$112,000	$100,000
Securities	$38,000	$38,000	$38,000				
Loans	$40,000	$52,000	$52,000				

12-13 (**Key Question**) Suppose the simplified consolidated balance sheet shown below is for the entire commercial banking system. All figures are in billions. The desired reserve ratio is 25 percent.

Assets	(1)	Liabilities and Net Worth	(2)
Reserves	$ 52 ___	Demand deposits	$200 ___
Securities	48 ___		
Loans	100 ___		

a. What amount of excess reserves does the commercial banking system have? What is the maximum amount the banking system might lend? Show in column 1 how the consolidated balance sheet would look after

this amount has been lent. What is the monetary multiplier?

b. Answer question 13a assuming that the reserve ratio is 20 percent. Explain the resulting difference in the lending ability of the commercial banking system.

(a) Desired reserves = $50 billion (= 25% of $200 billion); so excess reserves = $2 billion (= $52 billion - $50 billion). Maximum amount banking system can lend = $8 billion (= 1/.25 × $2 billion). Column (1) of Assets data (top to bottom): $52 billion; $48 billion; $108 billion. Column (1) of Liabilities data: $208 billion. Monetary multiplier = 4 (= 1/.25).

(b) Desired reserves = $40 billion (= 20% of $200 billion); so excess reserves = $12 billion (= $52 billion - $40 billion). Maximum amount banking system can lend = $60 billion (= 1/.20 × $12 billion). Column (1) data for assets after loans (top to bottom); $52 billion; $48 billion; $160 billion. Column (1) data for liabilities after loans: $260 billion. Monetary multiplier = 5 (= 1/.20). The decrease in the reserve ratio increases the banking system's excess reserves from $2 billion to $12 billion and increases the size of the monetary multiplier from 4 to 5. Lending capacity becomes 5 × $12 = $609 billion.

Chapter 13

13-2 **(Key Question)** In the table below you will find simplified consolidated balance sheets for the chartered banking system and the Bank of Canada. Use columns 1 and 2 to indicate how the balance sheets would read after each transaction in (a) and (b) is completed. Do not accumulate your answers; analyze each transaction separately, starting in each case from the figures provided. All accounts are in billions of dollars.

a. A decline in the bank rate prompts chartered banks to borrow an additional $1 billion from the Bank of Canada. Show the new balance-sheet figures in column 1 of each table.

b. The Bank of Canada sells $3 billion in securities to members of the public, who pay for the bonds with cheques. Show the new balance-sheet figures in column 2 of each table.

c. The Bank of Canada buys $2 billion of securities from the chartered banks. Show the new balance-sheet figures in column 3 of each table.

d. Now review each of the above three transactions, asking yourself these three questions: (1) What change, if any, took place in the money supply as a direct and immediate result of each transaction? (2) What increase or decrease in chartered banks' reserves took place in each transaction? (3) Assuming a desired reserve ratio of 20 percent, what change in the money-creating potential of the commercial banking system occurred as a result of each transaction?

CONSOLIDATED BALANCE SHEET: ALL CHARTERED BANKS

		(1)	(2)	(3)
Assets:				
Reserves	$ 33	___	___	___
Securities	60	___	___	___
Loans	60	___	___	___
Liabilities:				
Demand deposits	150	___	___	___
Advances from Bank of Canada	3	___	___	___

CONSOLIDATED BALANCE SHEET: BANK OF CANADA

		(1)	(2)	(3)
Assets:				
Securities	$60	___	___	___
Advances to chartered banks	3	___	___	___
		___	___	___
Liabilities:				
Reserves of chartered banks	$33			
Government of Canada deposits	3	___	___	___
Notes in circulation	27			
		___	___	___

(a) Column (1) data (top to bottom): Chartered Bank Assets: $34, 60, 60; Liabilities: $150, 4; Bank of Canada Assets: $60, 4; Liabilities: $34, 3, 27.

(b) Column (2) data (top to bottom): Chartered Bank Assets: $30, 60, 60; Liabilities: $147, 3; Bank of Canada Assets: $57, 3, 30, 3, 27.

(c) Column (3) data (top to bottom): $35; $58; $60; $150; $3; Bank of Canada: $62; $3; $35; $3; $27.

(d) (d1) Money supply (demand deposits) directly changes only in (b), where it decreases by $3 billion; (d2) See balance sheets; (d3) Money-creating potential of the banking system increases by $5 billion in (a); decreases by $12 billion in (b) (not by $15 billion—the writing of $3 billion of cheques by the public to buy bonds reduces demand deposits by $3 billion, thus freeing $0.6 billion of reserves. Three billion dollars minus $0.6 billion equals $2.4 billion of reduced reserves, and this multiplied by the monetary multiplier of 5 equals $12 billion); and increases by $10 billion in (c).

13-3 (**Key Question**) Suppose you are the governor of the Bank of Canada. The economy is experiencing a sharp and prolonged inflationary trend. What changes in **a** open-market operations and **b** switching government deposits would you consider? Explain in each case how the change you advocate would affect chartered bank cash reserves and influence the money supply.

(a) Sell government securities in the open market. This would immediately decrease the money supply by the amount of the securities sales. If the banks had been fully loaned up, they would now have to decrease their loans by a multiple (because of the money multiplier) of their bond sales. This would force up interest rates (this, added to the immediate effect of the bond sales, would tend to drive down their prices, that is, drive interest rates up), and decrease aggregate expenditures.

(b) Switching government deposits from the chartered banks will reduce excess reserves, thus banks could loan out fewer funds, thereby decreasing the money supply.

13-5 (**Key Question**) Distinguish between the overnight loans rate and the prime interest rate. In what way is the overnight loans rate a measure of the tightness or looseness of monetary policy? In 2001 the Bank of Canada used open-market operations to significantly reduce the overnight loans rate. What was the logic of those actions? What was the effect on the prime interest rate?

The overnight loans rate is the interest rate banks charge one another on overnight loans needed to meet desired reserves. The prime interest rate is the interest rate banks change on loans to their most creditworthy customers. The tighter the monetary policy, the less the supply of excess reserves in the banking system and the higher the overnight loans rate. The reverse is true of a loose or easy monetary policy, which expands excess reserves, and causes the overnight loans rate to fall.

The Bank of Canada wanted to increase excess reserves, increase money supply growth, and lower real interest rates. In 2001 the U.S. economy was in the midst of recession, with spending in decline and stock prices falling. The terrorist attacks of September 11, 2001, added further uncertainty to the already weak economic outlook, and an easy money policy was seen as a way to boost confidence. The prime interest rate fell as a result of these actions

13-7 (**Key Question**) Suppose the Bank of Canada decides to engage in a tight money policy as a way to reduce demand-pull inflation. Use the aggregate demand-aggregate supply model to show what this policy is intended to accomplish in a closed economy. Now introduce the open economy and explain how changes in the international value of the dollar might affect the location of your aggregate demand curve.

The intent of a tight money policy would be shown as a leftward shift of the aggregate demand curve and a decline in the price level (or, in the real world, a reduction in the rate of inflation). In an open economy, the interest rate hike resulting from the tight money policy would entice people abroad to buy Canadian securities. Because they would need Canadian dollars to buy these securities, the international demand for dollars would rise, causing the dollar to appreciate. Net exports would fall, pushing the aggregate demand curve farther leftward than in the closed economy.

Chapter 14

14-1 **(Key Question)** Use graphical analysis to show how each of the following would affect the economy first in the short run and then in the long run. Assume that Canada is initially operating at its full employment level of output, that prices and wages are eventually flexible both upward and downward, and that there is no counteracting fiscal or monetary policy.

 a. Because of a war abroad, the oil supply to Canada is disrupted, sending oil prices rocketing upward.
 b. Construction spending on new homes rises dramatically, greatly increasing total Canadian investment spending.
 c. Economic recession occurs abroad, significantly reducing foreign purchases of Canadian exports.
 (a) See Figure 14-4 in the chapter. Short run: The aggregate supply curve shifts to the left, the price level rises, and real output declines. Long run: The aggregate supply curve shifts back rightward (due to declining nominal wages), the price level falls, and real output increases.
 (b) See Figure 14-3. Short run: The aggregate demand curve shifts to the right, and both the price level and real output increase. Long run: The aggregate supply curve shifts to the left (due to higher nominal wages), the price level rises, and real output declines.
 (c) See Figure 14-5. Short run: The aggregate demand curve shifts to the left, both the price level and real output decline. Long run: The aggregate supply curve shifts to the right, the price level falls further, and real output increases.

14.3 **(Key Question)** Suppose the government misjudges the natural rate of unemployment to be much lower than it actually is, and thus undertakes expansionary fiscal and monetary policy to try to achieve the lower rate. Use the concept of the short-run Phillips Curve to explain why these policies might at first succeed. Use the concept of the long-run Phillips Curve to explain the long-run outcome of these policies.

In the short-run there is probably a tradeoff between unemployment and inflation. The government's expansionary policy should reduce unemployment as aggregate demand increases. However, the government has misjudged the natural rate and will continue its expansionary policy beyond the point of the natural level of unemployment. As aggregate demand continues to rise, prices begin to rise. In the long-run, workers demand higher wages to compensate for these higher prices. Aggregate supply will decrease (shift leftward) toward the natural rate of unemployment.

In other words, any reduction of unemployment below the natural rate is only temporary and involves a short-run rise in inflation. This, in turn, causes long-run costs to rise and a decrease in aggregate supply. The end result should be an equilibrium at the natural rate of unemployment and a higher price level than the beginning level. The long-run Phillips curve is thus a vertical line connecting the price levels possible at the natural rate of unemployment found on the horizontal axis.

14-5 **(Key Question)** What is the Laffer Curve and how does it relate to supply side economics? Why is determining the location where the economy is on the curve so important in assessing tax policy?

Economist Arthur Laffer observed that tax revenues would obviously be zero when the tax rate was either at 0% or 100%. In between these two extremes would have to be an optimal rate where aggregate output and income produced the maximum tax revenues. This idea is presented as the Laffer Curve shown in Figure 14-8.

The difficult decision involves the analysis to determine what is the optimum tax rate for producing maximum tax revenue and the related maximum economic output level. Laffer argued that low tax rates would actually increase revenues because low rates improved productivity, saving and investment incentives. The expansion in output and employment and thus, revenue, would more than compensate for the lower rates.

Chapter 15

15-1 **(Key Question)** What are the four supply factors of economic growth? What is the demand factor? What is the efficiency factor? Illustrate these factors in terms of the production possibilities curve.

The four supply factors are the quantity and quality of natural resources; the quantity and quality of human resources; the stock of capital goods; and the level of technology. The demand factor is the level of purchases needed to maintain full employment. The efficiency factor refers to both productive and allocative efficiency. Figure 18-1 illustrates these growth factors by showing movement from curve AB to curve CD.

15-5 (Key Question) Between 1990 and 1999 the Canadian price level rose by about 20 percent while its real output increased by about 33 percent. Use the aggregate demand-aggregate supply model to illustrate these outcomes graphically.

In the graph shown, both AD and AS expanded over the 1990-1999 period. Because aggregate supply increased as well as aggregate demand, the new equilibrium output rose at a faster pace than did the price level. P2 is 20% above P1 and GDP2 is 33% greater than GDP1. Note that it is also possible that in early 1990s when unemployment was above natural rate that some of the expansion of AD took place in the horizontal portion of AS curve, but that is not the situation depicted here.

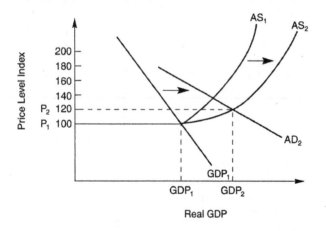

Real GDP

15-6 (Key Question) To what extent have increases in Canada's real GDP been the result of more labour inputs? Of increasing labour productivity? Discuss the factors that contribute to productivity growth in order of their quantitative importance.

Refer to Table 15-2. Productivity increasing factors in descending order: (1) Technological ad-

vance—the discovery of new knowledge that results in the combining of resources in more productive ways. (2) The quantity of capital. (3) Education and training. Since 1940 the proportion of those in the labour force with a high school education has doubled from 40 to 80 percent. And those with a college or university education have more than doubled from under 10 percent to over 20 percent. (4) Economies of scale and (5) improved resource allocation. Workers have been moving out of lower productivity jobs to higher productivity jobs. Part of this is associated with the increased efficiency often derived from production in larger plants, in which specialization of labour and productivity-increasing methods are possible.

15-9 (Key Question) Relate each of the following to the New Economy:

a. the rate of productivity growth
b. information technology
c. increasing returns
d. network effects
e. global competition

Each of the above is a characteristic of the New Economy. The rate of productivity growth has grown substantially due to innovations using microchips, computers, new telecommunications devices and the Internet. All of these innovations describe features of what we call information technology, which connects information in all parts of the world with information seekers. New information products are often digital in nature and can be easily replicated once they have been developed. The start-up cost of new firms and new technology is high, but expanding production has a very low marginal cost which leads to economies of scale – firms' output grows faster than their inputs. Network effects refer to a type of economy of scale whereby certain information products become more valuable to each user as the number of buyers grows. For example, a fax machine is more useful to you when lots of other people and firms have one; the same is true for compatible word-processing programs. Global competition is a feature of the New Economy because both transportation and communication can be accomplished at much lower cost and faster speed than previously which expands market possibilities for both consumers and producers who are not very limited by national boundaries today.

Chapter 16

16-7 **(Key Question)** The following are hypo-thetical production possibilities tables for New Zealand and Spain.

New Zealand's production possibilities table (millions of bushels)				
Product	Production alternatives			
	A	B	C	D
Apples	0	20	40	60
Plums	15	10	5	0

Spain's production possibilities table (millions of bushels)				
Product	Production alternatives			
	R	S	T	U
Apples	0	20	40	60
Plums	60	40	20	0

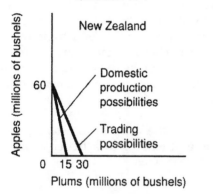

Question 16-7

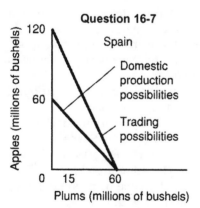

Question 16-7

Using a graph, plot the production possibilities data for each of the two countries. Referring to your graphs, determine: (a) Each country's do-mestic opportunity cost of producing plums and apples. (b) Which nation should specialize in which product. (c) The trading possibilities lines for each nation if the actual terms of trade are 1 plum for 2 apples.

(a) New Zealand's cost ratio is 1 plum = 4 ap-ples (or 1 apple = 1/4 plum). Spain's cost ratio is 1 plum = 1 apple (or 1 apple = 1 plum). See the graphs.

(b) New Zealand should specialize in applies, Spain in plums.

(c) See the graphs.

(d) Total production before specialization and trade: 40 apples (20 + 20) and 50 plums (10 + 40). After specialization and trade: 60 ap-ples and 60 plums. Gain = 20 apples and 10 plums.

16-9 **(Key Question)** Refer to Figure 3-6. As-sume the graph depicts Canada's domestic mar-ket for corn. How many bushels of corn, if any, will Canada export or import at a world price of $1, $2, $3, $4, and $5? Use this information to construct Canada's export supply curve and im-port demand curve for corn. Suppose the only other corn-producing nation is France, where the domestic price is $4. Why will the equilibrium world price be between $3 and $4? Who will ex-port corn at this world price? Who will import it?

Question 16-9

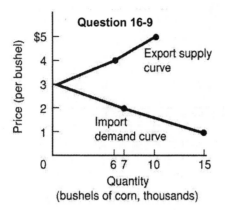

At $1: import 15,000. At $2: import 7,000. At $3: no imports or exports. At $4: export 6,000. At $5: export 10,000.

Canada will export corn, France will import it.

16-10 (Key Question) Draw a domestic supply and demand diagram for a product in which Canada does not have a comparative advantage. What impact do foreign imports have on domestic price and quantity? On your diagram show a protective tariff that eliminates approximately one-fourth the assumed imports. What are the price–quantity effects of this tariff to (a) domestic consumers, (b) domestic producers, and (c) foreign exporters? How would the effects of a quota that creates the same amount of imports differ?

Question 16-10

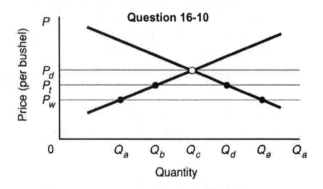

See the graph. Canada does not have a comparative advantage in this product because the world price P_w is below the Canadian domestic price of P_d. Imports will reduce the price of P_w, increasing consumption from nontrade Q_c to Q_e and decreasing domestic production from Q_c to Q_a. See the graph. A tariff of P_wP_t (a) harms domestic consumers by increasing price from P_w to P_t and decreasing consumption from Q_e to Q_d; (b) aids domestic producers through the increase in price from P_w to P_t and the expansion of domestic pro-

duction from Q_a to Q_b; (c) harms foreign exporters by decreasing exports from Q_aQ_e to Q_bQ_d.

An import quota of Q_bQ_d would have the same effects as the tariff, but there would be no tariff revenues to government from these imports; this revenue would in effect be transferred to foreign producers.

16-15 (Key Question) Identify and state the significance of each of the following: (a) WTO; (b) EU; (c) euro; and (d) NAFTA. What commonality do they share?

(a) The WTO oversees trade agreements reached by member nations and arbitrates trade disputes among them. (b) The EU is a trading bloc of 25 European countries who have agreed to abolish tariffs and import quotas on most products and have liberalized the movement of labor and capital within the EU. (c) The euro is the common currency that is used by 12 of the original 15 EU countries. (d) NAFTA is a trade bloc made up of the Canada, the United Sates, and Mexico whose purpose is to reduce tariffs and other trade barriers among the three countries.

All of the above have the goals of increasing international trade and leading to a better allocation of the world's resources.

Chapter 17

17-2 (Key Question) Indicate whether each of the following creates a demand for, or a supply of, European euros in foreign exchange markets:

a. A Canadian importer purchases a shipload of Bordeaux wine.

b. A Swedish automobile firm decides to build an assembly plant in Nova Scotia.

d. A Canadian university student decides to spend a year studying at the Sorbonne.

d. A French manufacturer exports machinery to Morocco on a Canadian freighter.

e. Canada incurs a balance of payments deficit in its transactions with France.

f. A Canadian government bond held by a French citizen matures.

g. It is widely believed that the international value of the euro will fall in the near future.

A demand for euros is created in (a), (c), and (f). A supply of euros is created in (b), (d), (e), and (g).

17-3 **(Key Question)** Answer the following questions on the basis of Alpha's balance of payments for 1998 as shown below. All figures are in billions of dollars. What are (a) the balance of trade, (b) the balance on goods and services, (c) the balance on current account, and (d) the balance on capital account? Does Alpha have a balance of payments deficit or surplus? Explain.

Merchandise exports	+$40	Net Transfers	+$10
Merchandise imports	− 30	Foreign investment in Canada	+ 10
Service exports	+ 15	Canadian investment abroad	− 40
Service imports	− 10	Official international reserves	+ 10
Net investment income	− 5		

Balance of trade = $10 billion surplus (= exports of goods of $40 billion minus imports of goods of $30 billion). Balance on goods and services = $15 billion surplus (= $55 billion of exports of goods and services minus $40 billion of imports of goods and services). Balance on current account = $20 billion surplus (= credits of $65 billion minus debits of $45 billion). Balance on capital account = $30 billion deficit (= Foreign investment in Canada of $10 billion minus Canadian investment abroad of $40 billion). Balance of payments = $10 billion deficit.

17-6 **(Key Question)** Explain why the Canadian demand for Mexican pesos is downsloping and the supply of pesos to Canadians is upsloping. Assuming a system of floating exchange rates between Mexico and Canada, indicate whether each of the following would cause the Mexican peso to appreciate or depreciate:
a. Canada unilaterally reduces tariffs on Mexican products.
b. Mexico encounters severe inflation.
c. Deteriorating political relations reduce Canadian tourism in Mexico.
d. Canada's economy moves into a severe recession.
e. The Bank of Canada embarks on a tight money policy.
f. Mexican products become more fashionable to Canadians.
g. The Mexican government encourages Canadian firms to invest in Mexican oil fields.

h. The rate of productivity growth in Canada diminishes sharply.

The Canadian demand for pesos is downsloping: When the peso depreciates in value (relative to the dollar) Canadians find that Mexican goods and services are less expensive in dollar terms and purchase more of them, demanding a greater quantity of pesos in the process. The supply of pesos to Canada is upsloping: As the peso appreciates in value (relative to the dollar), Canadian goods and services become cheaper to Mexicans in peso terms. Mexicans buy more dollars to obtain more Canadian goods, supplying a larger quantity of pesos.

The peso appreciates in (a), (f), (g), and (h) and depreciates in (b), (c), (d), and (e).

17-9 **(Key Question)** Diagram a market in which the equilibrium dollar price of one unit of fictitious currency Zee is $5 (the exchange rate is $5 = Z1). Then show on your diagram a decline in the demand for Zee.
a. Referring to your diagram, discuss the adjustment options Canada would have in maintaining the exchange rate at $5 = Z1 under a fixed exchange rate system.
b. How would the Canadian balance of payments surplus that is created (by the decline in demand) get resolved under a system of flexible exchange rates?
See the graph illustrating the market for Zees.

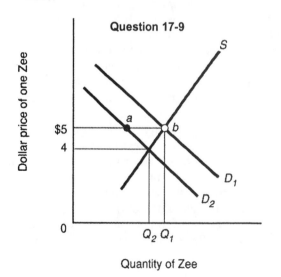

Question 17-9

Dollar price of one Zee / Quantity of Zee

(a) The decrease in demand for Zees from D_1 to D_2 will create a surplus (*bc*) of Zees at the $5 price. To maintain the $5 to Z1 exchange rate, Canada must undertake policies to shift the demand-for-Zee curve rightward or shift the supply-of-Zee curve leftward. To increase the demand for Zees, Canada could use dollars or gold to buy Zees in the foreign exchange market; employ trade policies to increase imports from Zeeonia; or enact expansionary fiscal and monetary policies to increase Canadian domestic output and income, thus increasing imports from Zeeonia. Expansionary monetary policy would also reduce the *supply* of Zees: Zeeons would respond to the resulting lower Canadian interest rates by reducing their financial investing in Canada. Therefore, they would not supply as many Zees to the foreign exchange market.

(b) Under a system of flexible exchange rates, the *bc* surplus of Zees (the Canadian balance of payments surplus) will cause the Zee to appreciate and the dollar to appreciate until the surplus is eliminated (at the $4 = Z1 exchange rate shown in the figure).

Chapter 19W

19W-1 (Key Question) Use the aggregate demand-aggregate supply model to compare classical and Keynesian interpretations of (a) the aggregate supply curve, and (b) the stability of the aggregate demand curve. Which of these interpretations seems more consistent with the realities of the Great Depression?

(a) Classical economists envisioned the AS curve as being perfectly vertical. When prices fall, real profits do not decrease because wage rates fall in the same proportion. With constant real profits, firms have no reason to change the quantities of output they supply. Keynesians viewed the AS curve as being horizontal at outputs less than the full-employment output and vertical only at full employment. Declines in aggregate demand do not change the price level because wages and prices are assumed to be inflexible downward.

(b) Classical economists viewed AD as stable so long as the monetary authorities hold the money supply constant. Therefore inflation and deflation are unlikely. Keynesians viewed the AD curve as unstable—even if the money supply is constant—since investment spending is volatile. Decreases in AD can cause a recession; rapid increases in AD can cause demand-pull inflation.

(c) The Keynesian view seems more consistent with the facts of the Great Depression; in that period, real output declined by nearly 40 percent in the United States and remained low for a decade.

19W-4 (Key Question) Suppose that the money supply and the nominal GDP for a hypothetical economy are $96 billion and $336 billion, respectively. What is the velocity of money? How will households and businesses react if the central bank reduces the money supply by $20 billion? By how much will nominal GDP have to fall to restore equilibrium, according to the monetarist perspective?

Velocity = 3.5 or 336/96. They will cut back on their spending to try to restore their desired ratio of money to other items of wealth. Nominal GDP will fall to $266 billion (= $76 billion remaining money supply x 3.5) to restore equilibrium.

19W-7 (Key Question) Use an AD-AS graph to demonstrate and explain the price-level and real-output outcome of an anticipated decline in aggregate demand, as viewed by RET economists. (Assume that the economy initially is operating at its full-employment level of output.) Then, demonstrate and explain on the same graph the outcome, as viewed by mainstream economists.

See the graph and the decline in aggregate demand from AD_1 to AD_2. RET view: The Economy anticipates the decline in the price level and immediate moves from *a* to *d*. Mainstream view: The economy first moves from *a* to *b* and then to *c*. In view of historical evidence, the mainstream view seems more plausible to us than the RET view; only when aggregate demand shifts from AD_2 to AD_1 will full-employment output Q_1 be restored in the mainstream view.

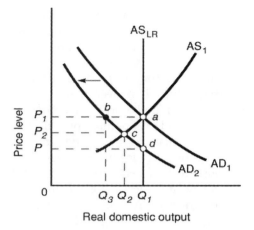

Real domestic output

19W-13   (*Key Question*) Place MON, RET, or MAIN besides the statements that most closely reflect monetarist, rational expectations, or mainstream views, respectively.
   a. Anticipated changes in aggregate demand affect only the price level; they have no effect on real output.
   b. Downward wage inflexibility means that declines in aggregate demand can cause long-lasting recession.
   c. Changes in the money supply M increase PQ; at first only Q rises because nominal wages are fixed, but once workers adapt their expectations to new realities, P rises and Q returns to its former level.
   d. Fiscal and monetary policy smooth out the business cycle.
   e. The Bank of Canada should increase the money supply at a fixed annual rate.
   (a) RET;
   (b) MAIN;
   (c) MON;
   (d) MAIN;
   (e) MON.

Chapter 20W

20W-3 (*Key Question*) Assume an DVC and an IAC presently have real per capita outputs of $500 and $5,000 respectively. If both nations have a 3 percent increase in their real per capita outputs, by how much will the per capita output gap change?

Rise in per capital output gap = $135 (= 3% × $5,000 - 3% × $500).

20W-5 (*Key Question*) Contrast the "demographic transition" view of population growth with the traditional view that slower population growth is a prerequisite for rising living standards in the DVCs.

Demographic transition view: Expanded output and income in developing countries will result in lower birthrates and slower growth of population. As incomes of primary family members expand, they begin to see the marginal cost of a larger family exceeding the marginal benefit. The policy emphasis should therefore be on economic growth; population growth will realize. Traditional view: Developing nations should reduce population growth as a first priority. Slow population growth enables the growth of per capita income.

20W-6 (*Key Question*) Because real capital is supposed to earn a higher return where it is scarce, how do you explain the fact that most international investment flows to the IACs (where capital is relatively abundant) rather than to the DVCs (where capital is very scarce)?

Capital earns a higher return where it is scarce, *other things equal*. But, when comparing investment opportunities between IACs and DVCs, other things equal. Advanced factors filled with specialized equipment require a productive work force. IACs have no abundance of educated, experienced workers; these workers are scarce in DVCs. Also, IACs have extensive public infrastructures which increase the returns on private capital. Example: a network of highways makes it more profitable to produce goods that need to be widely transported. Finally, investment returns must be adjusted for risk. IACs have stable governments and "law and order," reducing the risk of capital being "nationalized" or pilfered by organized crime.

20W-12   (*Key Question*) Use Figure I2-2 (changing box labels as necessary) to explain rapid economic growth in a country such as Chile or South Korea. What factors other than those contained in the figure might contribute to growth?

To describe countries such as Chile and South Korea, we would need to change labels on three boxes, leading to a change in the "results" boxes. "Rapid" population growth would change to "low" rate of population growth; "low" level of saving would change to "high" level of saving; "low" levels of investment in physical and human capital would change to "high" levels of investment in physical and human capital. These three changes would result in higher productivity and higher per capita income, which would produce a rising level of demand. Other factors: stable national government; homogeneous population; extensive investment in infrastructure; "will to develop"; strong private incentives.

Chapter 21W

21W-5 (Key Question) Use a supply and demand diagram to explain why persistent shortages of many consumer goods occurred under central planning in the Soviet Union and in pre-reform China. Why were black markets common in each country?

See Figure Web-1. Because Russia and China set prices and did not allow them to change as supply or demand shifted, prices were below the equilibrium price for most goods and services. When the fixed price, *Pf*, is below the equilibrium price, *Pe*, there will be a shortage since the quantity demanded will exceed the quantity supplied.

Black markets are common where prices are fixed below equilibrium levels. People can buy goods at the fixed government prices (or pay off clerks to save such goods to sell to them), and because of the shortages at the low fixed price, resell these goods at a much higher price to those unable to find the goods in government stores at the controlled prices. This reselling is said to occur on the black market.

21W-6 (Key Question) What have been the major components of economic reform in Russia? What is meant when these reforms are described as "shock therapy"? How successful has Russia been thus far in its reforms?

Privatization of state-owned businesses; market-determined prices; promotion of competition; integration with the world economy; and price-level stabilization. These reforms are referred to as shock therapy because they were dramatic and quick rather than phased in over many years. Russia's reform has nominally privatized much of the economy (but property rights are still not clearly defined), establishing market-determined prices, and setting the stage for future prosperity. But the transition has resulted in declining living standards for many and increasing income inequality. Also, the government still does not have a successful program for collecting taxes.

21W-8 (Key Question) Relate each of the following items to the success of market reform in China: (a) leasing farm land, (b) price reform, (c) private rural and urban enterprises, (d) special economic zones, and (e) corporatization of state-owned enterprises.
  (a) Leasing of land resulted in individually operated rather than collectivized farms; this greatly increased production incentives and boosted farm output.
  (b) Price reform established market-based prices. These higher-than-government prices provided incentives for enterprises to expand output; they also enabled market-determined allocation of resources to replace inefficient central planning.
  (c) Private rural and urban enterprises absorbed workers released by greater productivity in China's agricultural sector and established competition for China's state-owned enterprises.
  (d) The special economic zones—with their private corporations, free trade, and foreign investment—established the workability and benefits of "near-capitalism."
  (e) Corporatization focused the goals of state-owned enterprises on providing high-quality, minimum per-unit cost goods desired by consumers.